A NAVAJO LEGACY

The Civilization of the American Indian Series

John Holiday of Monument Valley (Photo by Stan Byrd)

A Navajo Legacy

The Life and Teachings of John Holiday

John Holiday and Robert S. McPherson

UNIVERSITY OF OKLAHOMA PRESS : NORMAN

Also by Robert S. McPherson

The Northern Navajo Frontier, 1860–1900: Expansion through Adversity (Albuquerque, 1988; Logan, Utah, 2001)
Sacred Land, Sacred View: Navajo Perceptions of the Four Corners Region (Provo, Utah, 1992)
A History of San Juan County: In the Palm of Time (Salt Lake City, 1995)
(with Navajo Oshley) *The Journey of Navajo Oshley: An Autobiography and Life History* (Logan, Utah, 2000)
(with James Aton) *River Flowing from the Sunrise: An Environmental History of the Lower San Juan* (Logan, Utah, 2000)
Navajo Land, Navajo Culture: The Utah Experience in the Twentieth Century (Norman, 2001)

Library of Congress Cataloging-in-Publication Data

Holiday, John, 1919–
    A Navajo legacy : the life and teachings of John Holiday / John Holiday and Robert S. McPherson.
        p.   cm. — (The Civilization of the American Indians series ; v. 251)
    Includes index.
    ISBN 0-8061-3668-5 (alk. paper)
    1. Holiday, John, 1919–   2. Navajo Indians—Monument Valley (Ariz. and Utah)—Biography.   3. Healers—Monument Valley (Ariz. and Utah)—Biography.   4. Navajo Indians—Religion.   5. Navajo philosophy.
6. Blessingway (Navajo rite)   7. Monument Valley (Ariz. and Utah)—History.   8. Monument Valley (Ariz. and Utah)—Social life and customs.
I. McPherson, Robert S., 1947–   II. Title.   III. Series.

E99.N3H67 2005
979.2'590049726'0092—dc22
[B]
                                                        2004058008

A Navajo Legacy: The Life and Teachings of John Holiday is Volume 251 in The Civilization of the American Indian Series.

The paper in this book meets the guidelines for permanence and durability of the Committee on Production Guidelines for Book Longevity of the Council on Library Resources, Inc. ∞

1 2 3 4 5 6 7 8 9 10

Contents

Illustrations

PREFACE

Books, like experience, sometimes have their own unplanned ways of beginning. John Holiday's autobiography is a good example of this evolutionary process, with the project taking on a life of its own. It began when translator Marilyn Holiday and I visited John in September 1991 to collect material for a county history for Utah's 1996 centennial celebration.[1] I remembered him as a very knowledgeable man with a wealth of information about the Monument Valley area and a treasure trove of traditional Navajo beliefs, but I was focused on my work, time went on, other projects followed, and I forgot about him.

In the early spring of 1999, while finishing the Navajo Oshley manuscript, I was stumped. Oshley had died in 1988, just as the translation of his tapes was being completed. He had made reference to numerous geographical places and historic people that were difficult for me to identify yet commonplace to him. Joanne Oshley Holiday, his daughter, suggested I see Little John in Monument Valley. John was a close relative to Oshley and had lived with him in the sheep camps of yesteryear; he also knew many of the personalities in the region.

That June, Marilyn and I sought John's help in identifying some of the places and people. Not only did he know everyone mentioned, but he also told, along with a little story, how each received his or her name. I was elated. Here was a man conversant with a past that otherwise would have been lost, and his information was highly accurate. During the interview process, several unplanned occasions testified to the high validity of what he recalled. John watched my pleasure at discovery, laughing heartily while reminiscing with obvious relish about people he had known and loved but who were now gone.

At the end of the interview, as I paid him for his time, he said that he would like to have a similar autobiography done for him. I was surprised. Not often does a practicing medicine man of his stature approach a white man to write his life history. I told him I would see what I could do but realized that compensation for his time and for translators would be expensive. Still, he had offered, and if it could be completed, the project would have great value.

I applied for a grant from the Utah Humanities Council, an organization that had always been helpful in matters like this. While the committee for funding grants was in session, a council member called me and, almost sheepishly, asked how I would feel about receiving an additional $500 beyond that requested. The committee had a few ideas to further the project. More than pleased with the news, I applied for a permit (C9923-E) from the Navajo Nation Historic Preservation Department (NNHPD) to do research on the Navajo Reservation. I also requested permission from the Oljato Chapter president, Neal Crank. With both documents of approval in hand, I began the project in November 1999.

During the interview process, I occasionally asked John whether he would like to make a statement about what these interviews meant to him. Not until I told him that part of the agreement with the NNHPD in Window Rock was that I send the manuscript to them for review did he give his most complete response. What follows is his translated statement, given November 9, 2001:

> I live here at Standing Train, also known as Among the Small Junipers [on a plateau approximately two miles north of Train Rock]. I came to live here when I was ten years old. I also lived in a place called White Streak of Cattail Coming Out, by VCA [Caine Valley]. One was our winter camp, and the other, our summer camp. But right now, I am here permanently, and I am getting old, so I will probably remain here.
>
> My name is John Holiday. People from everywhere—men, women, boys, girls, many leaders, and associates—know me as this. I have been interviewed several times, since two years ago, by this white man [Robert McPherson].

This is what I think. I am getting old. Many of our great ancestors were very knowledgeable in many areas, but they did not leave us these important teachings about and within these four sacred mountains, our land. Our ancestors took it all with them when they died. So presently, we live as if we are blind and deaf. This is the reason why I think I will not let this happen. I will not depart from this life without leaving my teachings behind. I want to be remembered through my life story and teachings.

My life story interviews begin from the time I was born and taken in a cradleboard [to Tuba City], to being a toddler, through adolescence, to my present life. In my interview, I told my life story and everywhere I have been. I want this to be my autobiography, in my name, and to be remembered forever by all those who read this book. This is what I had in mind, and that is why I agreed to do the interview with this white man.

This book consists of my life's teachings, how to make a living—the past, present, and future. I talked about many of our important people of the past, their names, where they lived, and what they did. I also talked about many geographical names of this area and how my stories are associated with each site. I told about what names we have given to our mesas and land formations around here. I want all this important information to be available to all. This is why I agreed to do the interview.

To my tribal leaders, the chapter president, vice president, council delegates, secretary, treasurer, all my officials and leaders in our tribal government in Window Rock, and to whom it may concern hereafter: I want this autobiography to remain as it is. I do not want anyone to change or rewrite any part of the book. I want everyone to take care of this book and to use it as a teaching tool and reference. Teach our people from all the teachings of our ancestors—the good knowledge. This book will be available to all the children of our schools and in educational libraries. Our children will read and learn the important teachings, language, and history of our people. These teachings of life are from the past, but they are still good for the present and future. Our children will benefit from them. This is what I have in my interview, my tribal leaders. It is all based on my very own life story and my teachings, and I want them preserved as such.

John had spoken, and the NNHPD listened. I received permission to publish the manuscript without any changes. The next step was to write something that would reflect accurately both the information and the feelings as John desired.

◆ ◆ ◆

Navajo biography and autobiography is a small but growing genre. In *The Journey of Navajo Oshley,* I outlined a brief summary of some of the more important works, with others having since been added, most notably Charlotte J. Frisbie's *Tall Woman.*[2] Each person's life history is unique, of course, but I believe John Holiday's to be an important contribution to Navajo studies for two reasons. First is the way he approached the task. John is as much a philosopher, teacher, and advocate as he is an elder, medicine man, and traditionalist. There is little doubt how he feels about a topic, and he instructs accordingly. I have found in working with medicine men that as a general rule, their interpretation of events and understanding spring from the training and world view associated with their ceremonial knowledge. Why something happens, its importance, and its aftereffects are explained from a religious perspective. John does this beautifully.

This is not to suggest that he is the only medicine man who views things this way. Indeed, in the first chapter we see his father and grandfather attending gatherings where many medicine men collected to compare thoughts and practice a ceremony before "going public." What make John's account important are the unvarnished explanations and the voice with which he describes what he saw taking place, based on his religious perspective. In Navajo autobiographies such as those of Left Handed (Son of Old Man Hat), Old Mexican, Tall Woman, and Oshley, the philosophical and religious world view does not emanate as strongly as it does here.[3] This is not to suggest that these books are unimportant. They are excellent works, wonderful additions to understanding daily Navajo life, but the narrators do not philosophize or ruminate over their experiences in the same way that John does.

On the other hand, the autobiography of Frank Mitchell and biography of Hosteen (Hastiin) Klah draw closer to Holiday's views.[4] Speaking from a ceremonial background, these two men provide a religious perspective, and even though Klah's thoughts are sifted through Franc

Newcomb's voice, the thinking and logic that are distinctly Navajo remain. I have worked to maintain a similar presence in John's story by preserving Navajo thought with its holistic, religious perspective. The reader receives a powerful glimpse into this perception through autobiography.

Numerous works explain Navajo philosophy and performance of ceremonies, compare beliefs, analyze lifestyles, catalog material culture, explicate social systems, and study gender. These are valuable, as the notes in this text attest, in explaining various aspects of Navajo life. But John rolls many of these topics together, synthesizing his explanations of how the world works. His voice is clear and vision sharp as he explains his rational world based on traditional teachings. Although this world may be discordant with beliefs from the twenty-first-century scientific world, John's views make sense.

Obviously, because this is one man's story, individuals will disagree with some of his views. In an oral tradition, where teachings are personal, there are bound to be differences. While working on the book *Sacred Land, Sacred View,* in the late 1980s, I had an experience that provides a good response to those troubled by a perspective not in tune with the way another might have explained some aspect of Navajo culture.[5] I had compiled a series of teachings that expressed how Navajo people felt about the land in southeastern Utah. Men and women had shared their feelings about the mountains, rock formations, rivers, plants, and animals, and now it was time to see how they felt about my compilation. I asked a group of elders and medicine men, who would be meeting at Monument Valley High School, whether they would be willing to listen to an hour-long cassette retranslation in Navajo of what I had learned. After listening to most of it, a spokesperson for the group said that he recognized much of it, but there were other things that he did not know. Then came his point: "That is how you were taught; then that is correct."

The information in this book reflects how John was taught and how he views his world. The vast majority of time spent in the initial interviews was under his direction and not based on a series of preconceived questions derived by the interviewers. John had a clear idea of what he considered to be important, what he wanted to say. Not until I returned with a number of points that needed clarification did the interviews take a question-and-answer format. Even then, John found opportunities to share new insight. I know, with surety, that what appears here is only the surface of his teachings, which go in many directions with greater depth. He invited Marilyn and me to learn more, if we so desired, but that will have to occur another time. In terms of his life story, I believe this to be as complete as he would like.

John chose to leave out some elements. The reader may find it surprising, for example, that there is so little mention of his family. His wife and children are almost invisible in this narrative. When asked whether he would like to include more in this book, he decided not to, and so their story will be left for them or others to write. I believe the reason for this is that John wished to make sure that his grandfather's, his father's, and his own teachings remained central and undiluted. His story is primarily a story of men, of ceremonial practitioners, and of teachings that have been passed down through his family line. It was his responsibility to see to its preservation, which became a personal task.

This was not the first time that I had encountered this perspective. A number of years ago, I interviewed a woman about her life, the history she knew, and traditional knowledge. Marilyn and I sat with her in one room, while her husband sat in another. Her low voice was difficult to hear as she whispered softly into the microphone. I later asked Marilyn if this woman was speaking that way because of the nature of what she was saying. Perhaps it was so sacred that she lowered her voice in reverence. Marilyn smiled and said no, that was not it; the woman did not want her husband to hear her teachings. This was somewhat ironic, considering I was a stranger to her and that she understood this information was intended for public instruction. Some things are shared within the family, and others remain the domain of the individual. The choice to share private information with the public rested solely on her shoulders.

The second reason this book is an important contribution to Navajo studies is its emphasis on local history and culture. Because of my experience with John during the Oshley interview, I knew that he understood the Navajo map of the past. Today, people pass through Monument Valley and southeastern Utah oblivious to the names bestowed upon the land by previous generations. When listening to older Navajos talk, one cannot help but be impressed with the rich ethnographic understanding associated with what seems like every rock, mesa, spring, and mountain.

Indeed, just as Anglos navigate in the city by street numbers, store locations, and traffic lights, Navajos in the past were specific in their use of geographical landmarks. Some names were given because of physical characteristics—the type of rock, the color of a mesa, the flow from a spring. Other places received names because of an event or incident—where two people met, an accident occurred, or something was lost. Still other names recall seasonal events or natural phenomena. Whatever the reason, this identification system was clearly specific, varied, and pervasive for Navajos in the past.

The information from this understanding is powerful. Keith H. Basso's study of the Western Apaches in *Wisdom Sits in Places* illustrates exactly how informative a cultural map of the land can be in grasping another's world view.[6] Teachings and history imbue the landscape with values established as mnemonic devices. An individual is reminded of his or her heritage by associating mythological stories or human events with a lesson about life. This is a way of learning that spans many cultures. As readers absorb the text and notes in this book, they will encounter a rich understanding of what the land meant to Navajos in the past. The land is personalized and instructive, the teachings from which need to be preserved as much as any other type of cultural information.

John provides such an understanding. My hope is that someday in the not-too-distant future, these places can be named on maps by elders who remember. From this information comes a product that will tie cultural values to a rich history in the land. This knowledge needs to be put in the hands of young people, not just as a school project, but as a tangible tool that pries open the doors of the past to a wealth of understanding. John's concern about instruction for future generations can be addressed, in part, through opportunities to engage students with the world beyond the classroom.

I have left in the text many names of people who are now gone. Perhaps some of these names and descriptions will be helpful to Navajo families tracing genealogical roots. John certainly assisted me in understanding individuals and relationships as I browsed in Navajo Oshley's world. Of equal importance is the reader's understanding of the complex flow of people and events so much a part of traditional culture. Anthropologists and sociologists write about a "web of relations," but John shows us what that means. His insider view provides much more immediacy, more fabric to the culture, as he tells of real people making a living in the livestock economy of the 1920s and 1930s and in the uranium industry of the 1950s.

This book, in addition to being about the life of a man, is a history of the Monument Valley community. John experienced so much over the past eighty years that he is, in a sense, a representative figure, a spokesperson for those now gone. His family teachings hearken to before the Long Walk (early 1860s) and Fort Sumner (1864–1868) periods and the Navajos' return to their land. He describes daily life in the livestock industry, livestock reduction, work for the Civilian Conservation Corps (CCC) and war industry during World War II, movie making in the John Ford years, and uranium mining. Woven throughout these everyday and landmark events are his training and practice as a medicine man in the context of daily life with the people, a way of life that changed rapidly from one that evolved over hundreds of years to one that dramatically shifted within two decades in the twentieth century. John tells what this was like.

The second half of the book consists of John's teachings about the land, self-discipline, traditional culture, ceremonies, and the future. Didactic at times, always a storyteller, John discusses what he sees happening today. He is concerned about, but not yet ready to pass the torch to, the younger generation. The loss of language and traditional values, a fragmented work ethic, weakening self-discipline, and decreasing ceremonial knowledge seem to be fulfilling the prophecies of earlier generations that these changes would eventually happen with catastrophic results. He is very much aware of what is to transpire before, as he describes, the "medicine men are placed in the mountains," but he also hints that it is not too late to reverse the loss. His words are offered to other Navajos as a means of reversing this trend.

EDITORIAL NOTE

Readers, especially scholars, are often anxious to know how much of an editing hand has been applied to a manuscript. Oral interviews are a wonderfully rich source of information that flows from the speaker recalling the past. Personal accounts bring immediacy to a topic and re-create what the individual recalls. This selective process encourages the art of storytelling, kinetic animation, and vocal renderings that give even more life to the flowing personal narrative. From the mouth of a gifted raconteur spring images, thoughts, and feelings that paint verbal pictures of the past. John Holiday is such a person.

Still, even with the best mind at work, the oral interview process allows errors to creep in, single-vision recall, magnification of an individual's role, and a generally slanted perspective. John's story is his as he remembers it. I have added notes to provide explanation of some things that may be unclear to the reader or to assist with another perspective. This is not to suggest that what he says is wrong, but only that others have viewed the same incident or phenomenon differently. No attempt has been made to change the feelings or direction of his instruction. His passion for certain subjects, the delivery of that passion, and the solutions to problems are his. This is his story.

One of the biggest problems I faced as the editor is that of maintaining an accurate chronological order. The fluidity of oral interviews—jumping back and forth between topics as well as starting up at another time where the interview left off—lends itself to shifts in subject. Between interviews, John would think about things that he wanted either to add or to clarify. Consequently, when it was time for me to put events in order, I had some questions about John's age when they occurred. I also added an earlier interview, conducted in 1991, that had rich information that expanded or clarified certain topics he had discussed more recently. Add to this issues inherent in translating from one language to another, and one can see how the task of editing becomes complicated.

I chose the least obtrusive course. After Marilyn translated the interview, I started moving elements around to fit what I felt was the proper sequence in his life. In a few instances, a particular type of event appeared to be in the same period as other events, yet in the interviews, it was mentioned later. To avoid switching subjects only to return in a few pages, I clustered some of these short stories together, placing them under the same rubric. I then identified in the manuscript the major events in John's life and asked him to respond to the accuracy of the sequencing. To my relief, he said that, with a few exceptions, the age and order that I had determined were satisfactory. After I made those corrections, I felt that the manuscript accurately reflected what he said and the way he had lived the events.

Sentence patterns and word choice were another concern. The Navajo language reflects an entirely different way of viewing the world than that provided by English. The latter does not even come close, in many instances, to relaying the precise meaning or connotation of Navajo words and thoughts, even in the best of translations. Also, the spoken word is different from the written word. Sentence structure and patterning fulfill different expectations in each form so that if the spoken word is transcribed verbatim, a very intelligent person may sound stupid. The repetition, vocables, and kinesics, so much a part of talking, do not transfer well to paper either.

What I have chosen to do is a light editing of what Marilyn translated. I moved about some sentences, replaced some word choices, and combined or restructured sentences to provide a better reading pattern. In general, however, I left pretty much alone what and how John spoke. In many instances, John responded to questions for clarity, and I incorporated his answers, added information, and shifted sentence sequence as necessary. Marilyn has read the finished manuscript for accuracy and given her nod. In turn, I accept full responsibility for errors of interpretation or in the chronology of this work, but I believe John is happy with what is here.

There are still some unsolved conundrums. Even after clarification interviews that questioned such things as the machinery that distinguished between Mexican and Anglo flesh, the sacred shields and medicine bundle created at the time of the Long Walk, and the mysterious wagon trains that passed through Monument Valley, there remain some unsatisfactory answers. Those things and events will probably remain a mystery, although I do not doubt John's perception of them. Possible explanations for some of them are in the notes.

Another problem was that John did not have many family photographs. Some older Navajo families have extensive collections stashed in trunks under a bed, but not so with John. To remedy the situation, I obtained pictures from the Utah State Historical Society and Northern Arizona University, both of whom have extensive collections of Navajo life in the Monument Valley–Four Corners region. Fortunately, I found many of the things that John talked about portrayed in these photos. He has approved their use and was even able to identify some of the people in them.

Sprinkled throughout the text are Navajo names provided first in English, then in Navajo. Since the work of Robert W. Young and William Morgan, Navajo orthography is standardized. Still, there are a number of ways to indicate a person's name when it is tied to a characteristic or event for which that person is named. Taft Blackhorse, a Navajo ethnographer who works for the tribe and is very familiar with Navajo names and spelling, helped with this part of the text. Garth A. Wilson, a Navajo linguist at the College of Eastern Utah, checked the final proof to ensure accuracy. Their expertise filled a gap.

In summary, this book is the result of a joint effort by many people. John has told his life history and teachings as he would like them to be remembered; Baxter Benally and Marilyn Holiday have performed a great service in the interview and translation process; Taft and Garth provided technical expertise; and I have moved the text to a published form. I believe John summarized the most important point for this manuscript when he said, "I know that my teachings, my words, my songs, and my prayers will live forever, because they will be written with my name on them. This is what I agreed to have done, and that is why I told my story."

Acknowledgments

Writing a book is both an exhilarating and a painful process. Working with people—interviewing, questioning, learning, assisting, and being assisted—is one of the most enjoyable parts of the experience. This book is no exception. There are those who played a crucial part in bringing this text forth, and my gratitude for their assistance is embedded within the pages of this manuscript, for they are a part of it.

Most obvious is my appreciation for John Holiday. Not only did he share his knowledge and personal experience, but he also patiently answered questions and clarified concepts for an outsider deeply interested in what the inside looked like. When other obligations got in my way, he patiently waited for me to return to the project to do my part in bringing it to fruition. We both recognize the importance of what he has shared.

The Navajo language, whether oral or written, is difficult for a non-native speaker to master. I am often asked, "Do you speak Navajo?" and respond with "Just enough to get in trouble." Pronunciation, spelling, vocabulary, and verb conjugation, just for a start, seem almost impossible for a beginner to grasp. Add to these the level of complexity when spoken by an elderly medicine man, and one can be quickly overwhelmed. The salvation of this project lay in the assistance of experts. The roles of Baxter Benally and Marilyn Holiday are explained in later pages. Others need to be recognized here for their tremendous help: Taft Blackhorse, Navajo ethnographer who works for the tribe; Garth A. Wilson, author of the popular *Conversational Navajo Dictionary*;

and Linda Keams, Navajo linguist employed by Utah State University, all assisted with specific aspects of translation and orthography. I greatly depended on their expertise in avoiding the linguistic swamp I found myself approaching.

I owe thanks also to others who extricated me from the ruts and bumps along the road to publication. Charlotte Frisbie and Peter Iverson gave excellent advice on cultural concerns, writing points, and aspects of presentation. Andrea Carpenter, a friend, helped organize the chapters on computer, and Jo Ann Reece, from the University of Oklahoma Press, allowed sufficient time to work on the manuscript during a period of transition in my professional life.

Organizations also made this work possible. The Utah Humanities Council funded much of the project; the Navajo Nation Historic Preservation Department approved it; the Utah State Historical Society and the Special Collections Department of the Cline Library of Northern Arizona University provided many of the historical photographs; and the College of Eastern Utah–San Juan Campus gave general support. Without the logistical pieces these agencies provided, this book would not be in your hands now.

Finally, there is my family. They contended with two problems. The first was my absence on those Saturdays when I should have been out playing instead of at the office working on this manuscript. The second was my unbridled enthusiasm for what John had shared. I hope, as they glimpse into his world, it will make theirs better. I know it has made mine.

A NAVAJO LEGACY

Introduction

Leslie Marmon Silko introduces her novel *Ceremony* with Thought-Woman saying, "I will tell you something about stories; they aren't just entertainment. Don't be fooled. They are all we have, you see, to fight off illness and death. . . . And in the belly of this story the rituals and the ceremony are still growing."[1] Each person's life is a story, John's being no exception. He is an excellent storyteller, who will start his account in the next chapter. This chapter is devoted to those who worked with him. They have their stories, and these stories, too, "are still growing."

Rarely, if ever, has the translator of a Navajo autobiography had much space devoted to his or her experience in or understanding of the project. Often relegated to the acknowledgments, a translator's voice may thread through a narrative, but only as a whisper compared to that of the editor. What follows are two stories of how this manuscript evolved from voice to tape to page. The first is an anecdotal rendering of how Baxter Benally and I interviewed John. Its purpose is to paint a picture of the circumstances under which the initial interviews occurred. Baxter is an excellent field man. He loves to joke, seems to know everyone within a 150-mile radius of Bluff, Utah, his home, and responds well to storytelling. He is the type of person who enters a home, senses an atmosphere, and determines what is appropriate for the situation. He is sensitive yet gregarious and enjoys visiting with everyone. In short, he is a people person.

When we visited John, I instructed Baxter not to interrupt the flow of speech, that I could catch up later, and to ask clarifying questions only after John had finished talking. Consequently, there were long stretches when we both just listened, Baxter understanding every word but silent, and me catching only snatches. On the way home, Baxter provided some details, and I made note of additional topics for later discussions. As for the laborious task of actual translation from tape to page, Baxter had no interest.

That task fell to Marilyn Holiday, whose explanation of her experience constitutes a major portion of this chapter. Fluent in Navajo and English, a keen observer, and having known John since she was a little girl, Marilyn approached her work with sincerity and devotion. Her countless hours of listening to tapes have provided the heart of this book. Her recollections of John as a community member, medicine man, and distant relative ring with authenticity. I have incorporated her words, with light editing, the way she wrote them. They are instructive, giving an insider's and translator's view not often found in Navajo autobiography. The reader can sense that, especially in Marilyn, John's stories "are still growing."

BAXTER BENALLY: SEEKER OF STORIES

The sky seemed particularly blue that November morning as Baxter Benally and I drove past Eagle Mesa and headed for the junction. The sun, still low on the horizon, cast long shadows from the sagebrush and fence posts along the way, while the red sand, damp from an evening shower, lightened as it dried. Train Rock loomed large from the desert floor to the west. Its familiar outline pointed to our destination—John Holiday's home, directly to the north. A few skinny cows grazing close to the fence line paid no attention to the traffic speeding down the paved road, then turning off for Monument Valley Navajo Tribal Park, with its famous red rock formations to the east. The sun crept above the Mittens, Coyote and Rabbit, and other sandstone monoliths, so familiar to tourists.

Baxter, dressed in blue jeans with three-inch rolled cuffs, a white long-sleeved thermal undershirt, white socks, and low-cut hiking boots, munched on pepper jerky we had bought in Mexican Hat. He was about my age, but not a trace of gray streaked his dark black hair. I am convinced that he has given me at least some of my gray hair from the "situations" he likes to create. A long-time friend, he loves to joke. Today the joke was about a movie we were going to make sometime in the never-to-be future. The plot revolved around the reversed roles of the Lone Ranger and Tonto, with me being the fall guy and he, as Tonto, the hero who makes things right. His humor seemed always to find its best points at my expense—setting me up for a marriage to some unsuspecting woman we were visiting; asking our host to serve me coffee, which I do not drink; announcing at the door that we were the Internal Revenue Service; or reminding me of my nickname, Jeeshoo (Buzzard), which he had given me because of my less-than-abundant hair.

I had opportunities to return the favor. When he needed an occasional pit stop on some lonely desert road, the truck I was driving would mysteriously edge away from him, the distance depending on how long he took. There were times when he actually had to run to catch the vehicle. When crossing the San Juan River, I threatened to drive to the water's edge long enough to baptize him, so that we both would not end up in hell, stoking the furnaces for all our friends above. And there was the long-standing ritual at the end of the day, when Baxter received his pay. I always provided a lengthy explanation about how he was overpaid, which obligated him to feed me, now that he had broken the bank. There was no doubt in my mind that his nickname, Golizhii (Skunk), was well deserved. Once we started doing interviews, however, we both assumed a more serious tone.

As we turned off the paved road and headed north, we could see the mesa where John's home sat. His yard was well kept. The hogan, reserved for ceremonial occasions, had a fresh coat of dirt, and the cars parked outside his two houses were lined up near the doors. This was our first day of interviewing John Holiday, a Navajo medicine man with a well-established reputation in southeastern Utah.

Upon entering his home, we sat and waited for him to finish breakfast. When he came into the living room, I gave him four strands of turquoise, two arrowheads, a deerskin, and some money to communicate the value of the time and information he would share. He seemed pleased but said little. Before getting started, however, he wanted to watch his rented World Wrestling Federation videotape. This came as a surprise. I was intent on what I wanted to ask him about his life and traditional Navajo culture, yet here was a medicine man, knowledgeable about many interesting and important things, wanting to watch Hulk Hogan. The three of us sat for almost an hour, peering at sweaty bodies tossing each other off the ropes, then pounding each other onto the mat for a pin. Ordinarily this would have been amusing; now it was just irritating.

Finally, he turned off the one-eyed monster. There we sat in his living room, a turquoise rug beneath our feet, flower-patterned couch cushions at our backs, and pictures of John riding a bull, a Plains Indian face with eagle, an American flag, and family photos hanging on the walls. John presided from a rocking chair, his hands sporadically gripping the arms only to glide off into a gesture to illustrate his story. His five-foot-six-inch frame had eased into the chair slowly, reminding us of his eighty-plus years. A small bun of gray hair, tied in the back, had wisps sticking out above and below the turquoise and dark blue headband. White teeth, framed by the wrinkles around his mouth, sat like white shell in sand, while his glasses suggested modernity. The necklace of white coral interspersed with turquoise, as well as the large silver and turquoise bracelet and watchband, spoke of tradition, and his gnarled bare feet whispered of years of hard use.

John's voice raised and lowered, illustrating an art of storytelling born of the oral tradition. At one point, he actively gestured with his right hand, then dropped it, only to raise it again and point in an arching movement to accompany his words. The smooth skin on the backs of his hands and his carefully clipped fingernails became another part of the picture he painted as his hands moved quickly, then slowed in pace. Often his left fist gripped the arm of the rocker, seeming to allow even greater freedom for his right. Baxter and I asked few questions then or on subsequent days as John continued to tell his life story. He needed little prompting, having a clear idea of what he wanted to share. A half hour between questions was not uncommon, as he outlined events from his birth to adulthood. Through it all, he maintained animation.

Few actions were surer signs of John's delight than when he would reach a critical point in his story and burst out with a throaty, chest-pulsing laugh that ended in a falsetto. He had many distinctive traits, but this was the most prominent. He loved to laugh and did it often. He also delighted in taking up where Baxter left off with humor. He would ask us what we thought about something. Did we understand? Agree? Looking at me, he would ask, "What are your beliefs concerning . . . ?" Always interested in learning, he seemed to be storing our replies in his philosophical locker. Soon I became "Big Mormon," and again the give-and-take banter resumed, though I must admit, I was not as quick with a reply as I was with Baxter. More questions followed, along with commentary. I felt that he enjoyed the interviewing process—all six hours that day; he agreed to our next return.

And so we did. This time Baxter and I met in the living room of John's other home. John ate a hearty breakfast of bread, meat, and potatoes, washed down with a final cup of coffee before his wife and son left to care for the livestock. The home was extremely warm, the stove having been lovingly stoked with juniper and coal before our arrival. John, perched on a recliner, was dressed in a pink shirt, blue pants, the same jewelry as the day before, and well-worn Navajo moccasins. A black Harley Davidson headband contained his gray locks, giving a kempt appearance, while a single crutch he used to hobble about his home rested against the arm of the chair.

Today, he paused more as he spoke, closing his eyes often to gather his thoughts before continuing. John spoke only Navajo, but there was not much need for questioning; he appeared to view a screen that dropped down in his mind, portraying events from the past. The details of this moving picture were extensive. How he recalled incidents, provided conversation for his characters, and cross-referenced one thing to another was delightful. His knowledge seemed limitless. Always there was a story, always a philosophical point for our instruction. Never did he hesitate to answer a question.

Finally, Baxter broke the spell long enough to open the outside door and allow a flow of cool air to enter. Through the crack, I watched the sun move toward its zenith and the puffy clouds pushing themselves about on their way to the east, with massive Train Rock beneath them, so large it seemed about to chug into the yard. Heat waves shimmered off the red soil, adding little distortions to the pinyon and juniper trees surrounding the camp. The tape recorder rolled on.

At noon, Bessie Blackgoat arrived in a new white car. A tan coat covered her short stature and thin frame, and a kerchief covered her hair.

John Holiday and Baxter Benally, November 16, 1999. Always there was a story, always a philosophical point for our instruction. (Photo by author)

She was feeling the effects of old age and needed help. Baxter and I paused for a half hour as she and her daughter asked John to perform a ceremony. Even as a medicine woman, she sought his help as a specialist in the Blessingway. For partial payment, she offered a turquoise string necklace; John accepted with a promise to hold the ceremony later. When she left, we again plunged into the past, ending the interview with three full tapes in the late afternoon.

And so the days went—four of them—with six hours of interview each time. This, added to a session conducted in 1991 and two later clarification interviews necessary to ensure accuracy on my part, form the basis of this book.

MARILYN HOLIDAY: THOUGHTS FROM A TRANSLATOR

The collection of this oral history was just the beginning. The most time-consuming and skilled part of the project lay with Marilyn Holiday, translator of the tapes. Five foot seven, with short permed hair, she is adroit in her ability he is saying." If there are people like him attending, others are more serious about how they handle business.

When I listen to John, his words are like opening a book that has much to teach. Every time I start translating, I cannot wait to hear the end of his story. I have done a lot of translating and transcribing over the years and have learned that my best time for concentration is early morning, when everybody is asleep and it is peaceful. My parents talked a lot about their childhood years and how their parents used to tell them to get up early in the morning. I used to think of it as a hardship, but to them, it was something to strengthen their personal being, to be healthy, and to have a strong mind and body. This is true for me now, so I get all of my materials, sit down, listen to the tapes, and start writing. I listen to all of John's stories, every word, and try to picture things as he describes them.

When he tells his stories, it is like sitting in a theater with a picture. He describes every little detail and provides a soundtrack, too. I hear and feel and see things as if I am there. Whatever story he tells, whether it is of his childhood or later in life, I experience seeing it through his mind and eyes. I learn a lot from doing the transcription, but once everybody starts stirring in my home, it shuts off something really good. I put the tape recorder and writing materials on the shelf and wait to get back to them to see what happened. Late at night, after I finish my daily work and everybody is in bed, I take them down again and continue to walk through history. The feelings from this work give me goose bumps and the type of exhilaration that comes from winning a race.

Sometimes I feel as if his words are saying, "Go, go, go." Early in the morning, I listen about how the ancestors lived and prepared themselves for their day. When I translate, although I may just be sitting on my bed, I take these words in, and they are good. I get up, go outside, and think how my ancestors had this kind of morning too. These feelings are real, and this is what they talked about. If you are up at four in the morning, you get the first of the blessings, and it is as if the Holy Beings talk to you. You present yourself to the morning. The Holy Ones say that the only way to be recognized by them is to be out and about. When John talks about these things, I know I need to do them.

His teachings and comparisons about his younger days and the present are powerful. He teaches with love, and at times, his words brought tears to my eyes. I knew he spoke the truth, but we do not practice those things today. We are going in another direction. I do not know where the change came, but things started turning another way.

John's teachings about the whip are a good example. Today we look at the use of a whip as abuse, but if one really thinks about John's perspective, it is an object of love. The whip provides strength for living and growth in knowledge. There is no hate in this, and these kinds of ideas make me think. If our whole society changed its perspective, our minds would be turned around, and we would go back to the way it was in his younger days. Children and adults who get in trouble because they are not disciplined could change.

He also talked about different religious experiences of his elders. He heard these things from his parents and other people. This knowledge he has learned since he was young, but it has gone through a big transition. I admire those people who lived these teachings. Listening to John is like walking through a history book with a philosopher. There is always a lesson in everything he says, and his words are important.

The Navajo language is very descriptive, drawing a picture as one speaks. English does not achieve the same kind of inner depth. John would at times describe a setting or person which implied much that needed to be brought out in the translation. When I tried to say it in English, it was hard to be accurate. I wanted to transcribe it to ensure this same feeling or what he saw was there, but it is difficult. Some words are strong in Navajo but cannot really be said in English. This is especially true when telling a story or describing a myth. At times I felt like I was not doing enough to draw a picture through words. John provides a whole scene, and that is what I wanted to grasp, but it was hard.

Not everybody understands elements of the Creation, because in Navajo, it is very complicated and deep. John would say there were certain parts of the story that were sacred and should not be shared, and then he started talking right in the middle of it, and I wondered what preceded it. He makes it known that he will not talk about sacred things, then he says this thing or person or Holy Being did this, and I am thinking, "Which Holy Person?" Later, he resumed the story and related back to some of those things which clarify what he was talking about, but it was still hard to find the words in English.

At times I asked other people or John who did something, and they would say, "them." So I think, "This must be sacred, so I'm not supposed to know or mention it." John would continue the story to a certain point, and then say, "All this pertains to this point, but I cannot go beyond. You will just have to understand." In Navajo tradition, a person can only say so much before getting into trouble. A lot of times a person will say that what is known is a shield in front of them that protects from harm. So if this sacred information is divulged, they become vulnerable. A lot of things cannot be talked about in detail.

When John told us stories from the Creation, he would say, "There are some things that we can only talk about in the winter, but not now while it is warm outside." He then asked us to return at the right season so that he could tell us more. Most medicine men still respect this view and will not talk about things unless it is the right time.

I feel like John means what he says. He is very concerned about what is going on today and really wants people to know about now and the future. Everything that is happening will affect the future, and we cannot be left to blow in the wind.

I always felt like he invited me in as his little sister. He would say, "Come in and sit down. You need to know about this." He made me responsible to make sure that his words went out just as he taught. I felt that if he was going to be talking through me, then I was going to do what was necessary to tell it as he wanted. We have explained from the very beginning what this project was about. I think that after he saw the book about Oshley, he thought that he had something to say too. He knew we were coming there for educational purposes and looked at us as a team that would do the job. He also felt comfortable talking to us. I believe he was grateful that there was somebody who cared enough to do this kind of work and share it with others. There was nothing negative during the interviews, never a time when he said anything about our working on this project. When he sees this book finished, I hope he feels it is actually like he told us. I wish he could read so that he would know, word for word, what is in it.

He examines a lot of things, and I am sure he found out a lot about me, too. He wanted to know what kind of a person I was, and there were times when he challenged me. He tested me to see what kind of

Marilyn Holiday: "I have learned from him that we are not here on this earth just to live and die, but that there is a purpose in our lives." (Photo by Stan Byrd)

head I had on my shoulders. I liked that; I wanted to be tested to know if I knew what he expected of me. I want to be in somebody else's mind and have him think, "She knows a lot and is understanding." He really respects people who are well educated and at times asked how you [Bob] thought about certain things. There were also times when he challenged through questions. That was when I really had to think and make sure I made sense.

I have learned from him that we are not here on this earth just to live and die, but that there is a purpose in our lives. The way John presented his life story, with its different teachings from many generations, made me look inside and search myself as a person and as a woman. I looked at the role I play in my family, as a mother and wife, as a person in public, and how I present myself and respect others. I think a lot of his teachings made me look deeper as to who I really am in the tradi-

to span, through language, the traditional and modern world of the Navajo. I had worked with Marilyn for years, conducted numerous interviews with her in the field, and knew of her love for the People and the responsibility she felt in preserving accurately their history. As translator, she performed the clarification interviews. If there was one key person in this project besides John, it was Marilyn.

I paid her for her time but knew that her service was as much an act of love as it was a means to meet economic necessity. Page after page rolled out from under her steady hand, and when she was not sure of something that John had said, she made note; if a thought needed to be inserted to clarify his comment, it went into parentheses. Marilyn never seemed to tire, although she was tired. She never asked to quit, although it would have been understandable, given her hectic daily schedule and family responsibilities.

I often stopped to visit her at work to see how the translation was coming and how she was feeling. On more than one occasion, she started telling me about something that John was "talking about" that morning and how good the things were that he taught. Tears welled up in her eyes as she grabbed for a tissue. His teachings and the beauty in parts of his life had spoken strongly to her. In the turmoil that surrounds each of us in our daily existence, she had found peace in the roots of her shared heritage. Although a distant relative of John, she was now close to him. I could not help but think that this was one of John's stated reasons for entering into this undertaking.

Realizing how involved Marilyn was with this project, I asked her to record her feelings and describe the experience. At first she was shy, asking if I could help with the writing. I switched tactics and suggested we do an interview, to which she consented. First, she wanted time to collect her thoughts. Then one day after work, she stopped by my office and announced she was ready. What follows are her recollections of her experience with John Holiday and this project. Not surprisingly, she begins by identifying herself through kin relationships.

◆ ◆ ◆

I am related to John Holiday on my father's side through the Bit'ahnii Clan, translated as Within-His-Cover People. Since my father, Fred Yazzie, is a Bit'ahnii, I am born for the Bit'ahnii Clan, as is John, making us clan brother and sister. He greets me as his little sister, and I greet him as my big brother. His wife, Lula, is a daughter of one of my great-grandfathers, Hastiin Water under the Cottonwood, of the Táchii'nii, or

Red-Running-into-the-Water People, Clan. My grandmother, Sally Grey, and my mother, Suzie Yazzie, are, therefore, from the Táchii'nii Clan, which makes Lula my mother. She calls me her daughter, and I call her my mother. So in a roundabout way, I am related to John and Lula through the clans, which provide a long stream of relatives on both sides of my family. This is how we respect each other in our greetings.

My father remembers John and his father, Hastiin Billy, moving back and forth through Monument Valley, where my father lived. The Holiday family would stay for a night or a week at my paternal grandfather's homestead as they passed through. In those days, a lot of people did that, spending time with their relatives as they moved to other pastures for food for their livestock or for special occasions like ceremonies or Squaw Dances. My dad was about the same age as John. They took care of the sheep, horses, and chores together. They knew each other in that way.

My mother, who was also about the same age, remembers seeing John from a distance at activities in Monument Valley. She saw him at ceremonies when he was a young boy, practicing to become a medicine man. They always greeted each other, and since the people were all related in one way or another, the community was like one big family.

There were many places where people would meet during the week. The trading post was one spot where they bought food, brought in wool or sheepskins, and exchanged whatever they had. Even as I was growing up, my family did this. I remember it was like a general meeting place, with individuals and groups coming to visit, telling about their family's activities, and catching up on the latest news. My parents were very involved when the folks from the Oljato and Train Rock area—which included John, his family, and in-laws—came over to take part in community events. Harry Goulding in his trading post became heavily involved in celebrating Christmas and the Fourth of July with the Navajo people.

I think the first time that I heard of John was when people asked for his services as a medicine man. My parents lived close to the Monument Valley highway, where the junction is now. Whoever came on that dirt road heading for the trading post or clinic stopped by our house to eat, ask directions, or locate a person. I was about thirteen years old when I learned of John, but did not see him until a movie company was in Monument Valley working on a film. There were a lot of people gathered at my Aunt Julia's home near Goulding's. I remember John Ford and John Wayne passing out money. A dollar went to the little children, while the older people received five. My sisters and I each got a dollar, but as I was standing in this long line, I saw a very distinctive person wearing a red velveteen shirt, a lot of turquoise and silver, a scarf around his head, red moccasins with silver buttons on the side, and a large concho belt. His traditional dress showed that he was well-to-do. He laughed often and appeared to be a jolly man with whomever he talked. He seemed to be respected and known by everyone. The silver, turquoise, coral, and mother-of-pearl he wore stood for a lot of things in Navajo culture, and when I saw him standing out from the crowd, it occurred to me that he was somebody. Knowing he was a medicine man also brought respect, and yet he was such a cheerful person that people laughed wherever he went. That was my first impression, and from that point on, I thought of him as someone to be respected. I still do to this day.

I think, sometimes, that people respect John to a point that they want to ask him questions but shy away, feeling that he may not have time for them because he is important. They may believe they will ask the wrong question or he might lecture them down to the ground. But he is the kind of person who really likes to share his knowledge. That is what I found when we were doing interviews; he is a walking encyclopedia or history book, and everything he says is backed by philosophy or has a teaching. He is hungry for students and wants to be heard. People respect that.

When you start talking to him, he tells you a lot, but there are some things that are very serious and should not be joked about. For instance, one time he talked to me about my ancestry. My grandmother on my mother's side had ancestors who came from the Paiute. This happened when the tribes were warring amongst themselves, and they used to steal little children. Great-Great-Grandmother was taken, grew up in the Paiute Tribe, and as a young teenager, married and became pregnant. After a while she was mistreated and so ran away and came back to Monument Valley. From her pregnancy came my great-grandmother, and after that, my family members considered themselves part Paiute. So we are Táchii'nii Paiutes.

John teased me a lot about that in a way that I thought he was joking. Once I met him at a restaurant, where he and his brother, Willie, were eating hamburgers and fries. I walked by his table, and he said something about me living in Blanding and being a Ute from White Mesa. Navajos sometimes classify the Paiutes and Utes as one tribe. He said, "Oh, so you're living here in Blanding or White Mesa." I replied, "Yes. I live here, but not at White Mesa." Brothers and sisters always tease each other about being from somewhere they are not. That is a traditional form of teasing, and so I said, "No, I'm not, but you are from White Mesa. You are from here." So they started laughing, when suddenly John's face grew serious, and he said, "You know you are from the Paiute Tribe." It was funny, and I kind of laughed, but it turned out he was serious. I thought, "Okay, it's funny, and yet I know it's true. I know he is speaking the truth," and so I respected that and stopped laughing. The teasing part was over. The conversation ended on that tone, and I understood how he can tease and joke, but one has to be very careful how to relate to things. Not everybody is like that. He is a respectful person who is also respected.

This attitude goes back in his family. People respected his father, Hastiin Billy, who was a great medicine man. John followed in his footsteps, learning the teachings of a medicine man. A lot of these things are very serious and complicated when dealing with illness or psychiatric problems. These issues cannot be resolved with simple medicine or thinking. People understand he has the power and the treatment to overcome these ills and that his medicine works.

He is a part of the community, and at our chapter meetings, he is respected. If he has something to say, people listen and take him seriously. Most chapter meetings are a time to resolve problems. There are disputes over land, housing, and issues among the people. Sometimes everybody is frustrated as the meeting goes in the wrong direction. I have seen John stand up and comment as a peacemaker, saying, "Let's not talk like little kids; let's look at this whole thing seriously and remember that we are all relatives. We all came from the same clans. Let's look at it that way rather than losing our mind over these things. We are just blindly talking, saying what we want. Let's think more about where we came from." I think a lot of people stopped and thought, "Here's a man who is right. Here's an elder who knows what he is saying." If there are people like him attending, others are more serious about how they handle business.

When I listen to John, his words are like opening a book that has much to teach. Every time I start translating, I cannot wait to hear the end of his story. I have done a lot of translating and transcribing over the years and have learned that my best time for concentration is early morning, when everybody is asleep and it is peaceful. My parents talked a lot about their childhood years and how their parents used to tell them to get up early in the morning. I used to think of it as a hardship, but to them, it was something to strengthen their personal being, to be healthy, and to have a strong mind and body. This is true for me now, so I get all of my materials, sit down, listen to the tapes, and start writing. I listen to all of John's stories, every word, and try to picture things as he describes them.

When he tells his stories, it is like sitting in a theater with a picture. He describes every little detail and provides a soundtrack, too. I hear and feel and see things as if I am there. Whatever story he tells, whether it is of his childhood or later in life, I experience seeing it through his mind and eyes. I learn a lot from doing the transcription, but once everybody starts stirring in my home, it shuts off something really good. I put the tape recorder and writing materials on the shelf and wait to get back to them to see what happened. Late at night, after I finish my daily work and everybody is in bed, I take them down again and continue to walk through history. The feelings from this work give me goose bumps and the type of exhilaration that comes from winning a race.

Sometimes I feel as if his words are saying, "Go, go, go." Early in the morning, I listen about how the ancestors lived and prepared themselves for their day. When I translate, although I may just be sitting on my bed, I take these words in, and they are good. I get up, go outside, and think how my ancestors had this kind of morning too. These feelings are real, and this is what they talked about. If you are up at four in the morning, you get the first of the blessings, and it is as if the Holy Beings talk to you. You present yourself to the morning. The Holy Ones say that the only way to be recognized by them is to be out and about. When John talks about these things, I know I need to do them.

His teachings and comparisons about his younger days and the present are powerful. He teaches with love, and at times, his words brought tears to my eyes. I knew he spoke the truth, but we do not practice those things today. We are going in another direction. I do not know where the change came, but things started turning another way.

John's teachings about the whip are a good example. Today we look at the use of a whip as abuse, but if one really thinks about John's perspective, it is an object of love. The whip provides strength for living and growth in knowledge. There is no hate in this, and these kinds of ideas make me think. If our whole society changed its perspective, our minds would be turned around, and we would go back to the way it was in his younger days. Children and adults who get in trouble because they are not disciplined could change.

He also talked about different religious experiences of his elders. He heard these things from his parents and other people. This knowledge he has learned since he was young, but it has gone through a big transition. I admire those people who lived these teachings. Listening to John is like walking through a history book with a philosopher. There is always a lesson in everything he says, and his words are important.

The Navajo language is very descriptive, drawing a picture as one speaks. English does not achieve the same kind of inner depth. John would at times describe a setting or person which implied much that needed to be brought out in the translation. When I tried to say it in English, it was hard to be accurate. I wanted to transcribe it to ensure this same feeling or what he saw was there, but it is difficult. Some words are strong in Navajo but cannot really be said in English. This is especially true when telling a story or describing a myth. At times I felt like I was not doing enough to draw a picture through words. John provides a whole scene, and that is what I wanted to grasp, but it was hard.

Not everybody understands elements of the Creation, because in Navajo, it is very complicated and deep. John would say there were certain parts of the story that were sacred and should not be shared, and then he started talking right in the middle of it, and I wondered what preceded it. He makes it known that he will not talk about sacred things, then he says this thing or person or Holy Being did this, and I am thinking, "Which Holy Person?" Later, he resumed the story and related back to some of those things which clarify what he was talking about, but it was still hard to find the words in English.

At times I asked other people or John who did something, and they would say, "them." So I think, "This must be sacred, so I'm not supposed to know or mention it." John would continue the story to a certain point, and then say, "All this pertains to this point, but I cannot go beyond. You will just have to understand." In Navajo tradition, a person can only say so much before getting into trouble. A lot of times a person will say that what is known is a shield in front of them that protects from harm. So if this sacred information is divulged, they become vulnerable. A lot of things cannot be talked about in detail.

When John told us stories from the Creation, he would say, "There are some things that we can only talk about in the winter, but not now while it is warm outside." He then asked us to return at the right season so that he could tell us more. Most medicine men still respect this view and will not talk about things unless it is the right time.

I feel like John means what he says. He is very concerned about what is going on today and really wants people to know about now and the future. Everything that is happening will affect the future, and we cannot be left to blow in the wind.

I always felt like he invited me in as his little sister. He would say, "Come in and sit down. You need to know about this." He made me responsible to make sure that his words went out just as he taught. I felt that if he was going to be talking through me, then I was going to do what was necessary to tell it as he wanted. We have explained from the very beginning what this project was about. I think that after he saw the book about Oshley, he thought that he had something to say too. He knew we were coming there for educational purposes and looked at us as a team that would do the job. He also felt comfortable talking to us. I believe he was grateful that there was somebody who cared enough to do this kind of work and share it with others. There was nothing negative during the interviews, never a time when he said anything about our working on this project. When he sees this book finished, I hope he feels it is actually like he told us. I wish he could read so that he would know, word for word, what is in it.

He examines a lot of things, and I am sure he found out a lot about me, too. He wanted to know what kind of a person I was, and there were times when he challenged me. He tested me to see what kind of

Marilyn Holiday: "I have learned from him that we are not here on this earth just to live and die, but that there is a purpose in our lives." (Photo by Stan Byrd)

head I had on my shoulders. I liked that; I wanted to be tested to know if I knew what he expected of me. I want to be in somebody else's mind and have him think, "She knows a lot and is understanding." He really respects people who are well educated and at times asked how you [Bob] thought about certain things. There were also times when he challenged through questions. That was when I really had to think and make sure I made sense.

I have learned from him that we are not here on this earth just to live and die, but that there is a purpose in our lives. The way John presented his life story, with its different teachings from many generations, made me look inside and search myself as a person and as a woman. I looked at the role I play in my family, as a mother and wife, as a person in public, and how I present myself and respect others. I think a lot of his teachings made me look deeper as to who I really am in the traditional sense. We all experience tragedy in our lives and things that we do not understand. His life and teachings made me understand that it is all right to have problems. There is always a way out. He is very sincere about things like faith and beliefs. We must be at peace with ourselves. John gave the feeling that a person can do anything, but that what you do is what you are, and that is what you will be in the future. This is the kind of thing he wanted to relate in the interviews. This is really important to him.

I think the younger generations need this kind of teaching. A lot of youth are turning back to study their history. They really want to know where they came from. John relates his life so that these students, in times of trouble, can be reassured and have hope. We are not lost, because our history is strong. Navajos can see for themselves the roots of their history. Many of these things are only being repeated in a modern setting, but the inner self has not changed. John has brought this out in his teachings, showing that we are each important and should not feel lost. This is not the first time that troubles have arisen.

I think it is very important that our culture be preserved. Everything from the day that we are born to the day that we die is an important part of history. Even if we are not public figures, we are still a part of history within our own little family. We need to be remembered just like John said: "I want to be remembered somewhere even after I'm gone. I want to hear somebody say there was this man named John Holiday who did or said this. I want to hear my name even after I'm gone, make myself known, and not be forgotten." I know John will be remembered and appreciated by a lot of people for a long time.

ANOTHER EVALUATION OF JOHN'S TEACHINGS

An experience I had on November 30, 2000, illustrates what Marilyn said about the importance of what John has to share. It was a time I had looked forward to with some reservation: I was to give a public program in Monument Valley on some of John's teachings. I had seen other, similar lectures and discussions given by scholars go sour, with much resentment generated against "white men who have no business talking about such things." I fully realized that in spite of my teaching and interviewing in the community, I was still very much an outsider to many Navajo people. For that reason, I had a certain amount of anxiety about going into the "lion's den."

The advertising was somewhat unorthodox, with flyers in trading posts, post offices, gas stations, and legal offices, and announcements by word of mouth, the latter being the most effective on the reservation. I drove out to John's home, gave him an announcement, and invited him to attend, though I realized that as a practicing medicine man, his work might call him away.

Giving programs on the reservation is always a flip of the coin. We set up about fifty chairs in the library and decided not to use the auditorium, based on the experiences of the principal of Monument Valley High School, the librarian, and a college student who helped with advertising. One man pushing through slides in a big room with ten people present can get lonely. As the bewitching hour of seven o'clock drew nigh, however, we decided to bring in more chairs. By the time the program started, we were hauling piles of chairs from neighboring classrooms, and by the end of the presentation, there were so many people crammed into the room that many either stood in the doorway or pressed their faces against the library windows. The final count was 146 people, which does not include a dozen or more children who faded in and out of the crowd. People had come from Mexican Hat, Halchita, Oljato, Douglas Mesa, Monument Valley proper, and camps spread throughout adjoining areas. I was surprised at the response. There were grandmothers and grandfathers who spoke little or no English, those who were highly educated in terms of formal schooling, mothers and fathers with their children, college and high school students, and numerous Monument Valley tour guides. This was truly a community response—75 percent of the people attending were Navajo. John Holiday presided.

When time for the question-and-answer period came, I took a deep breath and opened the floor for comments. John addressed the people in Navajo and talked about the importance of sharing his teachings with others, so that this information would not be lost. From there, the group moved into an emotionally charged expression of appreciation for what had been shared that evening. Indeed, there was a man and a woman who could not hold back tears in thanksgiving for the preservation of the things John had talked about in the program. Others wanted to know about plans for the translated interviews: Could some of this be put on video? Could his life story be written in Navajo as well as in English? How could this information be transformed into teaching materials for the schools? The people's acceptance of what had been done was overwhelming, and although I explained that I still had a great deal more to accomplish, I also told them that once the book was available, they would be able to develop what they liked from an extremely rich bank of knowledge. I believe John's teachings and life history can play an important role in helping his people.

This may sound self-congratulatory, but John has opened a door to preservation that has been closed by many other knowledgeable people. As Leslie Silko suggests, these stories are what stand between a very real "illness and death" that affects traditional cultures steeped in the fast-paced twenty-first-century dominant society. John's teachings hold the potential to benefit others as they thread their way through the difficulties of life.

I

John's Life and Experiences

CHAPTER ONE

DAWN

John actually tells two stories in the following pages. The first, which starts in this chapter, is about his life; the second is about his teachings and how they apply to his experiences. The two stories are really inseparable, but to provide a focus that avoids repetition and gives a clearer sense of meaning, I have divided the book accordingly.

John begins his life story by identifying spiritual and family roots, expressed through clan and extended family relations. The long list of kin and elders he discusses gives a sense of the richness of his heritage. It is not exceptional for a Navajo elder to trace his or her genealogy on both the mother's and father's sides back five or six generations. When one considers the complexity of Navajo kinship, the tremendous emphasis placed on social identity and relations is apparent. These connections hold Navajo culture together through bonds of blood and sharing. Some readers may question the wisdom of John being "loaned" at such an early age to one of his paternal aunts living near Tuba City. On the other hand, what a testament it is to the trust of his family to have him stay with his father's sister for so long. He certainly was loved and warmly welcomed on his return from this experience.

Some of John's earliest recollections are associated with the profession of being a medicine man. His father and grandfather introduced him early in life to the teachings and practice of the art of healing. Even when his patience was tried as they traveled, with frequent stops, John maintained a curiosity about and fostered a growing knowledge of the practice. His mother also encouraged this interest, through her teachings, which inspired John to seek his own formal training. At one point, he equates this to what his brother received in boarding school. John obtained his own education, but in a traditional form.

PARENTS, FAMILY, AND BIRTH

I am John Holiday of the Bitter Water Clan (Tó Dich'íi'nii), born for the Within-His-Cover People Clan (Bit'ahnii).[1] In 1919, I was born under the trees near what is today a catch-basin dam by Train Rock, Monument Valley, Utah.[2] This is the home in which all my sisters and brothers were born. After me there were two younger brothers, Sam and Joe Holiday, and a younger sister, the youngest of all of us, who has since died.

My father, Billy Holiday, was of the Within-His-Cover People Clan, born for the Many Goats (Tł'ízí Łání).[3] His Navajo name was Yellow Hat (Ch'ah Łitsoii), or Hatty (Ch'ahii). He was born just east of Train Rock, by a small rock mesa called Sitting Red Rock. This site has an extended rocky ridge leading from it, where one can still see traces of hogans along the horse trail that leads to Owl Springs. His father, my paternal grandfather, known as Aching Stomach (Tsá'dinihii), or Tom Holiday, was of the Many Goats Clan and born for the Water's Edge Clan (Tábąąhá). He came from Shonto, Arizona. His first wife's name was Woman Who Was Hit (Asdzáán Bidoobeezh).[4] My paternal grandmother lived in Monument Valley throughout her life.[5]

My mother, Black Hair Clan's Daughter (Tsi'naajiní Bitsi'), was a Bitter Water and was born for the Black Hair Clan at Baby Rocks, west of Dennehotso, Arizona. Other names for the Baby Rocks formation are Woman Holding the Baby, Streak of Red, Wide Rock, Rocks Protruding, and Rocks Scattered Down. Mother's father was called Black Hair [clan name] Laughing (Tsii'łizhinii) and was of the Red-Running-into-the-Water People (Táchii'niitó Nát'oh Dine'é).[6] He was a cheerful person, always laughing when he talked.

My great-grandmother was named Woman Who Shoots (Asdzáán Adiłt'ohii), because in those days, she used a muzzle-loading rifle. Woman with the Four Horns (Asdzáán Deedįį'ii) was my maternal great-great-grandmother and received her name because she owned many four-horned sheep when she returned from Fort Sumner during the Long Walk period [1860s]. She had three daughters. There was Streak Running Red Grass (Asdzáán Tł'ohyiichíí'í), my mother's mother. Another daughter was Mourning Dove (Asdzáán Hasbídí), mother to Navajo Oshley.[7] The third daughter was Woman Who Owns the House (Asdzáán Bikinii), my maternal grandmother's little sister. She married my father when she was young but was given back to her stepfather in marriage. Then I had an aunt who had a limp, and she was also my father's daughter. Their son, Mister Yellow (Hastiin Łitso), who was born for the Red House Clan (Kinłichíí'nii), was my stepbrother. My grandmother was pregnant with him at the time she met my dad. These three were separate from my real father's children. My mother and her sister were daughters of One Who Goes Up and Down (Dah Nááneesii).[8] One Who Goes Up and Down was from a different Indian tribe but claimed Many Goats as his clan and had a sister named Barren Woman (Asdzáán Doo Ałchííhí). A man named Short Hair (Tsii'agodii) was also his brother.

My maternal grandmother, Streak Running Red Grass, was born for the Towering House People (Kinyaa'áanii), and her paternal grandfather was from the Water's Edge People. My father was first married to my grandmother, which was a custom practiced back then.[9] Relatives say that when my mother was twelve years old, she was given back to my father through marriage. My older sister was born first; she grew old and died recently.[10] There was another older sister, who died at a very young age. I have another older sister, Lucy Atene, who lives in Oljato with her grandchildren, an older living brother, and another sister who has passed away.

We had many elderly men living around here in those days. Some of these were Black Water (Tó Łizhiní), Changed Clothes Again (Há'di-ijáahii), Point of the Mountain (Dził Deez'áh), Husky Man (Diné Dííl), Little Gambler (Adika'í Yázhí), Aching Stomach, Mister Lefty (Hastiin Nishtł'ahii), "Haawoohi," One Who Owns the Small White Horse (Bil-įį'łigai Yázhi), Giving Out Anger (Hashké Neiniih), One Who Did It (Hastiin Át'į), Cottonwood Coming Down (Hastiin T'iis Ádah Íít'í'í), Without a Hat (Ch'ah Ádinii), Descending Red Mesa (Tséyaaniichíí'nii), Husky Bitter Water (Tó Dich'íí'nii Dííl), and Mister Once a Leader (Naat'áaniishchíín).[11] They all had their way of teaching and lived well, proving that their teachings were valuable and true. Some of their children and grandchildren are still here today.

My father took my mother and his children to Hat Rock, eight miles west of the former Monument Valley Mission and Hospital and southeast of the Episcopal church, toward the Oljato Trading Post. Their winter camps were west of Train Rock, at a place called Thin Standing Rock and

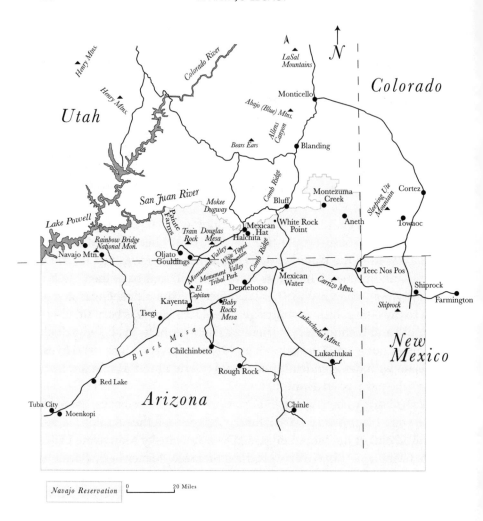

John Holiday's World

at sites on the San Juan River, part of which is now covered by Lake Powell.[12] They also lived behind Train Rock Mesa, on the east side.

My paternal grandmother, Father's aunt, was named Coughing Woman (Asdzáán Dilkosii), because she always coughed. When I was born, she helped my mother by washing me as soon as I arrived and talked to me during my bath. She said, "Dear little baby," as she wrapped me in a sheepskin, and that is where I got the name Baby (Awéé'). There was no such thing as diapers then, so they took the bark from cliffrose bushes, rubbed it together until soft, put a thin layer of it under the baby, covered the bark with a thin sheet of cloth, and wrapped it around to the front. They put me on a cradleboard, but I guess I did not like it and cried all night. The next day they took the bark out from under me and replaced it with soft layers of cloth. Then I slept well and did not cry. My grandmother took care of me for several days while my mother got better.

LIFE WITH THE HOPIS

I was less than a year old when an aunt took me to Tuba City and the Hopi villages in Arizona. This aunt, one of my father's sisters, was married to a Hopi who lived there. Her husband worked at the trading post, but I guess they met while attending boarding school in Tuba City, where they later married. I was told that she came and took me in a cradleboard on horseback to her home.

My aunt and her husband lived south of Tuba City, in the valley where the Hopi village is. I grew up there until I was four or five years old, but I can barely remember it. I do remember how the Hopis held their yearly dances, and that I went to observe them. I dressed in dancing costumes, which were heavily decorated and beautiful. These were worn for the Snake Dance. I usually stood at the very end of the line of Snake Dancers, which was said to be good luck. I remember very clearly that I was instructed to yell loud, and so I did.

While I lived in the village with my aunt, I observed a lot of the Hopis' daily activities. I remember one incident clearly. The Hopis make a paper-thin bread by spreading a shallow layer of raw corn batter over a heated flat stone. They are very careful in making this bread, because it is sacred to them. They make it away from their home, sometimes in a distant little hut in the sagebrush. A single person did the cooking.

One day while playing outside, I noticed some smoke coming from the little huts in the sagebrush. I was curious, so I investigated. I slowly peeked over the bushes and saw a Hopi lady cooking some piki, the paper-thin corn bread. She sat close to a mud and rock wall and was so busy with her batter that she did not see me. Behind her was a basket heaped full with bread. I slowly crept along the wall and came within reach of the basket. Very slowly and quietly, I grabbed an armful of bread, ran home, came through the back door of the house, then to the trading post where my aunt's husband worked. As soon as I reached my room, I got some water, dipped the bread, and ate. It took only a few minutes for the lady to appear at the trading post to see my aunt and her husband. She was furious! My aunt came to my room and asked what I had done, saying, "That lady said you stole her bread, which made the rest of her bread turn out badly. It was ruined because you stole some." The Hopis believe this, and the woman was angry because of her ruined bread.

My aunt and her husband insisted that I go back to the hut with this old white-haired woman and have a prayer to correct the problem. I did not want to, but they got after me, so I followed her. Once there, she told me to take a horn ladle with holes in it and spoon the corn mixture onto the hot stone four times before she spread it thinly over the surface. We did this four times, which corrected the problem; the cooking returned to normal, and she let me go. I stayed in the Hopi village with my aunt for a number of years and learned enough Hopi words to understand their language. Unfortunately, I have since forgotten and no longer understand it.

Some of my free time was spent playing with Hopi children. We pretended we were farmers working in a cornfield and made toys. We took a large base of tall grass, broke it up, and made play figures of men, women, and children. Then we built little hogans and adobe huts. In the summer, when the frogs came out, we caught them and pretended they were horses. We made little saddles for their backs, then placed our stick men on top and let them go. It was like a rodeo with bucking horses. The frogs hopped until the man fell off, and we laughed hard; it was fun. There were a lot of small springs in that valley back then, and we had plenty of things to do. I still remember those days when I was small.

As young children we were told to run and shout as loud as we could. This was done at the break of dawn, when we faced toward the east and yelled, then to the south, west, and north, then we ran back home, yelling all the way. The Holy People recognized us and brought good luck and the blessings of life. This yelling was also good practice, because that is what I had to do during the Snake Dance.

Another interesting place that I remember was called Line of Adobe Houses, which had a kiva with prayer sticks. The Hopi priests sang and sang without stopping and said that this continued on and on. There was an elderly man and woman in the kiva, too, and the priests said the very old people would remain underground and never come to the surface again until they died from old age.[13] I can still remember all these experiences as part of my life with the Hopis.

INTRODUCTION TO NAVAJO MEDICINE

When I was about four or five, my father and his uncle—my grandfather, named Metal Teeth (Béésh Biwoo'ii)—stopped by our house in Tuba City.[14] They said they were on their way to perform a ceremony farther south. Metal Teeth lived near Rocks Spread Out, a canyon below the Lukachukai Mountains. Father said, "We'll be back soon and take you home with us." I was so excited and anxious to return with them, I could not sleep or eat for about eight days. But the time came and went, and they had not come back. They finally arrived, sitting side by side in a one-horse buggy the People [Navajos] (Diné) call Wagon that Runs Fast. My aunt's husband had scrubbed me clean and dressed me in fresh clothes. I left behind my Hopi ceremonial outfit hanging on the wall. Father and his uncle stayed overnight, and my aunt really took care of them, serving hot coffee and food. I remember she had some type of prayer ceremony performed for her while I dozed.

We left at dawn the next morning, and they put me and all my belongings in the little luggage box in the back of the small buckboard. We stopped at White Hill at Big Policeman's (Siláo Tso) place. He wanted to have a ceremony performed for him, too, so we spent two days there. They blessed some sacred mountain soil, and even though I was small, my father told me what was going on.[15] The first daylight came, and the patient washed himself in the Navajo basket full of yucca suds as they sang a song and said a prayer from the Blessingway (Bijí) Ceremony.[16] No one could go outside. My dad told me, "My dear little one, observe all that goes on," so I watched everything. After the yucca wash, the patient was dried with cornmeal and had corn pollen applied to his whole body. They brought a blanket and covered the ground, then laid a tanned deerskin with a basket in the middle of it. They started cutting up the deerskin in preparation for blessing the sacred mountain soil. It took all day. Then the patient went through the routine of the basket blessing and prayers. I can still remember what they said and what they did. That night they continued the songs and prayers, but I fell asleep after a tiring day.

Early the next morning, someone fetched our horse and hitched it to the wagon in preparation for our departure, but we did not leave until just before noon. We passed through Tonalea, Arizona, by Red Lake, where we stopped at another home. Dad and Metal Teeth performed a ceremony for a man named Something Tied to Him (Be'estł'óoii). I don't know how he got that name. The ceremony was called the Sheep Way (Dibéjí) and helped this homestead, which had a lot of livestock. The two men sang and prayed all night, and the next morning they mixed herbs for the sheep. This, along with the songs and prayers, was done two days in a row. We finally left, I thought for home.

I was very excited about seeing my mother, although I had forgotten how she looked, because I left her when just a baby. I learned I also had a brother and sister, which made the trip home seem even longer. When we finally arrived in Cow Springs, Arizona, my father and his uncle performed another day and night ceremony. They said prayers and took sacred stones (ntł'iz) to a sacred place.[17] Once again we set out, heading northeast toward House in the Greasewood [Inscription House], to a place called Water Flowing Into. Here, a man called Green Grass Coming Out (Ch'ilhootsooí) lived. He was a very tall, handsome, rugged-looking person. While we were there, a man came on horseback and said he wanted a ceremony done for him, too. So my dad and his uncle spent another day or two performing the Blessingway Ceremony (Hózhǫ́ǫ́jí) for him. It seemed like it was taking forever to get home.

Early one morning, another man came with food on horseback. In those days, many people gathered for a Blessingway Ceremony to help each other by bringing meat, corn foods, and other items. They came by horses, wagons, or on foot. Today, people do not help out as much. The man who rode in was named Hole in the Rock in the Wash Bed (Tsé Atsisí). He was tall, handsome, and came from a place with that name. I was curious about this, so I asked my father what it meant. He said it was a hole in the rock, where the water pours into a wash bed and accumulates, giving it that name. "Where is this place? Was he born there, or is that where he lives? How did he get the name?" I was full of questions, too many questions for a small boy.

My father told me that the man had married a lady who came from that place, located northwest of Oljato, close to Lake Powell and No Man's Mesa. He married a woman from the Bitter Water Clan. He took his bride away from there and moved to Rock That Steals. Then I asked how that place got its name. "I can't tell you about it," said my father. "It's scary and bad; therefore, nobody talks about it." I begged him to reveal it to me. Metal Teeth said, "Oh well, go ahead and tell him; he'll probably forget it anyway." Father said people used to herd all kinds of stolen animals to the top of that mesa, west of Black Mesa. The men who captured the livestock brought the herds from Bodaway toward Cameron, Tuba City, Monument Valley, Navajo Mountain, Dennehotso, and Chilchinbeto [Sumac Berry Spring], then chased the animals to be killed to the top of this formation. The mesa had a flat top with a hole in the middle that was filled with sand, shrubs, and a thicket of tall trees. People drove the cattle, horses, mules, or donkeys to this hidden spot, slaughtered them, and hauled the meat down on packhorses. Nobody talked about this place, because it was to be kept hidden as a secret. "See, it's bad," said my father. "That's why we don't talk about it." I was frightened by the story and stood there wide eyed and scared.

When my father performed different ceremonies, he was paid in about everything, but most often it was jewelry and sheep. The patient told him what was given—sheep, goats, cows, horses, and so forth—but often we could not take it then because we were riding in the small buggy, so we received the animals later. My dad hired three men to pick up the "spoken for" payments, but there was no exchange of money.

We again started on our way, reaching Water Running through Rock Valley Wash, now called Tsegi (Inside [between] Rocks [in a canyon]). As you can see, we had traveled by many places with Navajo names that eventually took us all the way to Kayenta [Water Flowing Into]. Starting from White Top Mesa, we had gone to Tonalea, Talking-to-Each-Other Rocks [probably Elephant Feet], to Cow Springs, to Blasting Rock, the Rock That Steals, Black Mesa, to White Ledge, Rock Valley,

Many Peaches, Rocks Scattered Out, Fallen into the Water Hole, to Kayenta.

When we reached Tsegi, about twelve miles west of Kayenta, we came to Yellow Man's (Diné Łitso) house, where a Blessingway Ceremony was being held. Yellow Man was a brother to my father; they had the same father but different mothers. He was also of the Within-His-Cover Clan and was the father of Woman Who Gambles's (Asdzáán Adika'í) husband. His sister was Singing Woman (Asdzáán Hataałii). My dad wanted to get there in time to help perform the last night, but we arrived just as the sun was rising, and the ceremony had begun. The yucca wash had started, which my father said he did not want me to observe because children have a tendency to be restless and go in and out of the hogan. There are certain parts of the ceremony where this is forbidden, so he told me to stay outside. I sneaked inside the crowded hogan anyway and sat behind a group of people to watch. After the washing, they did the marking ritual on the woman, who was probably of the Many Goats Clan. She was pretty and must have been of that clan, because on our way home Metal Teeth started teasing my father about her.

Many people had come by wagon, horse, and on foot to attend the ceremony. Unlike today, the women and girls used to sing and fully participate. They also had activities like horse racing, tug-of-war with a rope, card games, and the stick game tsidił.[18] People sat in several different circles around the area and played. It did not occur to me until now how different it was back then.

Since I was small, I could not see over the crowd's heads and shoulders, but I heard laughter and the noise of bouncing sticks and shuffling cards. There were some ladies who always attended these activities. One's name was Woman Who Became Fat Again (Asdzáán Nááneesk'ahii), and another was Wide Lady (Asdzáán Niteelí). Other regulars were Big Redhouse (Kinłichíi'nii Tso), Woman with the Wide Teeth (Asdzáán Biwoo'niteelii), Where the Hill Ends (Niilk'idii), Woman Who Shoots, Singing Woman's Mother (Asdzáán Hataałii Bimá), and Woman Who Hears (Asdzáán Adiits'a'ii).[19] These ladies would form a circle and play the stick game. The men played a game like hockey, where they chose sides and competed against each other. They used curved sticks to hit the small ball until the opposing team was outmaneuvered. Everyone had fun together.

Participants in a game of tsidił. J.H.: "The women and girls used to sing and fully participate . . . [in] the stick game tsidił. People sat in several different circles around the area and played." (Photo NAU.PH.85.3.OO.201, Cline Library Special Collections and Archives, Northern Arizona University)

After the marking ritual on the lady, the men took a sweat bath, while I sat and waited in the buggy. They had brought the horse somewhere to graze, so I played, pretending I was driving the buggy by pulling on the reins. It must have been during the fall, because it was getting cooler after the days of warm weather. A group of women had set up the rocks in a circle to play the stick game next to the wheel of the buggy where I was sitting. I watched from above and saw the different bids made during the betting. There were all sorts of winnings that ranged from watches, silver buttons, and beads, to homespun wool, looms, and carded wool. The women set all these things in the middle, then played to win. They had a hilarious time, and I still remember their fun. I also remember my father was given a box of peaches, and I ate too many. I had not eaten any since the Hopi village. We stayed for the final ceremonial night, then left the next morning.

HOME

As we continued our travels, we passed through Many Peaches and Sheep Fallen into the Water Hole, then eastward to Rocks Scattered Out and Dam the Water. We arrived at Kayenta, where several white traders met us. Their Navajo names were Little Boy (Ashkii Yázhí), and his wife, Slim Woman (Asdzáánts'ósí), and another person called Tall White Man (Bilagáanaa Nééz).[20] They were all working at the trading post, came out to us, took hold of our arms, and led us into their back room, where we ate plenty of food. They gave hay to our horse, some more hay, and a bag of corn to take with us. Then Little Boy talked to my dad and his uncle, saying he wanted them to take about eleven white people to Navajo Mountain, and that they should be ready to leave in about four days. The group needed eight horses for the white men to ride and four packhorses or mules. Slim Woman was putting the travel plan together for them. My father got all excited about this. I do not know how much he was paid, but he was happy.

When we left the post and headed north to El Capitan, we traveled through many places with Navajo names. From Kayenta we went past Gray Ridge to Black Rock Sand, Much Wool [El Capitan], Greasewood Bush Coming Out, Black Rock, and through the desert, past the place called Standing Juniper Tree, and finally to Hat Rock, where my family lived. It was a happy reunion, an indescribable feeling and event for me.

A few days after arriving home, we moved to our winter camp at a place called Boulder Blocking Passage, southwest of the former Monument Valley Hospital. There is a narrow valley there and some pointed rocks. I don't know where my dad and his uncle went, but they probably traveled ahead of us. I went in a wagon with my big sister and her husband, my brother-in-law Billy Nez [Tall Billy]. One of the wagon horses did not want to go. I do not know what was wrong with him, but the other horse had to pull the wagon. My sister and her husband decided to leave the horse that would not work. We unhitched it and piled everything onto the other horse. My older sister, a tomboy, was already riding her own mount. She roped horses like a man, saddled and tamed wild mustangs, and was pretty tough. I sat behind my brother-in-law, riding the rest of the three or four miles.

But that was one of the longest trips I have ever had. It was torturous, because my brother-in-law unintentionally kept hitting me with his long horsewhip. This was at night, so he could not see and did not realize what he was doing. He told me not to cry but kept whipping me and the horse, then got so angry that he threatened to throw me off and leave me if I kept crying. So I sat very still and took the pain each time the whip hit my leg. He never understood that he was hurting me. We finally made it to camp.

Everyone had arrived before us and was setting up our temporary home. My father's one-horse buggy was parked there too. In those days, they practiced the "hiding from your in-law" ritual (Aadaaní doo jiníł'įį' da), so my sister's husband avoided seeing my mother, and vice versa. They had separate housing.[21]

A few days after we arrived, Slim Woman from Kayenta brought the tourists to the Oljato Trading Post for the trip to Navajo Mountain. The store was located where the current dam and some cottonwood trees are now, about three miles south of today's Oljato Trading Post. There are still some rocks left from the original building. Father made this trip and many others to Rainbow Bridge, on the other side of Navajo Mountain, and eventually made a trade of being a tourist guide. He owned at least thirty-eight riding horses; I remember having that many feed bags for them. He used to buy a lot of grain and had at least twenty 100-pound bags of corn he purchased from Dennehotso. He would mix the two together and feed it to his horses each day. They were fat all year long, because he took care of them for his tour business.

I remember father was away shoeing the horses and mules. He had a certain way to do this. He'd put a hood over the horse's head and tie him very close to a post, then pull the leg out in the opposite direction. It was an awkward position, but that is how he did it in order to have a steady horse or mule's leg while preparing the hoof for shoeing. He filed the hoof until there was blood, then asked for the horseshoe. One of my father's nephews, Hite Chee, assisted him in shoeing all the horses and mules.

Oljato Trading Post, 1909. J.H.: "The old Oljato Trading Post became an important part of the community." (Photo 11343, used by permission, Utah State Historical Society, all rights reserved)

The old Oljato Trading Post became an important part of the community. Two white men who lived in the small red stone building near the well at the point of the mesa operated it. One of the men was called Rug (Diyógí), and the other was Old Coyote (Mąʼii Sání).[22] My father, brother, and another man worked for them as tour guides. These two traders decided to bring water to their house from a distant spring by the trading post, so they dug a large bowl-shaped hole in the rocks to accumulate the water. From there, they carved a long, narrow canal in the rocks, then placed some thin, flat granite rocks on top with cement, shaping it like a pipe. Once this was completed, they built a dam at the end closest to their house. Navajo neighbors brought in logs to make the dam and fixed it with braided logs and sand to fill the empty spaces. The water came down the dug-out rock pipe and into the dam, filling it quickly. Rug and Old Coyote worked hard to build this water trough through the rocks.

An irrigation ditch watered their garden of corn, melons, squash, cantaloupes, tomatoes, carrots, onions, turnips, and sugar beets. They had their own machinery to make syrup from the sugar beets. These men also grew a variety of plants and flowers and canned their tomatoes and other vegetables. They often had a huge harvest. Rug was a kind, generous person, who offered melons, corn, syrup, and tomatoes to the Navajos. Old Coyote used to trap coyotes. When people had trouble with them, they called on him, and he would arrive with his pack mule, traps, and chains. He set up his equipment, and before too long, the coyote was sitting in the trap. He collected a lot of their skins. That is how these two white men lived among the Navajos, but I do not know what became of them afterwards.

But it was Little Boy [John Wetherill] who gave the area its name. One night, Little Boy, who spoke our language fluently, went with a Navajo man to fetch drinking water from the well near this post. There was a pool of water nearby with cattails growing in it. The full moon shone in the water, and suddenly Wetherill said, "Hey, look, Ooljéé'tó–Moon Water," because of the reflection. That is how the post got its name.

PRACTICING MEDICINE

One day when a group of men came to our home, my family butchered a cow, and everyone cooked stew and roasted beef. I wondered why they had come. My mother ground flour and made a lot of bread on the hot coals, as well as underground bread. Then she sliced up the meat into thin strands and hung it up to dry. Nobody said much about what was going on until later, when I found out that my father and Metal Teeth had made plans while in Tuba City for these men to come and have a nine-night Yé'ii Bicheii Ceremony.[23] The purpose of this gathering was to help some of them learn from each other all of the important things and the correct way to perform a ceremony. They held this type of practice in other places too.

There is an overhang of rocks not far from where our hogan was. I saw a light coming from there later that evening, when I was home with my little brother, so we decided to go over and see what was happening. In the dark, we ran through the hills covered with scrub oak brush. When we got there, we saw the men dancing around and could hear the songs echoing throughout the valley. We watched for a few minutes, until my mother found us and said, "You are not to watch these dances. It will make you blind!" She spanked us and sent us running back to the hogan, but we still wanted to sneak over there again. It was impossible, though, so we dozed off. The next morning all the men came in and ate. The practice continued for several more nights, until one day they left on their horses to attend an actual ceremony in Mexican Water. My father and mother went on horseback too, taking all the bread and meat with them and leaving us alone at home.

We three children decided to visit Woman Heat (Asdzáán Dóhó), who lived just around the mesa, not too far from our place.[24] She was of Paiute descent, and her mother's name was Woman Who Hears. When we arrived, we found her door blanket closed, with a log leaning against it.[25] We kidded each other, asking, "How hot is it?" as we lifted the log and blanket from the door. "It is hot in there."

My family moved around a lot, searching for good grazing land. There was an abundance of vegetation, and we traveled wherever we found pasture for the sheep. That was the main purpose for traveling so much. "It rained over there, and there is plenty of vegetation; let's go there!" Then in the winter, "The vegetation has not been touched over there. It's fresh; let's move there." We traveled everywhere, never staying in one place. My family moved from the Oljato area to Paiute Farms, past Standing Red Rock and a place called Where the Three Rocks Floated Ashore. As we went from place to place, I was too young to understand why. Our sheep were lambing, and we would have all the lambs moving with the herd.

The family spent a few days at Water under the Cottonwood Tree, then moved to the point of the mesa just northeast of Oljato, across from Train Rock, and camped by it, spending a short time there, too. There used to be a natural spring with a dam where we watered our sheep at that location. Then we moved northeast, across the plain to Sitting Red Rock, and set up camp among the big boulders, where water was very scarce and far away. But out of nowhere, Navajo Oshley found some drinking water. The names of other places we lived include a site along Comb Ridge called Soft Ground Water, Very Rocky Ground, and just below that Red Sand Rocks, and Little Coyote, Cottonwood Tree, and Black Streak down the Rock. At the base of Douglas Mesa is a place called Wind Blowing around the Rock, and near Train Rock is Water Streaming from the Top.

At one time, my father lived across the San Juan River to the north. There are still traces of the hogans, sheep corral, and sweat lodge. Just below that home, at a place called Dark Water, there was another hogan and sheep corral, which used to be my father's homestead until the white men started coming through there. My family was afraid of the Anglos, so they moved back to Monument Valley. I think they should have stayed across the river, like Mister Sakizzie and men like Bitter Water, Mister Jelly (Hastiin Jélii), and Old Eddie (Eddie Sání), who lived by the windmill. These men refused to move off their land. "We were born here," they said, and stayed even when the white men came to chase them off. If my father had remained across the San Juan River, he could be living there now. When the white men came, they told my family that they would be handcuffed and taken away, so my family moved. But Mister Sakizzie refused to move, and to this day, his children live there.

Long ago, when my family was living across the San Juan River, my paternal grandfather (Aching Stomach), Mister Starry (Sǫ'ii), my father, and his mother all shared a homestead. During that time, the Mormons stored their food in particular places here and there. Sometimes my grandparents ran out of food but found boxes of flour and food in these storage sites, so they would take a portion of it to live on. The only other place to get their food was the trading post, but they were too far away, and there was no way to cross the river when it was running high. Once the Mormons found out what was happening, they poisoned the flour.

MOTHER'S TEACHINGS

My mother told us about how the Navajos, in the distant past, used to move west of the Bears Ears and also in the red lands of Mexican Hat.[26] Many of our ancestors used to move there for the winter and sometimes remained there throughout the summer. She told us what happened to some Navajos living west of the Bears Ears. White pioneers moved through their area with their cattle and a wagon train. The people stole food from these wagons and stashed it under some rock cliffs. Later, they returned for the food but did not know how to prepare things like flour and coffee. The Navajos cooked and ate it anyway and must have done something wrong, because they all got very sick. They suffered terribly until they called upon my paternal grandmother, Woman Who Was Hit. After diagnosing their illness through hand trembling, she told them that the food they had eaten was contaminated with poison powder used for killing coyotes.[27] Someone saw a bag that she was carrying and asked, "What is in the bag that you have?" "It holds some plants, or herbs, that I add to goats' milk to make cheese and nothing else" was her reply. This was the herb called Yellow Eye, and she thought it might help.[28] It has dull gray leaves, yellow flowers, and is sometimes found in cornfields. When mixed with milk, the combination turns to a cottage cheese–like substance. The people suggested, "Let's try boiling some of it and see if it will help us get better." So they filled half a bucket with water, then boiled and drank the medicine. Soon the people started vomiting and had diarrhea as the mixture worked them over for several hours, but eventually everyone was cured.

My mother told me other stories from the past, about how my older brother had been involved in World War I, and how some type of poison gas killed many people. The Great Influenza Epidemic originated from this gas, causing Navajos to die in their sleep.[29] It killed most of our people. Their sheep, penned in the corrals, waited as if they would be let out to pasture any moment. At this time, my parents and their children lived near Narrow Canyon, at a place called Where the Sagebrush Comes Through. My mother always boiled Yellow Eye on her stove and had family members drink it in the morning or mix it in their food. She had heard about its use from her grandparents, and because of this knowledge, none of my brothers and sisters, my father, or close neighbors—Old Educated One (Ółta'í Sání) and his family—died during the epidemic. My big brother asked Old Educated One, "Grandfather, why haven't I gotten sick from the influenza yet?" "I don't know. It is not a good thing to wish for; our people are dying from the sickness!" he replied. "Yíiyá! (Scary!)" said my big brother and ran off. So you see, this plant is a strong medicine, can be used for major sicknesses, and provides good protection against most health hazards.

FOOD

Mutton and mutton stew, as well as corn, were our main sources of food. Corn can be prepared in different ways as dumplings, tortillas

Women shearing sheep. J.H.: "Mutton and mutton stew, as well as corn, were our main sources of food." (Photo SM 89583, Milton Snow Collection, Navajo Nation Museum)

made on a hot rock, as blue bread, underground bread, and in different consistencies as mush—thick; thin; very, very thick; or very, very thin.[30] During the hunting season, we also got deer meat, which was cut into thin strips and dried. Later, we pounded and cooked the dried meat. They called this "achxǫǫh," and it was good.[31]

Not until recently did we have flour. We bought it at the trading post for ten or twenty-five cents a cup or by the pound. This is also how coffee and sugar were sold. Coffee beans looked like juniper berries— small, green, and round. We roasted raw coffee in a pan until the beans popped open and split in half like pinyons, cooked them until done, and ground them in a grinder we bought from the trader. Before coffee, we drank Navajo tea made from wild plants collected, boiled, and served plain, without sugar. This was how food was prepared when we were very young children.

My family often went to the trading posts at Mexican Hat, which used to be called Metal Pipe Going Across, or Hat Rock, or Swirling Mountain.[32] People would say, "I'm going there to get some food," then ride their horses. In those days, they used to charge food and pay later with lambs, wool, cattle, and rugs, a system that worked well. The trader knew what was needed and filled up the sacks without being told. In the spring, people sold their lambs and were able to buy things on credit all summer long: coffee, flour, clothes, shoes, and other necessities. Then in the fall, when the lambs were bigger, they separated them from their mothers and took them to the trading post to pay bills and buy things for the winter, like quilts, clothes, gloves, shoes, and food. Since it was often a long distance home, they bought food in large amounts.

For instance, my father might purchase ten large sacks of flour, a bag of coffee and sugar, baking powder, shortening, and four 55-pound burlap bags of potatoes and onions. He spent his winters across the San Juan River, so he stocked up on food items and hauled them in a wagon to the river, then packed his mules and horses to cross the water. These animals were large and strong and swam well. He had several hogans and corrals in his distant camp, but I do not know what happened to them. The Mormons might have burned them, but I do not know. When the weather was very hot in the summer, he moved back again.

Back when there was no shortening, people used to melt the fat from sheep to fry their food. They filled a sheep's or cow's stomach and other large organs with the melted fat and stored it for future use in making breads, gravies, and fried foods. People used to camp just to gather onions. They would dig them up, fill large flour bags, and dry the green stems as well as the bulbs. The onions were powdered once they were dried, by pounding and grinding them on stones; the whole bag became a small package of onion powder, used as a spice in soups and stews. Little potatoes grew in abundance on the hill coming down from Black Mesa, close to Church Rock, east of Kayenta. People took their pack mules to gather sumac berries by the Bears Ears, at a place called Mountain Sheep's Testicles.[33] They ground the berries and made them into a delicious pudding or jelly. People camped at many different places just to gather natural foods.

When I was very small and herding sheep, I lived on little cottontail and jackrabbits. I caught them by pushing a rock at arm's length into their burrows, so that I could reach the rabbits after they ran into the hole. One time I placed rocks in four or five burrows, then herded the sheep in that direction. Sure enough, the rabbits jumped out of hiding and headed for their holes. They only got as far as the rock before I pulled them out by hand or with a stick. I killed and cleaned them, then took my catch home to deep fry and eat for dinner. One day I brought back seven cottontails and a big jackrabbit that I had gathered in the Red Ground [Halchita—near Mexican Hat] area. The jackrabbit I caught as I herded the sheep home. He suddenly jumped out of a bush in front of me. I threw a rock and hit him with a lucky throw. He fell over, and I finished him off with another rock. I removed his entrails, tied it with the other seven rabbits, and hauled the heavy load home. A person named Husky Man, my maternal grandfather by clan, was there, his mule tied outside. He was a medicine man who sang the Featherway (Ats'oseh K'ehgo), which usually lasts nine nights, as well as the Big Starway (Sǫ'tsojí). I brought the rabbits in and tossed them sprawling by the stove. Husky Man was playing cards, looked at the rabbits, and said, "What in the world is this? Hurry, we've been furnished with all these rabbits." "Hurry and fry them!" said another. "Aw, he's lying. He didn't catch those. He probably took them from the dogs. They probably caught the rabbits, and he's claiming that he did," said Husky Man. His comment really hurt me. He belittled me and my hard work and made the whole event worthless! My big sister took the rabbits out and skinned them, then brought all of them inside, except for the jackrabbit. She put some shortening into the deep Dutch oven pot and filled it to the brim with rabbit meat. The men played cards all night, and early the next morning, my sister boiled the jackrabbit in stew and added some cornmeal. My in-law who had belittled me ate breakfast to his heart's content. "Wow! This is delicious!" he said. He ate the deep-fried rabbits in the evening, then the rabbit stew in the morning. "You made fun of me, and now you're devouring my rabbits!" I told him. "Where did you ever find such delicious rabbits?" he asked, calling me his grandson.

LOOKING FOR SCHOOLCHILDREN

People used to teach against the white man's education in the old days. Two men, Charlie Ashcroft [a trader] and Old Policeman (Siláo Sání), went together looking for schoolchildren. They searched every homestead. I remember once when family members warned, "The children

hunters are coming! The police are coming!" At the time, we were living at Comb Ridge, where there was a big canyon close by. They took
me, my older sister, and two sheepskins to sit on into the canyon to
Sandstone Going Under, where we were hidden for about three days.
They brought us food and water and said, "These men will come back
through here once more." That is how our family kept us from being
taken away to school, so we never went.

The argument against education went like this: "School is not good;
it's worthless. Taking care of the sheep, that is worthwhile. It's a source
of life—food. School is nothing. The white men do not feed people, so
why learn from them? They stand by and watch you starve to death,
and then that is it! That's what they're all about. Only once in a while
do you find a nice white man. If you decide to go with them, you will
learn their ways, their language. Sure, you might gain some self-pride
and think you're better than everybody else, but once you fall into debt
or have problems, you will become a street beggar and die of starvation. The white man will watch you starve to death and will not help
you, so why bother to learn his ways?" That is what we were told and
why we were not educated. "Here are the sheep, goats, cows, horses,
and cornfields. This is life! You will have them until you reach old age.
You will raise your children with them." Because of these teachings, we
never went to school and remained hidden from school officials.

The children who did go were taken on horseback or wagon to a
school in Kayenta, Tuba City, Chinle, or Shiprock. My older brother,
Henry Holiday, who was born just before me, went and told us stories
about the boarding school. "It's awful. We were always being spanked
for every little thing. They made us chew on bars of soap and carry
around a heavy log all day as punishment. We were made to stand
motionless in one spot for a whole day, were not allowed to use the
bathroom, and ended up urinating or crapping on ourselves. We were
punished for getting into fights or talking back to our teachers. I was
pretty naughty and have been punished too many times. After the punishment, the teachers explained to me why I had been disciplined. It
was to teach me a lesson not to do or say naughty things. I was treated
like this because I had been bad. 'It's for your own good, to use in your
future.' It was a lesson to learn."

He said some people stole food from the kitchen, while others fought over girls and so were punished. He was told, "You will someday grow up to be a man, and what you learn here will help you to do what is right and make the right choices. What you learn at school will help you. You will not be the kind of person who beats his wife because of jealousy. You will have the willpower to stay away from trouble. The paddling you got here will be a reminder that you should not do wrong things after you graduate from high school and go on to college. Some day you may work at a school or be a teacher and share these same teachings with the young children, so that they will learn the better things in life." This is how they lectured him after every punishment. It was a good learning process, even when it seemed harsh to us at times.

Boys and girls did not hang around together like they do today—it was not allowed. There were many restrictions, so nobody did it. It is different now with boys and girls intermingling. That's what drives them crazy. They are distracted from the important things they should be learning. It ruins their minds and makes them careless, violent, disobedient, and deaf to sound advice. They think, "Why not? Why should I care? It's not my problem!" and so they do not care about anything anymore.

In the earlier days, the children were obedient and respectful. They were afraid to try anything that was wrong, because they learned through punishment. Yíiyá. They did not want to be spanked, or carry a big heavy log all day, or chew on a bar of soap with its ugly bitter taste, so they behaved. They always thought twice about being disciplined. These students have since become our leaders and officials in the Navajo tribal government. This disciplinary activity ended after my children went through the school system. They received this discipline, so they learned a lot from it. It all changed when Annie Wauneka became the council delegate.[34] She ruined our children.

Anyway, this is what my big brother told me about his schooling. He went with a lot of boys and graduated with them, and they all said the same thing about school. There was one boy, a cousin named School Boy Who Is Big (Ółta'í Nitsaazígíí), who was very naughty. My brother told me that it took the longest time for him to understand anything or learn his lessons. He was punished over and over again, many different

Children at the Tuba City Boarding School. J.H.: "My father and I went to the Tuba City Boarding School to pick up my big brother. When we arrived, the children were having a field day." (Photo NAU.PH.516.127, Cline Library Special Collections and Archives, Northern Arizona University)

ways, so he finally caught on. He had long hair and a Navajo bun when he left for school, but when he returned, his hair was short, and he brought back some green uniforms to wear.

Once school was out, the parents headed there to pick up their children. They would load several horses, some with saddles and some without, while others took wagons, including the two-wheeler type. Some children rode double on their horses. The children spent their summer at home and in the fall headed back to school on their horses or in wagons. This went on year after year.

One time when I was still quite small, my father performed a ceremony on a patient living near Tuba City, at a place named Peeking Bobcat, a hill to the northeast.[35] This was in the spring, and the children were ready to get out of school for the summer. My father and I went to the Tuba City Boarding School to pick up my big brother. When we arrived, the children were having a field day. They were happy and having a lot of fun! "Boy, if only I had gone to school, I'd be among those happy children having a grand old time!" I thought. I'd play basketball and run races. My big brother was a really fast runner and could outrun anybody. We also saw the tug-of-war, with the ropes and scarves, and the high jump over the bar. It all seemed like so much fun. I wished I had gone to school! They also had arm wrestling. The students were all bunched up here and there, observing and participating in all these activities. It was really something to watch.

After the field day, we saddled a horse for my brother and left. Every few miles, we stopped to do a ceremony, so it took us forever to get home. I really regretted not being in school. I kept wishing that I had gone, but on the other hand, learning about traditional medicine was interesting and exciting to me. That was my education.

When I was older, my parents separated. My father remarried, and so did my mother. I continued to visit my father. It wasn't any different with his new family, for we were still taught the same things. We had to fetch the horses at dawn and perform many other daily chores. My father spoke kindly as he asked us to do something, but if we failed to do as he asked, he silently got the whip and spanked us. He'd say, "If you can't be asked nicely, then I'll have to use more force with this whip." The snapping sound on your body will certainly send you running! But the punishment was not the final teaching. Once we had completed the chore, he would come to me, put his arms around me, and say that he was sorry. He then explained why this was necessary as a benefit in life, that I would not remain the same person, and that my father and mother would not be here forever. "Someday you'll have to live on your own. You'll get married and have children and grandchildren. You'll have your own home, livestock, and valuables. You might become a medicine man and heal your people." This is what my parents used to say to me.

My mother was also a kind person. She asked favors with love and respect. We obeyed by herding sheep, hauling and chopping wood, fetching water, planting the cornfield, and caring for it. It is nice for a woman or mother to speak kindly to her children and others. It accomplishes more. I was raised with this atmosphere in my home. My maternal grandmother was the same. She spoke kindly to us. I was raised in her home more than anywhere else, so she taught me more things. She was married to my grandfather Man with the Fuzzy Face (Hastiin Binii'ditł'oii). That is how I was raised.

CHAPTER TWO

LIVING WITH GRANDMOTHER

Being raised as a young boy in the traditional Navajo livestock economy of the 1920s and 1930s was not an easy life. Even with John's exciting adventures with animals, living as a "survivalist," "parachuting," searching for garnets, and seeing mysterious wagon trains, there is no missing the drudgery and danger that was so much a part of his existence. He testifies in a number of instances how divine intervention, coupled with desperate friends and relatives searching for him, was all that stood between life and death. By any standards, he was a lucky boy.

Mobility was the key to survival for all. When Gary Witherspoon noted that there are "356,200 distinct inflected forms of the verb 'to go,'" he identified an important motif in Navajo thought and action.[1] Water, grass, wood, and other resources necessary to sustain life in a high-desert environment did not come without effort. That meant travel. The daily quest for resources could result in suffering and death if these things were not found. John's discussion of farming, herding, and living off the land illustrate the facts of life of survival.

John's grandmother nurtured him in other facts of life. As a medicine woman skilled in healing with plants, she brought him along on some of her travels and took the opportunity to instruct about sex, proper behavior, and the consequences of misbehavior. Another aspect of life John learned during these trips was the importance of dependence on others, as he and Grandmother visited home after home in their journey to obtain herbs. He recalls the people and their personalities as Grandmother tightened the weave of friendship and relations with her visits.

EARLY MEMORIES OF THE LIVESTOCK INDUSTRY

I lived in my parents' home for three or four months. Then my maternal grandmother, Woman Who Owns the House, who had two of my sisters, decided she would raise me, too.[2] When my family heard that my sisters and grandmother were planning to come to our home, we were excited, and we prepared for their arrival. We fixed cornmeal and other foods, and a few days later they arrived. Grandmother and my sisters herded their huge flocks of sheep and goats into the canyon by our home. Their livestock could be heard throughout the valley. We lived there for a while, then decided to move to Oljato, where my father had a small alfalfa field. He said they had cut the hay but had not yet baled it. He had harvested it with a long blade that cut going forward and backward. Father then dug a hole in the ground that had boards and wires protruding from it. The alfalfa was pushed into the hole, packed really tightly, tied into a bale, and stacked. We were warned to stay away from the hole because we could fall in. "You'll never get out if this happens!" they said.

After moving to Oljato, where my paternal grandmother [Woman Who Was Hit] lived, we first herded the sheep and goats into the canyon to the north, then later to the San Juan River to a place called Water Flowing Into, which is past Standing Red Rock. They killed a horse just before we left, and everyone feasted on the meat. There was no seasoning except rock salt. We also lived in Paiute Farms, at a place called Bank Washed Ashore. People used to live anywhere, even in difficult places. They herded their livestock into a canyon and lived at the entrance, building homes out of rocks, mud, and debris that floated in from the river. That was what our home was like. A man called San Juan [River] (Toohnii), as well as Navajo Oshley and Randolph Benally, lived at Paiute Farms as young boys.[3] There was also Little San Juan (Toohnii Yázhí) and Little Mexican (Nakaii Yázhí), who had a stacked shoe sole.[4] They all helped herd my grandmother's large flock of sheep and goats.

One day there was a girl's puberty ceremony (Kinaaldá) held not too far from our place.[5] I went over there with my grandmother, and we met my father's mother's sister, my paternal grandmother, Woman Who Was Hit. She told my grandmother to let me stay with her, so I watched the ceremony. There were some little girls there, so we decided

Men and women preparing food. J.H.: "When my family heard that my sisters and grandmother were planning to come to our home, we were excited, and we prepared for their arrival. We fixed cornmeal and other foods, and a few days later they arrived." (Photo 14463, used by permission, Utah State Historical Society, all rights reserved)

to play in the sheep corral in the canyon. They painted my face with red mud, and when we went home, the people laughed and said, "Look at what happened to him." My paternal grandmother grabbed me and washed my face. I must have been around six years old at the time.

The people cooked the corn cake for the Kinaaldá and sang all night. Some Paiutes came from Navajo Mountain or Paiute Mesa. A Paiute man named Green Shoes (Kédootł'izhii), who could speak Navajo really well, was asked to start the songs for the ceremony. All the men got together and told him to lead out, so he agreed and began to sing. The Navajos were amazed and laughed but helped him finish the song.

The next day my sisters and the other girls from my grandmother's side went to feed the lambs. While they were returning, they saw Green Shoes sunning himself by the hogan. He said, "Hey, you little girls, come here." The girls did not like him and turned their heads away when they passed by, saying, "What does he want?" and went into the hogan.

Another thing I used to do was run away from home and follow the tracks of the sheep and sheepherder. When I found the person watching the sheep, I stayed with him all day. One time I was walking by a crack in the rock when I heard something that sounded like whistling air. I was told not to go near that place again. I was as small and helpless as a little pup. The sheep ignored me and strayed where they pleased. I could not do much except yell at them. I often heard the coyotes howling in the distance, but they did not bother me.

During my childhood, when I lived in Monument Valley, my big sister, Warrior Who Fought Her Way There (Baa' Kógibaa'ii), and I used to herd sheep all the time.[6] We also played a lot by making toy figures from grass roots. The men had pants and the women, skirts. Sticks, stones, and sand became hogans as we pretended to be the little people we made, to pass the time while herding. The day seemed shorter, because these activities helped me forget my hunger and thirst. Herding sheep can make for long, thirsty days. My sister was smart, because she hauled the toys around after the sheep, so we could play, play, play! I have herded sheep everywhere, and if you were to see my tracks all at once, they would cover this whole area.

I remember another time when it snowed in the early spring. My sister and I were herding sheep, and she tried to keep me warm. I wore a type of clothing that I had to keep the cover crisscrossed to prevent the cold and snow from entering. My sister fastened it for me, but after a while, it came undone, and I would not bother securing it. The snow fell inside, but I just walked and walked. She cried, ran to me, and tried to close my clothing and keep me covered. I followed behind, and she kept checking to make sure I did not get cold.

My maternal grandmother, Woman Who Owns the House, had a camp near Dennehotso at a place called White Streak of Cattail Coming Out.[7] She spent her winters at her home in Streaking Red Grass. This camp was located where the road comes down along the mesa, and there is a deep overhanging rock ledge in the canyon. It made a good winter camp. In the summer she moved to higher elevations, where she and her family planted corn and other vegetables. We never lived in one place but moved around a lot and lived in the rocks on top of the mesa, and sometimes near Dennehotso at a place called Sitting Red Mesa, or in the sagebrush near Baby Rocks during the winter. Our home was a shelter made from a circle of sagebrush and a tent.

When I was small, we moved around quite a bit. During our stay at Owl Springs, the sheep had their lambs. On one occasion, my older sister and I were riding the sheepherder's horse, named Little Red Horse (Łįį' Łichíí' Yázhí), and Grandmother stuffed a number of lambs around us as we moved along. The horse got tired, lay down on a sand dune while we were still on it, and the lambs jumped off and ran in every direction. We tried to gather them, but they scattered quickly. My sister started crying, and I did not know what to do, so I lay down on my stomach. It did not bother me a bit, but my sister was upset, swearing and yelling, "Help me!" I just gathered up the bushes behind me, lay back in the sun, and watched. Oshley came to our rescue. He gathered all the lambs and stuffed them around us again after we got back on the horse. We rode like that for some time, until my sister got off and led the horse with me on it. I must have dozed off.

We arrived at a canyon, which we herded the sheep into before making camp. We spent several days there, even though the water hole was a ways off. Early the next morning, the family butchered a sheep and left all the meat hanging out to dry. Red Dog (Łééchąą'í), a sheepdog, somehow grabbed some hanging sheep fat and ran off. We chased him, but he got away. Later, he came home and had his tail chopped off.

ADVENTURES HERDING

Some family members brought back donkeys and horses from White Streak of Cattail Coming Out, so that we could use them in our move eastward. I saw a lot of men herding sheep and remember being put on a pack animal called Donkey with the White Eye (Télii Bináá' Łigai). It would not stop for anything but just kept walking and walking. We halted to water the animals down in the valley and rode across the flat land to a bar of sand dunes. I was last in the line of packed donkeys, got tired, and jumped off my animal onto the sand. I landed with a "thud." The sun was getting ready to go behind the western horizon, but I just sat there as the donkeys continued on their way. Darkness came, and I was tired, not having slept all day. Then I heard loud noises

Horsemen in Monument Valley. J.H.: "'Where is the little boy? He's gone!' they said as they rode into the night. Later, these men said they had traveled all the way to the base of White-Tipped Mountain, looking for me and the donkeys." (Photo 19662, used by permission, Utah State Historical Society, all rights reserved)

and saw two men, Oshley and San Juan River, riding past. "Where is the little boy? He's gone!" they said as they rode into the night.

Later, these men said they had traveled all the way to the base of White-Tipped Mountain, looking for me and the donkeys. They found the animals and returned, coming closer and closer and yelling my name as they herded them. I was sleepy but dared not drift off, because I did not want to be left behind. Still, I did not say anything until someone yelled right next to me. I called out. "There he is," they said. One of the riders reached down and scooped me off the ground onto his horse. I sat on the front of the saddle and helped chase the donkeys back to camp.

We moved again, when the lambs were bigger and faster, to the lower valley by White-Tipped Mountain. I was told to walk, since I could not stay on a donkey. I walked after the sheep, as the rest moved our camp. While we were there, my paternal grandfather Folded Metal Belt (Béésh Ahaadeezdéél Sis), Little Mexican's father, came to visit us. He brought packed mules, saying he was coming from Black Rock, where he used to be married. He had left his wife, so he joined the other men to help herd sheep. His big white sheepdog took orders on what to do and was smart. Metal Belt had also moved his cattle toward my grandmother's home at White Streak of Cattail Coming Out.

That morning we butchered a sheep and prepared a big breakfast of mutton and bread. They cooked the sheep lungs and heart, which my older sisters took when they left to herd the livestock. Back then, we were fed like dogs. After they butchered a sheep, they would partially cook a portion of liver and throw it to us to eat as we went after the flock. I wanted to follow the adults because of their food. The sheep must have been lambing, because when my two sisters and I got to White-Tipped Mountain with the livestock, we built a fire in the black bushes and ate lunch.

Some sheep had their lambs while we were herding them, so my sisters told me to tend the newborns while they went to gather the other animals that had wandered off in different directions. I do not know where the men—the usual sheepherders—went and why only my two sisters were tending the animals. I sat alone by the fire and the newborn lambs, eventually losing sight of my sisters. All I could see were grazing sheep. I dozed off but awoke to loud noises all around me. Two coyotes were running among the lambs, and one of them had snatched a baby and was escaping. I shouted, "Hey-y-y," the coyote dropped it, and the pair ran off. This was my first time to see a coyote, so I was frightened. I felt like I had grown big, so I yelled at the top of my lungs, which was not very loud at all. I was still scared and about fainted, but it was a good thing I yelled, because it scared the coyote into dropping the lamb.

WAGON TRAINS

After that, I stood up and looked about to see where my sisters had gone with the sheep. To the southwest, toward where the Navajo Tribal Park now is, I saw a big cloud of dust approaching. I watched it come closer and closer. Just then, my sisters came running. "What is that dust? Someone is coming," they said. We were not very far from the wagon trail, which was hardly a road, used by the old Model Ts with wooden wheels. Some people were following that road toward us. We watched for a while, as my sisters built several fires and erected a post with something on it to scare away the coyotes and other predators.

By this time, the traveling strangers were right beside us on the road, so we went out to see them. Some of the white men were driving the animals pulling the wagons, the train being so long that it disappeared behind the distant hills. Two or three oxen pulled each wagon, and three men rode in front on horses, leading the wagon train. The white women wore dresses that reached to the ground, large bonnets, and carried their babies on their backs. The men had large beards, and some were riding and others walking. I think the men on horseback should have been carrying the babies instead of the women. Some were fixing the rough road as they moved, carrying picks, sledgehammers, shovels, and crowbars. The little children walked alongside as they passed. We stood behind big bushes and stared at the travelers for some time as they went north down the old road and disappeared in a cloud of dust toward Mexican Hat.

That was a large migration of white people, the biggest we had ever seen, so we forgot all about the sheep. We had a lot to say when we arrived home and told everyone what we had seen. Grandmother said, "Yíiyá! You are not supposed to go near those white men. They will grab the children and take them away on their horses!" My sisters told her, "We hid from the white men; they didn't see us!" "Even so," Grandmother said, "they will steal little girls, too!"

The wagon train went to Swirling Mountain [Navajo Blanket, east of Mexican Hat], then on to Salt Water, then Water Streaming Up in a Bowl, to Where the Water Falls, then Decorated Rock, and down to the San Juan, where Comb Ridge meets the river. They crossed there, went onto the other side and up to the ledge along the river, all the way to what used to be the Bluff City airstrip, and then to the north with their wagons.[8]

When I was a little older, I again encountered a wagon train, while herding sheep near the south end of Comb Ridge, near Dennehotso. I was riding my donkey and suddenly spotted a huge cloud of dust from the wagons. Many of the people were riding horses, sometimes double. This happened on a very hot summer day, but it had rained several days prior to this, and holes in the rocks had collected water. As I moved along, an individual rode his horse toward me as fast as he could. He reined up, desperately motioning with his hand. I interpreted his sign language to mean he was thirsty, so I motioned him to follow. I led him to some water in the rocks. When he saw one of the holes, he jumped off his horse and dashed for it. With his hands clinging on either side of the rocks, he drank and drank. Within minutes, the others from the wagon train reached us and were bunched around each water hole, satisfying their thirst. This wagon train, with probably 130 people in it, must have been dying of thirst. They hauled out buckets of water and camped there for two days. An in-law of mine, named Lived in the Same Place (T'áá Kééhat'íinii), understood English, so he rode out to see them.[9] He saw that the water was nearly gone, so he suggested they move down to another place called Water in the Clay, where there was a natural spring and plenty of vegetation. The horses were starving, too, and had eaten most of the brush around the first campsite. In fact, they left behind two huge dead horses. These white men stayed at Water in the Clay for the next two months. Their horses roamed the grassy lands, and everyone was happy.

At this time, the Monticello and Blanding areas were not well known. These towns were built in places with heavy sagebrush, so people cleared the vegetation to build homes and farms. There were only two or three shacks and several tents.[10] The Blanding area was called Amidst the Sagebrush, and I remember how Navajo men used to come by on their donkeys or horses and say they were headed there to clear land. They also helped clear the area around Blue Mountain, where Monticello sits today. That town is called Mountain or Hills Coming to a Peak. We later found that the people in this passing wagon train settled in these cleared areas.

These travelers played baseball, a game I was not yet familiar with. We were then living in our summer shelter, and these white men came to visit us often. They must have had plenty of food, because they shared some with us and were very kind and generous. Their horses, mules, and donkeys were overly burdened with food. They also had four oxen, two of which were bound together by a wooden yoke. Between them were boards, which formed a carrier loaded with belongings. I did not notice if the oxen's tails were tied. This wagon train finally went on its way to the north.

CAMP LIFE

When I was younger, we also camped near Snake in the Water Spring, where my family collected goosefoot, or pigweed [*Chenopodium fremonti*], in the spring and summer.[11] We gathered these plants and removed the seeds. They had a bitter taste that was bad. There was also a lot of rabbit thorn [*Lycium pallidum*], which was sun dried, then ground, boiled, and stored to make mush in the winter.[12] People gathered these in abundance at Snake in the Water.

One day, while living there, my grandmother told me and my older sister to get some water from a spring called Under the Chokecherry Bush, below Snake in the Water.[13] She said, "You two get some water, while I ride the horse up Crooked Road to Dennehotso to get some things." We took two gas cans tied together and used them to haul water. I do not know where they came from, but she instructed us to make sure we filled them evenly at the same time, and not to take them off the donkey's back. So my sister and I rode to the spring, where we filled up the cans, carefully and evenly on both sides, with good clear water. We were just about to return when we saw a herd of cows headed our way. They were running fast, a whole lot of them, and they were thirsty.

My sister and I got scared and ran toward Comb Ridge, leaving the donkey with the water standing there. I could not run fast enough and kept falling down. My sister came back, grabbed my arm, pulled me along, and carried me piggyback toward the high ground. We finally reached the rocks, looked down, and saw the donkey with the water cans still waiting in the bushes. We walked the rest of the way home to find that Grandmother had returned; the family had butchered a goat and were eating. "Where's the water?" she asked. "We left it down at the watering place, because there were some mean cows running after us," said my sister. "Oh no, those cows are not mean. They were probably running to get to the water, not you!" Grandmother replied. "No, they were mad at us," said my sister. Then one of the men went on horseback and brought the donkey and water home. Everyone laughed at us because we were frightened by the cows.

One spring day when I was herding, some sheep became separated from the flock, as they often do when things are green. They went behind

Young girl and boy on a barrel-laden donkey. J.H.: "One day, while living there, my grandmother told me and my older sister to get some water from a spring. . . . So my sister and I rode to the spring, where we filled up the cans . . . with good clear water." (Photo 14446, used by permission, Utah State Historical Society, all rights reserved)

the sand dune along Comb Ridge and all the way to Comb Ridge Mesa. I did not see them leave and did not realize what had happened until I got home and heard the lambs crying for their mothers. After getting scolded, I was told to go back and look for them.

My older sister and I started off. We were both very little, and she kept crying. She used to be very sensitive and cried about little things, but I never did. I just walked quietly beside her. "I believe I might have lost them when I turned back," I said. The moon was full, so we could see the sheep trail in the dark and found the tracks of a lot of sheep that had gone off by themselves. They had traveled all the way to the foot of Comb Ridge, then down and all the way up the canyon to its very end. As we came closer, we heard the chaotic sounds of sheep bells making lots of noise. We had come just in time! There were several coyotes that had encircled the flock and were trying to catch an animal, but when they saw us, they ran off.

At one point, we lived atop Comb Ridge, on a hill with some trees. This was when the rabbit thorn had ripened, and we had picked a lot to dry in the sun. Nobody bothered to build a shelter; we just moved around a tree, wherever the shade was, and built a cooking fire. In the morning, we would be on the west side of the tree, at noon the north, and at sundown the east side, as we sought shade. That is what people did back then.

One evening at sundown, a man named Curved like a Hook (Názhahii), from Black Mesa, rode his horse to our home. He is of the Bitter Water Clan and received his name because his foot was deformed [hook shaped] from an injury he received as a boy. He used to be a policeman, along with another man named Big Policeman. Grandmother cheerfully greeted him, saying, "my little brother," because she really respected and liked him. She was so happy to see him that she fed him a lot of mutton, but we did not get any and just sat there with our mouths watering, watching him eat.

Later, we moved to our winter camp at Rough Rock, on top of a hill. I was about seven then and was allowed to herd the sheep by myself, because I could now walk faster. From this time on, I herded and herded the sheep. Their corral was farther away, and so in the evenings, after I fed the lambs, it was dark before I finally started back. One evening as I walked home, I slipped on a frozen water puddle in the rocks, hit my head so hard that I passed out, and lay there for a long time. I almost froze to death on that ice. I do not remember everything, but I think a Holy Being came to me that night and awakened me. He jerked me, stood me up, and said, "What happened to you, my grandson? Go home; it is not too far, and you are freezing. Now go," then disappeared. I did as he said. So you see, there are Holy Beings out there. They look after little children, staying with them so they can live to an old age.

We stayed at that camp for the rest of the winter and summer, then moved to the west, back to White-Tipped Mountain, where we remained until the next spring. My grandmother had made some winter clothing for me, and I used to wear it all at one time because it was cold. But now that spring had arrived, and it was warm, I took off my coat, most of my clothes and shoes, and left them, never looking back to see where they were. I was wearing just one thin shirt but was more concerned about coyotes who attack sheep than about the weather, which at this time of year can be very unpredictable. Conditions can change from sunshine to snow within a matter of minutes. By that afternoon, clouds covered the sky, and without much warning, snow began to fall. It was a heavy snow, so thick that the sky was dark. I became very cold and could barely stand the freezing temperatures. Fortunately, I found a tree trunk with roots and dug the sand out from under it, making a hole big enough to crawl into. I lay there, dozed off, and must have slept for a long time because the snow was deep when I awoke.

In the meantime, the sheep arrived home without me, and my relatives were now worried and began a search. I eventually heard someone yelling. It was my grandfather Folded Metal Belt, who had given me my Navajo name, the Mean One I Fought For (Hashké Bá Nisibaa').[14] He called, "My grandson, where are you?" He kept repeating these words over and over. I crawled out and shouted, "Here I am!" He came riding, all covered with frozen snow on his big Levi coat, with the long-haired goatskins sewed inside. He lifted me out of the dugout, saying, "My, my. You didn't freeze to death, my little grandson." Then hoisting me up on his horse, he placed me sideways inside his warm, heavy coat and headed for home. When we arrived, he said with a deep tone of concern, "This baby was freezing when I found him. My, my!"

One day some people went to the trading post in Mexican Hat to buy food. There was no bridge over the river, only a box strung on a cable to take people back and forth. They took wool, skins, and rugs to trade for food at this post located on the west side of Mexican Hat Rock. One can still see the building's fallen bricks and debris close to where the highway goes up the large hill. Big White Man (Bilagáanaa Tso) ran the store.[15] When my family members returned that evening, they were all eating candy. Oshley came over and gave me and my big sister some. "Here. Have some candy," he said. I reached into the bag first, took some out, and put it in my mouth; my sister did likewise. The candy was caramel colored and looked good. We both started chewing, then stopped. "Ugh!" we said and spat out the gook. Oshley had fooled us by putting some lamb manure in the bag! It was terrible, ugly tasting, and my sister and I tried to get the flavor out of our mouths.

Another time when we were camped at Owl Springs, Oshley played another trick on us. One night, he went to get water from the spring, as my older sister and I sat by the campfire. From the dark came a loud "mooing" sound like a cow. He scared us to death. We ran crying and ended up among the sleeping sheep in the corral. Oshley laughed and laughed—he was always cheerful.

While we were living in Monument Valley, several white men came to our camp. They were surveyors working on land allotments. My older sister, Woman Who Went to War (Naazbaa'), and I were the only ones home at the base of Douglas Mesa. These white men were hauling around a lot of things, including metal posts, on their pack mules. They claimed to be surveyors from the government and said they put an allotment in my Navajo name, Baby. This happened many, many years ago.

We spent the winter months at the same camp and finally moved toward the southeast and the VCA mine area the next summer.[16] While we were moving along, I herded the sheep on foot all by myself. I became tired, crawled under a big bush, and went to sleep as everyone else moved past without noticing me. Not until they readied camp did they find that I was missing. They went all the way back to where they had last seen me walking and tracked me at night. There were no flashlights back then, so Oshley and the other men used torches made from cottonwood and bark. I was huddled under a bush and remained very quiet, like a jackrabbit. Oshley, who was ahead of everyone else, said, "Here's his tracks going this way. Here he is!" I thought he would scold me, but he just laughed and pulled me to my feet. We rode the horses to our new camp, where Grandmother had hot blue cornmeal mush waiting for me when I arrived.

One day we planned to shear the sheep at Where the Water Falls, because the rocks provided a lot of shade. We moved them—and there were a lot, probably in the thousands—down there. Many men showed up on their horses to help with the work. They raced as they sheared and sheared the sheep. My uncle Gambler (Adika'í) had brought big burlap bags, which they filled with wool. The names of some of these men were Little Water (Tó Ałts'ísí); Mourning Dove (Hastiin Hasbidí), Oshley's little brother; Four Fingers (Bila'dįį'í), also Oshley's little brother; Much Money (Beeso Łáanii); San Juan River; Water Trough (Tó Bá Az'ání); Little Gambler, the late Frank Adakai from Monument Valley, a medicine man who used to perform ceremonies for the Utes; Thin Yucca Fruit (Hashk'aan Ts'ósí); Little Nose (Bichįįh Ałts'ísí) [Clyde Tallis]; One Who Never Falls (Doo Dimáasii); and Crazy One (Doo Áhalyáanii).[17]

All of these men enjoyed working and received their pay in wool. They sheared for themselves, scrambling for more wool as fast as they could. When they were through, they hauled their pay away.

I do not remember how long we stayed there, but we next moved toward the ridge before Comb Ridge. There is not a very good passage in this area, but that is where we went. We set up camp at Wind through the Rock. As we were castrating lambs, One Who Plucks His Whiskers and his wife showed up. He was wearing a bandanna with holes cut for his eyes. The cloth was draped over his face, tied on his forehead, and hung down to his chin. He was wearing this because there were a lot of mosquitoes, and that is why we called him Little Mosquito (Ts'í'ii Yázhí).

Our next move was to the place where Blasted-Down Road on Comb Ridge would one day be built. At this point, there was only a rugged path up the ridge to the north. We moved to the top of Comb Ridge, where there were several houses that belonged to my grandmother. That is where she got her name Woman Who Owns the House. We moved into the hogans and put the sheep in a large canyon with a fenced entrance not too far away. Four of us—San Juan River's Wife [Oshley's mother-in-law], Woman Who Went to War, my older sister, and I—stayed by ourselves.

One night we heard a coyote howling in the distance, but it kept coming closer, so close that our house felt like it was vibrating. I looked into the moonlit night and saw it standing with its nose raised as it howled. This was scary. Someone suggested that my grandmother kept a handgun stashed away, so we searched for it. Finally, we found a small pistol with a white handle and inlaid turquoise. It was in a holster with bullets, so we loaded it. San Juan River's Wife opened the window, shot at the coyote, and fell to the floor because of the recoil. Guns were like that back then. The coyote's tail twisted into an awkward position, and it took off running. She was still on the floor, trying to get up, but Woman Who Went to War was laughing hard; I can still remember it.

BLACK WATER'S BULL

That spring, we moved to Between the Mesas and hired several men once again to shear our sheep. We herded the flock into the shady canyon, where the men sheared them. Black Water lived in this area and owned a big bull that was mean. People were afraid of it because it ran at you, even when you were riding a horse. One day, Black Water was chasing his donkeys to the water hole and came across his own mean bull. The area was rather narrow and rugged, and the only trail was down the narrow pathway to the water. He did not see the bull until it was actually upon him; then it rose up and gave chase. Black Water ran as fast as he could across an open area and up a sandstone embankment, then tried to reach some boulders. The bull ran down below, turning in the same directions that the man turned. My sister and I were herding sheep and watched from a distance above the canyon. Black Water ran from the bull, which almost caught him before he made it to safety, but he ran so fast that his thin trousers and loincloth flew around behind him. It was funny, scary, and exciting all at the same time.

This mean bull, for some reason, was afraid of Grandmother. Maybe it was because she used to carry around a wooden stick made from a sagebrush branch. It was very long and had a part of the root still attached at the tip. She had applied some cooked pine gum on it, so that it shone like a sword and was sharp, too. One day the bull ran at her while she was riding her donkey. She took the long stick and poked the bull in its chest. The animal let out a cry and took off running.

Another time, I was herding sheep with Grandmother, as I sat behind her on her donkey named Donkey That Bites (Télii Adiłhashii). We were just returning home to our round shade house on top of a hill when we discovered the bull was inside our home. "Stay on, because if you get off, the bull will run at you," she said. It saw us, came out to meet us, then stopped and stared, ready to attack. Grandmother's donkey was not afraid of the bull either and just walked past him. Grandmother carried the long stick, poked it toward the bull, and the animal ran away. I guess it had been poked with the sharp stick several times before and did not want to tangle with her. It dreaded the pain of that sharp stick.

WORKING AWAY FROM HOME

Many years ago, when the road to the Mexican Water Chapter House was being built, a lot of Navajo men worked hard on the sheer cliffs and rocky ground the trail passed over. The men received a large bag of flour after putting in thirty-one days of work. There was no money. I must have been around seven or eight years old, but I said I was fourteen. "You can be a water boy," they said to me. So I gave the men water from a handmade bucket, with cups made from tin cans, with wire handles. This was my first job where I began working for wages. I despised a Hispanic man named Mexican Who Runs Fast (Nakaii Dilwo'ii), who constantly yelled, "Water, water!" in Spanish. The men also got tired of hearing him.

We began working in the spring and labored through the hot summer months, pounding the rocky ground all the way to Cottonwood Coming Up, then across the canyon, and so on. It was rough ground most of the way. We were still laboring on that road in midwinter in very cold weather. Today, winters are usually warmer, but back then it was cold and snowed while we slept.

One day, we received a truckload of army surplus clothing—pants, shoes, and large coats. The pants were tapered at the ankle and had to be laced up. We also got high-top boots, heavy woolen socks, and hats we called "dog hats." They entirely covered a person's head and had a flap that extended over the neck. My brother-in-law took my boots and cut the tops in half, then put the tops inside the boot and sewed the boots, shortening them to fit me. I worked in these boots for the rest of the year.

It snowed a lot that winter, and one day, several men wanted to go home, in spite of the deep snow and the fact that they would have to go over Comb Ridge. I decided to go with them. We descended Comb Ridge at a place called Seeing a Moving Speck [Person] on the Face of the Rocks.[18] It was shorter to go this way than around through Kayenta. The men who came with me were my brother-in-law the Tall Man (Hastiin Nééz), alias "N" John; One Who Sits Upright and Tall (Yaa'áhii), also from Kayenta, a son of Woman Who Became Fat Again; Little Man's Son (Hastiin Yázhí Biye'); and CC, also called Luke Yazzie. Many of us left together.

We walked all the way to the edge of Comb Ridge, through the deep snow, and arrived at Seeing a Moving Speck. This place was especially dangerous in the snow. The trail turned into a series of foot holes, which led down a steep rock crevice that protruded from the edge of a rock wall. If one of the men slipped, he would slide over the cliff. They built a fire on the ledge in front of the foot holes but were hesitant to try the descent. I broke off a large juniper branch, took an axe, and brushed the snow out of the foot holes, drying them as I scooted my way down. I brought a sharpened stick to push into the ground and hang onto if I started sliding. As I slipped around, the stick came in handy.

The men on top cheered me on as I managed to go beyond the over-hanging ledge of the cliff and bypass the deep crevice. At the very end, before hitting the ground, there was another short drop. Prior to reaching the bottom, I turned around and removed the last few blotches of snow from the foot holes. The men were happy but nervous. They started scooting down the indentations, holding each other's hands, and using ropes between them. It was scary and dangerous because of the sheer cliff below these foot holes. We all reached the last ledge, which was not too long, but the men hesitated. "Now what?" I said. "This isn't so bad." I grabbed my bundle of belongings and threw myself down the rocky ledge and onto the sand dunes below. "This is fun, come on down!" I called. "This could be a real good spot to play." Then all the men copied what I had done and slid down. One Who Sits Upright and Tall was the last to come, and the men had to help him. I led these men home. I must say, I did a lot of un-ordinary things in my younger days.

ADVENTURES WITH CHEE BILLIE

I used to hang around with my cousin Chee Billie all of the time. He was one year older than me and had a different mother. Once, when we were boys, we chased wild mustangs most of a day. It was toward evening when we came upon two other boys, who were leading their tired horses on foot. My horse was tired too, but I was able to catch a fresh one. We had been riding so long that my tailbone was raw and painful. When you rub your tailbone raw like that, it is better to keep riding, because it seems to stay warm and numb. Once you get off the horse, you cannot get back on. These two boys had made the mistake of getting off, but once their horses were rested, one of the boys tried riding again. He could not do it, so they both ended up walking. I told them to get on my horse, with one up front on the mane and the other two behind. We lay forward and scrunched up to avoid more pain on our tailbones. When we finally arrived home, we were all hurting.

Chee and I herded sheep together, but he was a naughty boy, and I did not quite understand his behavior. One day while we were looking after the sheep, he caught several goats and tied their legs together. I don't know why, but we left them behind and moved the rest of the livestock home. By evening, when we arrived, the little baby goats were making a big noise, crying for their mothers. I just did not understand why Chee would do such a thing. We were both scolded and got a whipping for it. "Where are the goats?" we were asked. "Which way were they going, and where did you last see them?" I then had to tell: "My cousin brother tied their legs together, and we left them behind!" Then they got after Chee. "Where are the goats; you lead us to them!"

The men on horses followed him as he ran ahead in the direction where the goats were tied. He was whipped again and again as he ran, the whip being the kind used on wagon team horses. Later, family members returned with the twelve or more goats. I never figured out why, but I did what he had asked me to do by helping him catch the goats and tie them. It was a crazy idea, and I felt bad about it.

Chee was naughty on other occasions. One time our folks got after us because we were planning to become nomads in the wilderness and live off the land. It was during the spring, because we picked sumac berries and ate them. Our parents thought we were crazy, but I guess that is how youth are—they try weird things. We stayed on a tall thin mesa that had a round rock at the top. The rock had a hole in it, so we scooped out all the sand and made it our home. There was a water hole below the mesa, so there was plenty of water. We did not go home, and every time someone came close to us, we ran and hid. Our families thought we were lost, so they hired a medicine man to perform hand trembling and crystal gazing to locate us.

We ate mostly sumac berries, but that lasted for only a few weeks until we were barely making it. We began vomiting the sumac berries, which would not stay down. No matter how hard we tried to avoid vomiting, the saliva would start, we would begin to gag, and soon we would throw up. Still, we refused to end the adventure in our makeshift home on top of the thin rock pillar. Finally, Chee Billie said he was ready to give up the idea, but if I wanted to stay, I could. I believed I could stay longer, but we were both getting hungry. We knew of a hogan that served as a storage place for corn that had been harvested during the year. The only problem was the doors were locked, and only the smoke hole on top of the hogan was open. We decided to go there, and so we braided some long sumac stems, about four of them, and connected them together with yucca. By the time we were finished with this sumac-yucca rope, it was pretty thick and several feet long.

We draped the handmade rope around Chee Billie's shoulders and headed down the hill to the storage hogan. It was close to sundown by the time we arrived. Chee carefully lowered me into the smoke hole with the rope. The door was locked from the inside, so I unlatched it, and Chee Billie came in. We built a fire and hammered off the lock on the box of food. The two nomads were going to eat real food! We cooked some and ate, then Chee said we needed to take some with us and continue to live in the wilderness. "We'll cook more food and take it" was Chee's idea. He was the planner, so I was quiet and followed along as we sat and schemed. In the meantime, San Juan River, Oshley, and Mister Tangle People (Ałtaa'neeszahnii Dine'é) [clan name] had been searching for us. I guess they spotted the smoke coming out of the chimney of the hogan. They had been looking for us for nearly a month while we were out in the wilderness, wandering around and trying to live like survivalists.

The three men suddenly appeared in the opening of the chimney. "Open the door. Unlock the door!" they said. Chee and I looked up, probably with white rings around our mouths after eating the corn. We must have been a sight to see. I quickly jumped up and unlocked the door. San Juan, the meanest one, came in first. He had a rope in his hand, ready to whip us, but Oshley came between him and me. "No. Do not whip these two. They were sung after by the medicine man. The sacred prayers and songs of safe return have been said. They cannot be harmed. Put the rope away and leave them alone! You were one of those who prayed and sang for their safe return, and here you are ready to strike them," said Oshley. "You're going to destroy your 'answered' prayer, so you cannot harm these two. Don't you remember?" Oshley had spared us.

The men separated and took us home in different directions. Oshley took Chee Billie back to Chee Billie's grandmother's place, where he herded sheep. San Juan and Tangle People took me to White Stream of

Reeds. They were on horseback, so they put me behind one of them and rode home. My grandmother was so happy to see me that she ran and hugged me, then quickly cooked a hot meal so that I could eat until full. As I feasted, she sat in front of me and cried, saying, "We were so worried about the two of you. We thought you were lost forever. We searched all over for you and couldn't find you. Where were you?" "I was sitting up in the rocks with Chee Billie," I said. "Why did you do such a thing?" she asked. "Because San Juan spanked and beat me real hard with a stick," I told her. He was really mean and used to whip me and Chee Billie all the time.

"He is no good. He is mean and full of anger, especially toward little children. He's no good. I've told him not to be that way, but he continues to be mean," said Grandmother. So that was an experience Chee Billy and I had back then. I found that it is impossible to live only on sumac berries.

PARACHUTING

Another time, while I was a teenager still living at Between the Mesas, three of us boys stayed together. There was me, Big One (Nistsxaazii), who was a little younger than me, and CC, the son of Mister John of Kayenta. The three of us got together and stole from the women at home a man's Pendleton blanket and some wool rope used for pulling and holding up the rug loom. We walked to the canyon, where there were high ridges and concave cliffs, then took the blanket and spread it out, tied each corner with several rocks in a knot, and attached the ropes to the corners to form a harness. We made a parachute to jump off the cliff! "Who will be first?" I said. I then volunteered, got in the harness, tied myself up tight, walked to the edge of the cliff, and jumped. I fell for several seconds, then the wind caught the blanket, and I gently landed on the ground. I ran back up to the top. "It's your turn," I told CC. He got scared and did not want to, so Big One got in the harness, jumped off the cliff, and landed just fine. CC still would not give it a try. Now it seems impossible when one thinks of the ropes breaking and so forth, but we never gave it a thought.

San Juan River saw us and came galloping on his horse. He folded his rope and whipped us as we ran, listening to the crack of the improvised whip on our backs. He was furious, yelling, "Coyote, Coyote. Not even your grandmother would make mush for you if you do that kind of thing!" as he chased us home.[19] He lived close to our hogan, so he returned later and started lecturing us about what we had done wrong that day. "What you did today was very dangerous. You shouldn't be doing things like that, my children. I whipped you, not with hate, but because I care about you and don't want you to do that again. Never. It's dangerous. If the strings broke and you fell, you wouldn't survive. I don't want to see you hurt, so don't do it again." We all had a good lecture from him. That's how it usually was, whenever anyone got whipped. They always came back to talk to you and tell you it was for a good reason—love. Children were well mannered and obedient back then. They listened and obeyed after the first spanking. But children today do not listen or obey. That's how it is.

GARNETS

Another time while we were still living at Between the Mesas, I went to fetch the hobbled donkeys in the valley. I walked past the monuments and down into the Red Lands. As I was traveling, I saw a car slowly moving along the rugged terrain, but I got to the donkeys and started chasing them toward home. The car, which was an oblong shape, was very close. I saw someone waving a cloth at me, so I rode my donkey to where he was. A white man, with a cap, came out of the vehicle, leaving the others inside. He held out his hand and showed me some red garnets. "Where are there some like this?" he asked. I made gestures with my hands, pointing in the direction where I'd seen similar stones. Since I did not know any English, I talked with my hands. "You take us over to the garnets," he said. I had come for the donkeys, and now this, I thought. There were four men and one lady. The woman and her husband were an elderly couple.

I took them to the location, and they started picking up the stones, even the smallest ones, and ran everywhere. We ate lunch at noon, then they went looking again until after dark, crawling around, searching with a flashlight. They set up their tents and one for me and stayed the night; then the next day, they went and gathered more garnets. I just sat

One of the first automobiles to traverse Monument Valley, 1918. J.H.: "As I was traveling, I saw a car slowly moving along the rugged terrain. . . . I saw some-one waving a cloth at me, so I rode my donkey to where he was." (Photo 11328, used by permission, Utah State Historical Society, all rights reserved)

around and observed, picking up a few pieces and giving them to any-one. We stayed another night. The next day, they crawled around and picked up more.

For three days we gathered rocks. When we left for home, they took me back to my donkeys and went on their way. Before leaving, how-ever, they gave me a small cloth sugar bag filled with money. I was proud of myself and overwhelmed by this payment, as I spread the money out, then rebagged it. I was so preoccupied that I forgot I had come to get the donkeys, but I finally got them together and went home.

"Where were you? Where did you stay those nights?" I made up a story. "I couldn't find the donkeys so I stayed anywhere," I replied. "Are you hungry?" "No, I'm fine," I lied. My older sister's husband, Tangle People, was at home at the time, and I accidentally showed him the bag of money. When he saw it, he said, "Let's get some groceries."

Food was bought in a different way back then. Flour cost anywhere from a nickel to a quarter per cup. This bag of silver money was too much. A small bag of flour sold for sixty-five cents, while two dollars bought two and a half ten-pound bags. A can of coffee was fifteen cents, and coffee in a paper bag was a dime. Five dollars purchased a lot of groceries. All the money I received was silver coins, quarters, dimes, nickels, and pennies, but no paper bills. We went and bought a whole lot of groceries the next day, and the following day, I herded the sheep out to where the donkeys had been. That was my experience with these garnet hunters.

HEALING WITH HERBS

My paternal grandmother was a real teacher, lecturing everyone, even small children. "Don't do this, don't do that; it will harm you. You will not always be small but grow to be a young man, so learn these things and prepare for your future." She lectured us every day, saying we would become teenagers, young men and women, adults, and enter old age. She also talked about relationships with the opposite sex and how to respect everything. To me now, it is like she spoke just a few minutes ago, I remember it so well.

She taught us many things and told us that even a hogan is alive. It has a heart and lungs, breathes, and is very holy. That is why a person should have a home where a fire is kept burning. Everything within the home is holy—the valuables, food, blankets, fire poker—all have their songs and prayers and are alive. Therefore, you should never say unkind things in your home, or these things will hear you. They listen and know your thoughts. You should never think or talk badly about yourself or others. All that is within your home is with you in your feelings and actions, so be careful.

Grandmother taught us constantly. She rubbed her fire poker in the ashes, then thumped it in front of us as she lectured with a stern, almost angry, voice. She would say to me, "You are very naughty, very unruly, and immature. You should never look at or have an affair with a medicine man's wife. Yíiyá. You should never do such things!" I had at least five grandfathers who were very good medicine men, like Metal Teeth, Old Policeman, Boasts about Himself (Ádaaha'niihii), Mister Horn (Hastiin Dee'ii), and Towering House (Kinyaa'áanii).[20] "Medicine men are always on the road to help others, but they also have a way of spotting an adulterer, a thief, a peeping tom, a woman chaser. They can kill that person through witchcraft, so don't ever indulge in such activity. These medicine men, through their prayers, heal others of impurities, hate, crime, jealousy, adultery, abusive behavior, and divorce. It is easy for them to turn their power against you if you take their wife. I believe it's true because I've seen it happen too many times."

She also talked a lot about women and their activities. "If you see a beautiful woman, you can be deceived and catch some form of vene-real disease. You never know what she has. If you really want to know if she's okay, just touch her arm. If she scratches it, she will be unclean, so that is how you'll know." She used to lecture about these things from her long life of experience. It is good advice for everyone.

Grandmother had other teachings about adultery. She again pushed the ashes with her poker and pounded it on the floor in front of me, saying, "If you marry, you are to remain with your wife for life. Your mind and body will remain strong and healthy even into old age. But if you start fooling around with another woman, you'll never stop. You will lose your wife and children and family for as long as you continue. By age forty, you will have destroyed yourself and will wander about like an old bull, with no place to go and no hope for a decent life." Grandmother never hesitated to talk about venereal diseases, ensuring we got the full information. "Be afraid of such diseases. Do not associate with people who are wild and careless. They are the carriers of this type of sickness, so leave them alone." She said this to her grandchildren, both boys and girls, so this is probably why I did not get married too many times in my life.

There are four main types of venereal disease. They are syphilis, labeled as "the Man"; "the sore"—gonorrhea—as "the Woman"; "inter-nal bugs" is "the Young Male"; and "the itch" is "the Young Female."[21] "They are all dangerous to your body and health and can paralyze you for life," she used to say. The origin of these diseases goes back to the time of Monster Slayer (Naayéé' Neizghání), when he was hunting. He mused, "I wonder where I can find more monsters to kill; are any more around?" Then he was told, "Do not hang your deer on a tree while you are butchering it." But Monster Slayer was curious, so the next time he killed a deer, he hung it on a tree. As he removed the meat, he saw something moving in and out of the deer's groin. It was venereal disease. Something told him to use four different plants—white ground corn, chokecherry, spruce, and sumac—which caused the disease to leave him alone. He was told that someday the human race would experience venereal disease, and these plants would serve as a cure.

These diseases went to the north. For this same reason, no one is to bring the deer across the San Juan River—even a whole leg—without cutting it into very small pieces. If one brings back a whole leg with the skin intact and has not cut it up, that person will be cursed by venereal disease without mercy.[22] Another saying was that if a woman ever became a leader or council delegate, the curse of venereal disease would come to our people.[23] These two events—the deer and a woman official—are the same, and if we let them happen, then the curse will be upon us. We have been warned, yet we allowed it to happen, and so today, the disease is rampant. It was also said that there would be many who would become homosexuals, and even the dogs would be that way. We have broken the rules, and so now everything is happening.

Grandmother, Woman Who Owns the House, was also a great herbalist. Unfortunately, I did not learn her herbal mixes, because I was too young, but I do remember some of the plants. People in need of her services used to take her everywhere. Following the Navajos' release from Fort Sumner, many of the people returned to their land with serious diseases, like sores that don't heal [cancer] and advanced venereal diseases. Aching Stomach, who received this name because of his ailment, was so infected with sores that his family built a separate summer shelter away from everybody else for him. He smelled so bad that it was impossible to get close, except for Man with the Fuzzy Face, who stayed and cared for him.

Fuzzy Face kept coming to Grandmother for more herbs to treat the sick man, and I went with her to gather the medicinal plants. She had me pull them out by their roots, taking only the straight parts, and then she carefully replanted the rest. She offered sacred stones to these herbs, praying all the while for this sick person's recovery. She gathered many different kinds of plants, then pounded and ground them. Grandmother then told me to hunt for a lizard in the greasewood brush. I found a large one sitting atop one of the bushes. "Kill it with a stone," she said, and I did. She took the dead lizard, cut open its front, and gutted it. She then mixed its organs with the herbs in water and again pounded the ingredients. We gave the mixture to Fuzzy Face and another man, Mister Breechcloth (Tł'eestsoozii), and helped Aching Stomach for a whole week. After a while, he was able to get up, his skin color changed back to normal, and he got well. This herbal medicine was unsightly, but it cured the man. Who would think of drinking something like that these days? We were later told that Aching Stomach rejoined his family and had many more children. That is how some of our medicine was made and used back then.

When I was about six years old, I remember accompanying Grandmother on her visits to sick people. There is a thin pillar of rock called Red Rock Ending, where a man lived. His wife was badly infected. The family asked Grandmother to make some medicine to cure her, and so I followed Grandmother over there, even though I did not know what was planned. I wanted to go with her everywhere, because she was really nice to me.

When we arrived we saw a very sick, thin lady lying in the hogan. She had received a serious infection through sexual activity with her husband shortly after the birth of their baby. She was now in danger of dying. Grandmother treated her with herbs, having her drink the medicine for the next four to five days. At one point, some of the women grabbed blankets and carried her out to the ash pile to the north of the hogan. Out of curiosity, I went to watch from afar. I saw them holding the sick woman upside down, as they poured some herbal medicine between her legs. They then put her upright as it washed her out. They kept doing this for some time. She continued this treatment at intervals for seven days. After four days, she showed great improvement.

Eventually, her husband returned home on a big black mule and entered the hogan. My grandmother told the healing woman, "Go to your husband, my daughter, and see what happens this time. He will not harm you; he is not as great as he thinks he is. I will continue to treat you with these herbs until you are healed. Why don't you go get some more of 'his medicine' [sperm] and see if it'll work." This was considered medicinal too. Her family gave us some goats and food in payment, and the next day my grandmother and I went home. We walked for a long ways, carrying everything. Grandmother hauled almost all the food given to us, except for a bag of sugar I carried. Even that was too heavy for me; I must have been quite small. I got tired

Woman, young boy, and donkey. J.H.: "We had been told to hurry, but the traveling took a long time because of the donkeys." (Photo NAU.PH.97.9.453, Cline Library Special Collections and Archives, Northern Arizona University)

after a short distance and sat down while Grandmother went ahead. Realizing I was far behind, she started yelling for me. Grandmother walked with a slight limp but came back, asked if I was tired, took the bag of sugar from my hand, grasped my arm, and pulled me home. I was very tired when we arrived.

There was another woman who was suffering from the same infection as this first woman. She was living near the mesa at the entrance of Narrow Canyon, southwest of Moonlight Mine, when one of her family members rode to our home to ask for help. Grandmother's herbs for that treatment were gone, and the only place we could get more was near Dennehotso, at a place called Red Rock Point. Although there are several herbs that were mixed together, the most important one was there, and Grandmother said we had to get it. "Let's go, my baby. Let's go get the medicine we need," she said. I was happy and excited to be going on this lengthy trip.

We had been told to hurry, but the traveling took a long time because of the donkeys. We left from our home at Thin Standing Red

Rock, by the San Juan River, and headed toward Dennehotso. We did not get very far on our donkey, so we stayed overnight at Red Beard's (Dághaa' Łichíí') home in Oljato. The next day we rode as far as the mesa behind Goulding's store. We were on the south side of the long mesa when we went to a man named Weaver's (Atł'óhí) home, located under the mesa, where rocks could fall on it. His dwelling was huge, with plenty of room, so he said we could spend the night. He was Oshley's relative too, and was said to be homosexual, but I forgot how my grandmother greeted him as a relative and clan member.[24] He was a man but wove like a woman. Before we went to sleep, I watched him weaving at the loom. It seemed odd to see a man dressed in pants weaving. I whispered too loud when I asked my grandmother, "Why is that man weaving?" She replied, "Hehhh. You're not supposed to say that," so I kept quiet and watched him. He was very good. He stopped and turned away from his loom and went to get some blue corn bread and deer meat cooked with corn for us to eat. We then slept. There were other relatives living close by.

I remember just part of the trip, but the next morning we headed east, past where the Monument Valley Ranger Station is today, and into the valley to Gray Whiskers's (Dághaa' Łibáhí) home. He was very generous and fed us. We spent the night there because it got dark, and I was so tired that Grandmother kept waking me as we rode along on our donkeys. I do not know why she bothered to care for me so much, but she did not seem to mind that I came along. The next day we started east again and rode all day.

We came to Streaking Red Grass, my grandmother's sister's place, on the west side of Comb Ridge, past the VCA mines. The next day we ascended the rugged road going up Comb Ridge. The trail was winding and rough and took us most of the day to climb with the donkeys. Once on top, we headed for a place called the Point with Trees. We went through places like Small Rock Floor and Rocky Ground Waterfall, and on to Ground Soft with Water and Trail through the Middle of Man's Corn, close to where my maternal grandfather—Grandmother's brother's grandfather, One Who Plucks His Whiskers—lived.[25] He was a medicine man, and that is where we spent the night.

We were now close to our destination, where we could get the much-needed herbal medicine on top of Red Rock Point. The next day we picked these plants that look like wild rhubarb and that grew on the sand dunes. The leaves were wide but wilted, because it was getting cold, and the roots were short. Grandmother gathered a lot of roots from this plant, praying to it and giving it sacred stones and corn pollen before picking it. She filled a twenty-five–pound flour bag with these herbs. I should have been by her side to listen and observe, but I sat and waited in the shade of my donkey. She told me to sit still and be quiet, so I obeyed, and later we left. Today, the places where she picked those plants are filled with sand dunes, and there is no medicine.

On our way back, we took a route farther south than the one we had come on. We stopped at the Hunter's (Naalzheehii) home after dark. Another name he had was Baby Who Bites (Awéé'adiłhaashii). He must have been my grandmother's son-in-law. White Sheep (Dibé Łigai) was another man who lived close by, but Grandmother said she did not like him because he had an attitude.[26] The next morning, we got ready to leave but were asked to wait. The Hunter's family was going to butcher a fat sheep and make underground bread for us to eat and take with us for lunch. After receiving the food, we went toward Baby Rocks and crossed at a place called Waterfall on Rock Floor, then on to Black Rocks Jutting Up and Water Running through Rock, where Mister House (Hastiin Bikinii) [Ralph Gray] lived. He died of old age not too long ago, but back then he was young, kind, and talked a lot. The next day we left. That is how Grandmother was; she stopped at someone's home in the evening, visited, and spent the night.

Next we stopped at Woman with a Hat's (Asdzáán Bich'ahí), of the Salt Clan (Ashįįhí), who lived at Jagged Black Rock. Grandmother really wanted to stop there: "She might be stewing some meat." In fact, we had not eaten the lunch made for us, and even though I thought about it, I never said anything. Sure enough, Woman with a Hat was stewing horsemeat made like boiled sausage. She invited us to eat, and we did, then left for Kayenta and passed by the [Wetherill] trading post, where I was hoping we would stop and buy some candy. No such luck.

We went southwest of Kayenta to Fallen into the Water Hole, to a man called Rock Coming Up to a Point (Tsébaa'haschįį'), of the Many Goats Clan. We spent the night at his home, since we were traveling very slowly and spending a night at someone's house every few miles. It is tiring to do that, but Grandmother enjoyed visiting. She told me we were going west to Tsegi Canyon. That next morning we passed through Rocks Scattered Out to Tsegi and went to Yellow Man's home, where he had some cute little daughters. We spent the night there and left the next morning.

The following day, our journey took us up the wash at Tsegi to the north side of the canyon. There Grandmother showed me a formation of rocks, pointing with her finger and outlining what she said was a woman's placenta and uterus. It was hollow, she said. Right next to the uterus was the birth canal, a narrow ridge of rock, which is where the baby originates. Beside that rested the male's buttocks [pelvis], she said, as she pointed to the landscape. She never mentioned anything about this until we were actually on-site.

Between these two formations sat a hill of rocks with very dense brush. That is where we picked the medicinal plants. It took us a long time to reach the ones Grandmother wanted, because we were both slow. We finally got there, and she instructed me as to which plants to pull and how many. We also took some from within the "uterus" rock, but just as many from other places, which amounted to a lot. After we finished picking, we carried the medicine off the mesa and went to stay another night at the home of Rock Coming Up to a Point.

The next day we started home, going north from Tsegi toward Trees Going Up the Mesa, and down to Narrow Canyon to a place called Spring without a Penis, then down a narrow canyon to Mister Going Across's (Hastiin Tsé'naanii) home, where we spent the night.[27] He told us many stories, one of which was about a very young white missionary who came to preach to him every now and then. His name was Wow, That's Great (Hastiin Bił Hwiihii).[28] This missionary taught him about Christ but carried a bag of corn pollen because, he said, "Even the coyote used to carry pollen."[29] He did not shun Navajo traditional religion and was very helpful, visiting all the homes in the area.

All the next day, we rode our donkeys until we came to the home of Without His Hat (Bich'ah Ádinii), a kind and generous man. Grandmother wanted some dried peaches and garden produce, so his family boiled some peaches and served us. Now, she took out the meat that had been packed for lunch a few days ago and everyone shared and ate heartily. Grandmother had saved the meat and bread just to get some peaches. They also gave us food like coffee beans, flour, and sugar, until our round-bottom bags were totally packed and tied to the donkeys' sides. We then went down the narrow canyon valley, across it, and around a mesa, then through Spotted among the Trees. Finally, we had arrived at the sick lady's place.

After we dismounted, Grandmother unpacked the herbs and got things ready. She asked a young man to grind the plants. He brought in a homemade stone axe, which was not like the ones we have today. It was handmade from a piece of oak and had a smooth, round groove etched in the middle. He pounded the herbs into powder, then took them to the hogan where the sick lady lay. Some women carried her a short distance away and surrounded her with blankets to hide her while being treated. As they were busy working on her, my grandmother told me to stay in the hogan. This ceremony was off limits for children. I obeyed because I understood. She taught me a great deal, and why certain things do or do not happen, so I obeyed her. We stayed for five days, and I played with the children. After a while, the lady was up and feeling better.

As with the other woman she healed, Grandmother said, "Go to your husband; see if he can infect you again." She seemed to know that this woman had had plenty of medicinal treatment to make her immune to those types of infections. When we got ready to leave, they gave Grandmother sheep and goats, but she left them, saying she would send someone to get them later. Eventually, all of these animals, including the ones she had received previously, were gathered and brought back to her home.

By the time we arrived at our hogan, it was winter and cold. We stayed at Grandmother's home and did not go anywhere. The family decided to herd the sheep down to the San Juan River, so they moved again. I was told to stay home because of the cold, but I sneaked off after the sheepherders, even though everyone tried to care for me and make sure I did not wander off and get lost. We spent the winter along the river, and in the spring moved east toward Oljato. We had a lot of little lambs and goats and lived in a rocky area for a while during the birthing season, then moved to Water under the Cottonwood Tree for a while.

That was the place where I had a problem with my liver. Grandmother instructed the men to kill two goats and make their skins into bags for hauling water from Cottonwood Springs. She took the bile sack from the goat's liver while it was fresh and warm and made me drink it as medicine. As soon as I swallowed it, I fainted and do not remember what happened after that. But I know this bile was a medicine for treating my illness, and it healed me. I got sick again that same spring, and this time I was given herbal medicine that grew at that time of the year. She used a small plant that is very bitter and called the Plant That Smells like Coyote's Urine. For three days I drank it, then got over my sickness.

GRANDMOTHER NEEDS AN ENEMYWAY

We moved from place to place, winter and summer. Grandfather Metal Belt cleared land in the Dennehotso area for crops and planted a very large amount of corn, melons, and squash. He asked me to stay with him that summer to care for the field. A person named Man with a Fuzzy Face, of the Folded Arms Clan, visited us. I used to call him my grandfather too. Metal Belt had given him his adopted daughter, who had actually been fathered by One Who Plucks His Whiskers. My grandmother, Woman Who Owns the House, also came over to help watch the cornfield and cook for the workers Grandfather hired to hoe weeds. They would butcher a sheep and feed lots of food to these men.

One Who Plucks His Whiskers told my grandmother she needed an Enemyway Ceremony (Anaa'jí) performed, because she was suffering from some past experiences. "It is because I fought and killed some white men, when there were enemies around here. I have killed several white men, as well as Apaches, Mexicans, and Many Enemies [a generic term meaning Plains Indians]."[30] Woman Who Owns the House said, "I am ill because these enemies have come back to haunt me. They're chasing me and want to destroy me. This is why I have to have a Squaw Dance."[31]

So the people built some summer shade houses. I followed my grandmother everywhere she went but was told that I was not supposed to attend the ceremonies, because they were too sacred, and children were not allowed. I stayed at a distance in the cooking shade, but peeked whenever I could and listened to the singing and chants. Fuzzy Face came out from a hut dressed as a warrior, wearing only a deerskin loincloth, a bow hanging on his back, an arrow pouch on his side, and strips of deerskin wrapped all over his body. A lot of his young nephews rode out on their horses and started to chase and grab at him. They tore off his bow, then his arrow pouch. There I was, looking through the shade house and seeing the whole activity, even though it was forbidden! I watched as the nephews tore everything off him, right down to the strips of deerskin that covered his body. He ran around quickly, so they did not catch him for a while. Finally, just as he went past the woodpile, one of them caught him, grabbed the main knot of the deerskin, and pulled it, unwinding everything. The nephew took the deerskin rope, rewound it, and rode his horse back to the shade house. That is the way the Enemyway, or Squaw Dance, was done. This is how it is done for a female warrior, but not for a male.[32] It is a reenactment of the actual event of killing. That is what I saw as a little boy, and I remember it clearly.

CORN AND SHEEP

Next, we moved to a place behind Comb Ridge near Dennehotso called Little Rock Floor. This is where we brought all the corn, still on the cob, loaded in bags on the donkeys' backs. Once we arrived, the corn was spread all over a huge rock floor to dry in the sun. Only my older sister, Grandmother, Metal Belt, and I were at home working on it. Once the corn had dried, we removed the kernels from the cobs and put them in large burlap bags. We cut the squash and cantaloupes into very thin strips and dried them, to be cooked later in the winter for food. It was delicious, but I was not allowed to eat a lot, just small pieces. I loved to eat dried cantaloupe and often stole a handful, went outside, and hid while I ate. All the melons and squash were stored in small dugouts lined with tree bark. There were many storage places scattered all around.

We next moved down to the front of Comb Ridge, where the big house sat. This was a huge hogan with a stone wall around the bottom. One day a lot of people started coming, by horses and wagons. Some built makeshift homes out of sagebrush, but others moved into the neighboring vacant houses and hogans. I got to sleep in the new, big hogan, but I really did not know what was going on with all the people. I guess they were gathering to learn ceremonial songs and prayers.

Preparing food for storage. J.H.: "We cut the squash and cantaloupes into very thin strips and dried them, to be cooked later in the winter for food. It was delicious, but I was not allowed to eat a lot, just small pieces." (Photo NH 49, Milton Snow Collection, Navajo Nation Museum)

This yearly cycle associated with the big cornfield in Dennehotso encouraged people from the Oljato area to come to help us. My grandfather hired all of them to work. There were two plows for one horse, and my father used three plows for his horse. This outfit was bigger and better than a tractor. The field was very wide, so one might see about forty men plowing all at once, with others following, planting seeds. Everyone worked together, and nobody claimed what was theirs; it belonged to everyone. When harvest time arrived, everyone came to get their corn, melons, and squash, then worked together to make kneel-down bread and corn foods.[33] Even those who had divorced or separated received their share of food. Everyone was welcomed.

In those days, the roads were long, treacherous, and tiring, even when going from Oljato to Dennehotso. One had to go through a place called Horse Jumping Up Steps, where the wagon trail went through.[34] All of the roads in the area were only rough trails. I traveled many of them during my growing-up years.

EARLY POSTS

During this time, Harry Goulding (Tall Sheep, Dibé Nééz) was selling merchandise from several tents that he set up at what is now called Gouldings.[35] My mother told me how he had arrived earlier, when we were living at Dark Woods by the Monument Valley monuments. Goulding brought his young wife to our area on his back (piggyback). Some said the girl was nine years old, some say twelve.[36] I do not know. They lived close to my parents' home for a long time. We would see the two of them herding their sheep. She would get tired, and sometimes Goulding had to carry her piggyback after the livestock. Later, he returned home, leaving his young wife behind. When he returned, he and another companion brought a large herd of pack mules and horses, then made several more trips for other things. Goulding started searching for a place to live around the area, paying special attention to sites with natural springs. He improved our springs, connecting several of them together, so they fed into a single source. Next, he and his wife set up tents and traded with the People.

We did not have barrels then, so the Navajos used bags made from goatskin. These were fashioned by carefully removing the skin to prevent tears, so that all one had to do was tie the ends to make a bag. Navajos made other containers from livestock stomachs that were emptied and turned inside out; some made sumac pots covered with pitch, but these were too small to carry much water.

One day, a man went to Goulding's Trading Post (where it sits today) to see if there was any container for holding water. He returned with a couple of five-gallon, silver-colored barrels. These were good. A few days later, Goulding showed up at our home with his two pack mules. He had brought flour, coffee, potatoes, and other foods, then told my parents, "I want some sheep." He must have learned these first few Navajo words from someone. He wanted to trade only sheep but no goats.

One of Harry's nephews came later and joined them. This nephew used to go from home to home with three pack mules and a donkey, hauling groceries to the people. He delivered food to the Navajos, saying, "I want sheep, and I'll trade food for them." The man's name became I Want Sheep (Dibé Nisin). The people would say, "Here comes I Want Sheep again." By doing this, Goulding purchased a lot of livestock, and so his name became Tall [Many] Sheep. He herded them around the Monument Valley area, while other white people grazed cattle there too. In the spring, they moved the livestock back to their homes. These were big herds of cattle and flocks of sheep, which Goulding ranged all the way to a place called Moving Back. Navajos named Black Bag (Azis Łizhinii), Randolph Benally, and Thin Goat (Tł'ízí Ghanii) all worked for him when they were young boys.

Another experience I remember about early trading posts occurred at Mexican Hat. My family had moved across the San Juan. The river was louder and very full back then. I saw the waves high in the air and the water overflowing on the banks. Today, it is quiet with less water. I do not know what happened to it. At that time [probably mid-1920s], we were told that the Red Rock Ledge land in the Mexican Hat area was a part of the Navajos' land. My family spent the winter, spring, and summer there. We did our sheep dipping where the stores stand today. Mister Hungry's Son-in-Law (Díchinii Baadaaní) built a home and the sheep-dipping equipment there for the Navajos to use.[37] Other traders that lived next to Mexican Hat Rock, Big White Man and Ugly Back of the Neck (Tsiiyah Hóchxǫ'ii), had moved out of the area.[38] Their old buildings, which were once trading posts, were fallen in; only the ruins were left.

Mister Hungry's Son-in-Law had asked my folks if he could raise me. He said he did not have any children and wanted some, that he would take care of me and had everything I needed. He said I could be his heir and take over his belongings if anything ever happened to him, and that he would take care of the paper work with the tribe in order to adopt me. But my folks did not want to give me away. Who knows what would have become of me if that had happened. After a year at Mexican Hat, we moved back to Monument Valley.

When we had the sheep dipping at Mexican Hat, I remember how we all stood on both sides of the trough and held up the sheep's heads. "Don't let his head in the water solution," we were told, so we made sure their heads did not go under. It was hard work.

I was older when we moved back to White-Tipped Mountain. There were a lot of wild mustangs in that wide open space. Each stallion had several mares of a variety of colors: white, beige with black manes, beige and yellow with white manes, black, brown, and reddish brown horses, and spotted ones. Some of these animals belonged to a person named Yellow Man. We gathered these horses and chased them up through the monuments. There were so many of them that they had almost taken up the whole space between the rocks. We also used to gather wild mustangs. We'd chase these horses all day long, riding bareback. By the end of the day, our tailbones were rubbed raw and painful. We had to lie almost on our stomachs atop the horse all the way home. There was a man called Thin Yucca Fruit, who loved to chase horses. He did not want to stop, urging us to go again and again. His horse was slow and straggly, but he was proud of it.

We were living between two mesas at the time, where there is a long narrow canyon close by. In the narrow entrance we built a sheep corral, which served as a gate. It was made of juniper posts, which were high and thick. This was in the springtime, so I decided to plant a garden in the narrow canyon. I put in a lot of cantaloupes, melons, corn, and red squash. I wanted to know what would happen, so I experimented. Then I moved with the sheep to the base of Black Mesa. I returned to the garden in the fall and found that all the predators had missed my food. There were hardly any crows or rodents, so my field had flourished! The corn was tall, standing high above the corral and rocks. The melons hung from their long vines on the posts, which looked rather humorous. There was a wonderful crop to harvest.

MAN STOPS DROUGHT

Later, when I was about thirteen years old, Grandmother and I had an interesting experience. One noon, a man named Shepherd (Na'niłkaadii) came to our home. He was dressed in white, his shirt and pants being made from flour sacks sewn together. "He herds sheep just like you do, going to different homes and herding for everyone," I was told. I asked, "Can I herd sheep with him?" but Grandmother said, "Oh, no. This man is unusual and scary." She cooked him some blue corn mush, mutton, and bread, and so he sat and visited with her. She asked, "My paternal grandfather, can you do a ceremony for us, a rain ceremony (níłtsájí), so we can have some moisture? This drought is unbearable. We can't go on like this. There's no rain, and all the wells and troughs are empty, and the sheep are thirsty, and the livestock is hungry. Please help us. There's no vegetation or water." My grandmother knew he was a medicine man, so she gave him coral and turquoise beads as payment. The man agreed. "Okay. I can do that for you," he said.

The weather in mid-summer was very hot. Shepherd asked, "Where is some white clay?" Grandmother told him, "We use it to dye wool, and there's some under the ridge at the end of this gray hill." He went for the clay and returned with a bucketful, which he took into the shade house. Then he asked Grandmother if I could assist him. By the time I returned from herding and went to help, he had mixed the white clay with water. "Put this on my back, my grandson," he told me. There he was, all naked except for his loincloth. I applied the clay to his whole back side, while he did his front.

White with clay, he took off running toward a row of small hills leading away from our home. I was curious, so I decided to follow him without being seen. I went down a wash that led to the hills, watching as I ran. Then he stopped and sat down, and I did too. He put something in his mouth and howled like a coyote. He first sat toward the east, then scooted and howled to the south, moved and howled in the remaining directions, then straight up to the sky.[39] That is all he did, then he ran back home. I did not want him to see me, so I ran as fast as I could all the way to the shade house where the clay was.

He returned and asked me to help him clean up. I washed his back side, pouring water over him, before he got dressed. "There," he said. "It should happen pretty soon." I wondered what he meant, because there was not a cloud in the sky, and it was too hot. "You shall have plenty of rain in a little while, Grandson," he said as he got up and walked toward his home in Dennehotso. Within a short time, we saw clouds gather above, and without warning, hail and rain poured down. Water was everywhere, reaching the top of the sagebrush. Our elders were very knowledgeable in these sacred ways back then, but nobody ever says anything about it. I saw this happen when I was a little boy, but I remember it well enough for it to be a part of my stories even to this day.

One day when Grandmother was dying of old age, I was feeding her, and she forewarned me about what would happen with her sheep.[40] She said, "They will come and take them—maybe all or at least most of them—but all they will herd away is their shadows. What they leave you will be the real sheep, which you will have for the rest of your life." That is what grandmothers say to you before they pass on. When Grandmother died, all her relatives came and wanted to take the sheep away from us. They even brought the police with them. They took all the sheep except for the seven they left me and the seventeen given my older sister. She cried, but I was happy because now I had only a few sheep to tend, which meant less work for me, instead of a thousand or more to worry about. Sure enough, my seven sheep increased before too long. The hundreds that the people herded away from us vanished. My sister's and my sheep grew and grew.

CHAPTER THREE

GRANDFATHER TEACHES THE WAY

Faith is the root of most religious endeavors and the basis of what happens in this chapter. Metal Teeth, John's grandfather, taught by example and through faith—faith in the ceremonies, faith in the Holy Beings, and faith in John. What could be more intimidating than to be a very young apprentice medicine man performing before seasoned elders who are skeptical of your abilities? Yet here is Metal Teeth, pushing his grandson to the front, encouraging him to conduct a ceremony. Even John's eagerness to learn had to have been cooled by the situation. Yet miracles happen—rain comes, people are healed, and deer are successfully hunted when lives are aligned with the teachings of the Holy Beings.

John has learned to trust also in the symbols of faith. His world is steeped in the symbolic understanding of how and why things happen in the Navajo universe. Each action is prescribed in the teachings of the elders, which offer a cause-and-effect relationship according to underlying religious principles that work. Rather than surrender himself to self-doubt, John invested himself in action. The results were gratifying.

EARLY APPRENTICESHIP

I was nine and a half years old when my paternal grandfather Metal Teeth moved to the Monument Valley area.[1] As I grew older, he taught me his songs and prayers, which I still use to this day; they have become my means for making a living and helping others. I was seven years old when my father wanted me to become a medicine man and asked Grandfather to be my teacher. He wanted me to learn Grandfather's sacred prayers and songs, and I did. Father could not learn even one song or prayer my grandfather taught me. He tried but could not do it! The sacred songs have a certain order that must be maintained while singing. My father tried singing just one song, but he would lose his way.

At one point, he took off his beads of coral and turquoise and gave them to Grandfather. "Here, my uncle and brother, you can have this. They are yours so that you will teach my son to learn the sacred songs and prayers. I can't seem to catch on." Father knew some songs and did some ceremonies, but he learned them from his father, Aching Stomach. Since he had a different teacher, it was impossible to relearn them from another person for a second time. When a person gets used to singing one way, it is hard to change, and that was his problem.

So father paid for my learning with his beads, and I sang the sacred songs, once, twice, three, four times. The song my father tried to sing, I finished all the way to the end. Grandfather told me, "That's very good. You will continue to sing it over and over, and pretty soon it will all fall into place. It will become easier." That was many years ago, when I was only twelve. As soon as my lessons were paid for with the beads, I went to my grandfather's home every night. Metal Teeth, at times, lived near my father, so I herded the sheep in the corral for the night, then headed for his home to ask questions. "How does this song go? What about protection songs, Blessingway songs, and the sacred prayers?" We would go over and over them late into the night. I could not sleep because it was all I thought about. "I'm going to learn all these sacred songs and prayers, then become a medicine man," I promised myself. The next morning I would take the sheep to pasture but stay nearby so that I would have time to make it to Grandfather's home in Oljato before dark. I even made a shortcut over the mesa to get there.

When a ceremony was being performed, I put the sheep in the corral and quickly went to attend, because I enjoyed singing with the medicine man and his group. I attended all of Grandfather's ceremonies, no matter where they were, and remained up all night singing. The next morning, I sang the songs as I walked home. I'm sure some of those songs were very sacred and should not have been repeated just anywhere, but I sang them anyway. Once I had gotten the sheep, it was back to herding all day long, but I would ride my horse or climb the hills singing the songs from the night before. I sang so loud, it sounded like I was performing at a Squaw Dance. I forced out my extra energy and breath, which was a good way to build my voice and learn.

If I had to stay for five or six days to learn something, I would ask my older sister or some of the boys to watch the sheep. Old Metal Teeth would ask me to prepare the sweat lodge and build the fire. "We'll spend the whole day there, while we talk," he would say. After these preparations, we spent the entire time talking about many sacred things of the world, including teachings about the mountains, their names, songs, and prayers. Their sacredness included the mountain water, darkness, dawn, sunset, night, and all there is to learn until the end of the songs and prayers. Then we would go into the heavens with its names, songs, and prayers, identifying all the stars. I asked Grandfather about all of the heavenly bodies, then we returned to the earthly legends—what prayers to use, what words to say for protection purposes, the events that took place among the Holy Beings, and what had been passed to the Navajos from these events. Grandfather taught as we consumed our time in the sweat lodge. It is from these songs and prayers that I heal sick men, women, young people, and children, as well as livestock. It seems like I have done a sing or ceremony for just about everyone within the four sacred mountains.[2]

I was also taught to run at dawn, and I obeyed. I took ice baths after breaking a hole in the frozen pond, snow baths, and shook snow-covered branches on myself. I had to yell as I ran, for the Holy Beings, Talking God (Haashch'éélti'í) and Growling [or Calling] God (Haashch'éé'ooghaan), awaited me, bearing gifts of wealth, money, horses, cattle, sheep, goats, donkeys, mules, and beautiful songs and prayers of strong wisdom. These would be given to me if I yelled loud enough for them to hear. "Running will build your muscles and keep you fit as well as give you more energy, self-esteem, and endurance. It will enable you to live one hundred years or more. But if you sleep with your head in the ground, you will be overcome by the smallest obstacles before you turn thirty," my elders told me.

As time went on, Grandfather moved to Water Joining the River, now covered by Lake Powell, where he spent his winters. I went to visit him and my father whenever I could. My mother and father, by this time, had divorced, and both were remarried. Father married a

Horsemen near the Mittens. J.H.: "One fall day, five of us boys left with my grandfather to do a series of ceremonies, as we learned the ways of a medicine man." (Photo 14507, used by permission, Utah State Historical Society, all rights reserved)

woman from the Towering House People Clan and my mother married a man named Mister Red Sheep (Dibé Łichíí'), of the Within-His-Cover People (Bit'ahnii Dine'é). My biological father called him his uncle.

One fall day, five of us boys left with my grandfather to do a series of ceremonies, as we learned the ways of a medicine man. There was my clan brother Hite Chee; One with the Metal Teeth; One Who Does Not Speak Up (Doo Hahałtaahii), another boy from this area; and me. A man named Big Cowboy (Akałii Tso) also joined our group but left early in the journey. We started performing at Navajo Mountain, then traveled southeast to Bodaway to Good-bye Cattails, then into the valley called Among the Black Rocks, to Black Rock with a White Nose [this black rock is like the volcanic neck called El Capitan], to Striped [vertical ripples on the volcanic] Black Rock, to Yé'ii Dancers, Standing Horse, then Corn Disappearing, and finally Pipe Springs.[3] These are all places where we went to sing the ceremonies. A man named Pipe

Springs (Béésh Bitoohnii), a really close friend of my grandfather, used to go around and gather all the animals that we were given as payment. He kept them in a corral at his home while we went about our business of singing. By spring, we had completed our special trip and were headed back home. That is how I learned—by following my grandfather around and assisting him with everything.

Time went on, I turned twelve [ca. 1931], and we reached the period known as Horses Died of Hunger (Łį́į' Dichin Bíígháá'), when it did not rain for more than two years. Because of this terrible drought, there was no vegetation or water. Even the San Juan River stopped flowing, which created a real stench along the riverbed. There were a few puddles left in the river, but there were too many fish, so they died. We could smell them rotting when we went to Mexican Hat for groceries.

JOHN'S FIRST RAIN CEREMONY

One afternoon, three men—Thin Yucca Fruit [Clan], Black Water's Son (Tó Łizhiní Biye'), and Son of the Start-of-the-Red-Streak People [Clan] (Deeshch'íí'nii Biye')—traveled to our house on horseback. "They are riding this way. I wonder what they want," I thought. There was no vegetation, so the people had to take their livestock to find food. My father's horses were down in the washes along the San Juan River, where there were spots of green grass left from the river's moisture. Father also brought his horses plenty of grain to supplement their food. The three men came inside and sat down. "We need your help," they told him. "About six nights ago, a medicine man named Black Hair Who Laughs (Ts'ínaajinii Ánádlohí) began a rain ceremony that lasted for several days, but nothing happened. He had boasted that he was the best rainmaker around, but there is no moisture. His ceremony did not work, we have no rain, the clouds have gone, and it has only gotten worse. Can you make it rain? We had crystal gazing done, as well as having a hand trembler perform his sacred ritual. The crystal gazer saw a 'long white streak' come down in the area of your home, and the hand trembler 'pointed' toward your place.[4] 'What is over there? Why does it [the power] see over there? Why don't you three men investigate?' That is why we came here," they said.

My father gestured by pointing his lips toward Metal Teeth. The men turned to him. "Help us. Please help us, Grandfather. It hasn't rained, and we are suffering and cannot take any more. Please sing for the rain. Our horses, sheep, all our livestock are starving and dying. Even the juniper trees are turning brown. We are tired of chopping down trees for them to eat." Grandfather sat and thought. The men gave him a payment of a string of turquoise beads and other valuable items. I was getting anxious, because I wanted to watch him perform this ceremony and was happy about the prospect. "I will observe this and sing for rain too, like he does," I thought. Grandfather told them, "Okay. We'll be over in a couple of days," and the three men left on their horses.

"Here we go, here we go," said Metal Teeth. "This is your chance, a good opportunity to do a ceremony, Grandson! There is a first time for everything. Go heat up the sweat lodge; we have two days before we leave to do the rain ceremony. We shall take a sacred sweat bath and you will learn how to do what the men requested. You will learn all day and tonight, then tomorrow; we will repeat the sweat bath and rehearse the rain songs and That-Which-Is-Taken-from-Underwater songs (Táłtł'aa Sin), then perform them.[5] Your 'name' is 'Water,' and the Holy Beings have already approved for you to do it. I will be there by your side while you are performing the ceremony. You already know the duties and how to do things like the sacred corn pollen ritual and the separation and offering of the sacred stones. You know how to do this." I did, because I had assisted him with those procedures during his ceremonies, but I was only twelve years old. "You will perform the rain ceremony, my paternal grandson. The rain is not far away; it exists right here on the tips of all the bushes and trees."[6]

Following his request, I built the fire at the sweat lodge, and we took a bath. He gave me a piece of herb to chew as I performed the sweat. Before long, I began spitting up deep orange bubbles that looked like soapsuds. He had me chew some of this plant several times, because it had something to do with the sacred songs and prayers that I would soon be performing. This herb was used only while learning and preparing for the ceremony. The second day and night was more of the same, then the following morning we got ready to go. We rode our horses to the Oljato Trading Post, where we bought two large bags of grain, tied them to our saddles, and headed east. As we traveled, we sang the songs, passing Train Rock, going over the red sand flats to the northwest to Among the Small Junipers and Owl Springs, then Coyote Mesa Flats, and onto the southern base of Douglas Mesa, where the rain ceremony was to be held. Grandfather and I continually rehearsed.

As we reached the top of the hill overlooking Mister Red House's (Hastiin Kinłich'íí'nii) home, we saw a group of men working on the big summer shelter in which the ceremony would take place. Another large structure stood beside it, where people prepared food and ate. There were many, many visitors—too many—and wagons and horses. The news had gotten around, with travelers coming from Black Mesa, Teec Nos Pos, Lukachukai, and other distant areas. Some had come in the Wagon That Runs Fast. The people had already butchered some sheep, and a blanket of grill smoke came from the cooking shelter.

When we rode to the men building the large shelter, we saw that one of the men was Black Hair Who Laughs, the man who had tried to sing for rain but failed. We noticed that he was putting the shelter trees upside down.[7] They are supposed to be right side up. "No, no, take them all out and set them up right. They grow upwards!" said Grandfather. "We are going to sing for rain, and those trees are to sit upwards to grow! Black Hair Who Laughs probably did his ceremonies like that, so it is no wonder his rain song failed to work," Metal Teeth scolded him. Grandfather must have been a great man to have gotten after a medicine man who was knowledgeable. If he saw something being done incorrectly, he corrected it. He was just that way.

We brought our medicine bags inside the ceremonial place. There was a young boy and girl sitting inside, who would serve as the Rain Boy and Rain Girl. "These two will accommodate you in singing and praying for the rain," I was told. I was just as young as they were and was quite nervous. It was a critical time, with all eyes upon me, especially those of the knowledgeable medicine men who had come to observe and take part in the activity. I was led to my seat against the wall of the hogan, and my grandfather sat down beside me. I was scared!

The ceremony began. We performed the prayer and rituals, and the next day, at dawn, everyone took a sweat bath. There were two sweat lodges, one for the women and another for the men. In the men's sweat lodge, the medicine men and the people who sat in as the patients were the first group to go inside. For this ritual, men hauled barrels of water by wagon from Water in Both Directions, near Douglas Mesa. Water from Owl Spring and Salty Water Spring filled a dugout nearby. Both of these sources produced quite a bit of water.

We crawled inside the hot sweat lodge and sat down. Then out of nowhere, we heard a frog croaking. "Shine the light inside, open the blanket door. Let's see where it's coming from! These are the sounds of Female-Rain Girl (Níłtsą At'ééd) and Male-Rain Boy (Níłtsą Ashkii). There they are, sitting side by side in the farthest corner of the hogan. Catch them and throw them in the puddle outside!" they said. The men caught the two frogs and threw them in the puddle. The poor little frogs were taking a sweat bath, too, but were removed and thrown in the water with a splash! We continued our sweat while the frogs croaked in the puddle.

After the ceremony, I went to the water to wash and did the sacred wash ritual on the young boy and girl. There is actually no particular patient or client, just the two children who assisted, Female-Rain Girl and Male-Rain Boy.[8] After the bath everyone covered themselves with ground-corn powder and spread a large blanket outside for the offerings of sacred stones. This is the part of the ritual when the little stone offerings are selected and put together to take to a sacred spot, prayed over, and left. Before we went with these offerings, there was a request made by the men who came from faraway places. They wanted to take some of these sacred stones with them to their homes, because it was not raining there either.

They also suggested, "We'll walk and take these offerings to all the water wells in different places around here." Grandfather said, "No, I don't do it like that. I place all the sacred stones in one place only." We took them to one little spot near the mesa where there was a small oasis of water. I said the prayers as we laid down the offerings, speaking to the four sacred points of the earth. While I was doing this, there was a sound of thunder, then another, but there was not a cloud in the sky, and it was very hot. Suddenly a cloud began to form above us, and just as I finished the prayers, it started to rain! The clouds poured forth buckets of water. It was a long way back to the homestead, and our handmade moccasins became soaking wet. Streams of water were everywhere, going in every direction. Once we arrived home, we did

Sweat lodge. J.H.: "We crawled inside the hot sweat hogan and sat down. Then out of nowhere, we heard a frog croaking. . . . These are the sounds of Female-Rain Girl and Male-Rain Boy." (Photo 14501, used by permission,)

the one-night Blessingway. It rained so hard that it snowed, covering the sand dunes with a thick blanket of white moisture. Ribbons of water flowed among the sand dunes as it rained and rained for four days, proving our sacred songs and prayers a success. It was holy.

AN EARLY HEALING CEREMONY

That was my very first experience with conducting ceremonies through my sacred songs and prayers. In the spring, we moved back to lower Paiute Farms at the mouth of Nakai [Mexican] Canyon to a place called Water Flowing Into. Up to that time, I had performed only these healing ceremonies. One day a person came to our home bringing news that a six-year-old boy, Willie Holiday, had fallen off a cliff while trying to find some goats that had wandered out of a corral. Hite Chee also had his goats down there, and someone from his place found the boy lying below the ledge. He had been motionless for quite some time, and so the people thought he might be dead. They had covered him with a blanket and shirt and sent for Grandfather. "Please help us and do a ceremony for him, even if it seems hopeless." He accepted. We went together, but Grandfather asked me to conduct it. "As a medicine man, you will encounter such challenges, so you might as well start here with these special songs and prayers called An Aid to Cross Over (Bee Bitis Adiidááh)." I performed the ceremony, and after I said several prayers and songs, the boy began twitching and moving around, then sat upright, threw off his blanket, and looked around. We laid him back down and carried him home in the blanket. He had a number of serious injuries and a broken jaw. When we reached home, Grandfather instructed me to dig a yucca root and perform more healing. "Make sure you do everything thoroughly," he said. There was an extra set of special prayers recited after the sacred wash. For such occasions, this was a complete healing ceremony for the patient to mend the broken bones and flesh of the body. We now had a Blessingway Ceremony, which many people attended. Some knowledgeable men who came to observe and participate were Big Man (Hastiin Tso), Thin Goat, Red Rock Spring (Tsélich'íí' Bitoo'nii), Tall Man, Hoarse One (Bizhí Ádiniih), and One Who Does Not Speak Up.

Thin Goat said, as he looked at me, "You mean he's performing the Blessingway?" Grandfather countered, "Sure, he is. He's my boy."

"Impossible! How could anyone like him do a Blessingway?" Later, when everyone was taking a break or had gone to the sweat lodge, Thin Goat returned and said, "You can't do this; you're not going to last long." His remarks were unpleasant. "Well, I don't know. I don't even think about such unpleasant things when I do ceremonies," I said. "I'm doing this as a special request, and what you say is far from my mind." "We'll see what happens!" he said. "Okay, we'll see what happens," I replied. He went out the door and left for the hills, his mule's tail twisting this way and that. We continued with the ceremony, and Willie Holiday is still with us today.

Grandfather taught me about the relationship between a patient with an ailment and the medicine man who performs the cure. With special offers of payment, the sick or injured person asks for help. The payment could be an earring, money, cow, horse, sheep, goat, mule, or something else of value, but it is a special offering to the medicine man for a particular illness, a transaction between the patient and healer from beginning to end. The exchange is treated as an important item, and everything is performed accordingly. The medicine man requests the patient's identity, asking such questions as "Who are you? What is your name? How have your relatives identified you ever since you first fell to earth? What worthy things have you accomplished?" The name given by the patient will be used when the sacred healing prayer is said.[9] "So-and-so has this illness. He asks for help in healing his body. An offering has been made to you [Holy Being], and we ask for this healing."

The prayer is recited as the herbs are gathered and the corn pollen given with prayer. Every ritual is done like this. When there is a ceremony, an offering and prayers are made in a sacred place where lightning has struck.[10] Herbs and medicinal plants are gathered with prayers for ceremonies in the Evilway (Hóchxǫ'íjí). The medicine man prays to the herbs that the bad spirits of the dead will be removed from the body, piece by piece, from the soles of one's feet, to the mid-section, to the chest, to the crown of the head. They are taken out of the body from the heart, to the organs, out to the tips of the fingers, feet, and head. The herbal drink removes all impurity from the body and heals the person. This is what the medicine man says in his prayers as he gathers wood from a lightning-struck tree and surrounding plants. This is how the sacred herbs are gathered for a specific person—special purpose—and named in the request for healing. A medicine man needs to know how herbs are collected and whether prayers are spoken when gathering them.

Ever since I can remember, I saw many wise elderly men and women serve as healers. They had knowledge of the old legends, sacred songs and prayers, and knew the stories of Creation. They knew the stories about the underworld, the binding of life to this earth, and how the Holy Beings created the land and formed humans. Our ancestors had knowledge of all these teachings. They knew how to acquire livestock and care for it, plant corn and use it as their main source of food, and how to prepare it in a variety of ways. They had prayers and songs for all they did, understood how to bless people and objects, and how to become wealthy with jewelry and other riches. They knew much but hid their knowledge and died without sharing it. Some said they could not teach others and eventually died. Their life stories, from birth to old age, were never told. These elders never said much about their past, so we will never know.

Long ago, my maternal grandfather One Who Gropes Around with His Hand (Nahaghaazii) and another maternal grandfather, Under-the-Cottonwood-Tree Spring (T`iis Yató), who lived on Black Mesa, attended a ceremony. They were clan brothers. Under-the-Cottonwood-Tree Spring was performing the Nightway (Tł'éé'jí Hatáál).[11] One Who Gropes came to his home, where Under-the-Cottonwood-Tree Spring was resting on his mat. As soon as One Who Gropes entered the hogan, he began joking, saying all kinds of things. Cottonwood Tree sat up. "What in the world are you saying? All you ever do is talk trash. You are always so loud and telling jokes—you embarrass me too much. Everyone says that about you. I would never be that way!"

One Who Gropes said, "Ah ha! Have mercy on you, you poor person. All you do is lie around here quietly all day long. Who is going to remember you after you are gone? Your silence will remain, and you will not hear anyone mention your name or even remember what you have done. Let me tell you about me. I think of the future, my future, twenty or more years ahead, when I get old and gray, and then pass from this world. I'm thinking of my grandchildren and people who live near me, and my relatives—men, women, and children of all ages, from infants to elders. From this generation on to the next generation to come, they will say, 'A man named One Who Gropes used to say this or did that.' I want them to remember me even after I'm gone from this earth. That's why I say and do what I do. I'll be long remembered by everyone." Cottonwood Tree, solemn in his ways, sat there and listened.

One Who Gropes was right. A lot of people still remember him, even though he died many years ago. I cannot forget something he did one time when he was the leader of a Yé'ii Bicheii Dance. He started the dance by stomping his feet and singing. He made two or three stomps with his feet, then let out a loud fart. "Ahoo! The Yé'iis are bloated!" he laughed, then kept on dancing. People still talk about him and laugh. He was a character.

ISSUES OVER HUNTING

When I was around seventeen or eighteen, we moved to the San Juan River in the fall. It was hunting season, and my father, Metal Teeth, Hite Chee, Bahe Stanley, and Kee Holiday allowed me to go with them. As we were about to leave, another group of men who were also going hunting arrived from Navajo Mountain. They were well known, and the people spoke highly of them, such as One of a Kind (Áłt'éedii), Charles Drake, Man Who Limps (Hastiin Na'níłhodí), and Cold One's Uncle (Yídlóhí Bida'í).¹² From Monument Valley there was In Payment for Him (Bá Niná'ílyáhá), Mister Shonto (Hastiin Shą́ą́'tóhí), and One Across (Hastiin Tsé'naa). They have all since died. There was also Tall Educated One (Ółta'í Nééz) and Little One Who Hears (Aadiits'a'í Yázhí).¹³ These were all great men. They passed our camp, crossed the river, and camped on the other side.

An argument broke out among them as we were leaving. Grandfather had put on all his jewelry—coral beads, turquoise bracelet, and silver concho belt. The men were angry at him for wearing all this jewelry while hunting.¹⁴ "You shouldn't wear it. Hunting is not to be done like that," these great men told him. But my grandfather said, "No, I will hunt like this. The great deer will come forth, encountering me dressed this way. I will meet him like this." The men disagreed, "No, no, no. You are wrong, and you will not be able to kill a deer. You won't find any." Then Grandfather told them, "You are not in charge, I am. It

Deer hunters with game. J.H.: "The sun was barely above the horizon, and we had already killed four deer. They were big bucks, and we spent the whole day butchering them." (Photo NAU.PH.86.1.65, Cline Library Special Collections and Archives, Northern Arizona University)

is up to me how I hunt." It was now nightfall, and they camped elsewhere, while our group remained there for the night.

At dawn we made breakfast and ate. Grandfather sang a song, but I am not sure which one, because I was still asleep when he sang. Then we saw them, four big bucks, running right by our camp. We had not moved, and they were already coming our way! Our camp was across the San Juan at Ugly House, along the ledge of the river, where there used to be a road. One of the men and I were chasing the packed donkeys, but the other hunters left on their horses, with rifles in hand, after the deer! They kept after them through a stretch of bushes and over the big hill. We heard a shot, another, another, and another.

Within minutes we saw smoke coming from behind the hill. The sun was barely above the horizon, and we had already killed four deer. They were big bucks, and we spent the whole day butchering them. It took longer because we did not know the special [ceremonial] techniques for cleaning and cutting the meat, so we had to be taught. Sometimes the men yelled at us because we did something wrong. We

processed every piece of meat and intestines neatly, wasting nothing.
We did not just haul it back home. We had to cut the meat into tiny
pieces the size of little dried peaches and even pounded the bones. We
did not finish cutting and preparing the meat until late evening, since
the days are shorter in the winter. After finishing, we moved back to
our camp over the hill and spent another night.

The next morning we laid two blankets on the ground, then mixed
and piled all the meat on it in a big heap. These deer were very fat. The
hunters sang sacred songs as they sprinkled corn pollen on it from east
to west, north to south, in the four directions. Then they mixed the pollen
thoroughly into the meat and packed it into canvas bags for each person.
They placed the bags on the donkeys and horses, and we moved across
the river to the south side at Water Coming Together and arrived home
with our load of deer meat. "What? You're home so soon! Those deer
must have been in a corral or something!" family members said.

The men who had argued with my grandfather had not come back yet,
but two days later, two from their group returned to Navajo Mountain to
fetch more food. They had not gotten any deer, and they were out of pro-
visions and hungry. Grandfather laughed. "What happened to the great
hunters?" he said. "I thought they were very wise and knowledgeable."

Everything was done in sacredness and holiness. Deer bones were
not carried across the river in one whole piece. The men did not dare do
that because it was so sacred. Nowadays, hunters haul the entire deer, in
one whole piece, across the river and leave its skin on. Once they get
home, the women butcher it.[15]

Medicine men make their medicine bags from deerskins taken from
an animal that has not been shot. This is done by singing the sacred
songs and prayers to the animals, causing them to be caught on a
ledge, in a canyon, or trapping them in some small space. The songs
and prayers work like a fence to capture the deer. Without them, deer
escape highly sophisticated traps without difficulty. The deer is lassoed
or caught by hand, muzzled with a bag of corn pollen, and suffocated;
the sacred pollen kills it. This special procedure is called Not-by-an-
Arrow-or-Weapon Way of Killing (Doo K'aak'éhii).

Before the deer is butchered, pollen is used to mark all the places
where the incisions are to be made. This is done sacredly, because the
hide is used for a medicine bag and other ceremonial items. Cut into

strips, it may be used for ceremonial wraps in the Mountainway (Dziłk'ijí), Enemyway, or other nine-day ceremonies. These strips of hide are wrapped on ceremonial rattles and other equipment.

More recently, we went hunting and decided to do it in the sacred way. Big Man and Billy Yellow went with us and sang sacred songs while we built a shelter. Big Man kept singing, but the hunt was unsuccessful, with only one deer killed. We tried and tried to hunt, but there was nothing. We moved to another place where there was a large pond and set up camp. The group decided to perform a sweat-lodge ceremony for the deer, thinking that we would not bother them until after the sweat bath. We went inside the sweat lodge, then swam in the pond and washed our hair. We were not supposed to wash ourselves, but we did anyway. The men hunted in the woods right after they finished the sweat and killed seven deer all at once. It can happen like that. Everyone was amazed and happy.

Some people go hunting in what is now the usual way—without the sacredness—while others do it the sacred way. I have done it both ways. I have gone with some young men on their trips and taken care of their things while they hunted. It seems likely you can get a deer when it is not sacred. If you do it sacredly, it can go either way, and sometimes it becomes complicated. It is easier and better to hunt in an unsacred way, but always be careful when you butcher, because that must be done sacredly. I have gone hunting the sacred way at least four times. It is very dangerous, and people can make mistakes in the process. It was said that some hunters nearly shot each other by mistake because they "appeared" as deer. That is why. These two men died shortly after this sacred hunting incident. It is dangerous.[16]

CHAPTER FOUR

THE WORLD OF WORK

At this point in John's life story, he has reached adulthood and the world of work in the dominant society. This is the mundane world we all experience— long hours threaded with success and disappointment. Yet even with all his hard work caring for sheep, rounding up horses, and making a living, he still had time to practice his ceremonies and launch into a brief, ill-fated marriage. Still, daily life never seemed to dull his zest for accomplishment.

John also lived through some major historical events. His anger at the live-stock reduction of the 1930s is representative of how most Navajo elders feel today about the loss of their animals. This event and the Long Walk of the 1860s are counted by many Navajos as the two most traumatic episodes in their history. The reduction of the herds, the partitioning of the land according to the standards of the Taylor Grazing Act, and the loss of financial independence changed the Navajo way of life permanently. The wage economy off the reservation became the key to survival.

Work experience with the Civilian Conservation Corps (CCC), followed by World War II military mobilization or defense work, became the pattern for many Navajos. John had a little of each. He provides a good insider view of how foreign the whole experience must have been for the Navajos coming off the reservation for their first major introduction to the dominant society. He leaves no doubt that there were adjustments to make.

SHEEP DIPPING AND HERDING

I remember when people used to do their sheep dipping at Hanging Water, by White Rock Point, across the San Juan River, southwest of

Bluff. The sheep dip was located at Where the Flat Rock Ends, close to where a big circle of cottonwood trees is now located. I used to herd our sheep all the way over there for treatment. I would take a loaded donkey and my riding horse and spend the night somewhere along Comb Ridge, then go to Black Water and on to the sheep dipping.

During the winter, we had to be at the sheep corral all the time for lambing. We would bring in the cold lambs, dry them off, turn them back to their mothers, then help them nurse until full. At times, there were three or four of them born in one night, so I did not get to bed until morning. This process was repeated with the goats. I grew up this way, taking care of the sheep and goats, looking for good pasture, and increasing the herd. I was excited and happy to find good grass and plenty of water.

I sometimes camped with the livestock, just so they had plenty to eat and drink. I rode my horse and took a packed donkey, making a large circle on these trips, to White Rock Point for their dipping treatment. Then I went southwest, herded the sheep all the way to No Water Mesa, and returned to the Black Mesa area.[1] In the winter, I traveled to Douglas Mesa and stayed with the sheep until spring lambing, then headed for home. That is how I worked, thought, and planned for myself.

Once there was a coyote that continually stole from us. We chased him between the bluffs, some men going around one side, while others tried to cut him off by going straight after him. All we ever found were his tracks leading back into the canyon. One day we spotted him resting in the shade of a tree at the mouth of the canyon, where the smooth rocks are. When he saw us, he started running. I aimed my gun and shot several times, but he kept going until he ran off a cliff. Even then, as he hit the ground, he kept running. His pursuers caught him on horseback at Standing Slender Rock and finally shot and killed him. We did this because he stole a lot of livestock from us.

I remember one incident when I did not sleep for three days because I was too busy moving the sheep to the dipping tanks. I then spent the whole day there and immediately headed home. As I rode along, I went to sleep and fell off my horse onto a hard rock. It was a painful awakening. I was so tired, I just curled up and went back into a deep sleep where I had fallen. The horse, pack donkey, and sheep went on their way by themselves.

I suddenly awoke as the day cooled. "Oh no!" I thought, "Where have they gone?" I jumped up and started running after their tracks. I

Sheep dip and corral. J.H.: "I remember when people used to do their sheep dipping at Hanging Water, by Big White Rock Point. . . . I used to herd our sheep all the way over there for treatment." (Photo NN 11-41, Milton Snow Collection, Navajo Nation Museum)

ran all the way to Black Water before I caught up with them where, luckily, they had gotten stuck on the edge of the canyon. The horse's saddle and donkey's packs were still intact. I herded the sheep to a place called Willows Coming Up, then on to Lady Black Water's (Asdzáán Tó Łizhinii) camp for the night. She and her husband had a fruit orchard not too far from where I camped, so in the evening, I sneaked over and stole some ripe melons and green apples, then hauled them back to camp. I had a delicious feast of fruit. The next morning I moved the herd to a place called White Rock Coming Up, then to Rocky Road Going Up, and back home. I had a bump on my head from the fall, so I told everyone what happened, and they laughed.

Another time I was involved in sheep dipping, my grandmother and family had moved to Dennehotso. I took a different route, going through the mesas and valleys near Mexican Water to a place called

Extended Mesa with No Water. I took my usual camping gear, horse, and pack donkey. I also had a close companion, a goat that we had raised on a bottle. He was spotted black and white, castrated, and huge. Since I was a deep, sound sleeper, I used to tie him to my leg whenever we stopped for grazing or at night. The goat woke me up by tugging on my ankle when the sheep started to move. This goat came to me whenever we settled down, because he seemed to know. I traveled through Dark Water, Amidst the Sagebrush, and Among the Salty Bushes, Sitting Hogan, then to Pointed Rough Rock. There was no trading post there at that time. I next traveled to Many Cottonwood Trees, Sheep Manure Spring, White Hill Rising Up, Rough Rock, and Chilchinbeto.

One time I herded sheep near White Mesa, located about six miles northeast of Chilchinbeto Trading Post. A local resident named One Who Came Up (Haayáhá) angrily confronted me. "Don't herd your sheep around here," he said. I replied, "When did you plant this area?" Now he threatened me with a saddle rope folded in half. He rode his horse at me, acting as if he were going to whip me, so I rode away from him on my horse. Another time, a man named One with the Gray Hat (Bich'ah Łibáhii) did the same thing, threatening me with his rope. This time I grabbed the rope and pulled him off his horse!

These are the places where I used to herd and camp with my sheep. From Chilchinbeto, through the desert east of Kayenta and back to Horse Jumping Up Steps, to Where Water Accumulates, to Blasted-Down Road [which had not yet been made], to Hanging Water, San Juan River's Spring, to Buffalo Skin in the Water—these are the places where I used to move my flock. I spent the winter in Caine Valley amid all of the rocks and valleys.

Food was very scarce in those days, and there was little salt. I used to get alkaline salt from the sandstone ridges down below this red wash [near Train Rock], where some willows grow. The moisture never really dries up there. The Gambler's wife would say to me early in the morning, "Let someone else herd the sheep today, while you fetch some salt. We are all out. Have one of the boys take care of the sheep." For some reason, when others went to get salt, they did not have much luck, but when I went, there was a lot of it, hanging like icicles. I would take a rock and hammer off the salt crystals into a small bag, put it on my back, and haul it home.

FIRST MARRIAGE

I was but a young man, around eighteen years old, when a woman with children from Dennehotso stole me away to be her groom. She bore a son, Arnold Holiday, for me. She asked me to stay with her in Dennehotso to take care of her cornfield, saying she was single and did not have children. Come to find out, she had lied and had seven of them. She was often very jealous and got angry for no reason, accusing me of this and that which was not true. I guess some women are like that. I did not know what jealousy was, but as time went on, it got worse, so that soon I was afraid of her. She threatened to beat me to death, and I began having anxiety attacks, wondering what I should do to get away from her.

My friend CC was a constant companion. He asked me to travel with him to a card game held at some distance from my home. After the game, we headed back to our summer shelter on top of a rock hill. As we traveled, I told him how miserable I was with that woman and asked him to do me a favor. I suggested he ride ahead of me and get to my home first. "Take my wife to bed as soon as you get there. I'll come in with a flashlight and pretend to catch you at it." I asked him to do this because I was anxious—almost crazy—in sheer desperation to leave her. I thought she might kill me one day.

CC never hesitated, leaving immediately. I arrived home soon after with my flashlight, caught them, then pretended to be angry. I said a few words like, "I guess this is what goes on around here," and left. My horse was fenced in the alfalfa field, so I saddled him, took all my clothes, and departed, leaving the two in bed. I rode all the way to White Streak of Cattail Coming Out, where my folks lived. I guess that is what you call "yóódeeyá" (running away from your spouse—separation).

I was bad at times and did some harsh things, but I guess that is all part of learning life's lessons the hard way. When a person gets desperate from anxiety, he will do anything to get away. People should resolve their marriage problems the best way possible and not through violence or destruction. Today, a lot of the younger generation resolves its problems like that. They think they are right in doing this, but they are very wrong. It is not good.

ROUNDING UP HORSES

I rode my horse to Mexican Hat, then to the homes of a couple of white men living below the Mokee Dugway, in the Red Lands area.[2] One of the white men was named Billy Young, from Naturita, Colorado, and the other was known as Black Hat (Ch'ah Łizhinii) and also Mountain Sheep (Dibé Tsétah), because he hunted them.[3] Billy's wife was a very young girl who cooked for all the men. She also wrestled with them while Billy sat there, watched, and allowed the young men to put their arms around her. They were crazy. She was always bothering the men and boys and would disappear with them into the dark. She had some children who were dark complexioned, with black hair, like Indian children. Old man Billy moved south, probably to Phoenix, and died of old age. I do not know where his wife and children went.

There were a lot of wild mustangs in this vicinity, but I am not sure they belonged to these two men or their father. The horses were beautiful, strong, and big. The plan was to capture and sell them beyond Denver, in Texas or Canada, as riding horses. The Anglos asked me and five other Navajo men to herd all these horses into a corral. I was hired for this job after leaving my wife and went directly to it, not even stopping at my relative's home. Besides me there was Little Man's Son, also known as Luke Yazzie; Tangle People, my in-law; Tall Red Under (Tł'aachíí Nééz); Thin Yucca Fruit; and Mister Lefty from Douglas Mesa—six total.[4] Many of the horses were spread from Navajo Blanket behind Mexican Hat Rock to the top of Comb Ridge. They were everywhere. Once we completed the work, we would be paid with money and some of the horses.

The first day we rode out mounted on horses loaned to us from the ranch. They did not last very long and became tired before the end of the day. Swinging Arm (Bigaan Nidilch'ałí) [Ray Hunt] and his brother, Jim, each had two horses from there. Ray was still a young boy, and his father, Little Mexican [John Hunt], was still alive.[5] We each got a big fresh horse and chased the wild mustangs, beginning at Mountain Sheep's Testicles in the direction of the corral. The horses ran ahead of us in herds, each with a lead stallion, mixed with mares and some smaller stallions. My big horse tired easily, so I got my own.

I liked my little horse because, even though smaller and thinner, he was a good runner. He had a white streak down his forehead and some iron horseshoes put on him by a white man named Bent Over (Yaashiyishí), in Mexican Hat. This person got his name because he could not straighten up, but he was good at shoeing and a very fast worker. The other riders had not thought ahead, but I was prepared for the rugged land that damaged horses' feet. With all four hooves shod, my mount was a fast runner. I used to race him against other horses in the Dennehotso area during the summer and made sure I kept him fed and healthy. He was a nice horse, and I totally relied on him.

As we chased the herds of horses, we formed a long line down the canyons and across the open areas. Some horses were tricky and quick, backtracking when they could. The big horses the other men rode were played out by the time we reached Pipe Springs at Valley of the Gods Wash. If horses are kept locked up, they get too fat and slow, but if they are kept active, they will be fast and not tire as easily. I kept riding, staying up with the herd. None of them turned back or got away. I pushed them around the point of the mesa where there was a fenced-in canyon, then drove them into the corral. It was now close to evening, so I rode back to the white man's home. The rest of the riders came in much later, worn out and with no horses. The animals had escaped except for the twenty-nine I had penned in the fenced canyon. The white men were happy and excited about the horses I had managed to corral.

The next day the men worried about their jobs. It was not going as well as expected. Luke Yazzie decided, and the other men agreed, that they should go home and get their own horses. While they did that, I made another trip toward Navajo Blanket, found more horses—dark brown and beautiful—at the base of the mesa and drove them down. I chased them all the way to the fence. Once I started, there was no stopping, or else they would have gotten away. By the end of the day, there were more in the corral. The stallions kept their mares separated from the others in the herd, each group having one primary color.

The men returned with their horses, and soon we were off to get more. We filled the fenced area in the canyon, where there is a spring. Everyone talked about what they planned to do with their horses. Put ropes around their necks, we were told, but these horses were big and their necks huge! It seemed impossible to lasso them. Then two white

Men and horses resting. J.H.: "The men returned with their horses, and soon we were off to get more. . . . Everyone talked about what they planned to do with their horses." (Photo 14445, used by permission, Utah State Historical Society, all rights reserved)

men came into the canyon with us to see them. The men shot several of the good ones with tranquilizer darts that put them to sleep so they could hog-tie them. I captured the most horses, so I was given two, a grayish one and a brown one.

I was a good roper back then, and the white men watched me lasso a big, strong, stocky stallion. He stood like a tree trunk but soon tired and walked around in circles. The white men asked how I did it, so I replied that a man named Yellow Man's Son (Hastiin Łitsoii Biye') had taught me how to rope. This man had his hair tied in a traditional knot and was expert at handling horses. He showed me how to pull on the rope at the right time, when the horse is off the ground with all four feet, making it easier to control. We were able to rope many of them this way.

There is a rough wagon trail up the canyon where we corralled the horses. The white men asked us to improve the road alongside the ridge, so we worked all day, widening it and the narrow road to Mexican Hat Rock. The visiting white men, not the local ones, were the ones paying us. Two large trucks, which were something new back then, arrived the next day. Men shoved the wild horses, with their feet tied crisscross, into the vehicles. The big stallions went first, with the mares and colts filling the remainder of space. The men told us that the trucks would return in two days, and that they wanted us to gather more horses. We did, and in two days, when the trucks arrived, they were filled again. Altogether, these men hauled four truckloads.

Much later, I encountered these horses again. I have a son named Harvey who competes in rodeos as a bull rider. His participation took him everywhere, even across the ocean to other countries. He used to receive a lot of money for his travel, meals, and hotels. We went to Canada with him one time. My three sons—Harvey, David, and Douglas—went as rodeo riders. Following the rodeo, we went to a place where they sold horses. There were lots of them, and some were mares with their colts. They were beautiful, well groomed, and stocky horses with long legs. As we looked at the billboards advertising them, we read that these horses came from Mexican Hat and were bought from Mister Mountain Sheep. The owner of these horses was there and said that his father and grandfather had brought them from Mexican Hat many years ago. They had been transported from there to Oklahoma City, then to Canada. His father and grandfather, who came from Oklahoma, took a stallion and mare to Canada and bred them. The horses' offspring were very fast and good roping horses. I had some of their colts as my horses, too, and they used to win races. Some were grayish blue and others brown. One of them used to run races without a rider and win. When these horses were hauled away from Mexican Hat, they were destined for faraway places.

I stayed that summer and through the winter working for the white men in Mexican Hat. When that job was over, an older white man named Many Teeth (Biwoo'łání) hired me to herd sheep around the same area.[6] This was in the spring, when the sheep were lambing, and it was almost time for shearing wool. He paid me thirty dollars a month, which was a lot of money then, so I began herding.

Many Teeth was a heavy smoker. His bag was full of tobacco and wrappers. He smoked all the time, even while eating. He would spoon in the potatoes, and then puff on his rolled cigarette or draw on his pipe, then drink his coffee and smoke right along with it. At night, I would see the little red light from his cigarette go on and off in the dark.

He was expert at butchering and cooking sheep. After he prepared the meat, even if there was a thick layer of fat, he would eat it all. Many Teeth put a wooden stake through the meat or ribs and cooked the skewered piece in the coals to perfection. He cleaned the intestines and organs, the head and feet, as well as the sinew, and cooked them under- ground. He ate everything, which did not bother him one bit. He was something else.

We herded the sheep through Bluff City to a place called Water Frozen to the Ground, where there was a corral close to a windmill. The sheep had their lambs and were sheared. I decided to quit my job as his sheepherder, and so No Hat's Son, later known as Gray Hair (Bitsii' Łibáhá), took over and moved the sheep to the canyons around the Bears Ears. We were just young men then. Billy Young wanted to hire me again to feed and water his colts. I stayed in Bluff in a little house located across from the road that goes through Cow Canyon. There were eighty colts, future stallions, that he was getting ready to sell. I worked through the winter, caring for the horses, then one day a big truck came and loaded them up. The purchaser paid my boss, who then paid me.

One of Billy Young's brothers, who lived in Moab and owned a lot of sheep, came to Bluff and hired me to work for him. We went to Moab and the La Sal Mountains, where he kept his flock. Fred Yazzie from Monument Valley also herded for him, grazing sheep amid the jagged mountains close to Sunshine Mountain [Book Cliffs]. Fred said he was very homesick by himself.

This was the time America was preparing to go to war with Ger- many [World War II]. People said the Germans were coming to eat at the White House and were going to defeat the United States. People in Moab cried out, "We're not ready to go to war!" It did not bother me one bit, because I had not heard anything about it; the war was new to me. Mister Young talked bravely, saying the enemy would never con- quer him or the state of Arizona. He told me, "Don't worry about the war, just herd my sheep," so that is what I did. I also built a sweat lodge and took sweat baths regularly. For three months I herded sheep.

While I was there, Dan Hayes's older brother came to visit me. He hunted wolves and spoke pretty good Navajo, so we talked quite a bit. I began helping him set traps for wolves, coyotes, and bobcats. He paid me cash for this, so I earned extra money while herding sheep. I invited him to take sweat baths, but he was afraid and joked, saying it might shrink him and make his wife cry. He was a funny person. I moved back in the spring.

DAD AND THE SHIPROCK FAIR

Long ago my father used to drive his horse and wagon to the Shiprock Fair, and one year I went along. We started from Monument Valley and camped overnight at Mexican Water, then the next day traveled to Red Water Road, where we spent the night. It took us three days to get to the fair, since it was very slow going by wagon. Today it is just "over the hill," and one gets there within hours. The fair was not as crowded back then, with only a few people attending. There was no rodeo, but they did have horse races, foot races, wrestling, and tug-of-war with a scarf or rope.

We arrived at the fair, called Yé'ii Bicheii Dance, in the evening and pitched camp close to the fairgrounds. I was responsible for caring for the horses, so I took them to the water, fed them hay, and hobbled them. We had five animals, three for the wagon, one for me, and one for riding. Two horses pulled the wagon, and two extra horses trailed along. Horses used to do that, follow alongside the wagon. The fifth mount, a pale-colored horse, was for the races. It was a brownish gray, with a white spot on his belly, so we named him His Underside (Biyaa Likizh). A man called Twenty-five Cents (Naakíí Yáál) rode him in the race and won, but I do not remember the prize.[7]

The women who came to the fair wore their hair in Navajo buns, tied with yarn that hung down. They did not have short hair like men. They also dressed in traditional clothes and looked really nice. The vendors, who were mostly white people, sold fruits and vegetables by the road. We left the fair when it was over, and since we had a load of things, we hitched the spare horse to the wagon, so that now there were three pulling.

My father knew a man from the Salt Clan (Ashįįhí) who was originally from Kayenta but was now living in Teec Nos Pos. Father called him "my son" (shiye'). We went to his home and stayed there for two days; then they asked us to do an errand. The three of us rode back to the fairgrounds, while the women and children stayed in Teec Nos Pos. Once we arrived, my father asked me to herd some rams back home, while he and the other man rode there in a truck. The man in Shiprock who had been caring for the herd complained about not being paid in full and that he was short eighteen dollars. The man from Teec Nos Pos had to go and find the eighteen dollars but returned with only fifteen— still three dollars short. The herder did not release the rams until my father paid the rest of the money.

I was now responsible for herding at least 118 rams back to Teec Nos Pos, to the people who owned them. Early that morning, I started the livestock across the San Juan River toward my destination. It took me a long time to get to Standing Juniper Tree, about twenty miles west of Shiprock. A man from Teec Nos Pos met me there on his horse and helped herd the rams into a corral. There were some planted fields with lots of cantaloupes. We spent the night there and left at dawn, driving the rams westward on a wagon trail along the bank of the river. By the time we got to the intersection of Beclabito Wash and the San Juan River, people started showing up on horses or in vehicles to separate and take their rams. Some claimed two or three, others more, as we moved toward Teec Nos Pos. By the time we arrived, we had only a few left. I think the man who was helping me received pay, but I did not get anything. When I arrived where we were to stay, I had only four rams that belonged to the man. "What happened to the herd?" they teased me.

This man's family was planning a ceremony. My father and I went to the mountain to gather wood for the ceremonial fire. We performed the Lightningway (Ii'ni'jí), used when a person's face or side becomes paralyzed [a stroke]. The illness is called One That Twists You, but with this ceremony, a person is restored to normal.[8] Later, the family asked me to haul more wood and hitched a big horse to a wagon. I headed toward the mountain, looking for big dry logs, but all I saw were green trees and the stumps of dried ones that had been cut down to the base. The mountain, Turning Mountain [Carrizo], had no firewood!

I was trying to think of what to do when I came to a rocky canyon with a few dead, dry trees below. I immediately walked down and started chopping the wood, but it took me all day to bring up enough logs to fill the wagon. By late evening, two men from home came on their horses, because everyone was wondering what happened to me. The wagon was almost full, and there was only one more armload in the canyon. I told the two men to get the wood, because I was very tired, and that there was no more anywhere around. One of them pointed to a tree, a green one, and said, "This is good wood; that is what we get." I told them there was no dry wood anywhere, so they complimented me on getting the best kind of firewood and teased me, saying, "We'll keep you around here, and give you a wife."[9] They were very proud of me but never got me married.

We performed the ceremony for the next day and a half; then, as we were about to leave, my father suggested they do a sweat lodge so that he could relax and recuperate. His wife was in a hurry to leave, but he stayed in the sweat lodge all day and spent another night. The next day we left early and traveled all the way to Mexican Water, where we stayed the night. The following day we went to Cottonwood Coming Up, White Rock Coming Up, and Red Rock Sticking Up, where we stayed the night. We left early in the morning and traveled all the way back to Hat Rock, our home, southeast of Father Liebler's mission.[10] We arrived at midnight, ending our trip to the Shiprock Fair.

LIVESTOCK REDUCTION

Then there was livestock reduction many years ago.[11] The government said it was because of overgrazing and depletion of the soil, but in those days we had plenty of vegetation because it rained a lot. Of course, at that time, our traditions were strong and everything was in order.

John Collier really wanted to round up our people but could not do it, so instead, he took our livestock. He went through our land and forced the people to get rid of their goats and sheep, horses and cattle. Next, he littered the reservation with dead animals, leaving a stench of death everywhere. When the government officials took our livestock away and slaughtered them, it was heartbreaking. By doing this, Collier tried to destroy our freedom and dependence on our land.[12]

When the government drove the livestock into the gullies, then killed and burned the carcasses, only a few of the animals could be taken home for food. The people had to butcher the meat right there and could not bring any animal back alive. It was terrible and tragic for the Navajos. The government took 1,000 or 2,000 goats and sheep from each area, and about 50 to 100 horses, and killed them. This was livestock raised and cared for by the People, who were brutally mistreated.

This tragedy took place all over the reservation, and many men and women died from it. The Navajos have two terms that describe what happened. "Dying from depression" (yíní hwiisxį) and "suffering from depression" (yíní ho'niiłhį), meaning that a person died before his or her time because of extreme concern and worry. These terms explain the results of the slaughter that took place under John Collier. Many of our people died from worrying, because the turmoil was too great. Some of them suffered in prison for several months to a year, causing them to die shortly after their release. These words describe those feelings.

I was a young man when this occurred. I herded in our horses—all 37 of them were marked with paint. I also drove in more than 600 sheep. I have been a sheepherder all my life and told the government that I was not hiding anything. I wanted to wait and see what happened—either they would take some animals or leave them alone. Out of this herd, they allowed me to keep 13 horses and 354 sheep and gave me a permit to that effect. The other 300 sheep and goats, they took away and slaughtered in the washes.

Some of our people did not want to lose their livestock, so they claimed only one or two horses or ten sheep and received a permit for that amount. This lying about the number of animals, saying there were less than there really were, shortchanged the people when they actually owned a lot of livestock. Others gave up their animals and suffered their tragic loss.

I remember seeing some police or authorities taking goats away from a man named Tall Educated One. There were others at that time, such as Leader (Naat'áanii), Big Man, Husky Bitter Water, Big's Stepson (Nitsaaíí Biye'jíł'íní), and White Sheep, who were losing their livestock. There were lots and lots of animals that we saw being collected between Promise Rock and Goulding's Mesa. Three of us young men watched the authorities take the sheep and goats and decided to stop them. We knew that many men were being arrested for trying to prevent this thing from occurring. Still, we wanted to see what would happen if

Corralled horses during the livestock reduction. J.H.: "I herded in our horses—all thirty-seven of them were marked with paint. . . . Out of this herd, they allowed me to keep thirteen horses." (Photo NN 5-12, Milton Snow Collection, Navajo Nation Museum)

we retrieved the animals. Also, we had heard all sorts of rumors about the war coming toward our country.

We came upon three Navajo police helping with the roundup. I rode to the first man, named Jumps Upward (Yáhii Tsxísii), or John Long, threw him off his horse, then took away his gun and nightstick. Next, I went after the second officer, Lumpy Policeman (Siláo Neesk'ahí), alias Jack Holiday from Blanding, and did the same to him, and then the third one, Big Giant (Yé'iítsoh), a brother to Hairy Mexican (Nakaii Ditł'ooii), or Paul Goodman, from Douglas Mesa. I was frustrated with them, because what they were doing was not right. I shot in the ground at their heels. "You say these are U.S. government orders, but I believe they are coming from the Navajo Nation government," I told them. "I will shoot to kill." I told Jumps Upward, "You are wrong in taking our goats and sheep, so I am going to kill all of you. You have killed too much livestock, destroyed the livelihood of our people, and have broken their sound minds. Nothing is left. What have you got to repay for this great loss? Nothing! You'll never pay anything to make it up to them, so it is probably better to kill you." They started begging for their release, especially Jumps Upward.

The four men with me were Flips like a Rope (Yanáádiłii), Yellow Yucca Fruit (Hashk'aan Łitsoi), Crazy One (Doo Áhalyáanii), and One Who Never Falls.[13] All five of us went after the policemen, but the others in the group just stood by and watched me wrestle with the officers. They were all aroused to begin with, but their feelings did not amount to anything, so I ended up doing all the work. We took the goats away, and I told Jumps Upward, "If you ever arrest me or have me taken to jail, I will soon be out, come back, and shoot you dead!" He is my uncle, a brother to my mother, but I threatened to kill him anyway. "No, no, my baby, please, my little one, my little one. Go ahead and take your goats home!" he pleaded. "No, no, my big brother," replied Jack Holiday, while Big Giant said, "No, no, my big brother, please don't do anything bad, please, no, no." They all promised they would not tell anyone about what had happened and then left. We took the goats and herded them back home. I was "naughty."

Another time in Monument Valley, a white man from Bluff, who had a stubbed finger, was staying at Goulding's. He was some type of official who spoke fluent Navajo and was stationed at the trading post with another white man named Rough-Skinned Cowboy (Akałii Dích'izhii). One day I saw them herding horses a short distance from the Arizona-Utah border. I do not know where they got these horses, but they were herding them toward Goulding's. Once again, I became frustrated with this kind of behavior. I took a rope, folded it in half, and sped after them on my horse.

When I reached them, I whipped both white men with my rope and took the horses away. I know I was mean for doing this, but they had no right to help themselves to our property. The government did not know about their activity, and these men should never have tampered with the Navajos' property in the first place. I warned them, said they could arrest me if they wanted, but that I would prefer charges against them if they did. They gave up the horses, were red faced, and agreed I was right. The man with the stubbed finger went on to say, "It's true. The government doesn't know that we're doing this. We are breaking the law; it's true, and you are right." Then they rode their horses over the hill toward Goulding's.

I know I was mean, but what frustrated me was that these authorities had done enough damage, both physically and mentally, to our people, young and old. They had destroyed our livelihood and happiness. Some Navajos had even perished from this horrible ordeal. They suffered extensively, beyond words, when they thought of these unbearable things, and there was nothing to be done to pay for or cure this tragedy. My feelings were strong enough to make me not hesitate to act against this mistreatment. I reacted naturally.

One time there was a Squaw Dance in Kayenta. During the Midnight Ceremony (Jiji), a police car arrived with three officers. I became uncontrollably angry, went to their car, and started lifting it off the ground! Some men joined me and helped roll it. Altogether, we turned over three police vehicles that night. Men like Jack Crank; One Who Acts like a Man (Hastoii Adil'íní), alias Mister Pipeline; Yellow Water (Tó Łitso); and One Who Hits (Adiłts'įįhii), alias Mister Austin, were arrested and taken to jail. But not me, and I was the leader who started the whole incident. I do not know why I was never arrested. Perhaps it was because of the sacred songs and prayers I did for myself.

Livestock reduction was similar to what happened to the Navajos during the Fort Sumner and Long Walk years. It was just as torturous. I tried to suggest that something be done, but our chapters and government were weak and did not accomplish anything. Our people should have petitioned to be compensated for their losses and paid for damages. I tried to voice my opinion, but no one listened, so I stopped going to chapter meetings altogether. Our chapter officials did nothing about it, because they depended on the "greasy bag" [Navajo Nation Funds], and so they let the people suffer. It is too bad our officials were unwilling to speak up on our behalf; I think it was ugly.[14] Now, we are not getting anywhere; it is worthless.

The officials from Oljato have not said anything about this problem right up to this day. In other chapters, officials and community members spoke up for their people. For instance, Navajos from the Aneth area, like Mister Sakizzie; Old Eddie; Bitter Water; Mister Jelly; Old Educated One; Little Tachinie (Táchii'nii Yázhí); Sam Key; Big Yucca Fruit (Hashk'aan Dííl), who lived above Bluff City; Shiny Policeman (Siláo Disxǫsii); Randolph Benally; and Tall Man, all went to Washington, D.C., from Window Rock, the Navajo Nation capital. Government officials told them that not everything that happened on the reservation during livestock reduction was ordered by the Washington government, but rather from our own local governments. Some people in Arizona spoke up and were compensated for their loss, but our people did not say anything and so we lost out. They were afraid to speak, while the others entered a petition and were paid. We had no confidence in ourselves, none whatsoever, and so events overwhelmed us; the task was too much.

Several years following livestock reduction, plans were made to build group housing, the idea behind this being similar to Collier's plans. Our people were to live in houses in one area and leave all our livestock, cornfields, and land behind. Today, many live as it has been planned and have been tricked. Most of them now live in group housing, where they swell in numbers. Some of their livestock has gone astray, was not penned, and has been captured by the tribal livestock representatives because the animals roamed onto the highway.

Another major event that has threatened our people was their work in uranium mines. They are now suffering and dying from this experience. It has affected our children with birth defects. These three tragic events— livestock reduction, housing developments, and uranium—are identical in many ways. That is how we feel. Our people have suffered insurmountable damage and loss without any sort of compensation. I feel that John Collier has finally succeeded in his plans, but no one bothers to discuss these matters.

Even now, our children, once educated, return to our communities and tell us, "These are the policies, rules, regulations, the law!" Law? What law? The law has always been in existence.[15] We have lived by it every day since the beginning of time. Our educated children should be helping us, but they take sides with their teachers, the white man, and begin lecturing us about what is the law. The children should be using their energy and tactics to uncover and resolve many of our ongoing problems, problems that came into existence because of our mistreatment in the past.

I think there is a good possibility that something can happen to overcome these problems, but not everyone is honest. We are tricked or cheated right under our noses. It is hard to trust anybody these days. I tried my best, as an individual, to persuade the officials and community to get together and work at getting compensated, but nothing happened, so I gave up. "Go ahead and go about it your way. No one seems to want to listen to what I have to say, so never mind me!" That's how it all happened. Enough.

WORKING FOR THE CCC

In those days they had the CCC [Civilian Conservation Corps] if one needed it. People either signed up or were drafted into the military from there. We used to sell meat—a whole sheep carcass, leg of beef, or rump—at the trading post or CCC camps. The cooks at these camps often bought meat from the local people. One day my big sister told us that people needed meat at Road Coming Down, so we butchered three sheep, packed the carcasses on the horse, and took it to them. I arrived at the jobsite, brought the meat to the camp where they cooked their meals, and sold it to them. My brother-in-law received the payment for the mutton, and I did not get a nickel.

I stayed around the jobsite for a while, so I was asked to help by taking the horses to water at noon. The watering place was large and near a mesa. A man named Charlie Salt and I took them there every day. He used to talk a lot and tell stories, so he would ride his horse ahead, then stop in front just to keep talking. He might have been a little retarded, but he talked all the time, and that is why he was also called Talks a Lot (Ha'dilch'ałí). He told me, "I got married. I got married two months ago and became a son-in-law of Tall Educated One." I said, "Yeow," and he kept right on talking. "She is only nine years old.[16] My parents herded the horses to my bride's place as payment. She is still afraid of me. I haven't touched her yet. When I move toward her, she tries to run away from me, so I leave her alone. I'm still trying to get her used to me. I want to wait until she gets used to me."

Another story he told me was, "One day not too long ago, I was breaking a horse. I got on, and it started bucking, then headed straight toward my mother-in-law's hogan. We weren't supposed to see one another, but I ended up right in front of the home, with her head staring at me out of the half-closed door. The horse suddenly jerked and threw me backwards, with strands of turquoise beads breaking off my neck!" His stories made me laugh so hard!

Charlie said: "One summer I planted a huge cornfield at Red Rock Going Down [Mystery Valley] and worked in it all day, hoeing weeds. This particular time, I was working in the middle of the field when my mother-in-law, who was not so fond of me, asked, 'What is that out there, in the middle of the cornfield? Is it a kitten burying his feces?' She never really appreciated me."

Another time he recounted: "I decided to build a hogan in Mystery Valley. The trees were nice and tall—good logs for building a hogan—but they were quite close to the homestead. I was chopping away when my mother-in-law saw me. 'Who's that out there chopping the trees?' Someone said that it was her son-in-law. Then she said, 'It must be a beaver!'" I laughed and laughed and enjoyed working with Charlie for several days before getting paid in silver coins. I was so proud of myself that I took them out of my pocket every few minutes and lined them up to look at.

Later, I was herding livestock at the base of the La Sal Mountains when I heard that I had a letter at home. So I returned to Monument Valley and began working for the CCC. The program operated out of several large white offices in Kayenta. The BIA [Bureau of Indian Affairs] constructed these buildings just like the BIA boarding school, with a cafeteria where the workers lined up to eat. My clan grandfather Man with the Gray Face (Hastiin Binii'łibáhí) was our cook. He used to get up early in the morning, prepare breakfast, then come in and yell, "Come and eat!"

Many Navajo men labored on these crews. The metal census tags used to count and identify our people by number, when being paid for work or during food distribution, were also used when working for the CCC. We were asked, "Do you have your metal [census tag]?" The pay was only $1.25 per hour. We worked to "kill the washes" in Chilchinbeto by filling in the water-eroded land and by putting up fence barriers across gullies. Other men built water wells, the remains of which can still be seen in some places. Most of these structures have now fallen apart due to age. We also built many dams using wheelbarrows,

Civilian Conservation Corps workers on a fencing project. J.H.: "We worked to 'kill the washes' in Chilchinbeto by filling in the water-eroded land and by putting up fence barriers across gullies." (Photo 10-10, Milton Snow Collection, Navajo Nation Museum)

big trucks, as well as arm and leg work. Some dams are still visible, but others have filled in with sand and debris.

For relaxation, we played baseball. There were other CCC groups in Tuba City, Skinny Cottonwood, Shiprock, Teec Nos Pos, and by the Anasazi dwellings northeast of the San Francisco Peaks and Flagstaff.[17] There were other outfits in Blanding, Monticello, and Moab. In this last place, the houses were green, not white like other camps, and were located just across the bridge by the Colorado River. Each crew had a baseball team that played against other camps. We would pile into a long green bus and travel to our games. Sometimes we won, sometimes lost, just like high school students playing sports. We had games in Window Rock, Moab, and against a Mormon team. I was always asked to be the pitcher, because I tossed the ball fast, and the opposing team could not hit it, would get mad, and would throw their bats down. I offered to have others pitch, but they told me to do it, and I had fun.

On workdays, our supervisor loaded us in trucks and transported us to the site, wherever a well was to be built. One day we were working on a well at Sitting Willow Tree, just below Rough Rock, Arizona. Our foremen were Dressy Woman's Son (Asdzáán Hadit'éhí Biyáázh) and Little Tower House (Kinyaa'áanii Yázhí), from Chilchinbeto. We worked really hard hand mixing the cement because there were no electric mixers. The cement, gravel, and water, blended in a baking pan–like container, were mixed with shovels, then poured into the square frame boards and mesh wire prepared as forms.

One day, Little Wise Boy (Tsiłkéí Hoyáanii) asked me to stay at the jobsite with him to guard the equipment. We decided to go for a walk, and as we strolled along, we saw a tower of smoke rising in the distance. A man named What the Heck (Yáadilá) lived out that way, so we headed for his place.[18] He was thin, short, and he limped. When we arrived, he was taking a sweat bath, so we joined him and stayed until late afternoon, then walked home and made supper. I fried the potatoes, and Little Wise Boy made fry bread. He asked me to get more firewood, so I went out and chopped some dry branches off a tree not far from our camp. As I was working, a single bumblebee came out. It flew after me as I ran with an armful of sticks toward camp. Then it attacked Little Wise Boy while I was helping with the fry bread. He swished his dish towel around him and got rid of the bee, then had an idea: "Let's eat and afterwards go over and cut down the tree at its base. There could be more bees!"

Just the day before, someone had delivered to our home a load of military clothing—socks, and pants with lace-up strings, and high-top boots. There were other forms of padding and protection, such as dog hats, with their flaps that hung down and a visor that could be lowered to protect your eyes and hide your face. We decided to dress in these clothes and chop down the beehive tree. Little Wise Boy talked me into it, saying we might find honey and that it tasted sweet and good. I did not know anything about beehives and honey, but he said I would like it, and we could just steal it from the bees! He had worked for a white man before who owned beehive boxes and gathered honey from the hives. So Little Wise Boy knew all about it.

After we finished eating, we got dressed in several layers of military clothing, including neck scarves made from wool, goggles, and the dog hats. No bees could get inside, we said. Little Wise Boy sharpened the axes, then walked down to the tree. It was huge. We first removed all its branches, then chopped at its base. Sure enough, there was honey down by its roots. Little Wise Boy pushed the tree over and exposed the goods. We did not see any bees until the trunk hit the ground, split, and a huge swarm erupted.

We continued to chop, and I split the tree open for more honey. The bees were large and swarmed all over, blanketing us in their attack. Little Wise Boy wanted to make sure we got a good portion of the honey, so we carefully chopped the tree. He kept guessing where to find the most and the best place to cut. We managed to obtain an abundance of combs full of pure, sweet honey, which we carefully placed in four buckets. Little Wise Boy told me to be extra careful not to break these nice combs, built by the bees in geometrical formation, with each cup side by side. This is how we stole from the bees.

When we arrived home, we were still covered with bees. Little Wise Boy told me to get a pine tree branch, build a fire, and burn the branch. This made smoke, which we ran through over and over, finally forcing the bees to leave. In the meantime, we were suffocating from the heat inside the uniforms. We laughed at each other's appearance, then I had to taste the honey to see if it was sweet, and sure enough, it was.

WORLD WAR II

Time went on. Then we heard about the war with the Germans, of young men being drafted, and soon I was among them. It was scary to think about the war, especially when people talked about the enemy invading our country. The people were very emotional about the war, and I was frightened. The money in my pocket seemed worthless at that moment, but I thought, "It's up to the Holy One." As I got on the bus, I noticed there were a lot of young Navajo men who had been drafted and were coming with me. I recognized one of them, Joe's Grandson (Joe Bitsoii), who lived at Comb Ridge Going into the San Juan River, just west of Bluff.

We sat together as we traveled to Salt Lake City. Upon arrival, the military put us in a camp and began our processing. I saw a line of young men that stretched a long distance. They were taking their physicals,

John Holiday around the age of nineteen. (Photo provided by author)

stripped naked without a stitch of clothing. "They shouldn't undress until they are ready to be checked," I thought. There were too many men, and they had all different sizes and types of penises. This was something I had never seen before.[19]

It took a whole week to go through the line. It was finally my turn, but it was uncomfortable to be checked, as the doctors poked every hole in my body, from my eyes and ears to every other place. Joe's Grandson and I passed our physicals and were transported to a canyon at the base of the mountain. Also, during this time, someone stole my identification; the officials did not recognize me, and I was told my name was not mine. Things were different back then, and the paperwork was complicated and confusing, so I lost my real name. If I had shipped off with the other soldiers, who knows what I would have done or where I would have been.

Within two days, we received our uniforms and were told to train with the other servicemen hiking with backpacks into the mountains. There was a lot of strenuous physical training, and I did well, but Joe's Grandson tired very easily. I helped him, holding him up by his waistband and pushing him along, but he slowed down even more. I sat and wondered, "How are we going to do this?" They told us that the war was escalating and that soon we would be shipped off to join the main forces. They also said the Germans were coming to Washington, D.C., to meet our officials in some important event.

The men had a very short training time and were now preparing to leave for combat. The year was 1942, and the war effort needed them. Soon it would be our turn to go. We had been there for three and a half months when Joe's Grandson became sick, making everything harder and harder. The training was more strenuous as we learned war tactics. Physical training, backpacking, running, and so forth increased, and in one week and two days we were to go out to the lake for water training. It seemed impossible! I had my small corn pollen pouch, so my friend and I decided to perform some sacred prayers not too far from our base camp. That night I did a protection prayer (Shield Ceremony, Ach'ą́ą́h sodizin), and the next morning we climbed to the top of a small hill nearby, laid an offering of sacred stones, and prayed again. I prayed really hard and long.

The following morning, as we boarded transportation to take us to more training, a leader called out our names. The men were leaving in two days, but we were told that our inability to speak and understand English was something that could really hinder our training. "You two may go home now. Neither of you speaks English, and one of you is too sick." My friend was so happy, and we were both relieved. We were each paid seventy-five dollars and taken back to Monticello by bus, then to Bluff by mail truck. I asked my friend if I could spend the night at his home at Comb Ridge. He agreed, and we set out on foot with our backpacks. As we walked along the road, a car, driven by a white man I had worked for in the past, pulled up beside us. We got in, and he dropped off my friend at his place, and I continued on toward Mexican Hat. I believe Joe's Grandson got sick from being scared of the military and the war. He never recovered, and died not too long afterwards. That was my experience with the military.

DEFENSE INDUSTRY WORK: BELMONT

Another job I had during World War II was in Belmont, Arizona, on the other side of Flagstaff. The union had just moved there for the first time and was organizing the jobsite. The trader in Oljato named Big White Man and a missionary called One Who Bows Down (Yaa 'Át'éhii) tried to help me.[20] While he was in Phoenix, the missionary had heard about jobs working for the government, and he told the trader about the union employing people south of Flagstaff. This was when World War II was at its height, and men were being drafted. I went to the trading post one day, and the trader said, "Go to Flagstaff and get a job. People are applying for them now. The missionary said so." "Then take me over there," I replied. "I can take you as far as the Kayenta Post Office," he said. He gave me an application that the missionary had brought back for those who were interested. I had help filling one out, then caught a ride with the trader to Kayenta. From there I rode in a mail truck to Flagstaff, then hitched a ride with some people headed to Belmont. Many workers, some in cars, were arriving at the jobsite, but at this time, I had not been exposed very much to cars. I learned that applications had been sent to many of the traders, so that whoever wanted to sign up could.

When I arrived, I saw three large green tents, similar to those used in revivals. One of them served as the registrar's office and headquarters, with partitioned rooms and another small tent attached for additional space. I went inside, carrying my application. There were a lot of people organized in long lines, signing up. I turned in my already completed application, and a worker gave me a blank card, which I was to insert in a time clock hanging on the wall. He said, "Take this card and turn it in at the other tent when you're leaving for work. Once you turn it in, you can wait for the supervisor, who will take you to your jobsite." I threw my belongings in my assigned tent and left for work.

My job was clearing shrubs and bushes with a small axe to make room for the survey crew. I took one hit, and out came the bush. I worked for four days making a long, narrow clearance for the surveyors, but after that, I was told to carry around a black-and-white checkered stick. It was long, had numbers that lit up at night, and was powered by batteries I wore on my back. The other man had a long red rod with a light on the end, which he used to signal me when he wanted me to move in a certain direction. The survey crew measured the distance with the stick I carried. I worked at night, slept in the daytime, and labored as long as I wanted. We surveyed in really thick, brushy wooded areas, but I liked working at night. We covered long distances, and I worked until I dropped. This was a tough job, and I carried a small handgun, because there were wolves in the region.[21]

After we completed surveying, another crew cleared the area of pine trees and brush all through the valleys and over the hills. I earned lots of overtime, the pay was good, and we received it once a week. The union gave us coupon books that we filled with seventy-five-cent stickers. I completed a lot of them but have since misplaced them.

Other crews drilled and blasted, and every now and then, I worked with those men. There were no bulldozers, so the laborers used large hammers to crack the rocks into smaller pieces for removal. All the workers helped get rid of the rocks so it went faster, but the stone was very hard to break when done by hand. The survey team kept ahead of us as we followed them closely. When I first joined the tree-clearing crew, the men were cutting all kinds of trees and shrubs. This was in the early spring, and I did not leave for home until it got cold.

I also cut down trees, made large dugouts for bombs, and carried water to the workers who were felling trees. CC worked with a tall black man, removing trees. They worked as a team and always hung around

Woman and children in government tent. J.H.: "Women worked at the site, too. . . . They lived in tents and summer shelters . . . cooked for the workers and sold meals for twenty-five cents." (Photo NO 16-1851, Milton Snow Collection, Navajo Nation Museum)

together, even sharing their lunches at mealtime. One day we butchered a sheep. My family, mother, and sister's husband were also living close to the jobsite. We bought a sheep, and my brother-in-law, who was expert at preparing sheep, butchered it and even fixed the intestines.[22] CC was there, too, and wanted to have the big intestine, so he got it.

The next morning he turned the intestine inside out and cooked it on the grill over some hot coals. It was a long piece, and when it was done, he put it in his lunchbox. That day he again worked with the black man, and at lunchtime, the two friends picked a nice shady spot beneath a big oak bush. They opened their lunchboxes, and CC, not realizing what was about to happen, took out the long intestine. "A snake!" shouted the black man as he ran off down the hill, never to come back. CC had scared off his buddy.

Women worked at the site too, gathering oak brush into piles, away from the open area where the ammunition was to be stored. They also put small rocks into piles to clear the area. Many Navajo families moved from Gray Mountain, Tuba City, and the surrounding areas for employment. They lived in tents and summer shelters, where the women cooked for the workers and sold meals for twenty-five cents. So we spent seventy-five cents a day for food, but it was not expensive then. A man from Oljato named Red Goat (Tł'ízí Łichíí'), or George Tom, and his first wife used to cook for the men. He would be all sweaty, standing around the hot stove, cooking. There were many other nationalities working there too, like African Americans and Hispanics. The men would run around with the tall black women.

One day CC and I decided to go to Flagstaff after being paid. We had a group of men who hung around town together, but not all of them were good. There was one man who roamed the streets robbing people and was said to be really bad. He tried to steal from an old man, but the elder managed to call the police, who stopped the attack. Sometimes this man hung around the payroll office on paydays. Everyone was afraid of him.

At the end of this particular evening, CC and I left town for home. As we walked along the railroad tracks, this man, who seemed to come out of nowhere, attacked CC with a stick. Once CC fell to the ground, the man next came after me. He missed me with his stick, but I pretended to be hurt and fell on my side with the pocket that held my wallet. As I lay there, I watched him go back to CC, take his wallet, and put it in his pocket. He then started in my direction, but I had, in the meantime, picked up a rock from beneath me and was waiting. He started to search but had a hard time rolling me over for my wallet. When his face was close to mine, I swung my hand with the rock and struck him on the side of his head. He fell over, and I quickly got up. CC and I took our wallets and all the money from the robber's pocket and left. We went a short distance and hid behind some bushes to see when he would awaken. He finally stood up, then ran in the opposite direction, and we walked home. He got what he deserved.

At this same jobsite, we worked with a man who was short, heavy, and named One Who Pulls Things Around (Nahaadzįzí). One day we wanted to see how strong he was, so we asked him to have a tug-of-war. We put a rope around his shoulders and had two men sit on his back. Three strong men stood on the other side of a line drawn in the dirt. He strained really hard and moved back quite a distance with each pull, dragging his opponents over the line. He won every time. Later, several black men, who lived in their own tent, wanted to challenge him. These three hefty black men said they could beat him, so they and some white men and a few Navajos went to the opposite side. The men bet on the challenge and collected a huge pile of money. Since I already knew One Who Pulls was going to win, I put down twenty-five dollars.

Before the contest began, the men measured off the ground using a carpenter's level; it was that serious. I joined in on One Who Pull's side with some other men, and he told me to sit on his back while another man sat in front of me toward his neck. We put a blanket under us, and he put the rope around him. The two of us who sat on him went backward with our feet and braced ourselves each time he moved back. We started to pull slowly but gained ground quickly, pulling one man across the line, then another, and another, and eventually all of them. We won the match and left with our money.

The work continued. The union made a storage area of cement cells in the ground for the bombs, located close to another mountain. The cement was very thick, and all the way around the top, covered with dirt. Women worked there too, keeping the place clean. Eventually, the union moved on, and another company took over. The union used to move around a lot, completing a project, then starting a job elsewhere. It moved on to Fort Wingate and [union bosses] asked me if I was going with them, but I declined. After we completed these storage cells, we traveled farther south for another job.

This new company did not pay much, even though our job of clearing shrubs and pine trees was the same. It quickly built some houses, a store, a hotel, and military barracks. Those who lived in the barracks had to clean it and dress in nice uniforms. There were stacks and stacks of green military shirts and pants, but you had to keep very clean, shower, then dress in those ironed uniforms. It was important to be clean when handling ammunition. When we finished work for the day, we had to shower again and dress in our own clothes. This was too much to do just to get ready for work, so I stayed for only a short time. They told me I had to keep my clothes clean, but I did not want to be bothered with that, so I left. Besides, I had plenty to do at home, including my medicine man practice. I packed my bags and left for Flagstaff.

I got into town and met Hairy Mexican and One Who Flips Over (Yaahiidiłhii). They were driving around and asked me if I wanted a ride. I said yes, back to Kayenta, and climbed in. The two of them were drinking but were not too drunk. I had no idea what was about to happen. These men were older, but not wiser! We drove around for a while and at noon arrived at a loading dock and large receiving house for the train. The place was deserted because everyone was at lunch. We went inside and saw boxes and boxes of merchandise everywhere. The two men looked around, then grabbed some large boxes, threw them in their truck, and took off. I did not know what was in the cartons and what these men were up to, but they covered the containers with old clothes and blankets and left town in a hurry.

We did not stop until almost Gray Mountain, where we turned onto a dirt road, then drove far out behind some hills. One Who Flips Over said, "Let's get some mountain smoke herbs here." I knew he was joking. We stopped in a gully, and the two got out and began looking through the things they had taken. There were three large new saddles in packing and four boxes with four Pendleton blankets—some for men, some for women—in each box. There were also several unopened boxes of Levi Strauss jackets and pants, the old-fashioned kind that were narrow at the bottom. "My goodness," I thought. They took out the valuable things and burned the boxes, piled the merchandise in the truck, and covered it up like a bed, so that one could not tell that there was anything under all their old stuff. I remember One Who Flips Over really singing while we were driving over the mountain.

We arrived in Kayenta, and I got out at Frank Bradley's home. He used to drive a big truck and sometimes went to Monument Valley. He helped me out a lot and gave me a ride home. His wife and my stepmother were sisters. Before I left One Who Flips Over and his companion, they gave me a pair of Levis, a jacket, and a blanket. I thought about this afterwards. I believe they picked me up just so they could blame the whole thing on me if they were caught. Fortunately, that did not happen. Thieves always have their plans and schemes. They are like coyotes licking their chops. I was just a young lad then and could have become their scapegoat. It was not good.

CHAPTER FIVE

WORK IN THE LATER YEARS

This final chapter of John's life is a culmination of many of his earlier experiences.[1] He married, this time with his lifelong mate, Lula; continued with his agriculture in the difficult Paiute Farms region; practiced his Blessingway to heal people, renewed medicine bundles, and brought rain; and worked with the dominant society on the reservation in the movie industry, off the reservation on the railroad, and in the uranium industry. He has had a wealth of experience by any measure.

Weaving through it all are traditional Navajo values, which he relates to outcomes. For instance, cleaning up after two men are killed in a train wreck affected his health. Working on the movie sets of John Ford hurt other Navajos because they practiced dying and self-fulfilled their own prophecy. The grueling pace and constant labor in the uranium mines not only filled John with pride in his accomplishment, but also led to his undoing, with temporary paralysis and other health problems. Each experience exacted its price.

Today John resides at his home but depends on others to do much of his work. His health is gone, allowing him to practice only his ceremonies. He is not angry or bitter because of this situation, much of which stems from these earlier work experiences. He is a man at peace with himself, surrounded by sons, daughters, and grandchildren who appreciate him, but there is a frustration with getting old and a desire to be able to do what he used to do so well. It is difficult for a hard worker accustomed to independence to turn to others for help.

JOHN GETS MARRIED

At this time, I lived by Train Rock, was still single, and had gotten a job in the newly opened uranium mine on top of the mesa, near where Harvey and Ada Black now live. I worked at this mine for three years and used to walk all the way there every morning.[2] I woke up when the morning star (east star) arose. My older sister's daughter cooked breakfast and made a lunch bag for me. I must have been a fast walker, because I was the first to arrive at the jobsite; then after work, I walked all the way back home. Sometimes I traveled by way of the Oljato Trading Post and other times caught a ride with my supervisor to Goulding's Trading Post. The driver was a white man named One Who Spits All the Time (Dizháhí).

One day, while I was on my way home, I stopped at Goulding's and saw my future wife's father, Bob Atene, or Spring under the Cottonwood (Hastiin T'iisyaató), packing his horse with canned goods and other kinds of food. He and one of his sons had traveled from Paiute Farms to purchase groceries. He asked if there were any job openings at the mine, and I told him there were and that he could help me because I was working alone. My supervisor had said he was going to do some more hiring. I told my future father-in-law, "There is a job opening at the mine, and they want to hire two men in a couple of days." "Yes, yes. I'll be there to go to work, my little brother," he said. He asked Harry Goulding to help him with the job application, and we both left to see the supervisor. I walked while he rode his horse, and when we arrived, he asked my supervisor if he could be hired. My supervisor said yes. Spring under the Cottonwood applied, then left for home.

At dawn, the very next morning, the entire family returned, built a fire, and camped among the bushes close to where the new Goulding's store is now. The family had come to be with him at his new job, and my future wife and mother-in-law were among them. I learned that they had not come to this area very often. His wife and children did not have much variety in their food—only rice, flour, potatoes, shortening, and coffee—and were unfamiliar with different types of food, because they had lived in remote areas most of the time.

I came to their camp that morning, and Spring under the Cottonwood and I walked to work. We started mining together, and later his family followed. I worked with him all summer, and in the fall, he asked me to marry his daughter. He said he wanted some money and a large silver concho belt for payment. I soon married and began to have our children—seven boys and four girls—eleven children in all. Everything that my parents and grandparents had taught me started to become a reality as I began life with my own family. My father-in-law and I worked through the winter and summer until I left that job the next fall.

I continued to work in various mines. I brought home groceries— eggs, chicken, and oranges, and a variety of canned goods—but my wife did not touch them. I wondered why. "Why aren't you cooking these foods?" I asked. She took the eggs and broke them on my head, saying I was naughty. My children later laughed about us. She did not know how to peel an orange or cook an egg because she had never eaten them before. She also did not know how to prepare canned foods. Her family had no blankets to sleep on and, in general, had very little. I did not know this at the time we met and were married.

FARMING

After I stopped working at the mines, my wife and I went to the Paiute Farms area with her family. They lived in summer shelters and hogans that had, nearby, large underground storage spaces. There was also a big field where they planted lots of corn, melons, and squash, as well as peach and apple trees. Once we had been there a while, I was told to clear some land, so I did, removing willow roots and rocks. Next, I dug an irrigation ditch to the field. I worked very hard in the intense heat, but as time went on, I got used to it.

After completing the ditch, I had to figure out a way to get the water to come through it. My father-in-law's cornfield was beside the ditch and needed to be irrigated. I decided to gather willows, tie them in bunches with wire, and lay them in a row, side by side, all the way to the water, which was quite a distance. I packed the willow bundles tightly, upright like a corral, and banked them with large gravel stones. I used a canvas bag, called in Navajo "red stripes up the sides," to haul the gravel laid along the base of the standing willows.

Day and night for approximately nine days, I filled both sides of the willows with a ridge of gravel all the way to the water's edge. This ditch was just below the bend of the river, so I shoveled enough of the sand bank to ease the water into the willow embankment which, in turn, piloted the water into the irrigation ditch. It worked just as planned. As soon as I shoveled off the embankment, the water came crashing down the ditch and onto the cornfields. The willows worked well, and the gravel stayed intact, even when the river ran high. We had a big harvest at Paiute Farms that year.

It was around this time that an important event happened. My wife had grown up in the valley where the San Juan Marina on Lake Powell is today. Her father had had his farm by the river all this time. Later, after I had moved there, a man named Tall Educated One settled there too. About that same time, a white man and his Navajo co-worker, named Frank Bradley, came by with some papers. The white man said, "If you sign these papers, you'll have all rights to this land." So my father-in-law placed his thumbprint on the paper. The whole process was a lie, because nobody could read what the paper said. Today, the paper sits in Window Rock, stating that Tall Educated One owns the property instead of long-time resident Bob Atene. He was cheated out of his own land. My wife and other family members originated from there and were the real owners.

This place called Paiute Canyon was named according to a Navajo story that came from the great-grandparents of a previous era. It was said that Giving Out Anger adopted a Paiute girl. The girl's Navajo name was Woman Who Can Understand. My mother used to speak of this. She said this Paiute girl did not know the Navajo language at first but later learned it, and that is how she received her name. Woman Who Can Understand claimed that the Red-Running-into-the-Water Clan and many families derived from her.

Bob Atene got his name of Spring under the Cottonwood from this area and was the first to live there. Because of this, he wrote a statement, saying that all his children and future generations have a right to this land forever. This written statement is also filed in Window Rock. Today, newcomers claim this land. We feel cheated in many ways. After many years of living there, we had to move out of that area because of the building of the dam [Glen Canyon] and lake [Powell].[3] The newcomers, who falsely claimed ownership, were compensated, but Bob Atene did not want that deal. "I don't want the money; I want to

Man hoeing a garden. J.H.: "After I planted the big garden, I decided to grow alfalfa. Dan Canyon . . . helped me prepare the land." (Photo NA 4-14, Milton Snow Collection, Navajo Nation Museum)

retain the land," he told them. So he never got paid, nor did any of his relatives.

Returning to my story, after I planted the big garden, I decided to grow alfalfa. Dan Canyon, my brother-in-law (he had married my wife's sister Betty), helped me prepare the land. He and I worked clearing a large area, removing big trees whose roots were huge and tough. They were like boulders, and it took us until noon to take out four hard balls of roots. We rolled them to the edge of the riverbank, then went home for lunch. It was pure work. I also planted in this field some fruit trees— apples, peaches, apricots, and plums. They were small, but even though I planted them in the spring, they blossomed, and by midsummer, people were feasting on peaches and plums.

My brother-in-law asked me to look after his sheep, because there was nobody to care for them. He also asked me to repair his underground storage places. The corn had been gathered in bags and was still sitting out unprotected. He told me to load them on the donkeys and take them to the underground pits. There was a lot of corn, some still on the cob. The storage pits were large holes in the ground, the sides of which were patted hard, while still moist, with a piece of flat wood. The soil felt like clay when it was compacted and was as hard as cement, with no loose sand. It seemed like there were not that many rodents back then. I filled all three storage holes with corn.

Later, when we ran out of corn, I went to the pit and took some bags with me. I uncovered the top, crawled in, filled the bags, sewed the openings together, put them on the donkey, and took them home. You have to make sure you cover it back up really well. Sometimes we lived near Train Rock and had to go a long distance to get corn from these storage pits. My maternal aunt, Wide Rock Woman (Asdzáán Tséniteelii), lived close by, so I would spend two nights at her home and one day filling the corn bags before returning the next evening. It was a long ways, but that is how we stored corn.

A WINTER TALE

When we had plenty of corn, everyone had a good time baking kneel-down bread and other foods, but we had little else to supplement our diet except wild Mormon tea. If we had not been to the trading post for a long time, we would run out of food. At one point, I remembered I had some blocks of bacon stashed away, so I took them out and melted the fat. Dan Canyon was so hungry, he took the corn bread and dipped it into the hot bacon fat and ate it. Before long, he took off running to the bushes! He ate too much, too fast, which made him sick, heaving and vomiting. "What happened?" I said. "We were really enjoying our lunch, and now this! What's he doing that for?" The men nearby grabbed me. "You hate your in-law, especially when you act jealous of each other or compete. In-law, come on, give it up."[4]

This is a famous saying among the Navajos, and this is how it came about. Many years ago, several knowledgeable men asked about its origin. These men were Yellow Water; Pipeline Biegishie, also known as Short Hair; Eddie Austin, also known as One Who Hits; Ned Benally, named Among the Greasewood's Son (Dihwoozhii Biye'); and a man named Yazzie, also known as Grandson of One with a Wide Hat (Bich'ah Niteelii Bitsoi).[5] These men were inquiring among themselves where this saying came from. I was sitting in a shade close by. Yellow Water saw me and said, "My nephew knows where it came from. Let's ask him." The other men said, "No, we don't think so. He doesn't know, and he won't tell us." Yellow Water replied, "Yes, he does. Let's give him some money, and he'll tell us." They put together their money and gave it to me. "Now, tell us where the saying came from." "Yes, I know something about it," I said. Then I told them this story.

Many, many years ago, before humans lived here on this earth, it happened. Badger and his wife and children lived alone. Coyote [the trickster] came to visit and invited him to go hunting. "Partner, let's go hunting for rabbits." Badger: "No. I'm not fast enough like you." "Don't say that. Let's hunt." Coyote made plans and asked Badger four times to go. (Everything was said four times before it was approved or done.)[6] The badger finally agreed. "Okay, my partner, let's go hunt." Coyote said, "Let's sing the sacred hunting songs before we get our prey." Badger: "No, let's just go." Coyote said, "No, let's sing," four times, and the badger finally agreed. The coyote won again. Coyote: "My partner, you go first. You start the songs first." (He said this four times and won again.) The badger began to sing, "Let it snow, let it snow up to the level of short grass," because it was easier to track the rabbits with a little snow. Coyote: "Not the depth of short grass, not that little." But the badger kept right on singing his song to the end, repeating the words. Badger: "There. Now it's your turn, partner." Coyote: "Okay. Let it snow, let it snow up to the level of the curved grass stems. Badger: "Don't say that. We might fall, and break our foot, and have a stumped foot, and that won't be nice!" Coyote kept right on singing, "Let it snow as high as the curled-up grass, as high as the jackrabbit's hairy chest."

It snowed according to Badger's song, and they went off to hunt. Many rabbits ran into their underground holes, and the badger went after them, burrowing into the dirt. He would catch one, take it out, set it at the entrance, then climb back into the hole for more. When Coyote saw what the badger was doing, he decided to block the entryway with big rocks to trap his partner inside. Badger was busy gathering the rabbits deep inside the tunnels and never noticed that he could not get out.

Meanwhile, Coyote started back to Badger's home. He had caught a rabbit and removed the skin, except for the head. This he added to the ones badger had left by the hole. He arrived at the home and told Badger's wife that he had already killed some rabbits, but that her husband had not caught anything. He spoke proudly of his accomplishments. Coyote then put his catch in the ashes and cooked them.

Later that evening, Mrs. Badger and her children went to sleep; Coyote lay down across from the fire, but his teeth kept chattering. "I am very cold, my in-law." He said this four times to Mrs. Badger, then, "Can I just cover myself with the tip of your rabbit skin blanket?" and moved closer. Next he said, "Let me lay on top of you; I'm very cold." Then he asked Mrs. Badger if he could have her once, twice, three, four, five, six, seven . . . he lost count. He betrayed Badger by having an affair with his wife.

Shortly after, Coyote was walking along when he met Skunk. Coyote: "Ah, partner, where are you coming from?" Skunk: "I just came from Badger's home. I was visiting over there." Coyote: "Come now, my in-law." He acted as if he were a relative of Mrs. Badger and was accusing the skunk of having an affair with her. "Come now, my in-law," he kept saying. "You had an affair with my relative, so you better pay [give it] up." The double-crossing coyote had turned the tables on Skunk, while he was the one who actually had the affair!

"That's where the saying came from," I told the men. "I told you he really knows a lot," replied Yellow Water. This story should only be told in the winter.

I must have spent at least five summers at Paiute Farms, where we had our cornfields. I owned twelve horses, which people borrowed to go to the trading post. When not being ridden, the horses grazed in little pastures up and down the San Juan River. After five years, these horses were good at surviving the river's dangerous qualities. They wandered around in the steep canyons and in the quicksand. If they got stuck in the deep mud, they did not stand there and struggle but immediately fell sideways and let their feet slip to the surface slowly. Then they would roll sideways to drier sand and finally stand up, shake off the mud, and walk away. Horses can learn pretty fast about quicksand.

PRACTICING MEDICINE

My father-in-law said there was a Blessingway Ceremony west of Paiute Farms at Water Flowing Into. Metal Teeth was going to perform the sing. I did not waste a minute but headed directly there. When I arrived, the men were in the sweat lodge, so I joined them, and the ceremony started the next day. I sat down with Grandfather and asked questions regarding the procedures and ways of performing traditional medicine. There is always much more to learn.

While we were in the sweat bath, Grandfather asked me if I could do a Blessingway Ceremony for his wife. This request had been a long time in coming, since they now lived in Lukachukai. "She does not want other medicine men," he said, "and I've been trying to get a medicine man to do it all this time. We came here five days ago." Then he said, "Tomorrow evening you will do the protection prayer, and in two days there will be a Blessingway for her." We went back home, and I received an advance payment after agreeing to do the ceremony. I went to Paiute Farms on my horse but returned that evening, performed the protection prayer, and for two days conducted the ceremony.

A man named Thin Goat, who lived southwest of Nakai Canyon, also attended. He was quite surprised to know I was in charge. "Do you mean to tell me that this young kid performs such ceremonies? I don't believe I have confidence in him," he said. "It's impossible." I asked, "Why? Why don't you think it's possible?" He did not say any more. Grandfather told him I was capable, had learned everything, and there was no need to worry. "Just you wait and see. Someday you will ask him to do a ceremony on you. You had better be ready to hear his response, because he might turn you down, even if you beg him."

A lot of people attended this sing, some staying from the previous ceremony to be at the one I performed. Three of those present included Big Man, Red Rock Spring, and Tall Man. These men played cards at night in the warmth of the hogan. Back then, even the women would ride their horses to the ceremonies just to partake of the sacred corn pollen and to pray. Today, nobody does that.

The day after I finished my ceremony, we heard there was a five-day ceremony at Navajo Mountain. I brought my earnings of fabric, a wedding basket, and some mutton home, and shortly after I arrived, my relatives wanted to borrow my horses to go to the Oljato Trading Post. The horses had wandered off in my absence, so I chased them down from the side of the rocky mesas and up from the river's banks. They were really good swimmers, going sideways in the river, then rolling to the dry ground on the edge of the water before getting up. I had lived by the San Juan for about six years, so the horses had learned these things. My relatives took the horses they needed, while I got a fresh mount and traveled to Navajo Mountain for the ceremony. I stayed until it was done.

The ceremony repaired and restored several old medicine bags and helped create a new one.[7] The morning after the last night of the ceremony, I saw several ceremonial rattles sitting in the center of the hogan floor. "Who wants this rattle?" they said. It was a short, skinny one. "I'll take it," I said. It was made from the tail of a cow and was received from a client as payment. It was cut on both ends and sewn on top. Otherwise, it was all natural and colorful. The other men wanted it too, but I spoke for it before they did.

I came home from Navajo Mountain after the ceremony and began preparing the cornfield. My family had to clear the ground first, and then the irrigation ditch. We planted corn and melons, had a big harvest in the fall, and made many different kinds of corn food. With the rest of the corn, we stripped off the husks, filled big gunny sacks, stored it, and ate it all year long.

Grandfather constantly asked me to assist him with his ceremonies, so I did all the rituals and sang for him, saying the prayers and laying down the sacred stones. Soon, I was doing the ceremonies from start to finish by myself. I also started to sing again at the Enemyway Dances.

I'VE BEEN WORKIN' ON THE RAILROAD

I looked for work whenever I could. I would pack my horse, ride her to the road, and let her go. She was a very gentle, smart mare that I could leave saddled and bridled and send home by herself. When she arrived, someone unsaddled her and turned her loose. Once, when we were living at Water under the Cottonwood Tree, I worked at Mexican Hat, panning. I would ride her there, buy groceries, pack them on, and send her all the way home. Spring under the Cottonwood [John's father-in-law] was concerned about this and said, "Why do such a thing. The horse will stray with all the groceries!" She never did.

It was hard finding work around here, so I hitchhiked long distances to go job hunting. Sometimes I got a ride, but several times I walked all the way to Kayenta, about thirty miles away. I usually spent the night there at my older sister's place. Her husband worked at the hospital, putting coal in the furnace. Early the next day, I walked to the trading post to catch the mail truck going to Tuba City and Flagstaff. Other times I walked and walked with my backpack. The elders with old trucks were most likely to stop, whereas the younger people with new vehicles zoomed by really fast. I would cross the old bridge and on to Tobacco Mountain and to Wide Willow Prairie.[8]

I used to walk a lot. One time, when my eldest son was just a baby, my wife and I walked all the way across the valley. I carried him and some items piggyback, while she carried a pack of food, pots and pans, and eating utensils. We also hauled our sleeping blankets as we walked this long, long way. I had horses and could have used them, so I do not know why we walked. We hiked all day and reached my big sister's home by evening. I remember once when I decided to walk all the way to the old VCA mine in Caine Valley, south of Mexican Hat. I had attended a sing at Water Flowing Into [near Lake Powell], west of Paiute Farms. I got ready to go, but the men at the sing said, "That's too far to walk!" I went anyway and walked all the way, getting to VCA before sundown.

My uncle Oshley was a good walker, too, going from Blanding to White Streak of Cattail Coming Out and arriving in the early evening. He was fast. He would say, "I left from Amidst the Sagebrush (Blanding) this morning." That is how he was. One day I saw him herding sheep and taming two horses at the same time. The horse bucked a lot, and Oshley got bumped in the nose, breaking it, making it even more distinct, and changing his facial features. My grandmother placed pine pitch and some herbs on his nose. It healed because of the pitch and Lifeway Plants, which were our medicine back then.

One time I walked all the way up the road to the top of a hill in the mountains until it got dark. Pine trees were all around, so I went into the woods, built a fire, and spent the night. The next day I got back on the road and started hitchhiking again. A man stopped and took me as far as House in the Sagebrush. He worked there, so I started walking again and went up the canyon. I caught a ride with another person, who was going to Richfield. I got off at the edge of town, while he went back into town where he said he worked. Later, he came back and picked me up, but I did not understand what he said. He had a big blond beard, talked with a pipe in his mouth, and had a dog in the back. This time he dropped me off at a railroad site, where I went in and signed up for a job.

The next day I was taken to the base of the mountain to work on the railroad track. The crew, many of whom were Navajos, was replacing the old ties and rails. Another man and I were given the job of removing spikes and staying ahead of all the other workers. When we reached a marked-off place, we would sit, smoke, and talk until the crew caught up. We kept moving on and on along the tracks, past the big hills where the prison is now [Gunnison, Utah]. Taking out the worn materials and replacing them, then going back over and bracing them with spikes and screws, was a slow process. The work crew also moved slowly.

A white man we called Bald Eagle (Atsá), because his nose was shaped like a beak, brought us to work each morning. He drove a metal dump truck, the kind used to haul gravel. We would climb in the bed and ride back and forth to work. Bald Eagle was quite a character and treated us roughly; he was naughty. As soon as he arrived at the jobsite, he dumped all the men, rolling them out of the truck into a pile on the ground! This attitude was not appreciated by the workers, who cussed him: "Go to hell, Eagle." I learned my lesson and jumped before he poured me out.

While working on the railroad, one of the employees, an elderly white man who wore overalls like an apron, chose me to work with him on his small engine and two boxcars. My job was to shovel coal into the engine's furnace. This old man became a good friend. He brought me a single-wide striped mattress and laid it beside the furnace, because he was worried that I never slept. It seemed like he never slept either. He was such a hard worker, helped me with my job, and gave me extra overtime hours, even though I had not worked. I guess he had some sympathy for me, but we both worked hard.

One day, while we were working, our supervisor told us that two long trains had collided in one of the narrow canyons. They took us there to help clean up this messy sight. The rails were like pieces of wire tangled everywhere. Parts of the trains were scattered to the base of the mountain along the rails. The engine and one boxcar of the train going into the mountain were under the train headed out of the mountain. Derailed yellow boxcars were down in the river below.

We worked clearing the debris still on the tracks, including the two huge engines, as well as those in the canyon below. They were very big engines and required special equipment to dismantle them before being hauled off by a crane. Next we repaired the tracks and put the cars back on. The old man and I worked hard doing this. There were two sets of rails side by side, so we used one set of tracks and cars to move the other ones onto the track next to it. The job required two weeks of hard, continual labor to complete.

One spring day it snowed. That morning the water had frozen, and the breakfast bell had not rung, so the men waited. Eagle and two Mexicans from the kitchen crew decided to haul some water. They put a couple of barrels in the truck and left for the canyon. As they headed back, they drove halfway across the tracks but were hit broadside by a train. They did not have a chance. The Mexican riding on the back jumped off before the collision, but not the two men inside. Only one door of the truck's cab worked, and so no one got out. Eagle and a Mexican perished, with nothing left of them except scattered pieces of flesh.

Our supervisors gathered us together and asked who would volunteer to clean up the mess by picking up the remains. The older Navajo men said they would not do it and left.[9] A young man from Black Mesa and I stayed to help. He had a Navajo bun but was educated. The supervisors told us that whoever helped would be on leave for the next two weeks. We picked up the flesh because we wanted to spend time visiting the towns around there.

We both put on a harness that held a detector like a car battery, with a red and green light, and some handles hooked to it. One of the long handles had a fork-type tip, and on the other handle was a spoonlike tip used for picking up flesh. When the light turned green, it was flesh belonging to the white man, and if it flashed red, it was the Mexican's.[10] This is how we knew which belonged to which as we filled two different bags. It smelled terrible, even though the accident had happened only a few hours before. While the other men had lunch, we spent the time throwing up.

For two and a half days we picked up the remains. Our boss told us to be sure not to miss anything, so we were careful. Several of us young men went all over the area, even down to the bottom of the canyon, gathering flesh and bones. My friend and I put on some old shoes for this job and went back over the ground several more times, while other workers picked flesh and powdered bones off the train and truck. We were fortunate to be out on the ground, away from them.

We finally completed the job, got paid, and the next day went to town to spend two whole weeks exploring. We even took a train to Pocatello, Idaho, just to see the place. Our pay was cheap, fifty-seven cents an hour—hardly anything! Some railroad workers took home souvenirs, like a piece of the track. I did not take anything.

Nine or ten years ago, I began suffering from the consequences of picking up that dead flesh.[11] We had really messed up our lives by doing it. Both of my feet hurt, part of them turning dark up to my shin, and I could not walk. They lacked oxygen, and I could not sleep because of the pain. I had to have a lot of different ceremonies—a nine-day Enemy-way and many different kinds of sings—for several years.

I went to see a medicine woman, Daughter of Man with a Checked Shirt (Bi'éé' Łikizhii Bitsi'), who lived by El Capitan. She did the divining to find out what was ailing me and said it had something to do with picking up and walking on dead people—a white man and an Anasazi. "No," I said, "It was a Mexican."[12] "Yes," she replied. She had figured out why I was having these health problems.

On the other hand, the white doctors recommended amputating my feet because they were dying. I think these men only wanted money, so I totally refused their request. The medicine woman told me to hurry and immediately cut the sacred stick for the Evilway. This was the only thing that would cure my feet problems and health. Then I went to see Oshley for the other ceremonial thing, the scalp, or hair.[13] He got one and came back with me. It felt better when I moved around or went places, but if I sat down or kept still, the pain in my feet became unbearable and nearly made me faint. Once the Evilway began, I watched and listened to the singers perform the songs. I felt tired, so I decided to lie down on the blanket that had been laid out for me.

Before too long, I had fallen asleep, as the ceremony continued. I awoke at dawn, and there was still singing. The pain had subsided, but both of my legs were still swollen. They felt big and bulky, but there was no pain; the sacredness of the ceremony had stopped it. I got up from my blanket and started walking without crutches. I walked past some men playing cards. "Hey! Look! Our in-law has survived." They were awful teasers! From that day forward, I got better. I found out it is not good to handle dead flesh and the bones of white men and Mexicans. It is dangerous, and I learned my lesson.

I believe this is what causes a lot of amputations among our people, even the white man, but they do not realize it. These people make mistakes, and they do not get any ceremonies done, so their lives are shortened and amputations are performed. This is how I was healed about eleven years ago. Being involved with dead people—Mexicans—can really affect your health. Without exposing itself, the sickness works on your health in its secret way. The Mexican disguises itself as an Anasazi, is hard to detect and dangerous, while the white man's flesh is much kinder.[14] It does not affect you as badly as the Mexican's does.

As I was saying, we continued to work on the railroad all the way to Helper and Price, then on to Green River and Sunshine Mountain, northeast of Moab. That is where I and my companion left our job and came home. We stayed together for the entire eight or nine months before returning. We had plenty of cash.

I then stayed home, and that was when my oldest son was born. He was still on a cradleboard when I decided to go off again to work. I went to Salt Lake City to the railroad station and worked maintaining train engines. There were many other employees there too, washing the trains. I found one Navajo man, named Jay Yazzie, who came from Monument Valley. I worked with him from that day forward, washing train engines. We had to dress really cleanly. First thing in the morning, we took a really good shower, then slipped into our overalls, especially made for this job. Then, we each took a hose with strong pressurized water and sprayed the huge black engines. The pressurized spray took off the black soot and burned-on smoke. A big column of black liquid would shoot up in the air. Three of us worked in that section and did that every day. I started on an engine in the morning and finished it by quitting time in the evening. Each of us washed one all day.

I worked there for a while, then was moved over to cleaning and maintaining the passenger train. I cleaned all day long, but I sort of cheated by catching some sleep every now and then. I'd clean them as they came in, and they would leave to go on their way. Altogether, I worked with the engines for two months and the cleaning for one month. At the end of the day, we had to take another shower and put on fresh clothes before going home. That was the routine.

Later, my supervisor transferred me to another job at the same place. A tall Mexican man had become ill, so I was asked to work in his spot at the post office. This building was huge, and I saw a lot of mail, some of which were large packages, coming and going. There were lots of letters, too. It was confusing for me because it was a job for an educated person. I got some help from the man who had come to get me, because I could not read. He kept passing the letters to me, and I put them in the boxes for certain destinations. There must have been seven or eight cars full of mail that we had to unload and send. After two or three days, I understood the process. I memorized the writing, and sorted all the matching written addresses in their separate boxes, and got pretty good at it, managing to work by myself. I did not know what the addresses said, but I learned to match the same ones together. I had not gone to school, so I could only match them. I worked for a couple of months and decided to stay longer.

It was fun to watch the different people come on the train. Most of them were elderly. If there was no mail, then I dusted the floors with a duster made of feathers. One day some big shots came in on the train. They were staying in a blue building close to the station. The house had everything—beds, furniture, and so on. It was neat and beautiful inside. My supervisor asked me to stay and work until I retired. "You can go home and get your family, then live in that nice house." I agreed to do that, but I did not keep my word. He gave me transportation money to cover my round trip, as well as some extra spending cash. I was to catch the bus to Monticello, and from there take the mail truck to Oljato. My boss wrote a note for me to give to the mail truck driver, so that I could get all the way home. I received my paycheck for work. One man at the office cashed my check and gave me the money, but he left the check on the desk. I stuffed the cash in my pocket. Soon a lady secretary picked up the check and cashed it again, giving me money a second time. I had cash!

I took a taxi to the Greyhound bus station and was told the bus would leave at midnight. I sat and waited until it came, got on, and rode to Monticello. I arrived early in the morning and went to the home of a white man I used to herd sheep for. His name was Yellow-Spotted One (Łitsoii Bee Łikizhii), because he had freckles on his face and arms. I knocked on his door, and he opened it. "It's John. It's John. What are you doing here now?" he said. I told him I was returning from up north and needed a place to sleep because it was cold outside. He invited me in, I went to sleep, and bright and early the next morning, he woke me up. "Come have breakfast," he said. He told me he had plans to go to White Mountain that day to check on his sheep and wanted to have breakfast with me before he left. He had fixed potatoes with bits of mutton, some onions, and black pepper, then added honey and mixed it together. "Why the honey?" I asked. "You already have salt and pepper in there and now you are putting in sweetener?" "It all goes to the same place," he replied. "Try it." "I don't think so," I said and laughed. He was a character, and we teased each other a lot.

He told me that Oshley was at White Mountain herding sheep for him, and that he was going to check on him. They were going to castrate the lambs, cut earmarks, and paint marks on all of them. "I have to be there early in the morning or Oshley will be mad. He can be mean and tell you off; 'Not too good,'" he said in Navajo. "He doesn't want anyone to be late."

I ate breakfast and walked to the post office to catch the mail truck, using the note my boss had given me. I got on and rode to Bluff, where we stopped at the trading post. I went inside and saw the trader, who was deaf. He told me he was ready to go to Flagstaff, so I caught a ride with him and reached home in Monument Valley. There were a lot of horses in the corral, and my family had butchered a sheep that morning to sell at Goulding's. The mutton was packed, so I saddled my horse and rode to the trading post, where I bought more food. I then rode down to Paiute Farms, where my family lived, and brought a lot of food. I had not been home for approximately seven months.

MOVIES

I remember the very first movie crew that came to the Monument Valley area.[15] A short, stocky white man, John Ford, had a patch over one eye. The movie outfit camped at Tsegi [Canyon], about ten miles west of Kayenta. My mother's husband, Man between the Rocks (Hastiin

Tségiizhí), who lived in Kayenta, and I took his wagon to Tsegi, where people were being paid as soon as they arrived.[16] Many, many Navajos showed up—women even brought their babies on cradleboards—and were paid $3.50. To receive that much money was like receiving more than $100 now.

After a day of movie acting, we would go back to camp to eat. There was plenty of food, and we ate a lot. Everyone was paid at the end of the day; even the bystanders who watched us act received money. At first, I was not able to participate. Those being filmed went to the location by vehicles, with their horses. This site was close to where the Tsegi Café and Motel are now. The Navajo One Who Gropes Around with His Hand was in the movie. He had a hat that went over his eyes, rode a large black horse, and had a bugle to blow. The movie producers sent him to the top of a hill with some trees, where he blew his horn, and the fighting, with a lot of shooting, began.

As the filming progressed toward Kayenta, I was finally hired. The outfit was near a dam just west of Kayenta, and the fighting continued amid some sand banks. Again, One Who Gropes was on top of the hill, blowing his horn. We were made into cavalry soldiers, wearing blue suits with yellow stripes down the sides of our pants and coats. A Navajo man named Wooden Hat (Tsinch'ah) had his hair tied in a bun, which he pulled forward, upwards, and stuffed inside his hat so that his head looked shaven.[17] He had an attitude, quick to anger, and was a teaser. We were told to stand side by side, and when we heard the bugle, to get up and go into an open area. A cannon would boom, the enemy would fire arrows, and we were to fall down and die. When the horn blew, we ran out, fell dead side by side, and did not move.

But I was sometimes naughty back then. I spied a little rock, picked it up, threw it, and hit Wooden Hat. He was mad, jumped on me, and began fighting. "Cut, Cut! It has been ruined," they told us. We refilmed the scene after the director sent Wooden Hat to another group, but he was mad at me for the rest of the day. Later, we went into Monument Valley, where the movie company did a lot of filming in the canyons.

We changed our tribes during the different movies. Sometimes we were Apaches and wore braids, loincloths, and painted faces. I became the enemy, along with other Navajos, and we did plenty of scalping.

Wagon train and riders on a movie set. J.H.: "We changed our tribes during the different movies. Sometimes we were Apaches and wore braids, loincloths, and painted faces. . . . We were told to die each time the white man attacked, while the horses we rode were made to fall with us." (Photo NF 11-44, Milton Snow Collection, Navajo Nation Museum)

We were told to die each time the white man attacked, while the horses we rode were made to fall with us. Some of the film crew replaced the live animals with stuffed horses, and dead soldiers were strewn about the battlefield.

We once did a movie in the Monument Valley Tribal Park, where there is a sand dune. The movie people built a makeshift hogan, with willow branches and sand, at the bottom of the dune. The scene they wanted was for an Apache to ride his horse into the camp, be shot, and fall off near this hogan. All the actors hesitated. Finally, One Who Winks His Eyes (Nanilch'iłhii) volunteered to do it. He dressed in his Apache clothes, put on his braided wig, got on his horse, and the cameras rolled. We wore nothing but loincloths as we galloped down the hill toward the hogan. Winks His Eyes rode as fast as he could, shots rang out, and he fell. He landed on the side of the shelter, caving it in, while a number of Apache warriors popped out from the rubble and began shooting arrows toward the soldiers. The bluecoats fell off their horses too. I don't know how they did it, but the arrows appeared to have gone through their bodies, sticking out on both sides. It looked real.

I also worked on the movie set one winter as an assistant prop man. The movie outfits used to haul in horses from faraway places like Phoenix. These horses were trained to fall on cue. Their caretaker, a tall, slender, hairy man with a patch over his eye, stayed with them in the valley. Many white men, Mormons, used to come and act in these movies as soldiers too. Since I was not acting but working on the crew, I helped move around the equipment and carried cans of spray paint. I sprayed the bushes as necessary and helped paint red blood spills and blue bruises as a makeup artist.

In one scene I had to tie a dummy against a ledge of rocks and secure it with a long string, which I pulled on cue. The setting was near some overhanging rocks, with large boulders at the base. The script called for three actors to be around a water hole and be attacked by soldiers. The three men at the water were to try to escape but would be shot. Only one was able to make it to the ledge before he was shot. At this point, I was to pull a string that released a dummy to fall off the cliff. The mannequin was dressed just like the Mexican actor trying to escape. He climbed the rocks, I pulled the string, and the dummy fell. Other men handled the special effects of dirt and smoke spurting up where the bullets hit the ground. But to see it from the other side looked real. When it was time for the Mexican to fall, he went around the corner and snuggled against the rocks; then the dummy fell off when the shooting took place.

Later, we went down and put the dummy in a truck, while the Mexican actor continued to act by leaving on a makeshift stretcher of long poles and blankets, pulled by a large horse. When the scene ended, we moved to another location, closer to the Monuments, where the soldiers were now dressed in leather and pioneer clothing and torn hats. Both white men and Navajos dug a shallow grave for the Mexican. The actor lay in the hole for a few minutes, then rolled out and was replaced by the dummy, which was covered up with rocks. I fixed up some brush by spraying it to look like flowers, and it was placed on the grave. The actors hung his horn on the cross, because he was supposed to have played it all the time. These Hollywood actors were good at making things seem real.

Some of the medicine men and elders did not like all this pretend killing. Many of the Navajo men who acted in these movies have since died. There was John Stanley; his brother Yellow Hair (Bitsii' Łitsoi); and his father, Jack; as well as Talks a Lot; Lee and Frank Bradley; and Keith Smith, all of whom collected a lot of the profits from the movie outfits. They were always in front of the camera. So were their sisters. All of these people acted in death scenes and moved around with the movie crew wherever it went. They all died at a young age, because they had done what our people are forbidden to do.[18] I participated in some of these scenes when I was young and mischievous, but I did not know any better.

Once, when a movie outfit was filming in Monument Valley, Little Gambler rode into their midst and chased them away. He told them to clear out because they were not on their own land. He was very angry; he rode his horse and swung his leather whip around them until everyone left. They moved out that same day. Our elders were very much in control, and the white men used to abide by their rules.

I was in some movies that John Wayne was in, but I also did things like working in the kitchen and playing cards. He used to pass out money, about five dollars each, to everyone. People would stand side by side for John Wayne to hand them some money. Harry Goulding, Hungry Boy (Díchinii Ashkii), and Lee Bradley were there too. I was in line to get my five dollars, but when it came my turn, he pressed a crumpled bill in the palm of my hand and pointed in a direction. I went out behind some things to look at my money, and to my surprise, he had given me a fifty-dollar bill. I had never seen money like that before. John Wayne was a character.

We always had fun when the movie makers arrived and made extra money on betting. Men often played cards in the camp. A man named Mon Chico used to gamble a lot and was a funny person. He once asked Mister Red (Hastiin Chíí'), from Black Mesa, to loan him some money. Mon Chico told him, "Grandfather, lend me some money, about fifteen dollars, and I'll let you have that white horse as collateral." He pointed up to the rocks where there was a white rock that looked like a horse. Mon Chico said, "See that white albino horse? I just barely hobbled him up there. You can have him for loaning fifteen dollars." Mister Red got up, put his hand to his eyebrows, and said, "I see it! I never had a white horse before, especially an albino. Even when I was young, I never had one. How much do you want?" "Loan me fifteen dollars," said Mon Chico, "and you may keep it or see me after fifteen days are up." He laughed and so did the others. Mon Chico won enough games that he repaid Mister Red his fifteen dollars and got his "white horse" back. We all laughed at that one.

Another time, the men were playing cards far up in Spring Canyon, southeast of the hospital. They were hiding from the police, because gambling was illegal. A person named White Man (Diné Łigai), from Tuba City, nudged me. He secretly showed me his cards, and I saw that he had one that would make him lose the game! I paid in forty dollars, then blocked the other players' view of him while he quickly got rid of the card. Just then, two crows flew above us. "What are these two guys doing here, flying around these steep, dark canyon walls!" he said. All the players looked up! "You don't know it, but I just cheated on all of you," he said. He played his hand, and we won the game! He was funny but used to cheat a lot.

Another incident was when we had to haul firewood to camp. We were gathering it on the side of the sand dune as you come into the valley, when we came upon a log that was too big to carry. We were working with several white men from the movie crew. After many of them attempted to pick up the log, everyone gave up. Then a man named Billy Katso, from Owl Springs (west of Douglas Mesa), volunteered to pick it up and carry it. Everyone bet their money, a huge amount, on whether he could or could not do it. Billy took a horse harness strap and wrapped it around the log, because he could not reach around it with his arms, then stood it up on its end. He put a piece of cloth on his shoulder to pad it, hoisted the log, and carried it several yards to the truck. He won the bet.

One funny incident occurred when Ocean Water's Son (Tóniteelnii Biye'), serving as a tour guide, took a load of white men working for the movies down into the valley. They came upon some Navajo men taking a bath in a sweat lodge dug out of the side of a hill, with logs for a roof. As they passed, the guide explained to the white men what was

Three men outside a sweat lodge. J.H.: "He told them there were eleven men in the small sweat lodge, but the tourists found that hard to believe, even with eleven sets of clothing sitting outside." (Photo NAU.PH.92.14.93, Cline Library Special Collections and Archives, Northern Arizona University)

going on. He told them there were eleven men in the small sweat lodge, but the tourists found that hard to believe, even with eleven sets of clothing sitting outside. The white men decided to bet on the number of men who were actually in there. They each chipped in twenty-five dollars, and there were about eighteen of them in the long bus. That was a lot of money. "This is impossible," they argued. "There can't be eleven men in there." The guide approached the sweat lodge and told the men to come out. They were rather upset about the interruption but began crawling out one by one as the onlookers counted. The guide won the bet, and the movie makers paid. They took a look inside the sweat lodge and wondered how all those men could have fit.

Hungry Boy also wanted to make some money betting. He organized a wager for someone to wrestle the tall white man who took care of horses for the movie set. When the bets were in, the pile of money came to about $200. "Who wants to Navajo wrestle this man?" he asked. This type of wrestling was done by simply putting your arms around each other, then seeing who fell first. The winner is the man left standing. There were several husky men in the crowd, but none of them said a word. "I will!" I volunteered, because I did not mind losing.

The crowd cheered and screamed as we began to wrestle. I noticed he had a very narrow waist, which I grabbed for. I gave him a bear hug, squeezing firmly, as he tried to grasp me, but he gradually went limp, fainted, and I laid him down. People poured water on him, and he was up again, but I had beaten the white man. It was quite an event. This happened more recently, after I had a few children.

Another funny incident occurred with a different white man in the movie crew. He was really afraid of insects, lizards, and small animals. One of his friends came to visit us and suggested we play a trick on his co-worker. "Why don't you put a dead lizard or mouse where he works or in his toolbox," he said. The next day, as the worker was painting, someone put a dead rat in his toolbox. When we came back to work, we saw him sitting under a tree in the distance. In fact, he did not come near his work area all that day. Some of the white workers also asked two Navajos, Harvey Black and Cold One's Son (Sik'aazí Biye'), to follow him around while carrying knives. The others had told this worker that some Indians still killed white men, so he was scared stiff when two Navajos followed him. They pretended to be mean and aggressive. The other men laughed like crazy every time they saw this.

Later, I worked at Goulding's, in the kitchen, washing dishes and waiting tables. One afternoon, I was finishing my cleaning chores when some Navajo ladies came to the windows and were trying to see inside. It was so hot that I had taken off my shirt. One lady had her nose pressed against the glass, so I went up to the window and stood against it with my chest pressed to the spot where her face was. She screamed and ran off. That was funny, but I was crazy at times.

The filming of movies in Monument Valley has changed recently. Since Peter McDonald became our president, there has been much fraud, and the money has been misused by our government officials.[19] We no longer get involved in the local movies, but instead, film makers are guarded by the police force. We do not profit from it now, but the white men do when they leave here. The movies we took part in fifty years ago still reap profits worldwide for the movie makers. We receive nothing. A good investigation into this will turn up something for sure.

HERDING CATTLE AND SHEEP

One day, a man named James, who owned a lot of cattle in the Oljato area, asked us to round them up to be sold. Black Rock (Hastiin Tsézhiní) bought three large black-and-white castrated bulls. They were huge. We had to chase them back to his home and had the hardest time keeping them together. We finally corralled them, but in the process, a rope that had been around one of the bull's legs came off in the middle of the cattle in the corral. Black Rock went to pick it up, and one of the cows went after him. The mean animal chased and caught him before he reached the fence and boosted him straight out of the corral. He landed far beyond the fence, and we laughed about it, but he was mad. "What's so funny? It's not funny!" he said. "You're a funny cowboy," I told him.

For some time we herded his cattle, until a white man told us to bring them to Bluff City, where they would be loaded on a truck. Donald Atene and I moved them from Oljato, around Hat Rock, through what is now the Navajo Tribal Park, then to White-Tipped Mountain, where we camped. The next day, we got the herd of about eighty cows to Mexican Hat, where we had the hardest time crossing the bridge. We practically had to push the animals across. It was a lot of work. We spent the night there, the next night at Metal Post near Bottle Rock, and the next night below Comb Ridge in a small canyon. All of this time, the white man followed, giving us water and sodas.

The bull that had chased Black Rock was in the herd, and whenever we were on foot, it came running toward us, keeping us on our horses. It looked mean and scary. The next day we herded the cattle on the road to Comb Ridge. It was slow, hard work. We spent the night on the other side of Comb Ridge, where we chased the cattle into a canyon before we went to sleep. Early the next morning, we rounded them up, with Donald going up and me going down the canyon. After gathering them, we began our journey but later realized an additional five cows had joined the herd. The white man told us to take them, too, so we herded all of them into Bluff. The truck was two days late, so we stayed with the animals and waited. "Don't lose any of them," said the white man. The five cows that had joined the herd were the only ones that were fat, having spent the summer in their pastures. They were all one-year-old female cows, gentle, and not afraid. We found out then that even white men steal from each other.

While we were in Bluff, we met a number of people we knew. There was Big Yucca Fruit; Skinny Policeman (Siláo Ts'ósí), also known as Joe's Son-in-Law (Baadaaní); Black Spot [Birthmark] on His Neck (K'os Dah Lizhinii), Big Yucca Fruit's brother; a medicine man called Fat One (Ayóó Aníldílí) or Around His Mouth (Zee'názt'i'), because of a mustache and sideburns he had; and One Who Lives in the Shady Area (Hoonesh'oosh), whose home was on the hill above Bluff. There was also Yucca Fruit (Haashk'aan), Thin One ('Ałts'ósí), Mister Shorty (Diné Ch'ílí), Tall Man, and Base of Cliff (Tsétsịịh), who used to look up all the time because his neck was injured. He lived in Aneth, at the base of a cliff. The white men I knew in Bluff were Dan Hayes, who was tall—another trader who was hard of hearing—and the trader Four Fingers and his children. His family used to own a lot of sheep, so I herded for them.

The two trucks finally came after three days. We gathered the cattle, put them in the corral, loaded them, and they were hauled away. We got paid for our work and left White Rock Mesa [near Bluff] for home. We crossed the San Juan River and headed southwest, past Black Water, then onto the southern end of Swirling Mountain [Navajo Blanket] to White-Tipped Mountain, and back through the tribal park. We rode all day, nonstop, and arrived home at sundown.

Another time, four of us herded lambs from Oljato to Farmington, New Mexico. The lambs belonged to the trader Big Nose at the Oljato Trading Post. It was terrible because the sheep kept going in all different directions, and this time we were on foot. We left from Oljato, and went down the pathway leading through the tribal park, and camped there. The next day we traveled to Cottonwood, where we camped overnight. I am sure we lost some lambs, because they were everywhere. We had to run on either side of the flock just to keep up with them. All day we moved east, chasing animals, but at Red Rock Point, we managed to herd them into a corral for the night and got a good rest. The two previous nights, we had stayed awake because the lambs

Herding sheep, with Totem Pole Rock in background. J.H.: "Four of us herded lambs from Oljato to Farmington, New Mexico. . . . It was terrible because the sheep kept going in all different directions." (Photo 19786, used by permission, Utah State Historical Society, all rights reserved)

could not tell the difference between night and day and just wandered around. We continued on the next day to Cottonwood Coming Up, where we herded the lambs into a small canyon called Cattle in Abundance, then on to Mexican Water, and another corral and a good night's sleep.[20] The white trader we were herding for checked on us, fed us, and gave us water all the way over. There was one packhorse and a donkey that carried our belongings.

We next camped at Dry Lake with Rocks Coming Down, but there was no corral, and so the sheep were just in the open. We struggled all night to keep the lambs together and thought we were extra careful, but we found that a coyote had dragged one of them over the hill and devoured it. At dawn the coyote notified us with a howl, probably saying, "They have some of my animals in their herd."

We finally arrived at Black Hair's trading post, put the lambs in the corral, and slept well that night. From there we went to Teec Nos Pos and stayed overnight at my clan brother's place. He belonged to the Coyote Pass People Clan (Mą'ii Deeshgiizhnii) and was born for the

Folded Arms Clan (Bit'ahnii Lók'aa Dine'é).[21] I went ahead of the herd to ask permission to use his corral. He said it was fine, so we put the sheep in it and had another good night's rest. Next, we went to Beclabito [Water under a Rock] and into the canyon we call Red Water, where we camped at the mouth of a box canyon and watched the sheep. It had now been seven days since we had left. Before we arrived at Shiprock, we stayed overnight at Tall Policeman's (Siláo Nééz) home. He was of the Black Hair Clan and a grandfather to me, so we borrowed his corral for the night.

Once through Shiprock, we put the flock on the highway, while some-one carried a red flag ahead and another behind the lambs. It was hard work, but two men—Roy Atene's father and One with the Big Head (Bitsiits'iin Nitsaa), who was from Bluff—arrived to help us. Six of us now moved the herd, as I walked in front, carrying a red flag. We took the highway all the way to Hogback and camped overnight at Comb [Hog-back] Ridge Going into the San Juan River. This was very difficult because of the rock ledges close to the river, making it easy to lose sheep. We stayed awake trying to keep the herd together, but the animals kept going up on the ledges, while we kept herding them back down. It was tiring.

Crossing the San Juan River was a sacred experience.[22] Everyone sprinkled corn pollen and said a prayer as they passed over, both coming and going. No one crossed without this sacred ritual and prayer, because that was the only way to cross the river. We did it when we herded the sheep over. A man named One Who Keeps Himself Good Looking (Dilzhóní) performed the ritual for us before we crossed. The trail is no longer visible. Things have changed, and the trails are all gone.

The next night we camped at the base of the mesa close to Farming-ton, chased the lambs into a small canyon, and slept. There were white men who lived along the way, but they did not want to loan us their corrals, and asked for money if we did use them. They were no good. So we just camped out, left the lambs in the open, and watched them closely. We again headed east along the San Juan, staying overnight by the river and surrounding the lambs for protection. The next day we continued along the bank, where there was very thick undergrowth and slow traveling. We managed to take the herd through and reached Farmington and the railroad tracks, where we were to load the animals on a train.

Big Nose, the owner of the lambs, kept an eye on us and fed us all the way over. We were all very tired and left the donkey there for him to later bring home in his big truck. He paid us; then as crazy as could be, we headed straight for the Mexican bootleggers' homes on the outskirts of town. Liquor was not allowed and was hard to get, except through these Mexicans. Following our purchases, we walked to the bushes by the river, sat down to rest, and drank. Roy Atene's father and I did not drink much, so we kept our senses and watched the others. Roy Atene's father sat and smoked; I rolled up a blanket for a pillow; and we were both harassed by the large mosquitoes. We built a fire and cooked something to eat, while the other men passed out from drinking. "We are too far away from home for them to be doing this!" he said. We sat around and waited until the trader, many hours later, came back to take us home. As we packed our gear, Big Nose just laughed at the men lying around. We grabbed their upper bodies and feet to lift them into the back of the truck and laid them in one by one. They were all passed out, and some had half-empty bottles hidden inside their clothing.

We headed home. The trader offered us a meal, but Roy's father, who was in a hurry to get back, said, "We just ate." I wanted to eat, though, even if I was not hungry. I could have had it later for lunch, but we never stopped. We arrived home that night. Even riding in the truck, the trip seemed long. The entire experience took about sixteen days.

URANIUM MINING

Eventually I returned to work in the uranium mines.[23] Even as a boy, I was aware of the presence of uranium in the VCA area, across the wash from our hogans near Black Rocks. As adolescents, four of us children had the responsibility of carrying water in buckets from the holes on top of some of these small pillarlike formations. We ascended the mesas in the springtime, after it rained. While we were there, we played hide-and-go-seek. Luke Yazzie and I climbed into a large crevice that was narrow at the top, then widened at the bottom.[24] We climbed all the way down and found an overhanging ridge with a sudden drop and a high cliff on the other side. We looked around and found a layer of rough rock in the wall, where someone had dug here and there. Some layers of the rock were reddish in color and some black. I also saw a pillar of uranium ore that had been dug into quite deeply, by the Anasazi, I think. Luke and I wandered around for a while before the other two boys found us. We wondered what had happened here and said, "Hey! This would be good for clay to mix with seeds then eat." So we gathered some, took it home, and Luke took some samples to Harry Goulding. He and Goulding went to the spot where we had found it, and the trader probably struck it rich from there. Those of us who actually discovered it never got a penny. We also saw the strips of ore on the hills and mesa at Moonlight before it was mined. The uranium was very visible to the naked eye.

When the search for uranium became big business, some Navajos used sacred rituals to locate mines. People involved in the search might use medicine men to pray for an understanding, but in other instances, mines were located by just looking for them. Layers of ore were visible, and they also used Geiger counters.

I have worked in a lot of uranium mines in the Monument Valley area. I started working in a mine called Stumped Ears, behind Promise Rock. There were no hydraulic tools, so we had to hold up the jackhammer while we drilled. There also was no water to blow out or settle the dust, so the mine was full of it. Sand filled our throats, noses, and ears—it was a mess! After I set all the wiring and did some blasting, we immediately reentered the cloudy tunnel and hauled out all the muck with our wheelbarrows. This was the beginning.

The second mine I worked in was Rough Rock. I was one of the first workers to open this mine, and the job was just as bad as the first one. We had no hydraulic jacks and had to tie the drill bit to the tip of the jackhammer. The process was slow because of the inconvenient equipment, and sometimes we had to use hand shovels to complete the job. I next worked at the Moonlight Mine as a driller, then in several mines on the mesas above Oljato, where I was promoted to foreman. Later, I moved to the mouth of Narrow Canyon for additional work. Today, I sit here as if I had never done such labor.

When I was transferred to the old VCA mines because the work was slowing down, I rode my horse from Train Rock to the site and spent one week, sometimes two, then came home. My white employers would not let me go. At times I worked for fourteen days straight, then took a week off and performed several ceremonies before returning to the mine. Harry Goulding must have told my employers I was a medicine man and prearranged my busy schedule so I could perform the ceremonies and work in the mines at other times. Goulding was somewhat of a supervisor, and I am sure he invested a lot of money from his Monument Valley trading post into mining.

The white bosses who supervised the operation entered the mines only once in a while. They feared them and came in only long enough to give instructions as to what they wanted done. This was usually at the beginning of the shift, so that the miners could follow through with the job. I drilled most of the time and learned how to blast, even though I never went to school. Observation, specific instructions, and then working were how I was trained. I was appointed lead man several times and mastered drilling and blasting, vertically and horizontally. I really worked hard during my mining years.

One job I had was harnessing a mule and leading him down into the mine shaft to haul ore. The animal wore a huge light on his chest harness. Once he returned to the surface with a load, it was emptied, and he turned around, went back down the shaft, and waited by the loading machine. All day long I walked down, hooked up the buggy, and brought him back up.

After four or five months, my arms began to ache for no reason at all. I went to the hospital in Monticello, but that did not help. I then decided to see a Hopi medicine man named Willow Reed's Son (Lók'aa Biye'), who was well known among the people, and have him remove the illness by sucking it out.[25] I gave him the bow guard off my wrist and forty dollars cash, but he refused to take it, saying, "I only charge two dollars!" These days it costs too much for such rituals. He gave the bow guard and forty dollars back, and I paid him two dollars. He massaged me all over until he found the illness. He continued the massage and soon took out a long, swollen piece of cactus thorn, the type used for special ceremonies, from my aching arm. The pain subsided immediately.

Willow Reed's Son told me not to go back to the same jobsite, because someone had supernaturally shot the thorn into my arm since I had taken his job away.[26] The medicine man asked me if I wanted to see him, but I decided not to. This person was also a medicine man, who did the Windway Ceremony. I guess he wanted to test me. I did not go back but went to another mine, and later back to the Moonlight Mine, where I worked as a driller and set up the wires for blasting.

In this job, I waited for the men who did the blasting to come in and blow off the surface. One day I decided to dig a ditch along the base of the wall inside the mine tunnel. There were streams of water everywhere, so I thought I would make just a small canal to funnel the water into one stream. Just as I was about to connect the two streams, I heard a loud crack above, and in a matter of seconds, part of the ceiling came crashing down. The rush of air from the falling rock pushed me clear of the slab, wrenched my shovel out of my hands, and threw it several feet ahead of me. I looked up and saw a huge oblong piece of rock lying where I had been digging. The stone was so large and long that it covered all the ditches I had dug. This was a miraculous escape. I believe my sacred prayers and songs truly protected me, and I was meant to live this long. I was very lucky.

When I worked at that mine, I lived at the site during the week but went back to my home at Train Rock on the weekends. I walked back to the mine, many miles from here, leaving early in the morning but still making it on time. Today, our children refuse to walk even a short distance and totally depend on their autos. I sometimes walked to Goulding's Trading Post to buy things, and then carried them home; other times I took a shortcut over the mesa.

Once, while I was working at the mines, I stayed in a tent close to the jobsite where I had been working for only a short time. I had a dream one night that someone, maybe the Holy Beings, told me to make an offering of corn pollen and prayers to the cliffs and mesas nearby. "It will be dangerous if you don't," something told me. I thought that I could not make the offerings because my sacred corn pollen was in my medicine bag at home near Train Rock.

I awakened in the early morning when the dream was still fresh in my mind. There was no water in the camp, and the weather was windy with light rain showers. I grabbed a bucket and headed down the hill to where the big water barrel was. The wind and rain had erased our footprints on the trail, but as I walked along, I spied my sacred corn pollen pouch sitting in front of me. I did not believe it at first, because I knew it was at home in my medicine bag, but I examined it very carefully, and sure enough, it was mine. This was strange, but I picked up my pouch, put it in my pocket, and walked back to my tent with the bucket of water.

My dream kept bothering me. I made breakfast, then went to work, arriving at the sheer cliff wall close to the mine shaft just before the other workers. I stood at its base and placed my offering of corn pollen and prayed toward the mine, saying a prayer to the uranium and the earth for my safety on the job and other things. At this time, my job was to blast the ore, then help my father-in-law scoop it up with big coal shovels and take it out of the mine in a wheelbarrow, then down the hill.

I had just blasted a very thin layer of ore that my boss told me to remove from the low ceiling. I quickly shoveled the ore and thought I would help my father-in-law haul it out, since I was in a hurry to complete the work. Just when I left my spot, a large piece of rock came crashing down right where I had been seconds before. The slab was so huge that it nearly went all the way up to the ceiling and missed my back side by inches. I managed to climb out of the mine, with barely enough room to crawl around the fallen slab. I was saved by my dream and the Holy Beings because of my prayers and offerings that morning. Somehow, my pollen pouch had followed me there and enabled me to perform the sacred prayer. If I had not done so, I would not be here today.

Everyone was surprised and amazed to see me. They kept asking me how I had survived. I went back to the tent to look for my corn pollen bag but could not find it. I believe this experience turned out the way it was meant to, keeping me safe and alive. Something like this has happened to me three times during my work as a miner and is another example of why I believe that there is a god.

I often prayed before going underground, because I knew which prayers, songs, and offerings to make to the earth, mountains, or mesas. It was a sacred routine that I followed throughout my entire mining career. Many other miners had it done for them. It is said that the Holy Being Black God (Haashch'éshzin) was in charge of Black Mesa, where the present coal mine is located. Today, the Peabody Coal Company is mining all this valuable coal. Black Mesa has a prayer and song of its own, and some of the employees working there still use these sacred rituals. One of my sons works there, and I have often performed songs and prayers on his behalf.

Another time when I was mining, my partner from Chilchinbeto and I were putting in bolts and mesh wire on the ceiling and walls of a wide-roof shaft. Together, we put up a very wide sheet of mesh wire on the ceiling, as our boss had told us to do that morning. We bolted some heavy-duty boards against it every few inches all the way across. By lunchtime, we were finished in that area, so we moved all our equipment around the corner and went outside for lunch. After eating, we returned to the mine and our worksite, but there was none. The work area was replaced with a long, large slab, where the whole ceiling had fallen to the ground. The rock was as thick as this house.

My co-worker was stunned and frightened, quitting his job immediately. I never saw him again. It must have really frightened him, because I heard he never recovered from the scare and that he died sometime later. He should have had a ceremony or sing, but he did not. This incident did not bother me at all; I must have been crazy. I did not think twice about what happened, or how fatal it could have been, but just went back down alone, moved my equipment, and drilled farther down the tunnel.

I was that way because of how I was raised. I was tough because of all the physical and mental training—running, snow baths, ice baths, discipline with a whip, and so on. It had made me capable of facing anything without fear. The close relationship one has with the Holy One (Haashch'élti'ii Haashch'ééhwaan) pays off throughout life. He takes care of you, keeps you from harm and danger, and gives you strength and courage. Our full mental preparation rests on survival, whether it is for food, money, or wealth. It does not matter what it takes; we must be willing to make sacrifices. That is how I must have been, now that I look back on my life. My body must have been strong enough to withstand the trauma, so I continued to work, work, and work.

The only fatality I witnessed on the job occurred when I was in a mine near Durango, Colorado. A cave-in buried two Mexican miners. I do not know how the workers retrieved their bodies, but we heard it took a week to get them out. This scared us, so we quit, and our boss put us on a road crew. I did not witness any fatality in uranium mines around home, but I heard about them. One happened near the Narrow Canyon mines. A collapsed roof killed Paul Begay.

I had a close call underground one time when an oxygen tank lid blew off and exploded as I was passing by. These tanks are big and used to provide oxygen. The blast was so strong that it tossed me about, for I do not know how long, carrying me around the next corner to the ground. I got sandblasted, too, with sandstone embedded in my body. It was a painful and terrible experience.

Later, I was hired in Mexican Hat at the uranium-processing mill to work the graveyard shift.[27] The ore was ground to sand, sifted, and refined, then mixed with water and run through some pipes overhead. Underneath were huge pots of black tar heated by flames, which dried the ore all night long. Once it was dried, workers loaded the ore into wheelbarrows and dumped it in a pile. The sifted, powdered form was dried separately, and then shoveled into the dump trucks by hand. The ore was as fine as flour and covered us from head to toe in powder, but we never knew how dangerous it was to our health. Then I worked near Denver, in a place called Rico, Colorado, in another uranium mine. I spent about two years there before moving back to Train Rock, where I was hired at a new mine not too far from Moonlight. I worked there for about three more years as a driller.

One evening, a group of white men came to my home. They had been inspecting the drilled areas and told me to prepare a huge space. I began drilling with my assistant, and we hurried along as fast as we could, putting explosives inside the holes and preparing them for blasting. When the inspectors came around, they saw that I had finished and was waiting while the men in other areas were still drilling. They found that I had drilled 280 holes during my graveyard shift. The roof was fuzzy with fuse wires. The men could not believe that I had made so many holes; they counted all of them, and sure enough, there were that many. "How many years have you worked like this?" they asked. I told them how many, and they recorded it in their records. "This man can sure work! He does a job equal to that of four men. He's a real hard worker!" they said.

But they also told me I was working much too hard and warned me that I was overdoing it. So they transferred me to another job for five days, and gave me a raise, and had me haul ore. They said I must be working equal to one hundred hours each week. I remained in the

Miner and railcar. J.H.: "Soon my supervisor assigned me to care for the entrance of the mine shaft, where the workers brought up ore in small railcars." (Photo unlisted, Milton Snow Collection, Navajo Nation Museum)

haul-out area for some time, then was transferred to the lift-out area, where I took care of the machines. I worked there for about a month.

Soon my supervisor assigned me to care for the entrance of the mine shaft, where the workers brought up ore in small railcars. Some of the men who worked at the entrance did not break the large rocks into smaller pieces, which created problems, so my boss had me make sure the rocks were the right size. I worked there for two months.

One cloudy, misty fall day, a railcar came to the surface with a big slab sitting on top. I unloaded it and let the rock roll back down the shaft, then took the sledgehammer and walked down to where it lay. I hit it with the hammer four times, then felt a flash of electric shock go through my arm and body. My limbs fell to my sides, and I collapsed to the ground. I became paralyzed and could only move my head a little before blacking out.

A horn blew each time a railcar brought a load to the surface, and since I could not unload it, the whistle kept blowing and blowing. Two workers came running up the mine shaft, asked what happened to me, then quickly called for help. They tried to lift me but could not, so they summoned an ambulance, and I was taken to the Monument Valley Hospital. The doctors finally revived my body after two days, and then I spent several more days in bed. After that, I had to slow down in mining and could not work like I used to; it was the doctor's orders. My job had failed me, and now I could not work like that again.

My final mining injury occurred at a new mine that had just barely opened. The shaft had not yet become very deep, and we were preparing to blast. I drilled the sides of the high walls, then filled the holes with explosives and waited. I sat down on a pile of sand and rocks near three other men sitting on another pile. The wall across from me was very smooth but suddenly exploded, sending flying rocks at us. One of these rocks hit the wall behind me and came down on my back, knocking me out. I spent four days in a coma, while the doctors in Gallup performed surgery on my spine. They told me that one of my disks was destroyed, which made it worse. I should have stayed home that day; then I would not have had this injury and health problems.

I left mining for the last time after that back injury, which totally displaced all my vertebras and disks. I feared I could not return to a normal life, because it had affected my health so badly. My speech became distorted, I could not swallow properly, and the mist from the ore was dangerous. It nearly got me. I had to hire medicine men several times to get my health back to normal. Traditional medicine is very strong and healed me. It is good to have medicine men with their powerful songs and prayers and sacred herbs for healing. I feel very fortunate to be here and to be well again. That is what I used, and that is why I am here today.

So I have worked in many mines, but at the time, none of us knew how hazardous it was. Many of the white men and Navajo miners that I worked with during those years are now gone. The only ones that I have seen recently are those who were employed for a short length of time. I worked for over twenty years as a miner, but it was not as a steady job.

I have since had health problems, and I hold the mine owners responsible. Some injuries sustained from work in the mines eventually passed by unnoticed, but time has taken its toll. Now I feel the pain and suffering. There was the time that the rock hit my backbone, and the other time when the cap blew off the oxygen tank, throwing me several feet and embedding hundreds of gravel stones underneath my skin. These injuries were painful, but I never received any compensation for them. When I started mining, I had never heard of cancer, arthritis, lung disease, or heart attacks among our people. We had none, until the uranium mines.

Today, our people are suffering from these effects; many more have died. It is obvious in determining the causes, but somehow the Public Health System blames it on other things and turns its back on us.[28] At one gathering, I met many of my former co-workers. I saw some who used to drive dump trucks and others who worked outside the mines. They were hooked up to portable respirators, and these were the ones working outside the mines. They never did any underground blasting, where the air was thick with uranium dust. I must have seen about four of them, and they seemed so very old. In fact, one of them was my boss. It was quite a reunion.

We went for treatment of illness many times during our employment at the mines, but these medical records have been hidden. The people in charge do not want to research and reveal our past health history but rather base their diagnoses on the current illnesses, like arthritis. Miners' wives' and their children's health have also been greatly affected. Babies were born deformed or with abnormal health problems, and so the people are frustrated and try to get compensation for these damages but are told they are healthy and that there is nothing wrong. I don't know what will happen, but we are going to keep trying. Our people get shortchanged with funds, and the assistance meant for them vanishes before they receive it. This is miserable and disgusting to be treated this way, but that is how it is.

I recently had copies made of all medical records concerning my uranium-mining days, because I was applying for compensation. It cost me thirty-seven dollars to get them done, and I sent them to the office requesting them. Shortly after that, we had a big meeting in Shiprock regarding this compensation case, so I inquired about the records. The officials told me they did not have them and did not know where they were. The only ones I'd had were the ones I'd sent to the attorney. We have all been affected by the mines and now realize how dangerous it was to our health.

II

Teachings from the
Past and Present

CHAPTER SIX

TEACHINGS FROM THE FEARING TIME

Stories about the Fearing Time and the Long Walk period are a shared heritage for many Navajo families. Indeed, the tribe suffered during this time (1858–1868) to the point that it has become mythologized and recognized as one of the most traumatic times in its history. Historians still question how many Navajos did not surrender and go to live at Fort Sumner to join the more than 8,000 who did, but all agree that there was a sizable number who never left their homelands. John had family members on both sides of the event—some stayed, others went.

This collection of stories has been passed down from one generation to the next. One unique feature is that the stories are all connected as one family's experience. Each has differences, but they all share the common theme of perseverance through trials, dependence on the Holy Beings and ceremonies, and the necessity of being resourceful. The primary persons remain faithful in their trials and are rewarded by guardians or opportunities that lead to their freedom. Evil, on the other hand, is punished, so that good prevails—a common theme in many cultures' traditions that assures compliance and continuance.

There are other lessons for today's society: Peyote is introduced as an aid, prayers save lives, animals can be helpers, and the power of medicine men can last for centuries. To make this last point, John discusses the ceremonial taboos placed against Fort Sumner, which helps explain why there are contemporary problems on the reservation and in Navajo government. Teachings from the past must be applied to the present.

WOMAN WITH THE FOUR HORNS EXPERIENCE

My grandmother, Woman with the Four Horns, was born into the Towering House Clan, and her mother, my great-grandmother, was Woman Sheepherder (Asdzáán Na'niłkaadii). Woman Sheepherder was married to Many Goats with White Hair (Tł'ízí Łání Bitsii' Łigai). My great-grandmother's mother was Woman Who Watches (Asdzáán Ha'asidí). Her two brothers were Loud One (Bizahólǫ́) and Yellow Forehead (Bitáá'ii Łitsoi), and her two nephews were named Ropey (Tł'óółii) and Little Bitter Water (Tó Dich'íí'nii Yázhí).[1] All of these people lived southeast of Richfield, Utah, at a place called Circle of Red Rocks and in the nearby mountains. She said their home was where the river runs beyond the Mountain with No Name [Henry Mountains], which was also called White-Face Mountain.[2]

Other Navajo families also lived there in a long deep canyon with high cliffs, where a stone building sits on top, close to Richfield. The names of some of the other people who lived in this area were Aching Stomach, Cottonwood Coming Down, and Pine Tree (Ńdíshchíí'). My grandmother's family had herded their livestock by moving around in this area for quite some time.

One day, a family from Rough Rock, Arizona, came to visit. The couple came with their son, Small Boy (Ashkii Ałts'íísí), whom they wanted to have marry young Woman with the Four Horns. If her parents agreed to the marriage, then the other family promised to drive their horses, used as payment, all the way from Rough Rock to Richfield. This was the way it was done traditionally—the groom's parents asked the bride's parents for their daughter in marriage. It must have been a very long trip for the groom and his family, especially when herding all the horses. The wedding, where the young couple ate their sacred wedding cornmeal mush, took place below White-Face Mountain.[3] Grandmother said they were very, very nervous and shy with each other, because this was the first time they had met. In the old days, newlyweds were like that.

So the couple married and lived together. After two years, they still had not had any children. Woman with the Four Horns appeared barren. And like all marriages, there were little spats and quarrels. One day her husband decided to return to Rough Rock because he was upset. However, the families living in this area were not aware of the events back home on what is now the reservation. They did not know that there was a war going on between the United States government and the Navajos, and they now had enemies.[4]

This fighting occurred because the Navajos were stealing from the Mexicans and the white men. Just one incident of a person stealing something and everyone was to blame! That's how it is today; when one person steals, everyone gets blamed. Some people steal from others and do not care. The Navajos at this time were fighting and creating havoc among the white men and Indian tribes like the Utes and Apaches. When one person creates a problem, everyone pays for it.[5] I do not know who the individual was, but the people were paying for it.

When Grandmother's husband left on his horse and headed home to Rough Rock, neither person knew about this conflict. Woman with the Four Horns went after him, but before leaving, she put on all her jewelry—coral beads, a silver concho belt, and rings made by a man named Silversmith the Arrow Way (Atsidii K'aak'éhii), who lived among the Navajos by Richfield.[6]

Grandmother said she ran, following her husband's trail through the canyons and mountains until she finally caught him. He put her behind him on his horse and continued south until they crossed the San Juan River and camped overnight on the far bank. In those days, people used to travel only during daylight, so as soon as sunset ended, they built a fire and rested. Today, everyone travels at night.

They left the next day and stayed the following evening at Standing Red Rock, near Monument Valley. The couple found a homestead, but no one was there, and they saw no tracks. They departed, traveling past El Capitan and Horse Hops Up Trail, through Water Running over a Rock Floor, past Baby Rocks, between Kayenta and Dennehotso, then toward his home in Rough Rock. As they approached, they spied a big cloud of dust west of Kayenta. In those days prairie grass was tall, and there was rich vegetation. The cloud of dust came from a large group of horses traveling toward them. They wondered what was happening and thought that perhaps someone was holding an Enemyway [Squaw] Dance. Maybe it was the dust from horses as the people carried the sacred prayer stick. Grandmother and her husband had no idea that enemies were approaching.

The couple froze in their tracks, staring at the oncoming riders. A white man with a big beard, straggly hair, and hat came bursting out of the crowd and abruptly stopped in front of them. He pulled a gun, and at that instant, my grandmother "spoke to the gun" [prayed] and heard the click of the hammer, but no bullet fired. Three times he pulled the trigger, but nothing happened. Just then another horseman, a Mexican with a large sombrero, rode up and knocked the weapon out of the white man's hand. Then the gun fired. "I'll take her. She'll be mine," said the Mexican, as he hoisted Grandmother behind him onto his saddle. The white man left, and the whole group rode off, taking her with them. They camped that night east of Dennehotso at a place called Donkey or Handmade Spring. Her captors tied Grandmother's hands and legs, treating her like a hostage.

These men spent several days looking for more people to capture. Some Navajos were brought in bound, with shoes removed, just like Grandmother. The only time the prisoners were freed was to go to the bathroom, but even then, two or three guards accompanied them. The whole experience was torture and suffering. The guards whipped both young and old men and had no mercy for the people. The Mexicans stayed for at least five days, and each day they brought in more and more Navajos. The children cried, and very elderly men and women were killed.

The group then moved east and camped somewhere near Chinle, Arizona. They must have spent another five days there, while the Mexicans gathered more people from all directions. The bound prisoners were given very little food. They were thirsty and asked for water, but their captors did not listen to their requests.

One young Mexican woman became Grandmother's guard. As time went on, she became friendlier and gave her more food and water, and even untied her when the party went out to hunt for more people. Several times Grandmother thought of escaping, but her feet were still closely bound, forcing little steps. The Mexican woman did, however, untie Grandmother's hands when she walked with her through the sagebrush. When the Mexican woman heard the hunters approaching camp, she hurriedly retied her prisoner's hands. Still, she had compassion for my grandmother.

They stayed for about a week, then left, moving everyone along. They camped near Nazlini [Stream around the Bend, or Spread-Out Stream], Arizona, for about three days. They moved east again, camping on one of the lower mountains for a night. This long movement began with a large number of captives being "herded," but those who tired were shot to death on the spot.

The group camped near a spring in the vicinity of Window Rock, Arizona, where they spent two days before moving on to Gallup, New Mexico. While there, one of the Navajos' former traders, a white man named Big Mexican (Nakaii Tso), came to their camp. The People knew him because before their captivity, they used to sell wool to him in Gallup, and he used to keep them well fed. When he recognized them, he asked what was going on and where they were going. "We don't know," the People replied. "These white men are crazy!" he said. "You'll come home; you'll come back. Don't be afraid; somehow we will help you come home. There are some white people who are willing to help you. We are on your side. We will all band together and put in a petition for your release. We are planning to do this. Don't be afraid, you'll be safely home in a short time," said Big Mexican to my grandmother.

The journey continued, as the people camped overnight here and there. Grandmother and another person rode a mule but remained tied. They traveled through Albuquerque, then camped at the base of the mountains before going on. It must have taken twenty days traveling before they got to Texas. Once there, they reached a river with some rowboats. There were other groups who had been crossing for two or three days. The Mexicans loaded all their belongings as well as the captives and made several trips across. Then they tied two horses to the boats and let the rest of the horses and mules swim after them. There were so many of them that they spread across the water for some distance as the animals swam across. Once on the other side, the Mexicans saddled or packed the horses and mules and made ready to travel. I do not know the name of the river, but it was a large one, and the weather was warm, whereas back home it was cold.

They finally came to a big camp with large pointed tents, where the Mexicans who had captured the people gathered. My grandmother saw many more prisoners and learned that some of the Mexicans were jealous of each other's captives. The Mexican woman who took care of Grandmother continued to watch out for her, but the rest of the people were poorly fed. The captors lived in the larger tents, with big guard dogs tied at the entrance. These dogs were huge, and if a prisoner ran away, the Mexicans released them to hunt the escapee down.

One day the Mexican lady said through gesturing that she would untie Grandmother that night! She went through the motions of untying her ankles and hands, then pointed away from camp, as if to say "run" or "get away." Grandmother knew the sacred prayer to help her escape without being detected. This sacredness is called "Yaahoo'a'í," and it spoke to her while she was escaping.[7]

That night the Mexican woman brought Grandmother's shoes and told her, "Let's go use the restroom." The two women went out to the bushes quite a ways from camp, where the Mexican woman untied Grandmother's hands and ankles. As soon as they were out of sight, she said, "Now, go run!" and Grandmother began running. She ran and ran as fast as she could, a distance as far as from Train Rock to Gouldings [approximately eight miles], before she heard a commotion coming from camp. She saw an array of lights and heard dogs barking behind the hills. Grandmother wondered, "Now what can I do?" She looked around and saw a rock overhang close to the ground, with thorn bushes and cacti beneath. Close by were a lot of yuccas, cacti, and tumbleweed thorns. They hurt her, but she crawled deep inside and covered herself with the debris. She was in a lot of pain but ignored it.

This spot was actually a nest of thorns and cacti built by pack rats, so she said a prayer to the female rat. "Grandmother, female rat, withhold their weapons, protect me. I am running for my life; have mercy on me. Protect me with your shield of great strength, that I may be spared. Don't let the enemies see me; let neither the dogs nor bullets find me." She named each with their sacred names and pleaded for protection against being seen and killed.[8]

The hunting group and its ferocious dogs had caught up with her and were very close. She saw the dogs sniffing around and the riders on horseback, with their lights shining on the ground as they swarmed by her. She remained as quiet and still as she could. The dogs came very close but did not want to deal with the long thorns in the rat's nest. The stickers hurt her all over every time she moved.

Eventually, the riders went past, but still she did not move. With the approach of dawn, the party returned. Each rider passed, looking tired and exhausted. Then silence. They were gone, but she remained under the rock ledge all day, fearing they were close by, looking for her. Finally, as the sun went down, she slowly crawled out and started walking.

By now she was exhausted, so she sat down to rest. Her whole body and especially her feet hurt terribly. She found her body full of thorns and wracked with pain. She tried to walk, but it was impossible, so she sat down and removed the thorns from her feet. It was very painful because there was already infection. She did one foot then the other, taking out the stickers, then trying to walk again, but she could not. The pain seared up to her pelvis and was too much. She managed to walk a little ways, then stopped at a small marsh with some willow reeds and cattails. There she made a hideout by digging a hole among the reeds. The space was just enough for her to crawl into. She gathered leaves off the willows and cattails and covered herself.

She remained there for some time, covering her tracks each time she went out. Later, she made sandals out of cattail roots and reeds and searched for food. She noticed some small, round fuzzy cacti underneath the tall shrubs scattered here and there and thought they were like the cacti her family used to eat at home. She pulled one out with its long root, then two more before peeling off the outer part and taking them to her hideout to eat. The cactus was bitter but juicy and had the texture of cornbread. She ate one and felt full, as if she had eaten a big meal. This cactus turned out to be peyote.[9]

Soon she was hallucinating, having visions of her home and the captured people she had left behind. These captives were now in Fort Sumner, where she saw them saying prayers and songs on her behalf. In reality, that was what was happening in Fort Sumner. These people knew of her escape and were singing for her. She felt good, as if she could continue her journey, but her feet still hurt. She feared her captors might capture her if she traveled during the day, and so she thought it would be better to travel at night. The peyote told her, "It is better that you travel at night," and that she would get back to her home if she followed this plan. She settled back down and fell asleep. She had not slept at all before, but now she fell into a deep sleep.

Two days after eating the peyote, her feet began healing. She continued to pick and eat the cactus when she became hungry, remaining in her hideout as her feet improved. She tried on her handmade sandals after carefully lining the inside with split cattail leaves and the soft cattail tops, which she crumbled and laid on the sole inside. She took extra leaves and cattails for use when these wore out.

Hiding in this fashion for a month, she became stronger as her feet healed from the thorn infection. While making shoes and surviving, she gathered more peyote to eat on her long journey home and found a way to carry it. This peyote helped her to "see" the way home. She brought back from this experience two of these peyote buttons that were left over. They were once big but have since shrunk to tiny little things. These two small golden buttons are in the sacred bundle of my sheep replenisher bag. This is called Living Plant Mixture and is kept for the sheep.[10] I still have this bag. It belonged to her, but now I keep it with the two buttons in it.

The day came when she continued her journey. At sundown she started to run and walk, run and walk, in her sandals—five extra pairs, which she fastened to her belt. She walked and walked, ran and ran all night, and by dawn, she had reached the big wide river. It was too dangerous to cross now, so she crawled into a pile of soft willow shrubs and slept. The next morning at sunrise, she awoke, looked around, and found a large log floating close enough to the bank that she could grab. She planned to cross the river using the log, and so after spying a sandy point of land with trees and shrubs downriver on the opposite side, she dragged the floating log upstream.

Grandmother hoped to float across to the opposite side where the trees and shrubs were. She got on the log and started downstream toward the point of land, but she almost missed her target. The hanging willows she needed to pull herself out of the river were barely within reach. She grasped their tips, let go of the log, and sent it down the river, managing to get on shore and find a place to hide. As before, she pulled the shrubs over her and slept through the day, not leaving until sundown.

All night she walked. It was a long way home, so she kept walking until daybreak, then crawled inside more shrubs to sleep. At sunset, she began her journey again. Because she was taking peyote, she felt energetic, tireless, and could see in the dark. One morning after traveling all night, she realized she had gone in a circle, because she remembered stopping at a water hole to take a drink the previous evening, and now she had returned to that spot. She was very upset, thinking, "What can I do to get back on track and go in the right direction?"

The overcast sky had darkened, confusing her even more. She spotted bear tracks, so she decided to follow them, even though it was daytime. A fog limited visibility. She followed the tracks until dark, before digging a small burrow under a bush to crawl inside to sleep. When she awoke, she was not sure if she had slept all day, but the sky had cleared, and it was near evening. Again, she walked and walked until she recognized a mountain east of Albuquerque that she had passed as a captive. She knew she was getting closer to home. That night, she made her way toward the mountain but realized it was too far away and ended up having to sleep again, this time in the desert, where there were no trees or hiding spots. She finally came to a gully with bushes, crawled in, and slept.

The next evening she started walking again without water or food and only peyote. Once she reached the mountain, she searched for water, found a spring, and drank. This was a good place to rest and sleep because she was alone, far away from any road or people. Here she said prayers and made offerings from the highest part of the mountain, which helped guide her home. After she awoke in the evening and continued to walk over the mountain, she suddenly felt strange but continued to walk all night until she arrived in the desert once more. The only place to hide were some small bushes that she crawled under to sleep.

At this point in her journey of several months, she had shrunk to skin and bones, allowing her to sleep under this small bush and not be seen. It seemed like she had traveled all summer and fall, and she was now so weary from hunger and weakness that she did not know if she could last. Only her prayers to the Holy Beings helped her survive. They must have been very sacred.

She continued to travel through the barren desert, with nothing in sight. It was fall and getting cold, with cloudy skies and rain. Her body became numb to the cold as rain turned to snow and temperatures dropped. She dug a hole under some bushes and crawled inside, too weak to do much more. Fear replaced her bravery, and the cold convinced her that she would not last much longer. Then she prayed the owl prayer and sang the owl song. "Please, Grandfather Owl, cover me with your skin."[11] Next, an owl hooted nearby, flew to where she lay, and perched upon the bush she lay under. It spread its wings over her and sat there until she warmed herself. At dawn she awoke, the owl hooted twice and flew away, and she began traveling again. She walked until dark, sensing she was close to her destination—Fort Sumner.

By sundown it started snowing and was cold. Once again she dug a hole under a bush and crawled inside, freezing cold. This time she prayed to the wolf.[12] "You are my brother, my sister, my sibling. We are children of Mother Earth. Please help me. I'm cold." Before too long, she heard some noise in the inch-deep snow and looked up to see a wolf trying to flatten the bushes above her. It walked around and around, lay down on top of her cover, and was soon snoring. She was tired, too, and dropped off to sleep. Early the next morning, she awoke to find the snow still coming down and visibility poor. The wolf got up, walked away, and howled twice in a certain direction. "That is the direction I'll go," she decided, then continued her journey.

Grandmother knew the bear's song (shash biyiin) and prayer (shash bitsodizin), as well as the songs for the owl and the wolf when one is cold and freezing. At the beginning of time, when our language was first developed, Wolf said, "If anyone calls me by my real name, I will assist them." He dedicated himself to help. In addition to this, there was a special ceremony and song being performed for her by the people she had left behind. They sang her lifelong sacred songs, which had been with her ever since she was in her mother's womb. These helped her survive the ordeal. She knew the sacred ways of pleading for help from the Holy Beings. She sang and prayed sacredly and called all by their sacred names. She knew these beforehand and used them for her survival now and throughout her life.

After receiving this help, she felt much better and decided to eat her remaining peyote buttons for energy. She ran and walked, ran and walked, until she saw some dark objects in the distance on the flat desert plain. She was not sure what they were but thought they could either be the enemy, who had come to run her down, or people being taken to Fort Sumner. Then she saw some houses and people, ladies wearing skirts and men in thin pants. They were barely visible through the snow. It was Fort Sumner, where all the Navajos had been taken. She ran toward the camp, where two guards met and assisted her as she fainted from hunger and exhaustion. The smell of smoke and cooking meat overwhelmed her as the men carried her into camp.

The people and medicine men at Fort Sumner had been singing for her safe return and now gathered around as relatives greeted her. The medicine men that I had mentioned before—Yellow Forehead, Loud One, and Ropey—who had been singing and praying for her, now came to her side. Many Goats with White Hair, the main medicine man who led the prayers for her safe return, was also there. As the people gathered around, they at first did not recognize her. She was greatly changed from the last time they had seen her. They began to sing for her again, and as she awoke and sat up, a ceremony was already under way. Her husband was there sitting beside her, telling her how happy he was to see her again. "My dear wife," he said, as he placed a white shell necklace around her neck. She later took a sacred yucca bath and had a Blessingway Ceremony performed that night.

SMALL MAN'S EXPERIENCE

As Woman with the Four Horns heard of the things that had happened to the People, she learned that her husband, Small Man (Diné Yázhí), had been captured near Baby Rocks. The white soldiers took him east to a military base. There, many, many soldiers held him captive, but he had not suffered as much as his wife had. He even dressed up in their uniforms, rode with them, followed his captors wherever they went, and took care of their horses. He had just returned to Fort Sumner four days before she arrived. While in captivity, he found a whole storage house full of jewelry and other valuable things, which the soldiers had taken from dead prisoners. His captors gave him the job of keeping this storage house clean, but he also stole a lot of the merchandise inside— necklaces, bracelets, and concho belts. This is where he obtained the white shell beads he gave to his wife.

He planned how and when to escape. One night, he gathered all his stolen items and a saddle and took them to the horse corral at a distance from the soldiers' camp. He had trained two horses and kept them in good shape for his escape. These horses were big and strong, and he raced them every day. They were fast runners, but he told the soldiers he was training these horses for them to do their important assignments. The night he escaped, he hid all his belongings and some food where he could get them without being seen.

When dark came, and people began to sleep, he silently left camp to pack all his things on the two horses. He put a harness on one horse to fasten the sacks stuffed with his belongings, then tied them down as one would pack a mule. He mounted his horse, led the other, and began riding all night until he reached a mountain. He realized that he could easily be spotted on the mountain, so he kept riding faster and faster, traveling a long ways.

Eventually, he reached a wide river with an unstable bridge that shook with every step as he and the horses crossed to the opposite side. He next decided to topple the bridge with a small hatchet he had stolen. All day long he chopped on the metal cables, until the middle of the bridge finally tumbled into the river. Now the soldiers could not use it, and there were no other crossing points close by. Once the bridge was down, he began riding again.

He rode until he reached another mountain, where he could see far in the distance. He decided to camp and let his horses graze while he rested. It was hard for him to sleep because of his fear and the need to be alert for soldiers. He was armed only with a stolen gun, the kind that is filled with gunpowder down the barrel and is single shot. It was not all that dependable, but he would at least have a chance to defend himself if he had to. Earlier, he had thought of stealing a pistol, too, but his captors were very protective and hid them. The powder rifles were everywhere and easier to steal.

The horses were full now, so he decided to ride again. He repacked his belongings and left at dark. He thought about how the soldiers were tracking him and were probably stopped at the bridge. The destruction of it gave him a head start, and even though it only went halfway into the river, it had buckled under, and there was no way to fix or use it. He had been on the run now for several days—two days and three nights—and had felt it safer to travel in the dark.

Now he began traveling during the daytime, going as far as he could before camping to let his horses graze. On the fourth day he left at dawn and galloped, then trotted, all the way, as fast as he could. While still a prisoner, he had asked which horses were the best, so that he knew which ones could keep up the pace and never tire. Even when it became foggy and he could not see well, he kept going.

The weather became very cold, and it started to snow. He had stolen enough uniforms from his captors so that he did not feel the temperature because of several layers of clothing. He also had enough food, which he had stolen a little at a time and which the second horse now carried. The jewelry—silver necklaces, squash blossoms, and white shell beads—he packed in with tanned deerskins, cow hides, and goatskins. He had taken a lot.

For seven days he traveled, until he reached the mountains east of Albuquerque. He knew, from what his captors said, that all the Navajos were at Fort Sumner. "There are no more Navajo people living in their homeland. They are all at Fort Sumner," they said. He thought, "I don't want to be out there all by myself. I want to be with them," so he surrendered to the white men, who probably thought they had gathered all the Navajos in the outlying areas. There were actually some living in the Henry Mountains by Hanksville, others in the Escalante Mountains, and still others living by the Bears Ears, the La Sal Mountains, and behind Navajo Mountain in Utah and Gray Mountain in Arizona.[13] These people escaped being captured and remained behind. Small Man thought for sure there was no one living at home now, so it was best to go to Fort Sumner.

When he surrendered, he threw away his gun and hatchet so that the soldiers at the fort would not find anything during their search. He told them his previous captors had let him go from the other prison, that he was to go home, and a bunch of other lies that the soldiers could not verify. Once he rejoined his people, there was a sacred ceremony performed for him. This was what happened to Small Man, my grandmother's husband. They both found their way back to Fort Sumner after being taken as prisoners near Baby Rocks.

METAL BELT'S EXPERIENCE

Grandfather Metal Belt was an older brother to my grandmother and was fifteen years old when the Long Walk and Fort Sumner occurred. He fought enemies from other tribes—the Apaches, Plains Indians, Mexicans, and whites—and killed many of them. Even during the night, he quietly killed them with his bow and arrows. He was also a good horseman. He would set up posts and shoot an arrow in each one as he swiftly rode his horse while hanging down around its legs. He used this same maneuver during attacks and was able to kill many enemies.

He had two horses that he kept at Gum Point, Setting Mountain, Mount Taylor, Bluebird Mountain near Albuquerque, and at a mountain near Fort Sumner.[14] He hobbled his horses at all of these places, and when he traveled, he obtained a fresh mount until he reached his destination. He dressed in the soldier's uniform that he took off the enemies he killed, and by wearing these clothes, he was able to get in and out of Fort Sumner with all the People's stories to take back with him.

It is said he once confronted a large group of enemy soldiers on the plains west of Ganado, Arizona. They surprised him, charged, and chased him, but he killed many of them before climbing into some rocks. The soldiers camped at the base of the rocks for two days, waiting for him to come down. He squeezed liquids from plants to keep his mouth moistened, and on the third day, he looked down below to see that some tribal members were with the cavalry.

One Indian wore a huge feather and was dressed in beads as he sat on his horse. Grandfather looked down the other side, and there were more cavalry men; two of them were facing each other on their horses. Metal Belt shot one with an arrow. At this point, he had only three arrows left, and now he had used one. He launched another at the Indian below, leaving only one arrow. He used that to kill one of their horses. "We better go and leave him; he's dangerous," they said as they started moving away. The cavalry left a huge cloud of dust over the flat land as they traveled from the mesa and out of the area.

After everyone disappeared, he went down to the horse he had shot. He was hungry, so he cut off some meat. His eye had been pushed out of its socket during the fighting but was still dangling from his face. He cut it off with the edge of an arrowhead. Next he sliced off a piece of cactus, removed all its needles and skin, then cut it in half and stuck it in his vacant eye socket. Cactus is very sticky, like glue. He traveled to Los Alamos Mountain to get another one of his horses. His other mount had been killed, and so he left it behind with his belongings. He had taken the horse skin and cut it up to make a bridle and rope for this spare horse. Next, he rode all the way back to Woman Who Was Hit's great-grandmother's place, across the San Juan River, south of the Bears Ears. He arrived and told her what had happened. "My head hurts; my eye is gone, and the socket hurts. What can be done about it?" he said. Grandmother replied, "Go ask Silversmith the Arrow Way; he sings the special sacred way, the Lifeway Ceremony (Iináájí)." He lived not too far from there, so they went and got him to perform a ceremony for three days. At its conclusion, Metal Belt felt better and rode his horse to White-Face Mountain, near Richfield, where he stayed until he fully recovered. He then went to Fort Sumner again, but three days after he arrived, the soldiers released the people, because they had made peace.

TEACHINGS ABOUT FORT SUMNER

The People said that during this time, bread was all they ate, and they were closely guarded by the cavalry. Some of the elders were shot and killed because they were sick, old, and treated like dogs. Women were also mistreated, with many becoming pregnant with babies for the white men and Mexicans. There was one man from Dennehotso, whose name was Mexican (Nakaii), who was said to have been one of these children carried back from Fort Sumner by his mother, on her back. He died recently. There were others taken elsewhere who never returned. They probably became like white men or Mexicans or Plains Indians. There are many stories about Fort Sumner.

Not too long after this, in the spring, the soldiers released the Navajos from Fort Sumner after several of our men went to Washington to make peace with the U.S. government. These Navajo men were Loud One, Yellow Forehead, Ropey, Little Bitter Water, Many Goats with White Hair, Black Bushes Going Out (Ch'il Hajinii), Giving Out Anger, Wide Hat (Ch'ah Niteelii), Silversmith the Arrow Way, and my maternal grandfather Metal Belt.[15] (He told me he was fifteen years old then.) These men did a sacred ceremony "through" the famous Rainbow Bridge, on the west side of Navajo Mountain, to release the Navajos from Fort Sumner.[16] This was done before they went to Washington, where they made peace on behalf of the People. It was difficult and took a long time to get their freedom. The white men told the Navajos they were crazy.

Another reason for the captivity and eventual release of the Navajos from Fort Sumner was that an individual had been working against the people. This man had sacred powers to "talk," or pray, the Navajos deep into the ground.[17] He lived on the edge of Rock Canyon, at Twin Stars [Sonsela Buttes, Arizona] and a place called Green Cattail Flat. He encouraged the enemies against us who gathered at his place. There were many. The medicine men I mentioned went to the top of Navajo Mountain and performed crystal gazing. They saw this person coming in and out of his hogan, followed by a dog. "This is the man. The man who did this to the Navajos," they said. They did a ceremony, then departed, next going to Promise Rock, about eight miles south of Gouldings, by the windmill. That rock, or mesa, tapers at the end and is said to be a large snake or reptile. There is a small patch of sand, with some bushes on its mid-crown, where there is a hole-like spot. The men performed another ceremony there, singing to the person who caused all the friction. "If it is really him, he will not last but perish before dawn," they said. These medicine men had sacred powers. It is said that the person died early that morning. This must have been during the summer, because the man was out hoeing his garden when his dog went past him from south to north, singing a song about Mountain Boy (Dził Ashkii) and saying, "Mountain Boy, you will die."[18] The man who talked the Navajos into the ground, the one who sent the enemies, died.[19]

Then the medicine men traveled to Sitting Mountain, to the top of Marble Mountain.[20] There was also Mount Taylor, Gobernador Knob, and then the top of Corn Pollen Mountain, where they sang again. From there they could see Fort Sumner. They made offerings and pleaded with One Standing Inside the Heart (Yá'álníí'neeyąąní).[21] "You are holding the Navajos hostage with your talk, with your mind, with your harsh anger, and by your will." Four things were mentioned. "Our people are imprisoned in your heart, enclosed by a steel door. You will open that door and release our people back to their land," they prayed.

The medicine men arrived at Fort Sumner. Many Goats with White Hair knew about things with sacred power. He applied something to the palm of his hand, then shook hands with his captor and said, "You will release us now, my official, please. We will be free to return to our lands." Black Bushes Going Out was next, then Yellow Forehead, Loud One, Silversmith the Arrow Way, and Ropey. They all applied something to their palms and shook hands with the official.

As soon as they got through, the officer began running around. He started to tremble all over and was hysterical. "Okay, okay, okay. I'll let them go." Then he stopped shaking. He released the people, because he began to suffer. Two days later, they were free. That's what happened. They sang the sacred protection songs as the cavalry escorted them during their migration out of captivity. The people returned to their deserted land, where their homes had been burned to the ground and livestock stolen. They had nothing to return to.

Another event that happened around this time, and which has had an impact on Navajos, occurred with the families, previously mentioned, that lived near Richfield at White-Face Mountain. They owned a round buffalo-hide object decorated with many sacred things. It had four different names: Earth's Protective Shield [invisible], Heaven's Protective Shield, Mountain's Protective Shield, and Water's Protective Shield. These names are in pairs.

This object was magical. With it, a person could travel out-of-body anywhere. It also acted like a protective shield that medicine men used to enter a cave and shake the sacred dust off a bear's back. They would then take it to Black Rock and shake off the sacred dust, then go to Navajo Blanket [by Mexican Hat], said to be a snake, and shake off the sacred dust from its back. The collection of this sacred dust is called Sacred to Carry Around, and all medicine men have it with them. They then took the shield to Green Cattail Flat, where they shook the dust off the lightning's back. This lightning was a bird the size of a mourning dove and very bluish in color. When lightning struck the tree, the bird got caught in the tree bark and remained in it. The medicine men shook the sacred dust off the bird, then let it go. The lightning struck again, picked up the bird, and ascended.

Next, these medicine men went to Rugged Place with Rocks, located on the road southeast of Tuba City, near Coal Mine Mesa. Here there was a hole in the flat ground [Wupatki National Monument?], with a loud stream of pressurized air escaping. The men prayed, and a small, round crystal pebble came out of the hole. This stone was the air, so they shook the sacred dust off it, and the pebble fell back into the hole with a "plop."

The round shield Sacred to Carry Around was never found after it was lost near White-Face Mountain. Yellow Forehead had kept it at his home, but when he heard the people had been released from Fort Sumner and were returning, he went to find where it had been placed, somewhere in this area. Earlier he had left it behind, but no one ever found where the sacred object was hidden.[22] My grandmother, who lived where it was lost, said it was complete, containing the Sun's Roots—the rainbow. This is what she used to tell us long ago.

Following their release, the Navajos moved back to Fort Defiance, Arizona. All of the people hiding in the mountains left their secret places and came to meet them. To this day I wonder why our people moved out of the beautiful mountain lands to be in the Fort Defiance or Gallup area. This is where they reunited with the people from Fort Sumner. From that point on, they mixed in with each other and made homesteads. No one bothered to go back to the mountains, the beautiful land. That is what happened.

The people left Fort Sumner by traveling over the mountains in a narrow file. The medicine men marked a line with a knife, swearing their people would never be treated like that again. They drew a long zigzag line on the ground and set up two posts. The medicine men said, "Our people, the Navajos, shall never come back over this line, ever![23] They will never return to Fort Sumner as long as they live. Inside this boundary is where our people were tortured, butchered, and killed. This is the burial ground of our people, and no one shall return here. If anyone steps across this line, we will be prisoners again. Even in the future, we should never return. If anyone does, our people and their leaders will be in prison for the rest of their lives." Fort Sumner was like a curse. It is all right to go around it, but not within its limits. These were the commitments made by our people, who were told to do this as the medicine men sang their sacred songs and prayers.[24]

Many have returned to that place within recent years. Our Navajo tribal officials from Window Rock made a trip to Fort Sumner.[25] I told them not to, but they went anyway. They went a second time! Look where we are now. Our people are in prisons all over the country, bound by their hands and feet, lying in jail cells that are small—they cry and suffer. It is all because our leaders broke the commitment of the elders who drew the sacred line. Even our former tribal chairman Peter McDonald and his staff took several people back to that place, and now they are in prison. If the officials had not gone back to Sumner, this would not have happened.

So, today, we suffer again in jails for the smallest things. Some of our people are in prisons that are very far away, because they did not listen. This is why the medicine men warned us never to go back. I heard that a group went there again two years ago. They said they were reenacting the Long Walk, and many people went to Fort Sumner to do it. I personally do not think that was right. The medicine men have told the people that if any of them return, the tribal officials or leaders will have a conflict and kill each other. They were never to go back to Fort Sumner, or they would end up in prison. Now that is where they are. Our Navajo Nation officials do not hold office for very long. They come and go. Before the Long Walk, our people were accused of being thieves for stealing from each other and the white man. This became a reality, and they ended up in jail. So, it is true what the medicine men predicted would happen if we returned.

CHAPTER SEVEN

JOHN TEACHES OF THE LAND

American Indians are often popularly featured as the first ecologists. Although some detractors say they were not, few would argue against recognizing their distinct relationship with the land. John explains in this chapter many facets of this relationship from a Navajo perspective. Although the reader must consider the impact of the livestock economy and other intense uses of the land, one must also reflect on the philosophical and religious basis that allowed this use.

Underlying all of John's teachings about the mountains, weather, stars, animals, plants, and places of power, there persists the common thread of religious teachings. In many instances, humans cannot harm the environment as long as they follow the design established by the Holy Beings. Human corruption of nature occurs only when we depart from this well-defined path. Science, of course, with its empirical view, is at odds with this notion. Two different world views provide two different answers to the same question.

John refers primarily to the local landscape. To him, it is a place of power, where he has called upon the spiritual forces that reside there to bless the people who depend on them. The entire landscape is a reminder of humanity's relationship to the Holy Beings, who not only created it but still inhabit every rock, spring, and mesa. This vibrant environment also has its contemporary issues. John is concerned about those who control it when their values are at odds with traditional teachings. His desire is that the next generations apply the spiritual principles that first established the land.[1]

MOUNTAINS

I come from my mother and father, who blessed me with the breath of life. They taught me that I am in charge of my body and spirit. I am in charge of my thoughts, words, and songs. I sing holy and sacred songs that come from deity. I heal with the songs sung by the Holy Beings. My prayers were given by the Holy Beings. All these things are in my charge. I learned them by heart. I have helped many elderly men and women, mothers and fathers, young men and women, and children of all ages with these sacred gifts. I have helped leaders. I have helped the morally afflicted, some who have been to jail. I have helped all who needed it. By the will of the Holy Beings, I am able to serve others in need with prayers and ceremonies.

The land is said to be many buffalo skins of different colors—black, blue, yellow, white, camouflaged, and spotted—that were spread out for us to live on. This is where we live now. According to Monster Slayer and Born for Water (Tó Bájíshchíní), who visited their father, Sun Bearer (Jóhonaa'éí), no enemy shall take these lands away from us. Thus, the mountains are very sacred and holy. It is said that when Monster Slayer went to the heavens to see the sun and moon, he was tested by his father, who mixed up the mountains to see if Monster Slayer really was his son.[2]

Sun Bearer had put the Carrizo Mountains in place of Navajo Mountain; the Jemez Range had been placed in the Naturita Mountains, which had been placed farther north; the Henry Mountains and the Bears Ears were also misplaced. The mountain beyond Lukachukai is called Mountain That Lay Down [Roof Butte Mesa, Arizona] and was switched with Wide Belt Mesa. And many others like Gobernador Knob; Mount Taylor; San Francisco Peaks; La Plata Mountains; Sloping Rim; Sitting in the Midst of Mountains, a peak on the east rim of Black Mesa [Arizona]; White Spruce [Chuska] Mountain; Pollen [Navajo] Mountain; Corn Mountain [Dowa Yalani in McKinley County, New Mexico]; Bluebird Mountain [Cerro Berro, Valencia County, New Mexico]; Yellowbird Mountain; Corn Beetle [Jemez] Mountain; Blue Canyon [near Fort Defiance, Arizona]; Obsidian Mountain; Beautiful Mountain, and many, many more that are in this world. There were twelve different switches or mixing of the mountains in all.

Monster Slayer was quite familiar with the mountains in our area. When Sun Bearer pointed them out, Monster Slayer was able to name all of them, even though they were out of place. This story constitutes some of our sacred prayer songs. The lyrics tell about all of these mountains, in all directions, and from above and below. We make our offerings to them as we travel above or beside them. We pray with corn

Navajo Mountain, with sheep corral in foreground. J.H.: "The mountains are very sacred and holy. It is said that when Monster Slayer went to the heavens to see the sun and moon, he was tested by his father, who mixed up the mountains to see if Monster Slayer really was his son. Sun Bearer had put the Carrizo Mountains in place of Navajo Mountain." (Photo by author)

pollen to the young pine tree that grows on them, asking for good fortune, prosperity, and a safe trip. All these mountains have our people's medicine and herbs, so they are very important.

For example, the La Sal Mountains are sacred and are called Five Mountains, while Blue Mountain is called Furry Mountain. Traditional beliefs say that all the mountains—Black Mountain Sloping Down, or Sleeping Ute; Swirling Mountain [Navajo Blanket, a syncline east of Mexican Hat, Utah]; Black Mesa, near Kayenta; Head-of-Earth Woman [Navajo Mountain]; No Name Mountain [the Henrys]; and the Bears Ears—were gathered together to "make" one mountain, then placed to the north. This is the La Sal Mountains. It has several peaks because it comprises these combined mountains.

From these places, Navajos collect mountain soil, which is kept in bundles by many elders and medicine men. This soil represents and contains wisdom, sound language, sacred songs and prayers, the hogan fire with its fire poker, food, utensils, sacred mixing sticks, the two sacred grinding stones with their brush, the wedding basket, sacred grass brush, sheepskin bedding, valuables, one's spouse and children, livestock, vehicles, money, and whatever else—like saddles, blankets, and bridles—that lie in one's home. Everything good that makes up a person's life is represented in this sacred bundle. It keeps things in order, at peace, and prosperous. People live in harmony with their relatives, friends, and neighbors.

As long as the bundle exists, there will be no needs, because a person will have everything forever. The livestock will remain at home and not wander off. There will always be plenty of food and water, so the animals will not diminish, no matter how many are used for food, sold, or given away. People wonder about this and ask questions, because it does not happen to their livestock. This is why a mountain soil bundle is so very important. It is like holding one's life in one's hands.

Mountain soil bundles encourage unity, but this no longer exists. They kept families together. All of the children with their children would gather at home, even though some of them worked far away among the "enemy" (other races). The bundles maintained a cohesion that we no longer have. Our springs have gone dry, livestock strays and disappears, and families have no desire to return home. Only a few people keep mountain soil bundles, and as I observe, I can tell who does. These bundles have lost their sacredness to our people. When people travel or live beyond the influence of the sacred mountains, problems occur. We have done the forbidden, and now our enemies have crossed over and are on our side of the San Juan River. Some have become our in-laws. This would not have happened if we had kept the law.

The Sunshine Mountain, or Book Cliffs, was named because its ridge has no shadows, is continuous, and the sun shines on it all the time. This mountain is sacred and mentioned in prayers. They say a ridge coming from the Henry Mountains is the male, the Book Cliffs the female, and that their heads meet in the canyons of Price, Utah. The male ridge from the Henry Mountains is very rocky and rugged, while the female Book Cliffs is smooth and straight.

Comb Ridge, which extends south from Monticello, is said to be the backbone of our earth, and Sleeping Ute Mountain its arm. There are many different stories about these things. Some people say it is forbidden to have a ceremony beyond certain boundaries, but my grandfather Metal Teeth taught that was not so. One can perform sings and ceremonies anywhere, anytime in this world, even in China. There are songs pertaining to all walks of life, which he used to sing. Some people say that one should not conduct a ceremony on the far side of Totem Pole Rock [near Paiute Farms], which is also a boundary marker. Others mention that the nine-day Mountainway (Dziłk'ijí) and Enemyway should not be held on the other side of the San Juan River. But there are ways to do it—there are songs and prayers to use in crossing, but those who do not know these songs are afraid to do it.

WEATHER AND MONTHS

The weather has always been important to Navajos. People say that our ceremonies, such as the Yé'ii Bicheii Dance, the Fire Dance (Ił Náshjin), and the Squaw Dance, were to be done completely separate from each other. They should not be sponsored within the same season or even close to each other, just as a mother-in-law should not see her son-in-law, and vice versa. But today, our ceremonies have been combined. For this reason, our seasons have overlapped each other, with summer lasting into Christmas, snow in July, and everything being confused.

The sun and moon have lost their place in their travel from winter to summer, and in-laws no longer hide from each other. This is why our earth and sky, sun and stars, are all mixed too. In the early days, the spring showers went from south to north in an even pattern. It was said that the thunder was on its way to the north to spend the summer. The rains passed through at least four times, bringing forth an abundance of vegetation. Then in the early fall, the thunder headed back to the south to spend its winter. The seasons were beautiful and in order.

January is called Cook the Snow. A story tells how long ago, snow, having the consistency of dry flour, fell from the sky. The people gathered, cooked, and ate it. Coyote came walking by and said, "My, my— my feet are frozen; the snow is cold," so the dry snow turned into frozen water, the way it has been ever since. February is the month of Baby Eagles, and March received its name (Wóózhch'įįd) from the mother eagle's hoarse cry after laying her eggs. Little Leaves [April] is when small flower buds appear upon the bushes, and the baby eagle's growth coincides with the vegetation's development. Then comes Plants Blossom [May], when the eagle's wings start to mature. Next come Planting the Seeds [June] for a garden and Planting the Seeds Bigger [July], when we finish planting. This is followed by Small Thin Leaves of Plants [August], when growth causes them to begin to get bigger, and Big Leaf, or Harvest, Time [September], when we gather corn.

In the fall, we had snow-capped mountains, and that is why October is called Upper Portion, or Back to Back, or Parting of the Seasons. This is when all of the corn turns white, the mountaintops are covered with snow, and vegetation turns red and yellow. During Slender Winds [November], the wind starts to blow, and Big Winds [December] is when they become stronger. There are twelve months total, and they all have sacred songs and prayers. But today, no one seems to know what each name means or represents. Instead, we just have our eyes fixed on our wall calendars. We are about a month behind in time. Fall should have begun with the half moon, but it is still warm. The seasons are misplaced because we have done the forbidden.

When you look at our world today, it seems to be going in the wrong direction and impossible to change for the better. Can these problems be turned around to make it a better place? I often wonder about this. Things are going in the wrong direction because we fail to listen, abide, and obey. No one cares to look at the good ways, and that is what makes it seem impossible. I do not know what will become of this world.

In the time of Monster Slayer and Born for Water, the giants ate little children. Monster Slayer's mother hid the Twins underground and used a thick slab of rock to cover the hole. This is why they were called Raised Underground (Łéyah Nolyání). The Twins were just little boys at this time, so their mother and grandmother took them out only when it was safe. The grandmother would say, "My dear once-in-a-while grandchildren," then hugged and loved them whenever she had the opportunity. So the older boy [Monster Slayer] was named Raised Underground and the younger was named Once-in-a-While Grand-child (Achóóyáázh).

When the Twins became adolescents, they asked their mother, "Who is my father?" She replied, "Sun Bearer is your father, but he is too far away, and it is impossible to get to him." Then the Twins said, "We want to see him." The second child of the two asked, "How was I born?" Changing Woman replied, "I went to the waterfall and 'thought' of a male as the water dripped on my 'privates,' and I became pregnant with you. That is how you came to be." As he grew older, he received the name of Born for Water, or Born by Water. The two monster slayers were sent in different directions: Raised Underground went to the south, and Once-in-a-While Grandchild to the north. That is where the great winds come from. They are of Once-in-a-While and are the tornadoes.[3]

So when a tornado arises, the prayers name Once-in-a-While Grandchild, causing the tornado to return to the heavens. The Navajos will occupy this earth forever and not be destroyed. It is said that Monster Slayer went to the ocean in the east and south; Born for Water went to the west and north. This is why there are tornadoes and hail. These Holy Beings travel or move around in them, but these strong winds hear if one speaks to them.

I told my oldest son about this and taught him how to talk to strong winds before he went on a trip with his family to some mountain caverns. One of my daughters was caring for his house in Kayenta. One day I arrived there just in time to receive his telephone call. He said that his family had barely come out of a cavern when they were told that a tornado was approaching. He described its looks as a yarn spindle. People were panicked, crying and embracing each other. He, too, was frantic and wanted to know what he could say to the wind. I asked if he had his corn pollen, and he said that he did. I told him what to say and do.

He later told me how he had taken his family away from the place, did as instructed with his corn pollen, and instantly the tornado whipped back into the heavens.[4] When he looked up, he could see inside the funnel, which did not come down until it passed over them. "You are right, Father. It is true that it hears and obeys," he said to me. He told that story many times and keeps saying how true our elders were in their beliefs and how our people are protected by Holy Beings.

In the past, the medicine men were very strong doctors. They gathered at different places and taught each other about their sacred songs and prayers. Big Man used to sing the sacred way of the sun and moon. He made replicas of them in ground sandstone. People say that he tried getting a job from the movie company, but John Ford would not hire him. Then he tried getting his horses in the movies, but that also failed.

Big Man, Monument Valley medicine man. J.H.: "In the past, the medicine men were very strong doctors. . . . Big Man used to sing the sacred way of the sun and moon. . . . Even I do not know how or where he learned it, but he was very knowledgeable in controlling the weather." (Photo courtesy of San Juan County Historical Commission)

Then he went to see the manager and two other Navajo men working for him, Frank and Lee Bradley. They met at the main camp, which was situated near the present Monument Valley Airport. He told the manager, "Since you aren't going to hire me, there will be heavy overcast skies for a long time, and you shall lose a lot of money while you are waiting it out. The overcast will remain for one or two months, and you will not be able to complete your filming." He then left.

Soon there was the worst sandstorm, which lasted for a whole week. There were no clouds, but the sand was thick enough to cause blindness. Another week passed without letup. The actors tried riding their horses, but it was impossible. Then the clouds came and lasted close to two months. Finally the movie people asked someone to get Big Man. The film crew hired him and his horses, so he made offerings to the wind, heavens, and rain. Sure enough, the next day brought sunshine, and the filming resumed. Even I do not know how or where he learned it, but he was very knowledgeable in controlling the weather.[5]

Snow falls quite a bit in the area from the surrounding hills to Train Rock Mesa. It snowed like that last winter, laying down a blanket of deep snow right here. When one looked toward Monument Valley and Gouldings, there were only small patches of solitary snow here and there, and all the rest was clear. We also had a big hailstorm last summer, but it poured rain and hail only here. The place where we were going to plant our cornfield was flooded with water. We requested a tractor, to plow before planting the corn and melons. There was plenty to eat at harvest time, with all kinds of corn foods.

THE HEAVENS

The stars are also important and have their own laws and rules, similar to our planet Earth.[6] In the beginning, humans were created, and then the stars. As the stars were evolving, they became hairy, with long tails. Next, the humans developed in the same way, but most of their hair was removed, except for on the tops of their heads, eyebrows, eyelashes, and a few other parts of the body. The stars were implanted into some of these bodies, and their tails were trimmed, while others were not. Including the Earth, there were four stars created that, with others, took their orderly position in the sky.

By these stars one knows of the time. For instance, one tells each day that it is dawn, others indicate the months, others the year, spring and summer, fall and winter. That is how we know the time from day to day, month to month, year to year, and season to season. These stars follow a special pattern every day of the year. Some stars were made just like our Earth. One of the four stars does not leave; it is constant, fixed.

The stars received names: The Pleiades; First Slim One [Orion]; Pinching, Fighting Stars [Aldebaran and the lower branch of Hyades]; Man with Spread Legs [Corvus and Orion]; Rabbit Tracks [tail of Scorpius]; Revolving Ones [Ursa Major and Cassiopeia]; and Big Star [morning star]. While Big Star was being created, he wanted some people on his planet, too. All these stars were being fixed—some had their tails cut short, some had medium-length tails, and others did not have their tails cut at all. Then suddenly Coyote showed up. "Why don't you just do this," he said, and threw the rest of the stars into the sky without names or shape. They were randomly scattered about, putting an end to the plan.

Old Metal Teeth used to tell me how the Dippers were used in our sacred prayers. They are called the Female Revolver [Cassiopeia] and the Male Revolver [Big Dipper and Ursa Major].[7] So is the group of seven stars: Pleiades, First Slim One, Man with Spread Legs, First Big One, Awaits the Dawn [Milky Way], Rabbit Tracks, and Big Dark Stars, which are in line—Big Blue Star, Big Yellow Star, Big White Star, and Big Silver Star, the one we live on. That's how each one of these stars is named in our prayers. They are a prayer in themselves, too. There is also a Blessingway song for each one.

The elders speak of a time during this creative process when the Holy Beings were trying to figure out a way to keep the Earth going. "How shall we do this; what kind of air should we use?" they asked each other. But they had no answers. Among them sat Coyote. "Well, what about you, Coyote? What do you think?" Without hesitation, but with intense excitement, he jumped up and danced around. "How about that! How about that! I'm glad you asked me, my fellow men, because it is possible to make a Holy Wind for the Earth. It can be done! In this direction, I shall make the Earth turn with the white Holy Wind [east]; and in this direction [south], I will use blue Holy Wind; and this way [west], the yellow Holy Wind; and that way [north], the black

Holy Wind. In the middle will be the sacred heat wave, where they will all meet. Then in the heavens will sit the fixed star at my nose tip. This star will not go anywhere but will remain in one position and only rotate. It will turn as a sacred spindle stick, with my nose resting on this star as my axis." To this day, his "nose" is still against the star. The Star That Does Not Move [the North Star] still stays in the middle of the heavens and rotates in a circular, clockwise direction. That is where Coyote's nose is. The rest of the Earth spins around it like a sacred spindle stick, while the coyote maintains our Earth and keeps it turning. It is said that he will very likely drop the Earth, and that will be the end of it as we know it and the start of a new beginning. In spite of this knowledge, we tend to curse Coyote when we say, "That ghost! He stole from me!"[8] This is a teaching that our forefathers told.

PLACES OF POWER

The land is also filled with power and holiness. There are many sacred sites, one of which is the San Juan River. We sprinkle corn pollen upon each crossing, coming or going. Our ancestors used to do that whenever they forded the river with their horses. They treated the Little Colorado River the same. The Colorado is a female and the San Juan a male river. Both are considered very holy and sacred. They come face to face in a kissing position below Navajo Mountain. Just above their union sits Rainbow Bridge.[9] This rainbow is what they breathe through to live, but now the dam has been built, and water covers them.

When I was a little boy, my family used to live at a place called White Streak of Cattail Coming Out, where there are some really jagged rocks that stick straight up. If a person gets on top of these jagged rocks, he will see a lake. It starts making loud noises and creates large waves that go crashing out to the edge. These rocks usually have a cloud above them, which brings a lot of rain. One day when I was older, it rained really hard, filling the lake until it overflowed. That night a big river of floodwater went by our home at Between the Rocks. The wash beside our home emptied into where the San Juan River and Navajo Blanket meet. We could hear the cattle bellowing down toward Mexican Hat. The people said it could have been some other living creatures that were swept from the lake to the river and back to where they belonged.

Ever since this happened, the cloud never forms, and it does not rain. Things like this happen mysteriously, and that is why I think there must be something very sacred there.

Our great men used to give offerings to all the mesas and mountains around here, which made these places holy and sacred. I noticed these things and wondered about them. Even right here where I live, I can sometimes hear the wind blowing, with sounds down underground, and then it rains or the wind blows. I sometimes think, "Let it rain," and it does. It is strange, but this is the holiness of the place. This is what I know about the sacred places. They are holy.

There are also many stories about the rock formations in the Valley of the Gods. It is said that at one time, these figures were alive but turned to stone. Some were Holy Beings, while others were saddles turned to stone and a decoration. The same thing happened to many of the formations in Monument Valley. They used to be saddles, horses with wagons, and some ceremonial items, which still stand erect among our mesas. Some of them were bonded with the Daily Sunrise Earth, but they have since turned to stone.

The name of the place along the road south of Valley of the Gods is called Pipe Springs, Glass Rock, and Moving to Get Together. The water there is pretty salty. People say that long ago, when Navajo men went hunting, they used to gather there before they moved toward the Bears Ears and Cedar Mesa to hunt. One group would show up, and later another, and another, until everyone who was going to go hunting arrived. They camped there, and so that is why it is called Moving to Get Together. Usually they called the gathering place Pipe Springs, or Glass Rock. There is also a wash that comes down from the Bears Ears called Hanging Meat, because returning hunters would see the animals killed by other hunting groups.

ANIMALS AND HUNTING

During the time of Creation, our mother, White Shell Woman (Yoołgai Asdzáán), or Changing Woman, provided different sectors of life. She created sheep, horses, and their kind to the south. In the center were fish and their kind. Then to the north were deer, elk, moose, buffalo, and their kind. She created all these things for the human race. These wild animals still maintain their cycle, or lifestyle, as they were first taught. For instance, the deer and its family reproduce at the right season. Humans do not see it taking place, because the Holy Beings control the deer. How is this possible? No one knows. Scientists probably wonder about these things too. It is hard to believe how these bucks are naturally separated from the females, then reunited when the time is right.[10] But animals under human control have lost their way. Even our goats mate in mid-summer, at the wrong time and season. They have gone crazy just like humans.

Wild animals communicate in a sacred way. Before the hunters leave at dawn, they pack their guns and speak to the Holy Beings, like Talking God, asking for a big deer to kill that day. Talking God owns all these wild animals, so one has to ask before an animal can be killed. Black God and Talking God rule over these particular animals. They provide the deer just as a person would give you his or her sheep. That is why we have to be very careful how we butcher and fix the meat. Once a hunter kills a deer, he has to release its spirit back to the "owners," so it can form into another deer. This continues forever, so deer will never become extinct.

Hunting is sacred, so hunters treat deer with respect. A man should sing the hunting song when he hunts all kinds of wild animals. After killing a deer, its head is pointed toward home. Once its intestines have been removed, we place them back inside the cavity as they were. Our elders used to say that once this was done, it would transform into another deer, which could be killed again. This was a sacred belief that our ancestors practiced and taught on their hunting trips.

When the meat was cut into pieces, the bones were cleaned of everything but left unbroken and set aside. It was hung and dried, then shared evenly among all the hunters present. None of the meat was wasted but only cut into pieces as small as dried apricots. The group's leader divided the piled meat on a blanket and sprinkled it with corn pollen from west to east and back to the west, then from the south to north and back to the south. Over the entire pile he sang a song. Next, he thoroughly mixed the meat, put it in bags, loaded it on horses, and the hunters left for home. It was forbidden to cross the San Juan River if the skin and legs of the deer had not been removed. Not even two deer ribs were to remain connected before the crossing. That is how our forefathers used to hunt.

Hunters packing deerskins. J.H.: "Hunting is sacred, so hunters treat deer with respect. A man should sing the hunting song when he hunts all kinds of wild animals." (Photo NAU.PH.86.1.64, Cline Library Special Collections and Archives, Northern Arizona University)

They taught that if these rules were broken, many foreign people would cross into Navajo lands, take them over without hesitation, and become in-laws, mixing the races. This includes foreigners from Asia and Russia [Red Coats], our enemies. Our own people will start fighting among themselves and kill each other, as it happened a few years ago when our youth killed those policemen.[11] Evidently, this is what has happened. Our ancestors were afraid to break any sacred hunting rituals, but these days, hunters bring their deer across still in one piece, with the skin on.

Our ancestors were right; we should not have broken the sacredness of hunting and corrupted our society because of our ignorant mistakes. We have truly broken many of the forbidden rules. Today, nobody cares how they hunt, and so many things have gone wrong. It is obvious that this is where it all started, so that now it is as if a dam broke and many problems have been turned loose.

Today's hunting policies have been corrupted too. Our people from the Navajo Nation have had problems with the authorities concerning our hunting rules. The rangers [game wardens] lie just so that they can get money through fines. After the season is over, hunters stand in line to pay off their fines and get back their confiscated guns, while the meat they hunted rots in dumps. That is how our people are being mistreated. It has gotten as bad as our educational system.

I was involved in a hunting incident with my son during the fall of 1990. He and his companions killed and butchered a deer. They tagged the meat as required, but two rangers came by, confiscated their guns, and gave them a citation. My son and I and our translator went to court in Monticello, where we met the newly elected councilman from Montezuma Creek and a white man who must have been the attorney's assistant. The judge told us to pay $350 for the guns. When we asked about the meat, he said it had been taken to the dump. I flatly refused to pay the fee and demanded further investigation into the matter. I wanted to get to the root of the problem by letting it go to the Supreme Court in Washington. The court officials in Monticello backed off, agreeing to let me carry this on to the higher courts. We planned to take the translator and attorney's assistant as well as hiring three attorneys to help us. These men investigated all our records—those in the Monticello court and the laws and regulations in Washington.

From what I understand, our people have always had the right to hunt these animals for food.[12] The deer are free and belong to us. The lawyers wrote this statement down, then asked what else they might say for me in Washington. I replied that if these hunting rights were not permitted for our people, then the animals would become extinct before too long. This would be our defense. I then presented my side of the case by explaining the situation, all of which was written down. I requested they take photos of the wasted meat in the dump and on the mountain where dead does and fawns and bucks, minus their antlers, were left behind, strewn here and there. Every fall, approximately 70,000 foreign hunters are allowed to invade these lands. Talk about extinction—they certainly would be the ones to cause it.

The lawyers recorded this information to take to Washington. Last winter, when we were to go, we got snowed in at our winter camp and could not travel. The government held the proceedings anyway, and the court decided in our favor. Our local chapter supported us, and we received $10,000 from Window Rock to take care of the attorneys' fees. The last we heard, the government said our people could hunt free from the middle of Blue Mountain to the east side of the Henry Mountains. They told my son to hunt for free in this area, but so far he has not. The important part of this ordeal is that this case has now led to free hunting in the entire state of Utah for all our people.[13]

Ever since the government in Washington intervened in our people's affairs, they have asked us about what we used for food. We told them deer, elk, antelope, mountain sheep, buffalo, moose, rabbits, prairie dogs, rats, horses, sheep, goats, cattle, donkeys, and mules. This was our meat. Corn, pumpkins, watermelons, cantaloupes, peaches, apples, sumac berries, grass seeds, juniper berries, wild onions, potatoes, and a variety of grass plants were also recorded as our food in the past. Interviewers asked again, "What do you live in?" We responded, "Wood hogans are made of logs and also serve as the main frame of our summer shelters." "What is your source of healing and medicine?" "Herbs of all sorts, different trees, and berries are used in ceremonies and drunk for medicine to cure sickness." This has all been recorded by the government, but no one cares to ask about it, so it is left as it is.

The land provides other foods. Long ago, people used to hunt jackrabbits. "Let's chase some jackrabbits, so it'll rain," they said.[14] Men would fetch and saddle their horses and make stick clubs. Then they paired off on their horses and started looking for rabbits. Once they spotted one, the wild ride in a cloud of dust began. They chased a rabbit until they clubbed it down or the animal outran them. In the cool evening, the hunters rode home with rabbits dangling on the sides of their saddles. When they arrived, they built a huge fire, warmed the ground beneath, then buried and cooked the rabbits.

There were other animals important as food for the Navajo. I have never heard of anyone eating beaver, but I do know they ate porcupine and bobcat. They ate bobcats when there was a drought or starvation. People also ate mountain sheep, whose flesh is similar to deer and serves as a medicine, too. When a person gets injured, the healer puts this on him. Sand is gathered from the spot where the mountain sheep's horn touched the ground and surrounding plants. Herbs gathered there are called Plants around It. The vegetation and soil are gathered with sacred pollen, songs, and prayers to use in ceremonies like the Enemyway. Participants put it on the Mud Dancers (Chaaszhiní), the men who come before the dance.

These Mud Dancers wear nothing but loincloths and run and catch people to throw into a handmade mud pit.[15] They grab even the largest, toughest, meanest fighters and throw them into the mud. The men do not feel any pain when they are hit or fall. They are holy and part of the beginning Enemyway ritual. If a person does not want to be thrown into the mud, he needs to give them a cigarette. The ritual itself is a healing ceremony that makes one immune to sickness. This is one way the horn of the mountain sheep is used.[16]

It is also a medicine for a person who is mentally ill, loses his mind, and goes crazy with rage in sudden outbursts of anger. The medicine man burns the horn as incense to calm the person, who is healed and walks away without anger. Sheep are cured if they are sick or something is bothering them. Part of the horn is burned, and the animals are herded around in the smoke.

PLANTS AND HERBS

I have also been involved with sacred herbs. In the past, we were never diagnosed with diabetes, cancer, or arthritis. We did not have much of this sickness, but there were herbal medicines to be used as a cure if we did. An herb used to induce vomiting was used to clean out the body and rid it of impurities. These impurities included things like bile fluids, ash-colored substances, burntlike blood, blood clots, and worms. With all these types of impurities in the body, people feel ill, irritated, mad, and unhappy, so they cuss others and are dissatisfied with themselves and their surroundings. Once you partake of this herb and purify your body, you will be happy and able to think clearly to plan good things for the future. There will be plenty of food, and you will be satisfied with yourself and your life.

If you remain sick and full of impurities, you will be lazy and irritable. All you will want to do is sleep, so you will lie around and become antisocial. My grandfather had this herbal medicine all the time, and I used it often. I have not used it recently, and so that is probably why I feel irritable sometimes. This is how Grandfather taught me as I followed him everywhere.

Navajos used other herbs and natural foods. Some of the plants we collected included wild celery [*Cymopterus fendleri*], little onions, sumac

Mud Dancers at an Enemyway Ceremony, 1938. J.H.: "Mud Dancers wear nothing but loincloths and run and catch people to throw into a handmade mud pit. . . . They are holy and part of the beginning Enemyway ritual." (Photo 14475, used by permission, Utah State Historical Society, all rights reserved)

berries, rabbit thorn, small potatoes, and juniper berry seeds. People used to move around gathering juniper berries. There were wide cactus berries that we gathered from Black Mesa. These were cut, dried, and ground to mix with cornmeal mush. It was good. There was another type of cactus that grew around El Capitan that was nice and round and very sweet—sweeter than other cactus berries. People gathered them in buckets after removing their thorns. Wild spinach had to be picked early, then boiled immediately before eating or it became bitter. When prepared properly, it tasted good. Wild spinach and rhubarb provided dye for wool too. People moved everywhere in search of many types of plants for food and other uses.

There are many medicinal herbs for all sorts of ailments. For instance, sagebrush and pine-pitch resin can be used together. They are boiled and mixed with grease and can then be applied to the whole body.

Sweat baths were accompanied with drinking herbal potions. These were used whenever someone was sick, or for small children when they had measles or pox. For injuries, like a pulled muscle, sustained from lifting heavy objects, Navajos used the sacred Lifeway Plants. The patient drank this medicine. Pregnant women used another herb called Baby's Placentaway, which was boiled. The expectant mother drank it, then jogged or rode a horse to exercise. When her time came for delivery, she had no difficulty. In fact, the baby might come as she was walking.

For those who experience illnesses due to nightmares, sleep walking, and so forth, there is the Evilway Plant, also known as the Devil or Ghost Plant. There is also a medicine called That Which Is Caused by the Lightningway, used for head illnesses in the eyes or colds and allergies. And for internal ailments, such as gallstones, there is another herb. When the patient drinks it, the stones dissolve and pass from the body. If a person suffers from appendicitis, he drinks an herb that melts away the growth until it is gone. There were many plant medicines used by our people, who knew of their value.

Charcoal was used when a child or adult burned his or her feet, hands, or body. This special charcoal is made from the bark that the Holy Being Fire Dancers throw to the crowd.[17] The Fire Dancers cover themselves with charcoal or ash just before they dance. While they are performing, they throw this tree bark, called "rock bark," to the people. The bark is then burned again for ashes so that its charcoal can be used for burns. When it is applied to a burn, it dries and heals the blisters or sore, preventing further infection. The charcoal is also made from foxtail grass or snakeweed and is used as the charcoal in the Evilway.

A couple of years ago, a white woman from Washington brought her children to visit me. She had been here before with another group. I did the Charcoalway Ceremony (T'eeshjí) on her and her two daughters and later received a letter from them, telling me how they had been cured of their nightmares from the day that I helped them. These are the two main ways charcoal medicine is used.

I found out that modern white man's medicine does not cure any animal's sickness. The son of the late Joe Beletso lived in the Montezuma Creek–Hatch area. One time, he had a lot of cattle that became sick. He tried to heal them with modern medicine and had the veterinarian from Cortez treat them, but it did not work. He then went to a

Woman collecting herbs. J.H.: "Navajos used . . . many medicinal herbs for all sorts of ailments." (Photo NH 4-20, Milton Snow Collection, Navajo Nation Museum)

hand trembler, who referred him to me. "Please, help me, my little brother," he said. "Who is trying to beat you up?" I asked.[18] He replied, "My cattle are sick." "I don't know; do what you need to," I said. "No, please. I need your help." So we left for his home, and on our way, I made some herbal medicine from plants on the mesas, then went to the cattle. I told him, "You can give me cows as payment for this healing ritual," which he agreed to do. I mixed the herbs, added water, and mixed the medicine some more. The cattle were in the nearby desert, the calves standing by their sick mothers, which were lying down with their noses on the ground. "They've been like that for three, four, five days now. I don't think there's any hope. I've had three different doctors out here to help me, but the animals have gotten worse," he said.

I put several drops of the herbal mixture into their mouths, treating at least twenty sick cows lying around. There were others still staggering about, so we treated them. We blew sacred smoke on all of them, ended with a prayer, and went back to his home to eat. I saw a wire corral that had maybe seven cows standing inside. This was a portable fence that can be put up anywhere. After we ate, we went back to the corral and were astonished to find that the sick cows had returned home and were standing around the fence with their calves. We gathered them into the corral and once again sprinkled medicinal herbs on them, ran them through the sacred smoke, and had another healing prayer. Before too long they looked good and were well.

Another time, a short man called Black Hair, who lived on the other side of the mountain, asked me to come to his rescue because his cattle had been sick for several days. A young bull that he kept by his home was so ill it would not drink any water. I had the man hold the bull's head up so that I could give it some herbal medicine. I also treated some cattle lying sick out in the field. After treating the little bull, we went inside to eat. There was a young boy, chubby and short, who kept going outside to check on the animals. He ran inside, shouting, "The little bull is trying to get up, Father!" "That's impossible. That bull was ready to die!" his father replied. The boy kept going in and out. "There he goes down the hill to the corral!" he cried. "You're kidding! My goodness! I see it!" said the father, as the little bull trotted down the hill to the other cows.

The man could not believe what he saw, but he believed that the medicinal herbs and prayers were true, because they had healed his cattle. "Here I spent a lot of money for modern medicine and doctors. I could have done this to begin with!" he said. We gathered the cattle and treated them with more herbs, smoke, and prayers. They got well. I have done this type of medicinal treatment and prayers for livestock, including sheep, for many people in the past and have also performed it for people who are distraught, mentally ill, or angry. This medicine works.

PLACE NAMES

During the summer, when I was a child, our home was a tent and a circle of sagebrush that served as a windbreak. Back in those days, all families used to move around a lot. We lived alongside Comb Ridge at a place called Soft Ground Water. We also lived down by Very Rocky Ground, and just below that at Red Sand Rocks, at Little Coyote, at the Cotton-wood Tree, at Black Streak down the Rock, then at the base of Douglas

Mesa at a place called Wind Blowing around the Rock, and at Water Streaming from the Top. We lived in all these places. We searched for good grazing land, and when we learned where there was an abundance of vegetation, we moved to that pasture for the sheep. This was the main purpose for traveling around so much. "It rained over there, and there's plenty of vegetation; let's move there." Then in the winter, "The vegetation has not been touched over there; it is fresh. Let's move there." We moved everywhere, never staying in one place.

The land was filled with Navajo names. One place was called Silhouette of Person beneath the Rock along Comb Ridge. This came from a crevice that runs down the mesa. When someone went up or down it, the person would see his or her shadow or silhouette against the rock. As we moved from Where the Rocks Came Ashore [near Lake Powell], down by Paiute Farms, we headed east through Water under the Cottonwood Tree (the mesa south of Train Rock), Sitting Red Mesa, Owl Springs (that received its name from the owls hooting at night), then down into the valley on the northeast side of the Monuments of Monument Valley to Salty Water Spring, then White Tipped Mountain, and on to Wind Blowing Downward off the Rock, then to Wind Blowing through the Rock, and Canyon of Trees, and Road Coming Up. When we got to Wind Blowing through the Rock, we had to shear the sheep because it was nearly summer.

Other places around Road Coming Up are Mister San Juan River's Water; Rocks Fallen Down; Pointed Rocks Coming Up; Creviced Rock; Crooked Road; Between the Rocks; Beneath the Rock; Willow Springs; Swinging around the Rock; Water That Boils Out; Pointed Rough Rock; Black Spot on the Rock; Jagged Rocks; and Hole in the Rock. These were all landmarks or geographical names of the places where we moved in and around the VCA valley area. Near Train Rock are places called Red Strip of Sand, Scattered Little Juniper Trees, Water under the Cottonwood Tree, Red Hill, Stumped Ears, Salty Water, and Sitting Red Object.

There were also many water holes that the Navajos used. For instance, Bullsnake Spring in the Sand is located north of Totem Pole Rock in Monument Valley, and farther down the wash is Dune, or Sand, Springs. Where the Sheep Drowned is found in the farthest canyon of Mystery Valley, located southeast of Promise Rock. There were some deep and steep water holes there. They say one winter, when the water froze, some sheep got on top of the ice to drink. Since they were all standing on one side, the sheet of ice flipped over, spilling them into the water, then trapping and killing them. One spring was named Buffalo Skin in the Water because the moss growing on the ledges under the water looked curly and dark like buffalo hair. Near another spring called Mourning Dove Spring was a place called Hanging Paiute. This got its name because Paiutes used to pick berries off the trees there. One of them jumped off a branch, got his shirt caught on a limb, and hung there for some time.

A formation of black rocks near the VCA mine is called Rocks [volcanic] of Hunger for Meat. They were named that because when people grazed their flocks in the area, the sheep would not get fat enough to butcher. The land is harsh in this place. Just on the other side of that group of rocks is a place called Bent-Over Cottonwood Tree, located down in the wash.

Below my home near Train Rock is a wide open area called Red Meadow. On the northern side of this area is a catch basin with trees at a place called Stump Ears. It got its name from a spotted horse with short ears that used to go there to drink. Beyond that is Downward-Sloped Red Meadow, and across from it, Among Young Juniper Trees. Rough Red Rock Bluff acts like a mountain. Sometimes at night one hears a roar inside, making the sound of gushing water. This noise occurs when the wind is going to blow or when it is going to rain. Sure enough, it happens.

The name of an area northeast of Train Rock is Stones in a Line to the Top. This is where I lived with my older sister, my aunt, and her husband. The sheep corral was against the cliff. I was about thirteen years old when I lived there, and this is where I used to begin to run long distances. The name of the land next to Oljato Mesa is Downward-Sloped Red Meadow. On top it is flat and wide. My father and his father lived there. Other names associated with this formation are Twisted Rock and Road over the Rock, which has a horse trail going up the canyon. Nearby is Eagle's Home, and behind it is Far Corner, and behind that is Standing Oak Tree.

The rocks around Eagle Mesa have sacred teachings, as do Train Rock and Totem Pole down in the valley. The monument of the Bear and the Rabbit is also sacred. The bear is really a coyote, not a bear.

Hogan ring of John's home at Stones in a Line to the Top. J.H.: "The name of an area northeast of Train Rock is Stones in a Line to the Top. . . . I was about thirteen years old when I lived there, and this is where I used to begin to run long distances." (Photo by author)

Legend says that the coyote did not have ears at that time, and that he caught the rabbit for a meal. "I will eat you," said the coyote. "Wait. Let's talk first," pleaded the rabbit. "The Navajos usually wrap their arrows around their bow before eating," said the rabbit, as he pressed his hands and arms against the coyote's chest. Then they suddenly changed into rocks.

The coyote's ears used to be shaped like a bear's ears long ago and were not pointed like they are today. There is a story that tells how this change came about. One day, the coyote crept up on a sleeping bobcat. He pushed in the bobcat's nose and chopped off its tail to a length where it could not move anymore. Later, when the bobcat found the coyote asleep, he crept up to him and pulled his nose and ears very hard. The coyote awoke, but his ears were pointed. Stagecoach Mesa, next to the earless coyote and rabbit, was said to be the spectators watching what went on between these two, but they were also changed into rocks. All are sacred. If there is a drought, one can place corn pollen at these mesas and they will bring rain. El Capitan near Kayenta is also said to be either a coyote or a bear. I don't know which.

Approximately thirty years ago, Train Rock seemed to always have rain around it. A small cloud would gather just above the formation, and it would rain all the time in a little area surrounding the mesa. I had noticed it was this way for about thirty years. Then one day it rained, and a huge slab of rock slid down on the west side facing Oljato. A man named Gray Whiskers, my grandfather by clan from the southern end of Monument Valley, was asked to make a special prayer offering at this site. So he performed the offering, but there has been no rain ever since, and we do not know why.

Then about twenty years ago, there was another rock slide. This time it was toward my home. I went up there and gave the sacred offerings. I took a jug of water, which had a mixture of water from the ocean, sacred mountains, and local springs.[19] With this water, I "cooled" the area of the rock slide, prayed that the rain cloud would reappear, because it had been gone for so many years, and that it would rain again like it did long ago. The next day was the fair in Monticello, held in mid-summer. My oldest son, Albert, and I went to the fair and played cards with the Utes. He said, "I think it's raining at home in Oljato."

We left for Monument Valley after dark. There still was no rain in Monticello; however, as we got closer to home, we saw it had been raining here. We were just east of Train Rock when we noticed that the red sand was wet and muddy, and before we knew it, we were stuck in a large puddle. Gradually, we backed out of it by shoving brush under the tires, then took another route on sandy soil to get back home. It had rained really hard, and water was everywhere.

I recall seeing a little cloud above the Bears Ears while we were driving to Monticello that morning. I guess it moved to Train Rock that afternoon, but only a narrow strip of rain had fallen, all the way from the Bears Ears to Train Rock. People said the cloud dissolved there. Now it remains there, and each time the cloud forms, it rains. People often ask why it rains only on Train Rock. Teddy Holiday, from Douglas Mesa, asked me once, "Why are you getting all the rain? You're the only one who will survive for sure!" "I don't know," I said, "It's the rock that's getting blessed from above, not me." "But you're the only one to get all the rain! It's your fault." "You should learn the rain ceremony," I said. He did not answer and just walked away. That is how mesas are; they are naturally blessed.

Eagle Mesa is called Water Basket Sits.[20] People say there is a male hogan on top of it. A while back, when I used to live within view, we used to see moving lights on top. I do not know which direction the lights went down the mesa, and I do not know who it was. The rock standing by itself beside Eagle Mesa is the Key, and the one behind it that looks like a sitting bird is called Turkey [Setting Hen]. It was said to be a live turkey before it turned to rock. The red hill next to it is Porcupine, which also was alive but turned to stone. The three rocks [Big Indian] pointing up are people who came down from the top of the mesa [Sentinel] and were sitting together visiting when they turned to stone. If a person looks at it from a different angle, it appears to be a jackrabbit's head with three ears. That is why it is named Jack, or Big, Rabbit. Next to it is a formation [Castle Butte] named after the Featherway, Wide Wood, and next to that is another rock named after the Featherway.

Just above the Monument Valley High School is a formation named Rock Blocking the Way because it is in front of the two other rocks. It is a gate that protects the Oljato Mesa and other formations to the west. Husky Standing Rock [Mitchell Butte] is said to be where Talking God lives. He comes out at dawn to pray and bless all the rocks and mesas. It is a sacred place.

The mesa across from El Capitan is Changing Woman [Owl Rock].[21] If people observe closely, they will see her gray and red flared skirt, with white-soled moccasins sticking out from under her dress. A legend says that she was angry, sat down, and turned into a rock.

Nearby is a black jagged rock—these are two horny toads lying crisscrossed. It is said that Thunder is the ruler of all things. He tied these two toads with curled blades of grass, then another Holy Being finished by tying them to a bush. They were bound for twelve days, then released after pleading for their freedom. The other gray hills below that are two female toads lying face down. Farther down the road sits Turtle Rock, showing a turtle that has just left his home of piled rocks on the other side of the road. People placed their offerings there for rain. Nearby was a natural spring at Water under the Cottonwood Tree, but the water has since been covered. The water used to bubble up from the ground, but now it is pumped from the well. This was also a sacred place for offerings.

Near Much Fur, or Much Wool [El Capitan], people used to tan antelope and deerskins.[22] There was a lot of fur around the area, and so that is how it got its name. People were very scared of the fur, because they did not want the sheep to wander into the area, and they did not want people to urinate at that place, because it would get them sick, and they would not be able to relieve themselves.[23]

Coyote Rock [Chaistla Butte] has its head in the clouds, just as Winged Rock [Shiprock] sticks into the clouds. The legend says that when everything was scary, and monsters were around, the female bird called Rock Killer (Tsénináháleehii) sat on that rock and the male bird sat on Shiprock.[24] That is what those rocks were made for. There is an old trail along the ridge from there to Upward Golden Meadow [Dennehotso], to Pointing Rock [Rock Point], then down to Growth of White Reed [Lukachukai], and over to Winged Rock [Shiprock].

Merritt Butte is called Poking [Standing] Rock. The rock sticking up nearby is Desert Weasel, and next to that is a snake that was also sticking his head up and turned to stone. The weasel put his hands together, and that is how he was turned into a rock. There is a legend about this area that a long time ago everything was very small. That is when all these things happened. This entire area was once underwater, but it went away little by little. These were the only rocks above the water. Then the gods blew on this region to make it really wide. That is when these rocks and everything became big. Even the people became big people, tall people. The water ran out and made big canyons.

The Three Sisters formation is a lady walking toward us with her two children, while the rock that is in front is a man with a cane leading them. Right by Wide Rock Butte, or Holding Things like a Bowl [Rain God Mesa], are three standing rocks that are gods to whom the people pray.[25] Nearby is Tracks of Sheep Leading Down. The people used to water their sheep at a place called Bullsnake Spring in the Sand.

These rocks that are in a circle were a hogan.[26] In the middle there was a fire [the Hub]. One can see the remains have turned to stone. The pile of sand is there to make sand paintings at a No Sleep Ceremony

Left Handed Many Goats's hogan, with Three Sisters in background. J.H.: "The Three Sisters formation is a lady walking toward us with her two children. . . . The younger generation does not realize the sacredness of these stories." (Photo 19665, used by permission, Utah State Historical Society, all rights reserved)

(Doo Iighaashjí). The rocks that are sticking up in the middle of the flat were buffalo who turned to stone, some big and some small.

About five years ago, a medicine man from the valley came to visit me. He said, "We never have rain, we are experiencing drought, and the wind continues to blow for many days." We did not go directly to a water hole to give the offering but took the sacred materials to Totem Pole Rock in the valley, where we asked for rain in all four directions. As we returned home in his pickup truck, the rain came, and there were flash floods everywhere. It was pouring, and the washes filled with water. The rain started coming again to this area after that. It was truly a sacred and holy blessing. If these holy places are destroyed, then I do not know what will happen. They are sacred, so that when we lack rain, we can place our offerings there.

The rocks around Water in the Sand are said to be people standing near a hogan with a fire.[27] Nearby are the Yé'ii, who dance at dawn, and these people are watching them dance. They sing making the sound, "O hoo woo ho, I hii yee he." In the distance is Woman Holding the Baby. The rock that is near her side is the Water Sprinkler [clown].[28] He has the hide of a coyote. The rock sticking out in front of them is a traditional whistle, and the other rocks are more people standing and watching the dance, while the round ones [on the side of the mesa] are their heads. That is what I was told.

The younger generation does not realize the sacredness of these stories. When I start telling them, they begin telling their own stories and mock mine. There are Navajo people who live around here who do not know the traditional stories about these rocks and mesas. The old people who lived here knew, however, like Bitter Water, He Who Starts to Jog (Haalwo'ii), and Mister Lefty. These are the elders who have lived here. Today's generation does not know about the old stories. They only listen and do not know what to do with them. They only see the place, live there, and do not preserve the beauty of it.

The big hogan located by the road in the park is where two or three families lived even before there was a road there. They shared space and food and did not fight but lived peacefully. It first belonged to Mister Lefty, who was called that because he did things with his left hand. He was not a medicine man, but he probably knew about medicine man things. He had a lot of children whose last name is Cly, and he now has many generations of both paternal and maternal grandchildren. After he left, his son-in-law His Big Son Adopted (Hastiintso Biye' Íłʼíní) took the hogan.

In those days people did not claim ownership of the land or hogans. Whoever was moving to the area for the season and found the hogan empty got to live in it. People would say so-and-so is now living in the hogan. They were kind and considerate of each other. Back then they used to say, "Go ahead and bring your sheep and let them graze anywhere you can find good grazing area. There is water for your sheep." They never turned anyone away. The people were afraid to claim any piece of land, because they believed that when one died, the place where he or she was buried became his or her land. For this reason the people did not claim ownership, and one never said "my land." But

now everybody says this and is stingy and protective. As soon as someone argues about owning the land, it is for sure that not too many days
will pass before the person dies. It happens every time. So I believe
those old wise people and never say "my land."

Gray Whiskers used to move around this whole valley near White-
Tipped Mountain. There used to be a lot of wild horses there, and each
stallion had his own herd. Some were white, some were red, and some
were black. There were other herds of horses with black manes, golden
horses, yellow ones, pintos, and roan. Occasionally, the people rounded
them up. Some horses were butchered for meat, and others were tamed
for riding.

CURRENT CONCERNS

Today our land is overcrowded with tourists, and the movie outfits
secretly do their filming in our area. They are guarded by the police,
who keep the complainers, even those who live a few feet away, from
them. None of us gets paid for their use of our land, which is not good.
In earlier times, our elders were always in charge of such events, but
today it is not that way. The movie outfit informs our local people that
they have already paid the tribe in Window Rock, but we do not hear
anything from our chapter officials about how the money was used. In
fact, no one tells us about an upcoming movie. We no longer have the
rights to our land and are being trampled by everyone. Our forefathers
were quite stern, never letting any white men move in as they wished.
They must have had closer connections with the government, but
today we are not as close. We are in a difficult period and continue in
that direction.

Several years ago, during Chairman Paul Jones's (Big Lawyer's,
Agha' Hwidiit'aahii Tso) term, I was invited to join a crew of surveyors
to search across the land from the San Juan River to the Bears Ears and
Blue Mountain, to the La Plata Mountains and Uncompahgre Plateau
[Colorado], as well as Ute Mountain to the Book Cliffs, and as far south
as Mount Taylor.[29] We surveyed this entire area. During this process,
we sawed down hogans, sheep corrals, and sweat lodges; dug up some
graves; and found weaving spindles. We went all over and found evidence of what used to belong to the Navajos. This area truly was part

Old Navajo forked-pole hogan dating to about 1850, located along Alkali Wash, a tributary of Upper Montezuma Creek, San Juan County, Utah (April 1953). J.H.: "We went all over and found evidence of what used to belong to the Navajos. This area truly was part of our land." (Photo 20321, used by permission, Utah State Historical Society, all rights reserved)

of our land. Paul Jones almost succeeded in regaining this land for the tribe. In fact, it was surveyed three times, and I was taken along as a guide. We also surveyed the river canyon where Lake Powell now sits.

Paul Jones sent these survey results to the Washington office, which were later returned to the Denver office, with the agreement that the land belonged to our people. Next, this paper work went to Window Rock and our new chairman, Raymond Nakai. He was supposed to sign the agreement and send it back to Washington, but he sent it back without a signature. This was another scandal; we were cheated out of our land. This caused a commotion on our reservation lands.

The Utah Navajos requested that the oil royalties generated in this part of the reservation be sent to the Salt Lake office, and not to Window Rock, for safekeeping.[30] The tribe asked for sixty cents from each dollar. This agreement fell through, and the survey land results were sent back without the proper signatures.

Welfare assistance for the needy people in Utah has been switched back and forth between the state and our tribal government. We have suffered because of all these problems, and the royalties of 37.5 percent that belong to our people have either been misused or disappeared. Our local chapter requested some money from this fund for future plans; our people approved this plan, but by the time it got back to the Salt Lake office, the plans had changed to benefit other people and counties, and none of it came back to us. We were cheated again and have not made any progress regarding these funds.

I also do not like what the Navajo Tribal Park is doing. Our chapter officials and tribal representatives initiated the plans for this park.[31] They negotiated these plans under the table, taking sides opposite our people. The local people were shut out of the discussions and had no say. These secret negotiations have totally blocked our chapter officials' future plans on many things. The land now belongs to the government and the tribe. A lot of money is made in the park, but residents feel they do not get any and that nothing can be done.

Some people say the government does not do anything for us, but I say it does, because I see the government helping a lot of people. I see young pregnant mothers receive assistance with food to keep them healthy, and the money continues when their babies are born. There are funds that provide food stamps, as well as help with firewood, coal, and housing. The government assists with many things. I feel that we cannot say anything against the government, because the money made at the visitors' center goes back to the government, which helps us. That is my understanding of our government money.

Still, the sacred places have been trampled, and no one speaks up for them. Even if someone did protest, the opponents always say they are abiding by the laws. For some reason, our best-educated people agree with them and do not speak against them. I am sure there are other alternatives, but they do not look into them. There is nothing; it is hopeless. If only I could speak and understand English. Although I have to use an interpreter to communicate, I sometimes ponder a problem until I get it right, especially if it does not make sense.

I'm steadfast and observant. I might not go places or participate in planning activities, but I know what goes on. Even though I am uneducated and do not understand the English language, it is still obvious to me.

CHAPTER EIGHT

A CHANGING WORLD

When one considers the dramatic changes in traditional Navajo culture that John has witnessed during his lifetime, it seems appropriate to have a chapter dedicated to his understanding of these phenomena. Since the introduction of the first car to the shifting moral values and increased discipline problems of today, Navajos have been catapulted into issues that challenge the teachings of the elders. Even the stars in the heavens and the seasons of the earth have changed because of these differences.

At the core of the issues lies the discipline of the younger generation. John may prefer the view of the "good old days," but he worries about today's youth, who seem utterly bereft of traditional values. Discipline is at the core of what must be restored. Snow baths, long runs, application of the whip, respect for elders, proper dress, and rekindled work values—these are the things that provide self-esteem. People with a more modern perspective may cry child abuse or brutality in restoring discipline. John, however, is reacting from a life of experience, in which lack of self-control could result in death. His childhood and early adult years testify to that.

So where does one turn? John realizes that the clock cannot be wound backward, and that there are no easy answers. These current problems were prophesied at an earlier time, when medicine men taught of the earth in its final stages before a millennial-type change. This will be discussed in the following chapter. In the meantime, John believes that adherence to traditional values is the only safeguard against contemporary problems.

TECHNOLOGY

I was about five or six years old but can clearly remember the day I saw my first car. We were living by a totem pole–shaped rock at a place called Logs, or Objects, That Floated Ashore. This is a place on the way to Lake Powell, about six miles above Paiute Farms. There is a wash in the direction of the lake that, when it rains hard, fills with water, carrying large tree stumps and debris to a big curve in the wash bed. There, the water deposits materials on the banks. It was late afternoon when a few family members and I spotted some objects slowly moving along the rock beds. There used to be a camp farther down, where white men panned for gold or other valuable minerals. We named that camp Group of Tents, and this was where the objects were heading.

These cars looked very fragile, with spoke wheels similar to those of a wagon. The people called these first cars One That Sniffs Around, Nose to the Ground, or Smoky Butt. Later they were called "chidí," then "chogi," the name changing several different times.[1] People made songs for them: "The sniffer, the sniffer, I have made you a part of my mind; the sniffer, the sniffer, I am riding you."

My father was familiar with automobiles, because he had taken some white men down to the mining camp before and had seen autos elsewhere. They used to ship the panned gold by wagon to the old trading post that sat on a hill above the Oljato Reservoir. The traders Old John [Wetherill] and Slim Woman (Asdzáánts'ósí) [Louisa] used to do it. A man named Old Charles shipped the gold by wagon to Flagstaff, Farmington, and Gallup, to a white man named Big Mexican. It is from these bigger towns that the automobiles came, ending up on the wagon trails to the tent camp. One day father came home saying, "A thing called 'chidí' came to our area today. It runs on its own." I do not recall anyone being afraid of these automobiles. Father rode in them and told us how fast they went on smooth surfaces.

My grandfather Metal Teeth was one of the first Navajos in this area to own an automobile. The next person was Long Hill (Holk'idnii) from Dennehotso, a man from Kayenta named Man's Car (Hastiin Bichidí), and then Lee Bradley's father, Red Mustache, a white man from Kayenta. He brought many automobiles back to sell. Our local traders from Oljato,

An early car on the road leading to Mexican Hat, Utah, by the San Juan River, in the 1920s. J.H.: "The first type of car was like a wagon covered with a tent. Grandfather used to bring it here on his visits, and it was pretty fast. . . . We had no highways, only dirt roads." (Photo C-526, used by permission, Utah State Historical Society, all rights reserved)

John and his wife, also introduced automobiles into our area. Many others with cars followed after that.

The first type of car was like a wagon covered with a tent. Grandfather used to bring it here on his visits, and it was pretty fast. Two years later, he brought a truck. They called it Big Little Car, because they said it was big but without much room compared to a wagon. He packed the back with his belongings and cranked in the front to start it. The gas tank was by the front window, and a tall pipe stuck up in the front so that water could be poured in. It had other odds and ends all over. My older brother drove it around, and Grandfather would yell after him not to ruin it. There were only two or three electrical lines in it, which seems like nothing compared to today's cars. But it sure had power to run!

We had no highways, only dirt roads. I am not sure where people got gas, but it was probably from Gallup, because I have heard stories from others regarding this. People used to say it was quite dangerous to travel through Chinle, because some of the residents were bandits who chased a driver down on their horses and turned the car over.

My grandfather and Long Hill went on a trip to Gallup. They bought a small barrel full of gasoline from Big Mexican's store but accidentally lost it on the return trip. Long Hill had purchased some whiskey, buying two small barrels and four one-gallon jugs. In those days, people used to haul liquor from there to sell here. When Grandfather and Long Hill were passing through Chinle, they were attacked, just as they were about to run out of gas. The bandits were coming closer and closer when Grandfather remembered the whiskey. He quickly grabbed the bottles and poured the whiskey into the gas tank, and sure enough, they were able to escape, making it home to Dennehotso. They learned that whiskey works just as well as gasoline. So, I suppose if one knew how to make whiskey, he would also know how to make gasoline.

There are Navajo teachings about how a car works. This vehicle is very much like a horse, operating on the same principles. The automobile is considered more "intelligent," and we think of it in such terms. The automobile is made of iron and steel taken from the earth. This iron is the earth's spirit, which has been made into the body of the automobile. The trees, as vegetation, were also taken from the earth and made into rubber for the tires. The air, or spirit, is the same as that of a horse's breath of life, instilled in its body. The arms and legs of the auto make it move. Then there are the dark storm clouds and heavenly bodies like lightning, which are found inside the auto to give it power. This is exactly the same power the horse has.

Water, which comes from the earth, is put into the auto for its cooling system. Oil from the earth is similar to the fat from the earth a horse receives. Just as gasoline comes from the earth as fuel, plants are in a horse's body to make it operate. Therefore, horses and cars are the same in every way. Even the battery fluid comes from the heavens as an electricity maker. Humans possess that same lightning, or electricity, in their hearts to keep alive.

When one buys a new automobile, it is treated like a horse. The sacred horse song (łį́į' biyiin) is sung while one sprinkles corn pollen on it. We pray for its safety and for its productive use. We also pray that envious people will not do harm to it in any way. Every human is born with this ugly envy, or jealousy. Some people are worse than others and want to bring harm through these feelings. For all these reasons, one should always do a sacred ritual for a vehicle; never leave it undone. At the end of the ceremony, the mirage, or heat wave, is applied to the automobile. This is for its endurance and protection for as long as it is used. This song or ritual can be used for other things with the same results.

The feathers that hang from the rearview mirror are for speed and endurance on long trips. Some people will have sacred miniature bundles tied inside their autos. These will contain shake-offs from various sacred birds and creatures.[2] It is made from the horse's body dust and saliva; shake-offs from the rainbow; shake-offs from hummingbirds and small swallows that swoop down above the water; shake-offs from the gray bird that sits on the sheep's back or is found around homes; and shake-offs from the horny toad. These are all in the miniature bundles. Some people carefully fix these, but others do it any old way. In the olden days, people used to tie these bundles and feathers to their horses' tails. We do not know these things unless we ask about them.

As with cars and horses, lightning and electricity in our homes share similarities. Both are dangerous and harmful, but if a person has sacred corn pollen and prayers, he or she will not be injured. Electricity can hear and obey what one says and is like what I have described with an automobile. Electricity and air work sacredly together through corn pollen. A person can have his or her home blessed and a prayer performed to keep things safe. This includes the use of electricity.

I saw my first airplane at the airstrip at Goulding's Trading Post, when I was a man, but it was many years later before I was offered a ride in one. Several of us were invited, but the others were scared to try, so I went alone. We flew above Navajo Mountain and the San Juan River. The pilot told me to grasp one of the two control sticks, pull on it, and look down. It was quite an experience. I looked down at the landscape and bushes, a mass of dark colors all around. We flew some more, then came back to the airstrip. "It feels good," I told the others. The only scary part was descending to land. The sudden motion nearly took out my insides and breath. Back then, the planes were not equipped with all the modern comforts, so it was rough.

First airplane to land at Flagstaff, Arizona (1920s). J.H.: "I saw my first airplane at the airstrip at Goulding's Trading Post, when I was a man, but it was many years later before I was offered a ride in one." (Photo AHS.0003.00154, Cline Library Special Collections and Archives, Northern Arizona University)

UTES AND PAIUTES

The Navajos in Monument Valley say that the Utes and Paiutes in this area used to live north at Kanab [Flat Place with Willows Going Down]. Some migrated toward Richfield, some to the Uintahs, and others on the north side of Navajo Mountain. The latter moved east, making temporary camps on Douglas Mesa for two years before going on to Bluff City, where they split with one group, moving to Allen Canyon, and the other to Sleeping Ute Mountain.[3]

Randolph Benally, Navajo Oshley's father-in-law, married a Paiute woman, and Oshley later married a daughter from this marriage, making his wife half Navajo and half Paiute. Some Paiutes, like Joe Deal and many of his sisters, lived at the southern base of Douglas Mesa but have since moved away. They claimed to belong only to the Red-Running-into-the-Water Clan and to be separate from the Navajos. They are descendants of a Paiute named Dying of Thirst (Dibáá' Daatsaah), or I Am Working on the House (Hooghan Binaanish), also known as Posey.[4]

He received his name when he helped to build a white man's home at Willow Tree Flats. Posey would say in Ute, "I am working on the house." Later, he killed a white man in Bluff, and ran away toward Allen Canyon and the Bears Ears, but was killed in the area Navajos now call I Am Working on the House Lying Down.[5] They say he was a warrior who could shoot well. Little Rabbit (Gah Yáázh) and Wooden Foot (Tsin Bikee'ii) were also from that family and were Ute.

Another Ute named Labee had children who were Paiute, and people used to tease him a lot. My uncle Bitter Water People [clan name] married Woman Who Became Fat Again from that family. She was a sister to Weaver and Ugly Gay Person (Náádlééhii Níchxǫǫ'ii). My uncle, who belonged to the Bitter Water Clan, married his daughter and moved to the side of Black Mesa where his children and grandchildren now live.

There were a lot of the Red-Running-into-the-Water People scattered about. They came from a band that migrated from west of Kaibeto, southwest of Page, Arizona, where there are sand dunes and oak brush. These Paiutes moved through Navajo Mountain to Paiute Farms and the San Juan River. I do not know how long they lived there, but they later moved nearby, where there are many trees in a cluster. They got exposed to some warfare chemicals that killed many of them.[6] World War I was going on when they died, and many of them are still probably buried there. The survivors moved to the base of Douglas Mesa at Sitting Separate, where there was a spring. About that time, the state surveyors came through, giving them land allotments in that area. They then moved to Bluff and the sagebrush canyons close by, where they lived for several years. This was around the time that Posey got into the fight [1923] with the Mormons, and the trading post in Bluff burned.

The Utes who lived by Douglas Mesa claimed to be Red-Running-into-the-Water Clan. One Who Did It belonged to this clan. One day he was at Ute Mountain, also called Black Mountain Sloping Down, and asked the Utes for one of their daughters in marriage. He brought her back and raised her. The family told the Ute girl that she was now from this clan since they raised her. She did not understand the Navajo language, but she learned, and as years passed, became known as Woman Who Understands (Asdzáán Adiits'a'í) because she learned Navajo. Her children were Woman Heat, Black Rock, and Black Rock's Sister (Tsézhin Bilah).

Several generations passed, and they all married Navajos, some of whom were from this area. Mister Katso, known as Water Trough, married into that family, as did Mister Át'íinii, from the Reed People Clan. Spring under the Cottonwood was also a Ute from that family and is my wife's father. He had many sisters, maybe ten all together. Some of them married into the Many Goats Clan. Spring under the Cottonwood and How Great (Dooládó') were brothers.[7] How Great used to go looking for his horses by Douglas Mesa, and one day he came upon some Ute girls. He chased one of them and made her his wife. How Great had a child and was expecting another when the Utes moved away to Blanding. Both children were boys. One was Teddy Holiday's grandfather, and both boys kept in touch even after they moved away. His marriage did not work well because of the distance, so his family told him to marry a Navajo named Laughing Woman (Asdzáán Anáádlohó).

The Utes became a part of several different clans, depending on who raised them or whom they were born for. Some became Ute and Red-Running-into-the-Water Clan, raised by the Tobacco People Clan (Naat'ohnii Táchii'nii), while others were raised by Gray Rabbit Running into the Red Water (Gahłibáhii Táchii'nii). These people went their separate ways but are descendants of the two boys by How Great. That's what they told us.

UTE GAMBLING AND TRADING

My paternal grandfather Big Man told a story about several Navajo men who went to the Ute camp to play cards. The Utes were real gamblers. Big Man, One Who Did It, Red Rock Spring, Tall Man, Cold One (Sik'aazí), Cottonwood Coming Down, Pine Tree, and my father took wool, rugs, and hides—sheep, goat, cow, and horse—with them to the Bluff City Trading Post. Upon arrival, they started gambling with the Utes and played and played until the Utes beat them. The Navajos had given away all they had, including their saddles and whatever they had bought from the store that day. They had nothing left.

A person named Continuous Hills (Woolk'idnii), a large man with big scary eyes, joined the group of Navajos but later walked away from the camp to the gray hill that is now the Bluff gravel yard.[8] He hiked up to a big flat white rock that used to lie on the side of the gray hill and took a shot at it at close range. He went back to camp and told the men what he had done, then the group returned to the trading post to see if they could get the trader to help them with their plan.

The Navajos challenged the Utes to a shooting match. The Utes picked their best shot, Posey, saying, "He's the greatest." Everyone agreed to use the big white rock as the target. "We'll see who shoots the rock," they said. "You can't miss!" The Utes brought all they had won from the Navajos and more, including tanned hides and deerskin dresses, fancy beaded items, gloves, concho belts, and many other valuable things. Winner takes all was agreed upon, and they began shooting.

One of the Navajos went first, raised his rifle, and shot without really aiming, but the men shouted, "Yes, he hit the target! We can see the smoke rising from the rock! Sure, we all can see it!" The agreement was that they had to shoot the rock right in the middle, and the Navajo men agreed that it was right in the middle! Then it was Posey's turn. He shot and the bullet hit the dirt right next to the rock, with dust spraying into the air. Then two men got on their horses to check the target. "He sure did hit the rock in the middle," they shouted. The Navajo man had won the challenge; the Utes had lost! The Navajos took all the valuable items and stayed a little longer to gamble, and this time they won.

There are a lot of other funny stories, some of which I have heard from friends, and some of which I have seen. I went to Blue House (Kindootł'izh) [Towaoc] one time to watch the Navajos play cards with the Utes.[9] Chee Billie was sitting in the game, dealing out his cards, when he leaned forward to put his card on the table. A Ute lady, Marie, sat beside him. Chee reached again, leaning forward, and Marie remarked, "My, my, Chee Billie, you sure have a hot groin! I'm just giving my cards away to you!" Chee seemed uneasy and scooted over to sit closer to where I was, as he tried to think of what to say back. Finally, he responded, "I wonder who was the first to be her husband? Who was her first?" Marie replied, "It was you, you, you. It was in Allen Canyon, when I was a young girl.[10] Another girl and I were riding a white horse across the creek when you jumped us and fell into the creek." Chee retorted, "That's a lie; it's not true." "Yes, it is," and pointing to me she said, "John knows that too." I replied, "No, I don't," but everyone chimed in loudly, "Well, then, you men [Chee and I] will need to pay your dues!" They were all speaking loudly. Chee gave

Gamblers playing cards. J.H.: "I went to Blue House [Towaoc] one time to watch the Navajos play cards with the Utes." (Photo SM 54627a, Milton Snow Collection, Navajo Nation Museum)

himself away by saying the wrong thing, and we ended up paying our dues. People laughed about it. They are funny when they get together, and there are always things to laugh about.

Long ago, my grandfather (by clan) was married to my mother, who had remarried. His name was Man between the Rocks, and they both worked for the white traders in Kayenta, John and Louisa Wetherill. My parents used to dig pottery shards and Anasazi bones in the hills by Kayenta, then take them to the traders. My mother carried around two big buckets, and once they were full, she'd take them in. They did this for work, and that is what killed my grandfather—the Anasazi.[11] He went to a Squaw Dance one day and suddenly collapsed and died. Handling Anasazi things is dangerous and killed him. The same thing bothered my mother, who fainted quite often. I did an Evilway Ceremony on her and she got better. In fact, she lived to be 120 or so. Eventually, she just ripened, then fell apart because she was too old.

We used to pick pinyon nuts during the fall and take them to Blanding to sell to the traders. On our way back, we went via Allen Canyon to visit the Ute village, because they would have a dance or some activity at that time of year. The weather was different back then. The Bear Dance was done in the winter, when it was snowy and cold, but now, they do it in the heat of summer.[12] Back then, snow fell in the mountains during September and October, and it was cold. The weather has changed drastically. For instance, it is now winter, and it is still warm, and we will not have winter weather until after mid-winter through to July. The seasons have changed places. It is even hard to plant a garden because it will freeze. People cannot do the Squaw Dance Ceremony [a summer ritual] because it is usually still cold in the summer. The nine-day ceremonies, usually held in the fall, start while it is still warm. Now, Squaw Dances [Enemyway] are done until Christmas, because spring is more like winter. These ceremonies are supposed to be done only in summer. The nine-day ceremonies were held in September and October, but now it is too warm. Squaw Dances are performed only during the hot months, and it is forbidden for them "to see" the nine-day ceremonies. Their relationship is like in-laws; they are not coordinated anymore according to the position of stars like the Big Dipper and others. It has all been mixed together. You hear of a Squaw Dance at one place and a nine-day ceremony going on at another house nearby. It is all done wrong. The in-laws have been mixed together. This is true also of the sacred prayers and songs that we once kept distinctly separate.

SHOE GAME

The shoe game was a really fun activity. Legend says it began long before the Navajos were here. The Holy Beings created the game when they bet about darkness and daylight. The shoe game songs will never cease, but if they do, the end of time will have come, and we will be in another world. We have to keep them going.

People usually have these games at ceremonies or family gatherings. Friends and neighbors also come to the shoe game. The participants prepare a bundle of yucca needles, a yucca ball, a bat, the shoes, and a blanket or rug curtain to hide behind when placing the token in a shoe.[13] There is also a token that is black on one side and white on the other. The players toss this in the air, and the two teams have to guess on which side it will land. Some say, "White! White!" If the white side lands facing up, the team plays on the south side, and if black, on the north. As the game starts, the players spread a blanket and put in what they want to bet. In the past, there were no nickels, dimes, quarters, or dollars, so people put in valuable things like knives, bridles, and whips, but after several games, would start betting goats and sheep.

The game begins with seven songs. The first one is the shoe song, then the yucca ball token, then the yucca needles, bat, curtain, tossing the coin—about seven all together—and ends with the dawn song. Many were sung describing the losers and winners of the game—the birds, bears, and animals. One song describes how daylight came before the bear reached the mountains. These songs are sung in groups of four or seven verses, with other verses in between. There were enough songs to sing a complete ceremony. I learned them from my grandfather and used to know them all.

Long ago, when we lived at my grandmother's home at White Streak of Cattail Coming Out, people came from all around to play the shoe game. They played it at Woman Who Became Fat Again's hogan and small house where she lived. The people alternated where they played between her house and that of Fuzzy Face, depending on who won. One night they were having the shoe game at her home, and each time her team won, she acted funny. Fuzzy Face, who was playing on the opposite team, could not guess which shoe contained the token and lost the bets. He accused the other side of cheating as he searched, on his hands and knees, for the token in the shoes. Woman Who Became Fat Again grabbed the long flashlight and poked him in the buttocks and made sounds like a male donkey. Just to be funny, he threw up his head and pretended to be a female donkey. The people tried to pull them apart as they laughed about their craziness. People used to do silly things like that just to make others laugh.

When the road off Comb Ridge (Blasted-Down Road) was being built, we lived in several homes below the construction site. My brother-in-law Oshley, San Juan, and other men were employed with the construction crew. One morning, my sister butchered a sheep and asked me to take some mutton to the workers, about eight miles away. I set out with my backpack full of meat and added two jackrabbits I killed in the sagebrush along the way. I walked to the jobsite and arrived by late afternoon. The men were happy to see all the meat. "Let's cook these fat rabbits underground," they said.

It was winter, and the people were having a shoe game that night. By evening I did not feel well because of the chills, so I curled up and slept as the shoe game went on. When the players noticed I was sick, they suggested a sing on me with the shoe game, which is considered a sacred ritual.[14] Each time they found the winning token, a man named Mon Chico, from Dennehotso, massaged me. He died many years ago from alcohol at Water Frozen to the Ground, by Pipe Sticking Out. He was quite a character, very humorous. He's the one who cured my sickness. He would get me up and massage my body, and before long, I felt better and forgot how sick I was. It worked—the sacred shoe game ritual actually healed me.

GAMBLING AND A FIGHT

One day, I set traps for some badgers, caught two, and skinned them. I took one of the skins to the Dennehotso Trading Post, where I bought some scarves that were very popular at the time, and a leather belt. The next day I took the sheep out to pasture to a big rock mesa that had a small pond on top, called San Juan River's Spring. I took my traps and a pair of wire cutters and began looking for badger tracks on my way to the pond. While I was there, Chee Billie came by. He wanted to play cards with me, so I agreed, but he beat me at five-card poker every time. He took my scarf, leather belt, the remaining badger skin, my dog, and the wire cutters—everything I had! I argued with him about the game and got mad. "That's not fair," I said. "Give me back my belongings!" He refused and was about to leave when we got into a wrestling match. During the fight, he managed to get one of my scarves around my neck and choked me until I passed out. There we were on top of this great big rock, with a long drop to the bottom.

After several minutes, I revived and looked around, but Chee Billie had left. I jumped up, looked over the edge, and saw him walking down the trail, carrying all my goods. I was still furious and threw rocks down on him as he dodged about. The mesa was smooth, and he had no place to hide for safety. "Give me back my things or I'll push this big boulder on you!" I threatened as I set my foot on a large rock. "Please, little brother, don't do that," he pleaded, laying down my belt, wire cutter, badger skin, and dog. I waited for him to descend from the rock and walk away before I retrieved my possessions and continued to look for badger tracks.

Badger skins had a number of different uses. People sold them for food and supplies. The badger's penis was mixed with herbs as a drink to cure a man's impotency, so that he could have an erection. I do not know if this worked. People say that it was possible for a 100-year-old man to father children. One Who Did It was about 110 years old when he had his sons, Kitsii and John Yazzie Atene, and Sam Chee's wife. He was an old man, but he still was able to have children by a very young girl. He died of old age when the ripened flesh fell off him.

DISCIPLINE AND WORK

Long ago, the Navajos lived only in hogans, called Stacked Wood or Pointed toward Each Other, which were covered with sand.[15] For firewood, people gathered dried branches from bushes and trees. They pulled and broke them by hand, because they had no axes, then carried them home on their backs. That is how I first remember it being done when I was small. We also used donkeys to haul our wood, placing two bundles on both sides, then another bundle in the middle, making it a large load. Food was pretty scarce. We had small portions for our meals. There was very little of anything, and no sugar or coffee.

Our daily activity was to herd sheep, so adults asked children politely only one time. "Please, my baby, herd the sheep"; "Please, baby, bring back some wood"; "Please, my baby, bring back a pail of water." We had to hand-carry two large buckets to get water. When living near Train Rock, I walked long, long distances to fetch water at places like Under-the-Rock-Ledge Spring or Stumped Ears. Sometimes I tripped and fell, spilling the bucket of water, when only a short distance from home! That was so hard, because I had to walk back to the spring and start over again.

My grandmother raised me, and that is how she asked me to do chores. If I did not move, she whipped me. "I've asked you nicely before; I guess this is how you want it," she said as she whipped me with anything—a whip, a stick, or even the fire poker.[16] It was harsh, and I cried, running to get the water or haul the wood. When I returned, she would run to me and give me a hug, saying, "My dearly beloved baby, I don't whip you out of hatred. I do it because I love you. This whip, the one I spanked you with, is embedded with a lot of good wisdom, excellent teachings, a good life, wealth—beautiful horses, cattle, sheep, donkeys, mules, goats, money, and jewelry. That is what is inside this whip. There is no hate. You will benefit from it throughout your entire life. It will keep you healthy and strong, and you will avoid illness such as colds and flu, hunger and poverty. You will be free from these trials, so that is why I do this to you, my baby."

Then she would take me in her arms, hug me, and say, "My dearest baby, this is what I want for you, and you shall live by what that whip represents. It holds prayers, songs, and respect. It will help you to live and dwell among your people with great dignity and pride." This was her way of teaching. She never left me wounded but always came back to lecture. My grandmother was right, and so was my big sister, because they raised me.

There were other requests by my parents and grandparents backed by the silent whip. "Go after the sheep; chop the wood; haul the wood; hoe the weeds; plant the seeds [there were so many chores], but whatever and however you do it, I have asked you politely with love the first time. My first request was gentle, and I called you my son, my baby, do this or that, but you failed to act or do the chore; therefore, you'd rather respond through the whip. Is this how you want it to be?" That was usually enough to get me running, with my backbone curled inward, to get the job done.

One day, I got a whipping with a branch of sagebrush by San Juan River. It was freshly cut, had spikes, and really hurt as it was laid on my legs and buttocks. I never knew the reason for the whipping, since I had just come home from herding. I had not done anything wrong, so it was for no reason. After that painful lashing, he lectured me. "The elders say the whip or a folded horse rope holds valuable treasures and teachings. It does not contain hunger, poverty, covetousness, or envy. It does not contain suffering and has nothing bad in it. Someday in your future, you will have learned something valuable from this, my little brother," he said. "You will have endurance in your mind and body, mentally and physically, and you will be strong. I am spanking you with all these good things, which are in your future. You will have big cornfields and work hard plowing and planting your crops and hoeing the weeds. You will not be lazy. That is why I did that to you."

But I was in pain from all the thorns stuck in my legs and backside. Grandmother cried as she removed the prickers with a safety pin, and I felt the pain. If this happened to a child today, San Juan would be in prison for abuse. But when I think back on it, I am actually glad it happened; it was a worthy lesson and has done me good.

Another time, San Juan whipped me with a rope. He said, "This is not hatred. It is for your own good, my little brother. You will someday use these teachings to live a good life. It will keep you healthy and strong, and you might become a medicine man, receiving the blessings of learning, the sacred songs and prayers, to help relieve the suffering of sick men, women, and children, from infants to adolescents. You will save them from suffering. That is why I do this, so that you can understand and perform the people's healing process. Once you do, the earth, the entire world, and everything on its surface changes. You will learn the sacred prayers and songs to make it a better place to live and to protect the earth against anything that will harm it. These sacred songs and prayers will nourish it for the goodness of life. You will pray and receive from the higher power these blessings. This is all within the whip that I use to help my little brother, because I love you."

When I was about nine years old and living at a winter camp, San Juan chased us out of bed at dawn and told us to run. He was stern with children and chastened us a lot. As time went on, the weather got colder, and winter set in. There was a reservoir not far from our home, so he told me and Oshley to run and take a dip in the frozen ice water. Both of these men ran ahead of me to the pond, broke the ice, then jumped in with a splash. I was right behind them, an experience I will never forget. We swam around in the icy water for a while, but it felt more like hot water the longer we stayed in. Once we got out, it felt really cold. We had to pull off our loincloths or else they would freeze against our skin and force us to walk with our legs spread apart.

Another thing San Juan did was throw me under tree branches covered with heavy snow. The dry snow was the worst because it was very cold. He would shake and break the branches of the tree, laden with what was called top snow. When it fell on me, it felt like being hit with a rock or a hard slap on the back that really hurt. I wanted to fall down on my face from the torture. But he said it was for our own good and would give us discipline and endurance. "If you don't survive this, you'll be easy to sidetrack and fall prey to the bad things in life. I am not mad at you or hate you. What you learn will benefit your life. There are many things out there that will harm you, even kill you, if you are not careful. They are like sharp teeth, gnashing together, waiting for a victim. If you train your body and mind by swimming through icy water, having snow baths, and running, you will be strong enough to overcome all obstacles and live to an old age. It is out of love, not hate, and is for your own good. You will build a strong mind and body that can withstand all trials. That is why you do these things, my little brother," San Juan would say. He lectured me in all that I did.

My childhood was pretty harsh. We did not have much to eat, so I was given one small piece of bread, which was to last me all day as I herded sheep. Sometimes, when they butchered a sheep, they would hurry and singe the lungs while it was still raw inside and throw it to us—one lung for me and the other for my big sister—then send us after the flock. We wished they had left the windpipe on the lung too, but they made sure they took it. My upbringing was nothing but hardship. That's how it was.

This way of teaching makes a lot of sense, especially when I look back and realize how it has affected my life. I have endured thus far and been successful in my livelihood. Just as I learned through the silent whip, I have lived as my elders taught me, with dignity and pride to share with men, women, and children.

I raised my nephew John Yazzie Holiday, who now resides in Shiprock, in the same way. I used to carry him piggyback after the sheep, and later we would run together after them. I also used to put him on top of an untamed horse that bucked him until he fell. At first, he kept tumbling off, but the more he rode, the better he became. That is how I raised him, and now he holds a steady job as a police officer, which is

Child herding sheep. J.H.: "My childhood was pretty harsh. We did not have much to eat, so I was given one small piece of bread, which was to last me all day as I herded sheep." (Photo NAU.PH.413.150, Cline Library Special Collections and Archives, Northern Arizona University)

quite strenuous for most people, but he is doing well. It is true what our elders said: "One has to teach and train oneself to be mentally and physically ready to face difficulties in life."

Those who have never experienced these types of ordeals struggle. They do not own a decent home, so they live in other people's houses or are homeless. When you compare these two types of people, the ones who are disciplined are the ones making it in this world. People often ask, "How did you manage to accomplish so much in life, in spite of your lack of education? How did you have so many children who are well educated, have their own homes and good jobs? What did you teach them? Is it because of your sacred songs and prayers? And how did you get all your valuable belongings?" I tell them, "I'm not sure how it all happened. All I know is that life goes on each day, and I get up and face the challenges with a positive attitude and am strong in enduring hardships."

If you are mad or sad, cuss or are irritable, and do not listen to others, you will have a bad time with yourself and those around you. People hate to be near those who are irritated. One cannot be happy with himself or others if he has a negative attitude. That is what I tell my children, and it is true. In life there are sheep in the corral, a cornfield, horses, and cattle. There is wood to be cut and a fire to be built, but once you get old, there is no one around to help you take care of these things.

As an elderly person, it becomes more and more difficult to do even the simplest chores, like building a fire. One cannot even get up off the floor because of weakness. There are grown children and grandsons and granddaughters that you watch come and go, but they are always busy with their own business. You ask them to help, but they have excuses. "Can you feed the sheep dogs or chase the sheep out to pasture for just a few minutes?" "Can you split the logs of wood and bring in some coal for the stove? Will you bring it inside and stack it neatly in the corner, so then all I have to do is crawl in there and put it in the stove?" "The horses have gone astray for quite some time now. Why don't you go find them and bring them back and give them some hay so they'll remember their home?"

"No, I can't. I have to go. I'll be late. The clock is ticking; I have to go now." That is their reply.

"Why don't you go and gather up the cattle and let them stay in the corral for tonight?"

"I'm going somewhere. I'll be late." This is how our children respond, and they do not help us. "This man is mean!" they say, when all you are asking for is help. "The corn needs water. Go haul some and give each corn stalk a bucket of water, so it will grow big and we can eat it this summer. We'll make kneel-down bread and have a feast."

"I'm going somewhere."

"There are weeds. Can you hoe the weeds, my children, please?"

"We're going somewhere." Nothing. They do not help. This is how it is when you get old and are no longer able to care for your livelihood. It seems hopeless when you are helpless. Everything seems impossible.

When I was still young, healthy, and strong, I had several cornfields at different locations. I cared for them all by myself. There was no irrigation, because there was no water available, so I took a shovel and made small shallow ditches several feet apart all the way down the cornfield, so that I could water it. I did this for several days until finished, then hauled water in a bucket to each hole all the way around. I did this for each section until completed, then let it stand for two or three days, the water soaking into the ground. Next, I planted the field, row by row. As I watched everyone else go about their business, I did not ask for help. Occasionally someone volunteered to assist. That is how it was back then. Today, it is impossible for anyone to plant like that. They just are not capable of doing it.

When the corn grew, I watered it again a few more times. By the time it was big, the rain started, and everything grew until ripe. One year, the melons were big like boulders and just as heavy. It took two boys to carry one from the cornfield. They told me, "Why don't you take it to the Shiprock Fair? You'll win a prize! These melons are huge."

I used to get soil and mulch from the banks of the San Juan River, below Navajo Blanket in Mexican Hat. I put some of this soil with seeds in each hole and covered it with wet dirt. The melons and squash grew big, and at harvest time, the people feasted. This was in my younger days, but now, it is just wishful thinking. I remember those times, but I now feel like a prisoner because of my ailments. There is no freedom or activity, and the chores or responsibilities are left undone because of sickness and old age.

When a person grows up having horses, cattle, sheep, goats, donkeys, mules, and cornfields, it becomes an important part of life. They still are for me, and it is hard to be without them. When there are none, I am afraid. "What will happen to me if they are gone?" This is a frightening feeling. Horses, good fat horses, show they have been taken care of. One also wonders where the cattle are, if they are thirsty and all right. I wish I could ride my horse around to check on them. One looks after all the animals and loves them just as one loves his children. When animals stray for several days, my heart aches and longs to see them, because they are missed. When there is no corn in the field, not even one or two stalks, it makes one weary and uneasy in mind and body. But if there are two or three corn stalks, one can watch them grow and feel proud; it gives life, and one feels good. Old age without corn is awful. One's activities slow down, and life becomes hard. If only I could do all these things. It makes me weary. That is how I feel, as I sit here each day and wish that I could do everything I used to. Old age has diminished my livelihood, but there is nothing that can be done.

"Forget it, Dad. Sell all your animals. You're incapable of caring for them now. You're too old." "No, I will not do that. As long as I have eyes to see my animals, I will never give them up," I tell my children. That is how it is.

SELF-ESTEEM

Jewelry is also important. Without it, a person seems worthless. It is hard to be without it, because you feel naked and look gray and dull. Elders, adults, children, and young ones look good in it. I feel happy about myself when I put on my turquoise bracelet and necklace, so I wear them all the time. They are a part of me. This is also true of my hat. It seems like I am not worth anything without these valuables. People seem to kick you around, ignore you, and push you aside, because they do not see anything of value. When you are young, you do not realize these things. The youth do not stop to think about what is and is not important and so are ignorant. They do not know or care and go about their business, hesitating to get things done, thinking they are capable of everything.

Nowadays, I spend my time just sitting here looking out the window. It overwhelms me to think about it, but my thoughts go back to my maternal grandmother, uncles, grandfather, father, paternal grandfather and grandmother, and relatives, clan sisters and brothers, all of the important people who spoke to me as I was growing up. They taught me about life, and I learned from their advice. I lived according to what they said, and they have molded me into what I am today. I did what I was told; I was their gift—a valuable gift—to me.

With this gift I raised my children and had all that it takes mentally and physically to give them the best that I had. "Always keep them decently clothed. Don't have them in ragged clothes or shoes with holes and their toes sticking out. Have livestock. You will have food for them, and these animals will make them happy as they tend them. Never be lazy. Don't sleep. Do all that you have to, to keep happy and alive." This is what my children needed. I have lived it and now understand it.

Learning to be a medicine man is pretty challenging too. When your teacher instructs you, you have to abide by all the rules and make sure

Woman bedecked in jewelry. J.H.: "Jewelry is also important. Without it, a person seems worthless. It is hard to be without it, because you feel naked and look gray and dull. Elders, adults, children, and young ones look good in it." (Photo NC 8-18, Milton Snow Collection, Navajo Nation Museum)

it is done right. Once you are able to do it alone, he tells you, "I have given you the gift." Then you wonder, "What gift? I didn't get anything from him. All I got were the songs, stories, prayers, and rituals. That's it—nothing physical, not even an arrowhead."

"There, I have given you everything, all the prayers, the life, the shield—the protector of life—the gift of a healthy life. I have given you everything. I have bracelets, money, livestock, and my medicine bag. But I will give you none of them. It's all out there beyond that hill. You have the songs, prayers, and all it takes to get these things. You can receive these valuables, but you have to get them for yourself. You will use what I've taught, and if you do it right, you'll have what you need. Someday you'll know what I'm talking about." I now understand what he meant by that. It is true.

My teacher, Metal Teeth, told me these things. I met him one day, while traveling through the hills above Baby Rocks; he had all his valuable things with him, and people were herding his cattle, mules, horses, sheep, and goats. He had jewelry, rugs, silver belts, new cloth material, and deerskins all bundled up on the horses, and there I was in rags. I went with them on their singing and ceremonial trail, going from home to home to do ceremonies. He never gave us any money, even though I stayed with him through the winter and next summer. He received his wealth but did not give me a nickel, a blanket, or a piece of the cloth that his patients gave to him. He shared none of his earned wealth, but he gave, or taught, me his songs, prayers, lectures, and stories of how the sacred prayers, songs, and rituals came into being. That was the wealth he gave to me, and that is how I learned from him and his way of teaching.

In the spring, when it was warm and the people were herding sheep, we moved toward home, moving his livestock as we went. My clothes were in shreds, my coat and pants patched, and my toes hung out of the front of my shoes. I was a sight to see. Hardly anybody took a bath, and our feet and hands and faces were sandpaper-rough because we never washed them. "I'm ready to go home; I'm leaving," I told my teacher, and he agreed.

I had a worn saddle, which I put on my horse and rode to Red Rock Point, past Dennehotso, through Among the Salty Bushes, to Dug-Out Spring, Donkey Spring, Water Splashing Down, and the Mexican Water

Trading Post. I arrived at noon. There were a lot of horses outside the post, indicating many people were there. I was embarrassed to enter, even though I had credit with the trader and wanted to go in before I went home. I decided to wait until everyone left, so I sat in the shade of a large sagebrush, hidden from sight, and peeked over the bushes to see when everyone had gone.

Time passed slowly until finally the men departed, each with a bale of hay on his saddle horn, as they headed for the big cottonwood trees not too distant from the store. I hurried over on my horse, and the trader, Red-Haired Man (Hastiin Bitsíí'łichí'í), was surprised to see me. "Where have you been, John?" he asked. He was on his way to lunch and invited me to join him. "Come, come, come inside," he said. He served food and asked, "What happened to you? You look scary! Where have you been keeping yourself? Have you been dragged around in the rocks?" He was pretty fluent in Navajo, so we used to talk a lot. "Well, it's because I haven't bought anything for myself yet," I said. "Why?" he said. "There are plenty of goods here in the trading post."

I quickly finished my food, then followed him into the store. He told me, "I went out to your camp yesterday at White Streak of Cattail Coming Out and found that your family had sheared their sheep. I loaded thirty-seven 200-pound burlap bags with wool into my truck and brought the sacks in for them. Your family wanted to leave thirty-three bags of wool at home, to save for you. And where are you coming from?" he asked. "I came from the opposite direction." He handed me a pair of pants, a shirt, shoes, and socks, and I took them to the wool-packing room to change. I really looked nice. He stood there and waited for me, saying, "More people will be coming. You need to look nice." He gathered up my rags and threw them in the trash in the corner. "There, now you look really nice and decent."

I laughed at his gestures and did the rest of my shopping, buying a really nice coat, with a velveteen collar that felt like bat hair. I also purchased a new saddle, bridle, rope, silver concho belt, silver and turquoise bracelets, and hat with a silver band. I put it all on, even though I overdid it, and was standing around when all the men returned to the trading post. The trader said he was coming to my home the next day, so I told him to take my old saddle, bridle, and rope, as well as more food and other items I had bought, and bring them in his truck. I left for home, passing through Many Cattle, Highest Point, and Road onto the Rocky Ground. I arrived home, located at Hole in the Rock, just below the old VCA mine, around sunset. The next morning the trader came with more money and loaded the thirty-three bags of wool. Now I had cash.

TODAY'S PROBLEMS

Our schools used to be very strict, but not anymore. Several years ago, we were told not to use strict discipline, or we would go to jail for child abuse. I heard Annie Wauneka, a former Navajo tribal councilwoman, told a bunch of false rumors to the government in Washington.[17] She caused today's policies, rules, and regulations on child abuse, instead of implementing "discipline." The schools did away with teaching children through consequences by calling punishment mistreatment. This was a bad decision on her part for our communities. She claimed that our children were being oppressed, which has now caused them to suffer and become mentally disoriented and stupid. Everything changed for the worse for our children and their behavior. It is bad.

In earlier times, when children misbehaved in school, they were disciplined by spanking or other punishments. They listened and obeyed. We did not have problems with juvenile delinquency. The powers of the parents and grandparents have been diminished or removed. Blame is now placed on the maternal and paternal grandparents and uncles and aunts, but the real issues arose when the idea of child abuse was adopted into the law.

The children have been in charge ever since this was approved. A father cannot ask his daughter, or a teacher ask a student, to do anything without fear of being accused of child abuse or molestation. If a father asks his daughter to wash the dishes, and she refuses and gets disciplined, she is liable to lie and tell the authorities that she was fondled or sexually molested. The authorities are quick to respond and arrest the innocent man because of the lies of his accuser. They will question the girl, "Did he do this, do that?" She will answer yes to every question until it becomes a bigger problem, as the authorities lead her on. The larger the case, the more pocket money for the investigating authority. The court system is so unfair to our people. Many of our youth are in correctional facilities because of false accusations and the corrupted court system. I personally know this is how it is in our society. This is ugly but true.

Now, children have become our leaders, dictators, and are ruling us. They, not the parents, are in command, and so everything is out of order. Some parents defend their children's misbehavior when teachers are trying to discipline them. This has caused the teachers and administrators to refrain from strict discipline. Then the children become more prone to fight, steal, and be violent, which, in turn, leads to drugs and alcohol in our schools. Some students are sniffing and drinking hair spray. We see young men along the roads with long hair or shaved heads with tails, and their clothes are outrageous—they look unattractive and scary. Some of our children gather in the cities, portraying themselves as hippies. They have outgrown and now despise our traditional clothing. That is how the elders see it today.

The next step is our young men and women imprisoned for drugs and alcohol abuse. We see them working in their bright orange jail uniforms in Tuba City, Chinle, and Window Rock. Their relatives cry for their release, trying to gather enough money to bail them out. The government's idea to initiate new regulations backfires on the officials and on us. It makes one wonder if the government did this for its own profit. Officials are raking in our money all over the reservation. And to make matters worse, our tribal officials are not doing a thing to settle these problems. We hear about our students and their educational issues every day. Students are rarely taught about our traditional livelihood—involving livestock and cornfields—the sacred songs and prayers of our ancestors, or Navajo ways of thinking and doing. No one bothers to teach such things these days. Instead, our children learn other subjects at the high schools and colleges across the country.

We hold community meetings over the issues, stand our ground, and tell them, "Why are you [the authorities] always trying to look for ways to resolve this problem? The problem is obviously the child abuse law," but no one wants to argue the point. No school-board member, principal, chapter official, or council delegate will discuss it. The truth is that the law is the root of the problem.

When children were disciplined by the whip, they were afraid to do wrong. "Listen to what I'm saying. Pay attention and learn to understand what I'm telling you. Do you understand? Because if you don't understand, I'll have to use my whip on you," I would tell my children. "Yes, I understand," they replied. That is how I raised them, with discipline, and we understood each other. I told them, "I mean what I say," and that was the truth.

But these days, with the child abuse regulations, parents are afraid of being arrested by the authorities. This is why our children are always getting into trouble. They do what they please, get their way, and break the law, but parents and teachers are the ones held in bondage. Children sleep until all hours of the day, destroy and vandalize property without fear of punishment, then are protected against us. That is how they form bad habits and learn from each other without discipline, rules, and order. There is only chaos.

This leads to other problems, such as incest and marriage in their own bloodline. The children do not have respect for clan relations, causing them to have deformed or retarded children. They even lose their identity. Are they male or female? Things become confused so that boys act, dress, and talk like girls and vice versa. This problem became worse since the start of the child abuse law. Children have lost their respect for their relatives, and even worse, for themselves. When the parents or an elder were in charge, they taught the children, "This is your relative, your clan uncles, aunts, brothers, sisters, grandfather, grandmother—these are your bloodlines, your family." The children listened and had respect. But this is no longer the case. Now they ignore and do not want to respect their relatives.

It seems impossible to reverse the trend. Our law officials, judges, and police force are not trustworthy anymore; they lie too much. I do not know what will become of our people. It is obvious that the government has made a major mistake. There is a possibility that things will get back to normal, if we change this regulation back to the way it was before. The only way to resolve this issue is to reestablish disciplinary action.

Why can't the Navajo Reservation, within the four sacred mountains, abolish the child abuse law, so that we can better society for the future? The government should allow parents to discipline their children as in the past. I think it is the only way we can improve their behavior. Parents should have the right to use the whip, if necessary, to keep their children in order and out of trouble. It has to change soon, or within ten years, our children will be killing each other every day. If our schools returned to strict discipline, our children would straighten up. If they do not, it seems hopeless.

CHAPTER NINE

TEACHINGS OF LIFE

A common theme in Navajo thinking is that of cycles, or stages, that things, including humans, pass through. The world is in a cycle now that started with the Creation and will end with the establishment of a new, perfected state. The Navajo people will go through a similar metamorphosis, as will the animals and all living creatures. In a sense, the individual human life cycle that we live today reflects this pattern.

John provides specific teachings about how life is formed: that everything was created spiritually before it became a physical entity, that the Holy Wind inside each of us plays an important part in our lives before it leaves us in death, and that the ceremonies taught by the Holy Beings are there to bless people during earth life. Birth, naming, the Kinaaldá, weddings, marriage, old age, and death are just some of the stages in the cycle that John discusses. He is concerned that the important ceremonies and practices related to these stages continue.

There are indicators also that the world is moving inexorably toward its old age and eventual end. John's experience with the Diné Who Exist Elsewhere, in Canada, and the history he tells of the Great Gambler and the Anasazi are just two more indicators that the time of great change is approaching. There is a distinct feeling that the corruption he sees about him—from the seasons and the behavior of animals, to the loss of the Navajo language and the improper use of ceremonies—is hastening the world to its final state. Exactly when this will occur, he does not say, but the signs are imminent.

CREATION: THE WORLD

Some of the stories I am going to tell cannot be told in the summer. I am only sharing them now because it is winter.[1] We can talk about current events, but not stories of Creation, because if I did, it could cause tornadoes, hailstorms, and other disasters. Many of the elders knew our ancestral legends and stories, but they died and never shared them. Many had sacred songs and prayers that have since vanished. This is why I am sharing with you what I know. I want others to know about our people and culture and to be remembered in generations to come. It makes me happy to share all of this so that others can learn from these teachings. Even after I am gone, my stories will live forever. This makes me happy, and it is good.

Sacred songs, stories, and prayers are worth something, and people pay to learn them. They are sacred teachings that do not come from the people but the Holy Beings, and if one has an interest in them, he or she will pay.[2] This must be done by everyone. There are many stories and sacred legends. Some are kept as a protector or shield, and if one knows them, they will serve as armor. Others are for a healthy mind and prosperity. Young men and women familiar with these stories and songs have prospered. They have livestock, wealth, good jobs, and a happy family.

When the gods created the earth, it received different markings. It is said that the ocean was as thin as a blade of grass. The Holy One stretched all four sides of the earth to the east, south, west, and north, then blew over the edges, forming a nice round earth. Next, the ground was torn to the east toward Denver, at Pueblo, Colorado, where a volcanic rock sits in the shape of an arrowhead. Then the earth was torn to the south, to Albuquerque, New Mexico, near the Rio Grande, where sits another volcanic rock in the shape of an arrowhead. Then it was torn toward this side of Bluff City, Utah. The arrowhead used for tearing the ground was made into Comb Ridge. The ground was also torn between Moab, Utah, and Grand Junction, Colorado, where a red arrowhead sits along the riverbank on the other side of Naturita, Colorado. All these arrowheads surround the Navajos' reservation in the four directions.[3]

People say that these arrowheads stretched the earth for only a short distance at first, sending the earth's water in all different directions through its gorges and pathways. These are now deep valleys and canyons. The earth was blown into its proportions [by the Holy Beings], creating specific formations that became enlarged to the size that they are today. Metal Teeth said the earth was like a spindle stick [wool twiner]. He used to argue with others about how our world works. He told them it rotated around and around and did not stand still. "If it is round and turns, then we would fall off," they would say. My grandfather had these heated arguments back then, but we know today that he was right.

After the markings sank in the different directions, the Holy Beings brought up the mountains through the sacred passage from beneath this world and placed them in their positions to serve as guidelines. These mountains were Blanca Peak, Mount Taylor, San Francisco Peaks, La Plata Mountains, Gobernador Knob, and many, many others. They were set up as if on a sand painting, and that is why one does not see ripples on the mountains. The rest of the rocks have these marks because they were here when the water covered the land.

On this small piece of earth, the people emerged and migrated about. We were the Holy Beings but were smaller than the smallest ant, about the size of a tiny grain of sand. The place from which we emerged is called the Emergence and is where the animals and the Holy Beings came up together with First Man (Áłtsé Hastiin), First Woman (Áłtsé Asdzáán), Talking God, Black God, Male God (Biką'ii), Female God (Bi'áádii), and Bik'égochiidii.[4] All the animals and the People spoke one language—Navajo. The badger dug the passageway for everyone to enter this world, but when he appeared on the earth's surface, a couple of eagles swooped down from two directions and ripped a reed rattle in half, from its mouth to its buttocks, and threw it in front of him.[5] "Can you do this too?" asked the eagles. "Only if you can do this, can you live on earth."

The badger went back down and told the Navajos what had taken place. They asked the locust to go up to the surface, but when it did, not only was it ripped in half, but its heart was torn in shreds. "Can you do this?" The locust copied the eagles' action and won the earth for the people.[6] He beat the eagles' challenge, and the Navajos emerged upon the earth. The gods then decreed, "For those who will live upon this earth, your [eagle] wings, your tail, your claws, your lips, your body will be used for our ceremonial purposes. Leave all of these parts for the Navajos to use," which they agreed to do. All of the Navajos' sacred beliefs and rituals were given to the people at this time, and that is how we came to be.

Because the ground had been torn in the four directions, and the water seeped into the crevices, there was no vegetation. The Holy Beings built the first sweat lodge from mirage, or heat wave, and not from wooden logs as we do today. The first family—First Woman, First Man, First Boy (Áłtsé Ashkii), and First Girl (Áłtsé At'ééd), as well as other Holy Beings—existed, but humans were in the form of the Holy Wind and were not yet flesh.[7] The gods created the earth in its spirit form and were like a mirage, the kind you see on the horizon or in the distance at a certain time of day.

The Holy Beings were in the process of planning how to make the first physical sweat lodge. "How shall we make this structure?" they asked each other. Coyote spoke up and said, "Look at your own bodies. You have legs, arms, and a head, so build it accordingly. The logs will be stacked up like your head and shoulders, the legs will be down at the bottom, outstretched for support." So the sweat lodge was built according to Coyote's instructions.

From within this structure, everything was created: the mind, wisdom, sacred words, songs, prayers, the earth with its mountains, and the heavens with all its stars. The Holy Beings next decided that they would build a male hogan, where they could meet and continue to plan. This structure was also made from the heat wave and had a pointed roof, as today's male hogans do. They discussed many plans, among which was that this hogan, as a young male, would be alone. How will it reproduce and continue to thrive? Then Talking God said he would construct a young female hogan built from the ground up, with logs lying sideways, one on top of the other. He made it with sunrise, yellow ground sunset, blue ground darkness, and sunrays. Now there was a male and a female hogan.[8] Likewise, all different kinds of vegetation were planted as pairs of male and female.

CREATION: THE PEOPLE AND THE TWINS

From the beginning of time, the Holy Beings created the People as either male or female, but nobody knows for sure how the human race was started. Our bodies are divided down the middle—one half is male, the other half female—yet it is a single body.⁹ One foot, knee, and leg is male, and the other female; one pelvis is male, the other female; one nipple is male, the other female; one nostril male, the other female; one lung male, the other female; one eye male, the other female. Every part of our body is either male or female. We all have an eternal spirit— One That Never Dies [Holy Wind]—though our skin and flesh may eventually deteriorate. This is how our body was created. We were made from the heat wave, the same thing that our hogans were first made from. That is how it is.

People say Jesus Christ is a god, and they pray to him. Likewise, the Navajos have a god. He is an everlasting god who never dies, and we pray to him for everything. We were created from white shell in a sacred, holy way. Part of the white shell was taken and put in our bodies, but no one can see it. White Shell is a god. We pray to her "to give us the invisible white shell shoes, white shell socks, clothing, feathers," and so on—that is how the prayer song goes. This god is female and is out there, but we cannot see her. The Creator also gave to us belts and bracelets, long-sleeved shirts, pants, skirts, and woolen Navajo dresses. From white shell and turquoise, he made the females' earrings.

Turquoise is the grandchild and is a Holy Being, so we pray and sing to it for all our needs. A male's feet and bones are made of mirage stone, while a female has heat wave bones in her body.¹⁰ Both males and females have bones made from these two different things. The female is decorated in white shell, and the male in turquoise. White crystal is in the female's eyes, and blue crystal in the male's. Then white shell was placed in our brain to think and reason with. Finally, twelve hairs were placed on top of our heads.¹¹ This is what gives us the power to move around in a magic but holy way, and why Navajo men wear headbands and hats.

My grandmother used to teach that long ago on Gobernador Knob, New Mexico, the Holy Beings found a baby.¹² Talking God heard the baby's cries in the mountains, while he was running errands for First Man and First Woman. It was foggy, so the Holy Being followed the cries to find the baby. He located it quickly, tore off some bark from a cliffrose bush, and rubbed it together until soft. He next wrapped the baby in it and brought her back to First Woman, who had already prepared a cradleboard. She placed the little female in it, where she grew rapidly. This baby had been born to bear the Twins, who would, at a future time, destroy the monsters that roamed the earth. These monsters, such as Big Giant, Giant Elk [also known as Horned Monster] (Déélgééd), Giant Rock Birds (Tsénináháleehii), Walking Rock (Tsénaagháí), One Who Kicks You off the Cliff (Tsé Dahooziłtałii), One Who Kills with His Eyes (Nááyéé' Agháanii), Bear That Tracks You (Shash Na'ałkahii), and many others terrorized and ate the earth people.

The baby grew to become Changing Woman. She hid her twin boys underground, beneath the fireplace, putting a rock over the hole to cover them when the monsters appeared. They left her alone because Sun Bearer took care of her, but they often asked about the small footprints around her home. She told them that she made the prints with the side of her hand because she was longing for children of her own.

As the Twins grew to adolescence, they fixed two bows and arrows that were only half made, then said they were going to slay all the monsters on the earth. "It's impossible," their mother said. "These monsters are indestructible." "But we will slay them all," they boasted. The Twins grew to be adults and one day asked their mother who their father was. She said many things, but they did not believe her. Finally she told them that Sun Bearer was their father and how he had come down to visit her many times. The Twins wanted to see him, so she let them go. This is when they received weapons to slay the monsters. It was as if the doors of death had opened.

The Twins returned to earth at the hot water springs near Albuquerque, where the monsters usually drank. Monster Slayer watched Big Giant taking a bath in a large hot spring, but once he saw the Twins, he began throwing his club. He had weapons made of different types of lightning. There were bows and arrows made from the lightning that strikes crooked and the lightning that flashes straight, and clubs made of flint. He also had a suit of flint armor. The twins jumped as one club went under them; he threw another, they ducked, and it passed over them. They continued to dodge until all of Big Giant's weapons were gone. Monster Slayer then picked them up and killed the giant. This story should not be told in the summer, so I have told you only portions of it. From this time on, the Twins destroyed the other monsters. People say that the killers of monsters went off in all directions and later became the mountains that we see today. These beings are still present and holy.

THE GREAT GAMBLER AND THE ANASAZI

When all the monsters were dead, Monster Slayer said it would not be safe to keep the weapons that they took from Big Giant. "If we keep these weapons, we will destroy ourselves. We are not safe if we keep them here." So they stood them on the rainbow, and with lightning, shot them across the ocean to the bottom of the earth. They went to the white man's world, where they stayed. Following these events, the people flourished on the earth. It has always been forbidden to talk about these things, but today, like everything else, we have done and said all that is forbidden.

My grandmother shared teachings about the Great Gambler (Nááh-wíiłbįįhii), too.[13] She said, "Once upon a time, the white man's God, also known as One Who Wins You as a Prize (Naahwiiłbįįh), had beaten everyone and won everything. He even beat One You Gather Everything For (Bá Náhoodiidzid) and won as a prize the earth, its people, the heavens, and all that they contained. The Great Gambler was lying where Sleeping Ute Mountain is located when a rainbow suddenly struck him. Gathers Everything was victorious and took back all the prizes. Then the Great Gambler followed him and begged to be clubbed to death, but Gathers Everything refused. The Great Gambler asked him to recreate the slain monsters but was told that he could only make the Walking Rock monster, which he did.

"This creature, Walking Rock, started to move about but soon exploded into bits and pieces, and his remains seeped into the earth, becoming the coal, gasoline, oil, and uranium that we use today. The body of the Great Gambler is Sleeping Ute Mountain.[14] He was killed there, and only his spirit went down into the earth, while his body lies facing upward. His spirit had both female and male elements that went below. The body on the surface remained as the mountain."

People say that the Great Gambler promised to return. "I'll be back someday to win all of you again. I will earn your feet, your legs, your body, your arms, your heart, your head; your whole body I shall have. I will even take your language. I will beat you and win all these things back from you." Now, he has returned, this person who was sent to the other side of the earth. He is here trying to win us back, taking our language away so that we use only English. He is also taking our bodies, minds, songs, and prayers—everything from us.

It is said that once our language is extinct, the earth will change. There will be lightning strikes, all will be destroyed, and we will not grow anymore. This same thing happened long, long ago to the people before us. Their language, perhaps the Spanish language, became one, and the earth changed. This is what our ancestors told us. They said that no matter what happens, our language cannot become extinct. This is how we helped win the war [World War II]. But if it is lost, we will be lost, too, and our enemies will conquer us.[15]

There are also teachings about the Anasazi, who lived many, many years ago. They were small in size and said to have had wings, which enabled them to fly. After them came the Indian Mexicans, who lived during the same time our people were here.[16] They were dark skinned and short, a type of Indian tribe, but unlike the Mexican people today, who are light skinned and tall. These Indian Mexicans built stone dwellings and made pottery but were not the Anasazi. The Anasazi dwelled only in the high places of the canyon and mesa walls, then became extinct. I heard these stories from a man named Old Eddie from Aneth, who heard them from his great-great paternal grandfather Big Mexican Clan (Nakaii Dine'é Tso).

These Indian Mexicans were the ones who drew on the walls, made pottery, and lived all across this continent to the shores of the oceans. According to our people's timetable, these Indian Mexicans lived before the marking and stretching of the earth in the four directions, when the ocean was still as thin as a grass stem, and before today's lakes were formed. These people migrated back and forth at that time. Monster Slayer destroyed them, because they were killing off our people. He used the great winds to destroy them in a single day. This is what I heard.

Today, the remains of the Anasazi are used in cleansing ceremonies. It is believed that we chase the Anasazi's evil spirit away from our bodies when we perform the Charcoalway, or Evilway, Ceremony. This is done by using charcoal, a bull roarer [sounding stick], and herbs on the first day. The next day, the person has the Blessingway washing. This purifies a person of all bad things, similar to cleaning out the trash and

Anasazi artifacts. J.H.: "There are also teachings about the Anasazi, who lived many, many years ago. . . . Today, the remains of the Anasazi are used in cleansing ceremonies." (Photo courtesy of San Juan County Historical Commission)

throwing it away. After the trash is removed, the Blessingway songs and washing are done. The patient will then continue his or her life in a purified state. The same thing happens at an Enemyway Ceremony. At this ritual, the bones, representing evil, are smothered with ashes, shot with a gun, then discarded or destroyed.[17] These bones represent the enemy, whether they are Mexicans, whites, or Utes.

Once the ceremony is over, the person observes the four sacred days, during which there is a Blessingway sing on him or her. All these sacred rituals are done according to a step-by-step procedure. The first step in each one is to rid the person of his ailment, whatever that might be. Then, with the sprinkling of corn pollen, this person starts anew on this earth. All steps are equally important and must be performed according to the teachings.

DINÉ WHO EXIST ELSEWHERE

There are also interesting teachings about the Apaches and other groups that speak the Navajo language. People say the Apaches joined the white people and became the enemy of the Navajos and fought them. Because of the fighting, they moved away, but today, we still mingle with them. I have done ceremonies for Apaches three different times, and they still believe in traditional Navajo religion. I did these ceremonies on the White Mountain Apache Reservation, and just recently, I also performed a ceremony for a Sioux Indian. These people really respect and appreciate the Navajo religion.

There are also people in Canada who speak our language. They are called the Diné Who Exist Elsewhere (Diné Náhódlóonii). They are not Navajos and are from a different tribe. We call them Enemy People. In fact, there are some people who claim to be from the Hairy Ones Clan (Tł'ógí), associated with the Bitter Water Clan. Their ancestors must have been some of those who were kidnapped by our tribe or some other.

One time, I went with some family members to western Canada, where there were many cities and towns. There is a mountain that goes on and on and looks like Black Mesa from the south side, because it is wide and long. We came to an opening in this mountain that was the entrance to the reservation of the Diné Who Exist Elsewhere. After stopping by the entrance for a while, we continued on until we came to a city to do some shopping. I was having problems with my back, so I sat down on a bench and watched while the rest went about their business at a large flea market, where vendors sold ropes, jewelry, and many other items.

As I sat there, a couple of men from the Diné Who Exist Elsewhere approached. They greeted me with a language I understood. "Hello, my dearest. Where are you from?" "My dearest" is how they greet each other. "I'm a Navajo from the Navajo Reservation, my homeland," I replied. I thought these were some Navajos who were visiting there too. "I'm from the Bitter Water Clan, born for the Folded Arms; Many Goats is my paternal grandfather's and Black Hair is my maternal grandfather's clan," I said. "Well, some of the same clans live back there within those mountains," they said, pointing to the mountains through which we had just come. "And what clan are you?" I asked. "I'm a Mexican People (Nakaii Dine'é)," said one, and the other replied, "I'm a Water's Edge People, born for Rock House (Tséníjíkiní) and into Red-Running-into-the-Water People." They were also related to the Honey-Combed Rock People (Tsé Njíkiní), the Hairy Ones Clan, and One Walks

Around (Honágháahnii) Clan. Once we became acquainted, we all started talking. Unfortunately, my family returned too soon. I was prepared for a really good visit with them, but they only had time to ask, "Do you know the ceremony the Blessingway?" "Yes." Then they said, "Our people were separated from your people during Creation. Why? We don't know. The Holy Beings held us back and kept us here. We heard your people [Navajo] took most of the religious ceremonies like Blessingway and others with them. Our people still have a few ceremonies, too, like the Blessingway and Evilway. If a Navajo comes here, he will have to come to our home, perform a ceremony, and tell our people the history of the religion and their beliefs, before he can be released to go." This was disturbing information.

My family and I left, continuing our trip through the mountains. We came to a resort, where we had to pay a four-dollar entrance fee, and then saw "No Trespassing and No Camping" signs. There were all sorts of animals—lions, bears, wolves, mixed with other animals like deer, moose, and elk. A big moose stood in the water with its nose above the surface. There was such a wide variety of animals; some bears were spotted with different colors, others were white, black, and brown. And there were purplish wolves that walked in a zigzag motion, their hind ends twisting as they moved.

Next we came to a lookout tower. I must have been feeling better, because I chose to climb the winding stairs, while the rest took the elevator and beat me to the top, where there was a lookout platform with several telescopes. We looked through them and saw a couple of moose fighting in the water and hundreds of elk, buffalo, and other animals, some of which were animals from foreign countries. I looked some more and saw something strange. The water looked very close, and on the banks I saw huge alligators with their large mouths open and full of teeth! It looked very, very close! I told my family, "You haven't seen this yet," so they looked into the telescope and were as amazed as I was. It was very interesting to see all those animals. We then went down in the elevator and left.

We saw a bear eating something, stopped to watch, and I decided to give him an offering of sacred stones, because there was a drought at home. As I did this, he turned around, sat down, and ate as he watched us. More bears of all different colors appeared to watch as I sang my sacred song, prayed, and laid my offerings. I finished, turned around, and saw a wolf. I gave him the sacred corn pollen, saying, "Grandfathers, we need rain. Let the rain follow me home." The wolf left and crossed the road.

We also went to Yellowstone Park and watched the geysers. They were fascinating, but there were too many tourists. When we arrived in Denver, I suggested we sleep in the van, because motels were too expensive. But my children told me, "Let's go, Dad. We'll show you something." So they took me inside a building and up, up, up in a spacious elevator. We got off at the top floor and went to a room with beds! "You sleep here," they said. I looked out the window and could hardly see the cars below, they were so small. Here we were in one of the tallest buildings! My children laughed at me. Later, some bellboys brought food—a lot of food—and we ate. Then we left and returned to Farmington, New Mexico. That is what I saw, and that is what is out there. I know now.

BIRTH AND NAMES

People say that a baby is ready to be born based on the time of the half moon.[18] The pregnant woman and the unborn baby have a prayer and song about one month before the birth. They have the Birthingway (Ch'iljí, or Hodoolééljí) or Charcoalway Ceremony, and then the protection song. This is performed for the health and well-being of both the mother and the baby. Then there is the Blessingway Ceremony, so that there will not be a problem during delivery.

News spreads about a woman giving birth, and people come from all around to cook a big meal outside the home while the woman is in labor in the hogan.[19] Those helping with the birth cut down a nice, straight juniper sapling, forked at the top to secure a rope. They cut off the branches, leave the bark on, place it upright in a hole dug in the hogan floor, and fill in around it. While they are tying to the fork of the tree a sash belt or wool rope used to tighten a rug loom, they sing a song. The actual delivery is made to the beat of a drum and a song, while other women help the woman in labor. The ladies take turns assisting and get really busy helping when the baby is born.

The newborn receives its name at birth with its first cry. A relative gives this Navajo name as a type of blessing. No English names are

Woman with baby on cradleboard. J.H.: "The newborn receives its name at birth, with its first cry. A relative gives this Navajo name as a type of blessing. No English names are given at this time, but there are different ones for boys and girls." (Photo 14452, used by permission, Utah State Historical Society, all rights reserved)

given at this time, but there are different ones for boys and girls. Names such as She Goes Around and Around Them Warring (Naanázbaa'), and She Continued to War (Deezbaahii), and others with "baa" (war) in them belong to girls, whereas a boy's name might have "Mean One" in it. My name is Mean One I Fought For. My maternal grandfather gave it to me. He was a warrior involved in local conflicts with our enemies.

Later, I received my English name. One of my uncles was named just plain John, while his Navajo name was Gambler. When I was small, a white man, Herbert Redshaw, traveled about with a Navajo interpreter, giving census numbers and round silver census tags.[20] They came to White Streak of Cattail Coming Out, where we lived. My uncle told them, "My name is John, and so now I will name my nephew Little John, since he is little." That is how I got my name and my census number, but I was very small and barely remember it. My name was Little John for quite some time before they added Holiday to it. This last name came from my father.

KINAALDÁ

A man named Gray Whiskers used to live on the northeast side of the valley, below the Mitten monuments. He was of the Bitter Water Clan and married into the Folded Arms, my mother's clan. His family was sponsoring a Kinaaldá for his daughter, who was told to run every day.[21] For four days she did this; then on the fifth day, her parents held a sacred sing and made the corn cake. During the four days of running, she ran several times a day, with everyone—men, women, and children—running after her. Gray Whiskers's daughter ran fast for long distances, probably ten miles. Many people followed her, but she left most of them behind, except for three of us boys—me, Billy Yellow, and Old Educated One's Son (Ółta'í Sání Biye').

We followed her until she turned around, and on the way home, the others rejoined us. Some, who were not in shape to run long distances, did not come back until after sunrise, even though the girl and runners left before early dawn. The other runners could not get ahead of her, because if they did, they would reach old age faster. Also, no one can touch the girl, for whatever reason. It was not allowed, and if one did, there was not an easy way to correct it, because the mistake is complicated to undo. That is what people used to say.

Part of the ceremony includes the baking of a blue cornmeal cake in a pit in the ground. Some corn is roasted, ground, then put in a person's mouth for about ten minutes, until it is soaked with saliva. The mixture is spit into a cup and the process repeated until the cup is filled. This is next added to the rest of the ground mush and boiled. The mixture constitutes the sacred underground corn cake used in this puberty rite. The saliva and corn ingredient makes the cake sweeter in taste.

Back in those days, the women who made the sacred corn cake used to search out someone who produced the sweetest tasting ingredient and take him or her from place to place to help with the ceremonies. I was one of those sweeter ingredient boys and was invited to participate at the event. The women got me to chew the corn for the cooks. "Your ingredients really sweeten the corn cake. Come and take part in the process," they said. So I helped. I was small then, just a child.

Following the run, the girl performed the "tying of the hair" (tsii' bee'astł'ǫ́), where a medicine man or woman massaged her from head to toe, then tied her hair back up. Thus she would have a strong, healthy body. They massaged the face and crown of her head, so the girl would not be mean but intelligent. The area between the eyes is where language and wisdom sit, so they massaged it twice as hard as in other areas. If a girl does not have this puberty ceremony, she will be crazy, will not have the sacred blessings, and will grow up to be worthless. Also, she will not know how to do things, will take her children to other people's houses begging for food and shelter, and if she marries, the man will leave her as a single parent with children. It is like this today, because girls no longer have this ceremony. The young girls go from one man to the next, never settling down.

MARRIAGE AND UNWED MOTHERS

Mothers took great care of their daughters, ensuring they were protected, did not go out anywhere, and had no relationships prior to marriage.[22] The boys were looked after just the same. There were few unwed mothers, and the boys and girls were very, very shy. The only

Top photo: Grinding corn with mano and metate, Monument Valley, 1941. Bottom photo: Kinaaldá, with relatives preparing blue cornmeal cake. People identified are Harry Goulding (left) and Hite Chee pouring batter. J.H.: "Part of the ceremony includes the baking of a blue cornmeal cake in a pit in the ground. Some corn is roasted [and] ground. . . . The mixture constitutes the sacred underground corn cake used in this puberty rite." (Photos 14459 and 14486, used by permission, Utah State Historical Society, all rights reserved)

time the young people got together was during a Squaw Dance, but the parents watched them. The mothers told their daughters to dance with nonrelatives. "He is not your relative. Dance with him." A mother took her daughter and granddaughters to these dances and was very careful to make sure her children knew their clans—who they were, and whom they were born for—as well as their maternal and paternal grandparents. All of the clans of the immediate family were very important.

But one can be an in-law to his or her own mother by marrying into the clan of the mother's father or paternal grandfather. A girl can marry into her mother's father's clan and her mother's paternal grandfather's clan. As the saying goes, a woman once said to her daughter, "That boy over there with the sheep fat [sheep fat denotes wealth] around his neck is a Water's Edge [Clan]. Go over there and dance with him!" The people used to really dress up for special occasions back then, with the men wearing large hats and earrings, and the women adorned in earrings and rows of silver-coin buttons sewn on their blouses across the back and down their sleeves, collars, and front yokes. They were all dressed in money! That is what it was like when I was a young boy.

In my upbringing, I was prepared for marriage through discipline not to be jealous and to be patient. "If you don't receive any teachings, you'll be very lazy and just lie around in the shade of your wife, or cry and hang onto her skirt when she goes to leave you because you are useless or, even worse, abusive to her. So my whipping you is nothing bad. It's good to receive strength and courage from the icy water and snow baths. It holds the treasures of life and gives you a sound mind, body, and speech of great worth, as well as sacred songs and prayers. This is a life of strength and prayer, one of power, the kind that won't end until you grow old." These were the lectures given to us by those who meant well. There is no doubt in their teachings, and I believed every word. I approve of these teachings, and they remain with me still. They are true, so true.

WEDDINGS

There were a lot of things that the people were taught that they could and could not do. For instance, a man could not marry a widow without special sings, and a wife was slow to leave her husband if he was a medicine man, for fear that he would take the sacred songs out of the area. Before remarrying, a widow should have a three-day Evilway Ceremony. A prayer is said, pleading with the darkness, which frees the widow from the spirit of the deceased and sends it back to where it came from, putting it to rest. This is done in a humble manner, praying for a peaceful separation, so that the widow can live on this earth without worry. The ceremony serves as a protective shield for her and keeps the spirit of the deceased away. Songs, prayers, herbs, ashes, and the bull roarer scare away the spirit of the deceased. Not until this ceremony is performed can the widowed [male or female] remarry. If these rituals are not done, the new spouse can lead you astray to destruction, harm you, or even strangle you. That is how it is and how it is done. It is better to first have the sing to send the deceased on its way before remarrying.

Weddings are done with a sumac [Navajo wedding] basket that represents the world, with water inside it. There is a reflection off the water, and all appears backwards or reversed, including the feathers that point downward from the reflecting water. The reddish brown rim could be the dam holding the water. The white cornmeal mush is poured inside the basket as part of the wedding ceremony, representing growth, birth, and where all things will come forth. Yellow corn pollen is sprinkled across the mush from east to west, just as the sun goes from east to west; so shall the couple walk the path of life together to their old age. The pollen is sprinkled from east to west and back to the middle. Then more is sprinkled from the south to north and back to the middle of the mush in the wedding basket. All of this is done with prayer.

This is the holy way the couple will walk on the path from east to west, the female road of protectors and good. Both paths are sacred and holy. The prayer is for the good life of the couple, for health and prosperity from beginning to end. This is why the corn pollen is sprinkled in all four directions. The corn mush represents planted white corn, yellow corn, and melons, which depict the blessing of children who will be born from this couple. The purpose of the cornmeal mush is to represent the five-fingered human beings [children] they will produce. The prayers address First Woman, Corn Pollen Boy (Tádidíín Ashkii) and Girl (Aniłt'ánii At'ééd), Holy Protectors (Diyin Diné'é) and directors of goodness on the female and male paths.

The prayers are said as the couple takes the mush from the four directions—east and west, south and north corners—then feeds each other. Once the sacred mush is eaten, it is like planting within each other the ability to produce offspring, the blessing of reproduction, the exchange of each other's being in sacredness. It is important that this is done for the young couple. Today, our young people do not care to have a proper wedding ceremony. They get acquainted, and within one week, they live together.

If people want to be free of evil and venereal disease for their entire lives, then they should leave it [sex outside of marriage] alone. Even the girls were lectured about this. What was said was true, because one's marriage and liveliness depends on how a person takes care of him or herself. It is beyond all the wealth in the world, to respect yourself and keep your body clean. It is extremely important. If people engage in worthless activities, they will be ruined. That's how it is today. Many of our youth have fallen into this trap, and they are suffering. "You will lose your ability and your feelings for sex if you carry on in that manner," we were told. "So be careful! Develop a clean mind and body. Learn only the good in language, songs, and prayers, then dwell on it and live accordingly. Keep it all in balance, like a team of strong horses pulling a wagon." That is what Woman Who Owns the House used to say.

There were also two types of jealousy. One is worrying about your belongings, such as your house, livestock, and food, hoping that someone will not take them away from you. This pertains only to your livelihood. The second one is jealousy of your spouse. An example of this is when you grab your spouse's hair and make him or her stick beside you all the time, even when there is no one around. You keep him or her from doing the chores, seeking work, going to school, herding the sheep, hunting for lost horses, hauling wood or water—everything! This is not good. It causes the couple to go short on food and money for gas and have no visitors or social life. It is a miserable way to live!

A couple should talk about these things and solve such matters in a gentle way.[23] They should support each other's needs and feelings. There is a "brake" for both to use, when things get out of hand. It takes both to work it out. There is so much to teach and learn; they are all interconnected here and there, and it goes on forever. We have to teach our children about everything.

HOMOSEXUALS

The only homosexual I knew was a man named the Weaver. People said he was "made" because a nádleeh is not born but becomes that way.[24] He was married, had children, but did things like a woman. In those days, the Navajos did a ceremony that gave a male the gift of female skills, such as weaving. Rug-weaving equipment, such as the weaving board, weaving comb, loom, yarn, and special loom ties, were bestowed upon the person during this ceremony, enabling the man to become like, and work like, a woman. He has his own songs and prayers for that special sing, but I am not familiar with them. The man is still a male but is given the female skill of weaving, so actually a "homosexual," in our terms, was that way only for the sake of weaving rugs as a male weaver. He is still a man and a husband who has children, but since weaving is truly a female art, it is out of the ordinary. The special sing "made" him that way.

ENEMYWAY AND SONGS

As I was growing up, I attended many, many Squaw Dances at places like Teec Nos Pos, Lukachukai, Rough Rock, Black Mesa, Tuba City, Navajo Mountain, and Oljato. When a person decided to sponsor one, he planned to have it last three, five, or seven days. Two parties were involved in giving each other expensive gifts. The group that had the sick person asked the other group or families if they would be the receivers of the sacred ceremonial stick.[25] As soon as the sponsoring party brought in the scalp and sang a sacred song, the receiving party would say what it wanted for payment. The client would ask the medicine man to begin and conclude the three nights and four days of ceremony with all the sacred rituals, prayers, and songs. Not until this was completed would the payment be made. Possible gifts included a work horse, a cow with calf, a riding horse, a mule (this was a favorite), turquoise beads, blankets, hides, and so forth. No money was involved. The medicine man agreed to perform the ceremony and accept the payment.

Once the price had been agreed upon, the "giver," or group with the patient, traveled by horse, carrying the stick to the "receiver" party's home. The receivers accept it after receiving something of value—a gift called Put into Your Hands—as a gesture of appreciation. The first night of the Enemyway is an all-night ceremony at the receivers' homestead. On the second night, both parties camp and have a Squaw Dance part of the way back to the patient's home. The third night is performed at the patient's hogan, when the receivers ride in and are given gifts in return. On this night, the final songs at the end of the ceremony were completed for the recipient of the sacred stick. He or she was "decorated" with sacred songs on the last day, "undecorated" the next day, and the sacred stick put away. I have seen this done in the proper way by the great medicine men in the past.

During the four days and three nights, each group exchanges gifts of value. From that point on, these two groups continue to exchange gifts on a yearly basis. I once had such an exchange going with a person named Man of the Folded Arms Clan Who Is Light Complected (Bit'ahnii Łichíí'). We gave gifts back and forth for about thirteen years. This ended recently, when I outdid him. I had heard that he was in need of a sheepherding horse, because his had died of old age. I gave him my gentle, deep brown horse and put all the trimmings on it—a saddle, bridle, and rope. "Here, you may have this horse, my [clan] father," I told him. I visited him several times after that, but he never gave me his exchange gift in return before he succumbed to old age. That is how I outgifted him.

During the Squaw Dance, the people held a song session every night. In the past, people sang their hearts out. Many used to attend these dances with a lot of participation by everyone. The men sang and sang until dawn, but the women did not. Today, they sing too. The dance songs were basic but later were fancied up with more versions. I, too, did this along with everyone else. There were all sorts of songs describing things and events.

One time, people told us there was a Squaw Dance southeast of Mexican Water, at the base of Missing Mountain, between Chinle and the Lukachukai Mountains. My father, John Stanley, Black Hat, and I went by horseback on the long ride. We traveled nonstop all day and arrived for the first night of the dance. The second night, people started to sing a lot of nice Squaw Dance songs. I sang quite a bit most of the time. We sang the two-step young girl's songs to the beat of the drum, and since this was also during World War II, most of our songs pertained to the Metal Hats [Germans] or other foreigners. We sang songs about the war, saying, "The Germans can't make it; the Germans can't make it," and they were defeated. The same thing happened to the Japanese and the Russians. We overcame those enemies. The songs were holy, and that is why we won our foreign wars.

In the early days, when I was old enough to first notice things, the young girls used to dress very beautifully and modestly for these dances. They wore moccasins called Big Shoes, with deerskin wraps and silver coins on them, long-sleeved blouses, an assortment of jewelry, and their hair in Navajo buns. A man named Checked Shirt (Bi'éé' Łikizhii), also known as Mister Phillips, from Narrow Canyon, southwest of the Oljato Trading Post, came from a place called Fishhook Cactus. He knew a lot of songs but also made them up as he went along at the dance. He taught us a lot of fancy songs, some of which were about young girls and their characters.

These songs described and criticized the girls and how they dressed. "The girl was dancing in her white heels and miniskirt and had lipstick on her lips, rouge on her cheeks, and curly hair. She danced on and on." At that time, none of the girls looked like that. They were still traditionally dressed and had clean and respectful personalities—all of them. These songs became quite popular Squaw Dance songs and spread quickly to communities like Navajo Mountain. The Monument Valley people joined in and sang them too. Before long, the young girls changed their styles. They danced in miniskirts and curled hair, so that it became the trend! The songs were very effective and changed the younger generation.[26]

Then there were more songs. "I have but one horse. It has sores. Won't you take him to the water for a drink? He is still a horse." Our land had an abundance of horses at that time. "I chase only three striped-face goats." Then again, our horses and sheep diminished by the hundreds.

There was a song about alcohol. "I was on my way to see you, but I drank some wine and never made it there." People started drinking heavily, and many were killed in accidents. These songs set the pace, and everyone seemed to follow them. My, my, it was terrible. We should have known better than to sing such crazy songs, but we kept it up, and things got worse. More songs: "You were my sweetheart, but you left me and went to the city. I followed you there, only to find you had some little black children." These days, we see the young girls

Site of Squaw Dance, Monument Valley, 1938. J.H.: "Squaw Dance songs are sacred, and whatever is sung happens. . . . Squaw Dances are no longer done in a sacred manner and are considered just another social event." (Photo 14462, used by permission, Utah State Historical Society, all rights reserved)

going away to the big cities and bringing home their black offspring. Again, we sang, "The man is dancing; his woman gets mad and takes off in the car. She is mad." Women act like that these days.

We have certainly lost our sacred ways. The songs, we now sing any old way, the way we want to sing, and there is no more sacredness about them. Because of our songs, we are lost, our society has gone astray, and we allowed it. My grandmother warned us that these songs should be kept sacred and not ridiculed. We have brought about our current problems, and it is unfortunate that people do not realize what has happened.

Squaw Dance songs are sacred, and whatever is sung happens. One cannot sing just any song anymore, because it could be a mistake or a wrong decision. Squaw Dances are no longer done in a sacred manner and are considered just another social event, which is incorrect. Today, the ceremony is performed any old way and often improperly. People ask to take back the things they contributed to the ritual. They lend it instead of giving it, which is wrong. Going about it the wrong way has destroyed many lives and caused death for both young and old. This is not good, but it is their fault.

The Squaw Dance is viewed differently and has become a place of disrespect, violence, craziness, foul language—where people make fun of each other. We have used our sacred Squaw Dance in the wrong way, turning it against ourselves. All that has been said and done has certainly changed our society for the worse. It is awful when you think about it. I have since decreased my attendance, quit singing, and seldom go. It is better left alone.

TEACHINGS ABOUT ANIMALS AND OBJECTS

The teachings of discipline and life are good and were much stricter in my childhood. As I have mentioned before, they used to say, "A whip of discipline has within it the good sacred songs and prayers, the good teachings, the good mind, a beautiful way of life. If you are not whipped, you will suffer poverty, sadness, and misfortune. You will either be successful or a failure in life."

There were other teachings that prepared us for life. The elders say that when the very first corral was built, it was dedicated with the marking ritual, then the sheep song and prayers. It was blessed for that purpose, and soon there were sheep in the corral. It was early dawn during the Creation when the Holy Beings first heard the sheep "baaing," and we have had sheep ever since. That same corral holds the horses, cows, goats, donkeys, and mules. It is life. It is food. We survive with these foods, and we make a living, and so this is what we teach. Corn and the garden is another teaching source for food and religious activities.

Before one butchers a sheep, a piece of its wool is placed in the mouth of another sheep. This tradition has been going on since the beginning of time and is also used with cows, horses, deer, and other animals. It is done so that the animal knows that it will not be a loss to man, and that it will be reproduced to replace what you took. Life is continuous for them.

Dogs and cats were made as protectors at our door. People say they stand between humans and bad things, turning away that which harms us. But when a medicine man goes to a patient's home to do a ceremony, these protectors are to be removed or kept out of the medicine man's way. It is not good to have them interfere with a ceremony. Cats and dogs warn of dangers just before they happen. When they urinate on something in front of you, it is a warning, as if to say, "You need to get a medicine man to help you, so that you will not encounter evil." Thus, they foretell the bad things and save your life.

My grandfather felt differently about cats. He usually told everyone to let the cat be. When people tried to throw it out, he would say, "Leave it, leave it alone. Let him stay. The cat is valuable just like other things. Within the cat lies wealth; it comes first, before other things. This animal means no harm, so leave the cat alone."

It was said long ago, "Never be without a fire poker, because it is a protector, a shield." Women used to lay it beside their babies when they had to leave them unattended. They also used the grass brush, the sticks used for mixing cornmeal foods, the long wide stick used to hold the loom strings apart while weaving, and the wooden comb used to pack the strings or wool on the loom. These were all used for the babies' or children's protection. These objects were laid either on top of or beside the child.

Fire is said to be the heart of the home. The hogan is alive, just like a human being, and the fire is its heart. When fire does not burn, when the hogan is abandoned, the home starts deteriorating and falling apart. As long as the fire is going, the hogan stays alive. Without fire, the sand falls off, and the bark and wood show. If one keeps the fire burning, the hogan is in good shape and looks fine. My hogan sitting outside is like that. We build a fire inside every morning to keep it nice. If we were to leave it without a fire, it would start to fall apart within two months. The roof of my trailer would also start to fly off, but with a fire, it stays alive.

Water also has a name, prayer, and song. The rivers are formed by the streams coming together from all parts of the mountains. When it rains, the streams run together and form a bigger river, just as a tree has many branches joining into one trunk. The water coming together is what we call Water with Mixture of Debris.[27] At the beginning of each stream, it runs fast and rough, but as it goes farther down the mountain, it slows and becomes calmer and gentler. After the first rush of water, the stream softens and slows in the same path that the raging water took. This gentle flow is called Small Water.

Telling of your clan when you met a person was a practice of respect in earlier times. One would say, "my beloved big brother," but today, people say, "it is well, big brother." The earlier greeting always began with "my beloved," then added "my sister, my son, my daughter, uncle, grandmother, grandfather," and so forth. Our language has changed drastically. Now we greet each other with "it is well," using the words that describe someone who is well, healthwise. If someone asks about a sick person in the hospital, the response would be, "he is well." We use this word (yá'át'ééh) instead of the real greeting, which shows more love and respect. "Hózhóne'" is the right word for greeting. I wish more people would use it. To use "yá'át'ééh" is like bewitching ourselves to become sick.

People say that if a Navajo kills or steps in the blood of a white man, or sleeps with a white woman, it will kill him, and so he needs an Evilway Ceremony performed. These two situations are similar, and both require this ceremony. When the first white men arrived and exchanged smokes with the American Indians, they had a big feast. The Indians watched the white men serve themselves and eat the hot food, with the steam blowing in their faces. "Look at those people. They eat steaming food. Steam is covering their faces as they eat," and so they were named in Navajo One Who Eats Steam (Hasiil Yiyáanii). The whites sat around the fire, with their legs outstretched, so, again, they were given the name Ones with the Burning Knees (Godiniihí). These were their names.

SILVERSMITHING

A Navajo man named Muddy (Haashtł'ishnii) learned silversmithing from a white man, Missing Teeth (Wooshk'aalii), who used to come from Albuquerque to the Mexican Water Trading Post and Teec Nos Pos. He taught him how to make jewelry like bracelets, earrings, and turquoise beads. Muddy learned the skill and used to do silversmithing by the road, behind a store on the way to Teec Nos Pos. He used a half-underground hogan behind this building for his work.

Then a man named Son of Coyote Pass People (Mą'ii Deeshgiizhnii Biye') became a silversmith, as did many others.[28] They received cattle for selling their jewelry. They used a large round cast-iron pot and a hand-operated bellows to heat the coals under the container. The fire got red hot and melted the silver, and they took a thin wire or some wirelike metal from the coals and put it on the tip of the point to be melted. They made buttonhole loops on the silver buttons and melted silver coins to add to their work. Women used to wear these buttons on their blouses, but not anymore.

These men also ground and smoothed turquoise stones they got from Albuquerque into beads. The turquoise came from mines at a place called Marble Mountain, and people used to travel there on horses. They had songs and prayers before they went to purchase these materials. People did not take much with them for these trips, only a small lunch made from yucca fruit, pinyon nuts, juniper seeds, and wild rhubarb roots. These four things were mixed and patted together into a hard cake. It lasted a long time, was very filling, and made a good travel ration. This, plus water, was all they ate.

Just before arriving, the group of three to five people performed a small ceremony, went into the mines, and sure enough, found plenty of turquoise stone. But if they did not have the ceremony, they would not find much. If one person had evil thoughts, the group would find very few stones. It was easy to detect if anyone was not in harmony because mining turquoise was a sacred process. The same is true with salt—it must be gathered sacredly. Three men—Muddy, I'm Worried About It (Kébíni', or Ghaakébíni'), and Son of Coyote Pass People—were expert silversmiths back then and were the only ones who took others to gather turquoise.[29] Today, people do not do this, and it is no longer sacred. They use vehicles to go everywhere.

OLD AGE, HOLY WIND, AND DEATH

Another teaching was to respect the elderly people, especially if you are young. You are not to laugh at them, for you might look worse than the elderly when your time comes. Or you might become this elderly person's son- or daughter-in-law. A person is not to make fun of their carelessness or helplessness, or think badly of their personal hygiene, for these old men and women have survived everything in their life-times. It is said that you could pick up their spit and swallow it; this will make you live as long, or longer, than this elderly person. That's how respectfully we should think of them. These were the teachings of our people in the past, but today it is different because there are too many diseases, such as tuberculosis.

The teachings about death say that we all go back into the ground. We were given the Holy Wind and a body of flesh and skin, which is our outer clothing until it returns to the earth.[30] The Holy Wind, given to each of us at birth, will be taken away when we die, but it lasts for-ever. Nothing happens to it. Christian priests were called One Who Does Not Die (Doo Daatsaahii), not One Who Drags His Clothes (Éé'nishoodii), as they are known today. The Holy Wind given to our people is ever-lasting too.

Life was given to us from the tips of the white and yellow corn stalks, where pollen is found. People say there is a corn seed that exists somewhere as another world. The Holy Wind comes from there to give us life, entering our bodies when we are born. We use this Holy Wind as we live on this earth until we die from old age; then we go back into the tips of the corn stalk that produces pollen. That is why the Navajos use corn pollen to pray. As children of the Holy Wind, we are given life through it, so when we die, this life will return to the corn pollen stalk.

This is how it happens. Songs and prayers change us into people. The Holy Wind is placed in the soles of our feet, knees, lungs (front and back), necks, palms, and faces—from where we speak to the crowns of our heads. This gives us life, so we live accordingly. When we are born, one of these Holy Winds enters our body. It might come from the earth, heavens, sunrise, sunrays, sunset, the north, and the Holy Beings. Even a stillborn receives one of these. This is why small children have a Blessingway sing to send them on their way to old age. This is how our beliefs and practices work. The Holy Wind is both male and female. When we die of old age, it returns to the white corn stalk. It enters through the corn's silk and continues back down into the ground to the underworld, where a soft white corn is located. The Holy Wind will enter its soft heart and become at peace again. Then, if another human is born, it will come back out and reenter a newborn baby. That is the cycle.

Our teachings also say that Navajos have already been to the sun and moon. The footprints the astronauts saw up there are probably ours. We went there in our Holy Wind long before the white men did. We have also been to the center of the earth. I do not understand how, but that is what is said. All of these events happened shortly after the Creation. People often wonder, "What makes us live, how were we made, where did we come from?" It is the Holy Wind that stands in all the vital parts of our body that keeps us alive. All humans live like that, even the white man. There is more to this than just the Holy Wind, but I cannot say.

The Holy Wind communicates with us through the ways of super-natural power. It is also capable of picking up bad language or evil thoughts that we have in ourselves or that we speak to others. It detects cruelty and other bad things that a person does, and when that person dies, all these wrongful things will be a strike against him or her upon reaching the other world. Therefore, when we bury a person, we have to hold sacred the death and burial for four days. If it is kept sacred, the person will be able to go to the other world where the good people enter.[31] Our keeping of the four sacred days changes the deceased and makes a bad person worthy to enter the good world. That is why it is so important to observe this after the burial. Those who commit suicide have their own world. It is chaotic and wild. But for those who die a normal death and were good, there is a beautiful place.

We were made from the earth and its contents. The Holy Beings gathered the tiny particles of debris left by water and wind and the sacred mountain soil to make us. We are the children of this earth, which is our mother, and the sky is our father. The female mountains are also our mothers, providing food through a variety of plants and animals. Water Woman (Tó Yísdzáán) is our grandmother and gives us the water of life. The earth chose us people and took sand in the shape of round sandstones, which were made into our bodies.

It was said that shortly after the creation of humans, the very first death occurred, when a man lost his wife. Her Holy Wind left her body, and he wondered what happened to those who died. After sitting by his wife's grave day and night, the husband decided to follow her spirit to see where it went. He followed it to the white corn stalk and went inside, where he traveled down, down, and down, arriving at a new land where the dead lived. He recognized in this beautiful place many of the people he had known on earth. They rode in their wagons, had large fields of corn, and hogans spread across the land. It was a paradise, where there was no suffering.[32]

He saw many of his relatives and his wife and wanted to shake their hands, but they just floated away, because he was still a living human being. "Go home. You didn't come to join us. This is not the place for you," they told the man. He came back to our world and brought this story, and so it is said that the Navajos were the first to see what death was like and the world of the dead.

I have heard people suggest that things happen to individuals for a reason. One story is told of a woman who was very ill with diabetes and high blood pressure. When she returned from the hospital, she said, "My deceased father and mother, brothers and sisters, pleaded with me to go home with them. Since they were no longer loved or wanted as part of the human race, they invited me to go with them to get well. This is what they told me," she said. "I'm here getting well, but I didn't go with them. They have been dead for some time, but they all came to see me at the hospital."

Elderly people talk about such encounters, one mother saying, for instance, that her late daughter returned and asked her to come with her. This is an emotional thing, part of a process, and was meant to happen like this from the very beginning. All lives end at different times. A father and son will die at different times, which is how life is, with death a natural part of it.

In the old days, the dead were buried immediately. This was such a sacred event that no one was allowed to drink water or eat any food until the task was completed. Two individuals, wearing nothing but loincloths, did the actual burying. Once they finished, they returned home, washed with herbs, and ate but sat opposite and separated from the others in the hogan for four days. Only after the burial could the other people cook and eat and the immediate family members stop mourning. This was for everyone, no matter where they lived or where they were— they had to observe the mourning days. At the end of this period, everyone bathed in sacred herbs, painted their face with a mixture of powdered red sand and grease, and gathered together in one place.

At this meeting, the family talked to the deceased, had a big farewell, and talked the dead person into his or her resting place below. For traditional Navajos, this was not a big public event like it is today. People could still mention the deceased's name and tell stories about him, how he used to say this or do that, and how he used to sing and pray. They could talk about how he used to go after his horses, herd sheep, plant his cornfields, hoe his garden, and what a hard worker he was. This is how the people talked about their lost loved ones.

END OF THE WORLD

When the Navajos first entered this world, it was said that the seasons—winter and summer—would shorten. They would get to the point where they would pass over each other and change places. This changeover will signal the end of this life and a new beginning, which will occur without warning. There will be no suffering and it will happen as quickly as lightning. People will be sitting here, and the next thing they know, there will be a change. They will not feel or see what happened.

Shortly before this changeover, all of the medicine men will be taken alive and returned to the sacred mountains. These men will not die but will be put into the mountains and mesas around us and kept there until the changeover is completed. Those who sing the ceremonies like Blessingway will later be released to return and carry on the sacred religion of the people. We will once again live like we did before everything took place. Eventually, this will wind down again to repeat this course of events. It is something that has been going on forever and will continue. This is what our elders used to say. The Navajos will never cease but will live again after the new world has come.

Another teaching is based on children and age. In the early days, people lived until they were over a hundred years old. Their life span, once long, began to diminish. They are now growing older at a very young age. Eventually, infants will be born to young mothers who are eleven years old, then eight, then six, until there is no more, and the infants are born mature. The changeover will be complete when a child is born with gray hair, as with old men and women. We can see this happening now, as our children look increasingly mature when only

Horsemen in Glen Canyon area. J.H.: "Before this changeover, all of the medicine men will be taken alive and returned to the sacred mountains. These men
will not die but will be put into the mountains and mesas around us and kept
there until the changeover is completed." (Photo NAU.PH.96.4.215.42, Cline
Library Special Collections and Archives, Northern Arizona University)

ten years old. It is said that this trend will worsen until an infant will be
born with white hair and aged like an elder. This is the crossover of
human life, just as it will happen to the seasons. There are many similar
stories pertaining to this changeover and new beginning.

One teaching tells how, before this world had a new beginning, there
were things that happened to make it come about. It was through
White Shell Woman that this new beginning occurred. People in those
times could have been the Anasazi or the Mexicans. They began exper-
imenting and producing unimaginable things, just like we do today.
They kept at it and at it and at it, until they destroyed themselves. Now
we see their pottery shards and bones everywhere. People say it was so
destructive that the ground completely overturned, destroying all the
means of livelihood on this earth.[33] After the renewal was completed,
the medicine men with their sacred religion were released from the

mountains to live once again on the new earth. The same will happen again when this world ends after the changeover. Wow! Unbelievable, isn't it? This will happen after all the crossovers occur.

My elders taught me these legends long before much of what is now bad even happened. A lot has changed since I first heard these things. Last summer's season is still here today, and yet it is now mid-winter. And when mid-summer comes, it will be like winter. Things will freeze, and the snow will fall all the way to mid-summer. The crossover is happening. This is what my grandmother and grandfather used to tell me.

Today, we hear constantly that medicine men, the singers of the Bless-ingway, are dying. Even our younger generations are changing, because they have lost the sacred beliefs that are part of the changeover. Our religion will become extinct, and that is where we are headed now. We are experiencing the closure of the great changeover, so a new beginning is coming soon.

On the other hand, from my own observations as a medicine man, I see unusually holy young people who attend my ceremonies. They are strong believers and keep the teachings and prayers sacred. Many come on the ceremony's first night and remain to partake of the rituals and activities throughout. Some of them bring their belongings and food and eat with me. They ask a lot of questions about the prayers and songs and rituals that take place and really want to learn. I think the older people overlook these beliefs and do not observe and learn the sacred ways. They shy away, ignoring the traditional teachings, but I do not understand why. I experience this as I travel about performing ceremonies.

Some of the older people have thrown away or burned their sacred prayer bundles. They have burned the sacred mountain soil in their medicine bundles, which has caused wildfires in the mountains. We rarely heard about these fires before this happened, but ever since our people started throwing away or burning their prayer and mountain soil bundles, nothing has been the same. They have brought suffering and unhappiness to our people. Those who burned their sacred belongings are all dead, killing themselves before their time was due.

There are other teachings that show we are getting close to the new beginning. At the time of Creation, the white man's god, One Who Wins

You as a Prize (the Great Gambler), was defeated, and parts of him became the earth's oil (fat). His body is seen as Sleeping Ute Mountain, lying there like a small man. He is in a reclining position, with his head to the north and his knees and feet pointing upward. His wife lies beside him. Only his Holy Wind left him, going across the ocean. After the lightning bows and arrows, guns, sharp knives, long swords, bayonets, metal clubs, sunrays, and other deadly weapons were taken from the Sun's home, they were thrown down into the center of the underworld.[34] People say that this was at the same time the Holy One appeared on the other side of the world. It is also said that if anybody reinvented these deadly weapons, there would be more enemies.

The white man's god spoke four times and said, "I shall return someday to win back your language, mind, plans, songs, and prayers—everything." He returned, and today most of our people are speaking the white man's language. Even the smallest child speaks English. What happened? What's going on? The Navajos are holy, but if they outgrow their prayers, songs, language, and wisdom, it will be the end. There will be the new beginning and great change. This is how Metal Teeth explained it. Those who keep their traditions will survive. But even if we kept all of the traditional beliefs, there would still be a new beginning, because the earth continues to become overpopulated and its resources depleted.

Our planets and Earth will remain the same, even though we hear of earthquakes in many parts of the world. Our forefathers used to say, "Someday our whole earth will shake itself, as a horse shakes itself after it rolls in the sand." At present, only certain parts, maybe an arm or leg, of the earth shake in foreign territories. But if it shakes its whole body, there is going to be a major catastrophe and the start of the new beginning. This is the time, already mentioned, when certain holy spirits will enter the sacred mountains and return as human beings.

Last year I took a trip to California, down by the ocean, and saw the results of an earthquake. The houses were in shambles. I found a Navajo family, originally from Inscription House [House in the Sagebrush] living in the midst of the chaos. I saw that their home and surroundings were undamaged. It made me think that my grandfather was telling the truth.

CHAPTER TEN

THE MAKING OF A MEDICINE MAN

This final chapter speaks directly to the use of ceremonies and their relation with some nontraditional practices. John discusses his experience with peyote, for instance, a relatively new religion introduced on the reservation in the first quarter of the twentieth century. Although it is not part of traditional Navajo heritage, it has gained wide popularity on the reservation. He also discusses healing Anglo-Americans with his ceremonies. His success on a number of occasions is an obvious point of pride and proof of the universal truth of his teachings.

But the core of his instruction concerns the healing of his people through traditional practices. He tells of how he attempted to use the powers of hand trembling and sun gazing and what happens to those exposed to witchcraft. He shares his personal experience detecting and confronting skinwalkers, how sacred smoke can cleanse and settle a person, and various aspects of ceremonies. John has used his sacred knowledge for more than seventy years. His service to his people has been recognized on local and tribal levels. But what can be done to pass on this heritage?

The last part of this chapter discusses his training of new apprentices. John is impressed with the caliber of those who come to learn. He is excited at the potential for good that these young men exhibit and lives in the hope that they will pass on what he leaves behind. As John loses more and more mobility, the future will rest with this new generation of practitioners.

DIVINATION: HAND TREMBLING,
SUN GAZING, AND STARGAZING

Learning to be a medicine man is a lot of hard work.[1] It is similar to learning in school. I had plenty of instruction in discipline. My teacher cursed me from head to toe while I was trying to learn, and I had to withstand everything. Some people who undergo such treatment quit, but I believe if anyone wants to learn something, he or she should be taught in this manner and not be treated lightly. Today, some of our children drop out of school because it is too strict, or the teacher says something disagreeable. This same situation occurs when a person is trying to learn to be a medicine man. Eventually the teacher cools off, things get back to normal, and the student continues to learn. This is how I became a medicine man. It is like everything else; there is a challenge to be successful in whatever one does in life. I took it upon myself to accomplish this task, and today I help those who are sick and in need.

Hand tremblers have their own experiences. The sacred spirit of this power is called Gila Monster (Tiníléí).[2] This creature diagnoses a person's ailment and tells how to treat it by indicating the necessary ceremony or herbal medicine. The Gila Monster is like the discipline paddle at the old boarding schools. I do not think there are any more around. Even horny toads are almost extinct. Medicine men use the shake-offs from a horny toad by sprinkling it with sacred corn pollen and saving the pollen that falls from it. This shake-off is used for protection, and people tie a small bag of it on themselves and always have it with them when in public.

Hand trembling came about from the beginning of Creation. It has its own form of sacredness and set of rules. Anyone who has been bitten by any animal is forbidden to practice hand trembling. The gift itself has to be bestowed from above on certain individuals, but one can become a hand trembler through ceremonies, if the Gila Monster accepts the person.

Not just anybody receives these gifts. Young children can have them, but they are too young to guess what the diagnosis is and what to do about it. They are unfamiliar with the rituals or ceremonies used for healing. One has to learn all these things first, including all the different symbols that represent an illness, such as reptiles, the coyote, dogs, and so forth. If the hand trembler sees one of these, the patient is required to have it "remade" for him or her. Each one represents an ailment of some kind. So it is very crucial to know everything first, or else it will be useless. The medicine man usually instructs his students in what he expects them to do.

Nobody can learn or receive this gift without a reason. The only time one obtains it is when someone is ill or troubled. Several people may volunteer to try it at the same time. The medicine man sprinkles the corn pollen on their hands, then sings and prays for them. Once one's hand is "touched," he or she will be asked to guess the problem and diagnose it, then say which treatment to take. It takes a lot of concentration and energy to be a hand trembler.

Sometimes the hand trembler cannot find the answer or understand the impression, so the sacred spirit will let the hand and fingers grab the diviner's nose or ear, or poke his or her ribs, as if to say, "Here's the answer, can't you see it? Are you stupid? You can't even guess the answer!" The trembling will not stop until the answer is found. The hand trembler then recommends a ceremony—Mountainway, Enemyway, Lightningway, Holy Wind, Blessingway, or Tobaccoway—and protection prayers.

If you lose something, like a horse or valuable property, you can use a hand trembler. My son had lost some money one time and decided to call on his aunt to "ask" for him in finding it. They wanted to test the power to see if she could really locate the money. His aunt told him that this little nephew had taken his fifty dollars. She said he spent ten dollars on something but had the rest. The nephew denied he had it at first but finally returned it. Hand trembling works, and my son was amazed. Many practitioners have the natural gift, which is very powerful.

Hand trembling does not work for me. I wanted to be a hand trembler, but it would not go. They tried to instill that gift in me, as I sat with my hands up (in fact, I tried both hands), along with several other people being tested. It was working for some around me—their hands were touched, but mine failed time after time. The medicine man "asked" why it did not work for me. His hands trembled vigorously, tearing at my hands and arms. He finally received the answer. "You were once bitten by a jackrabbit on this hand and a prairie dog on the other," he said. "The Gila Monster doesn't want you. It is useless and will definitely not work for you." So that was the end of that. If only that crazy prairie dog had not bitten my arm, I probably would have received the hand-trembling gift. Those who receive it are truly blessed.

My wife was once naturally gifted with hand trembling. One day, my baby niece crawled outside, and something made her cry and scream in pain. Nobody knew what caused it, but she would not stop crying. Evidently, the baby had been bitten by a rattlesnake on the sole of her little foot. My wife, while doing her hand trembling on the baby, accidentally touched the blood on the bitten area and that ended her gift. She no longer had hand-trembling power. That goes to show just how important it is to be careful in retaining this gift.

When she failed to continue her treatment on the baby, they went to my wife's father, Bob Atene. He was a powerful medicine man and diagnosed that the baby's intestine had become twisted like a rope. He suggested that the hospital was the best alternative. There were no automobiles then, so they took her in a wagon. The hospital was barely established in a one-room trailer, but the physician was able to restore the baby's health.[3]

Another time, when our oldest son was still small, he became very sick. He cried and vomited, so my wife did her hand trembling and diagnosed him to have appendicitis. Sure enough, he did. We had to take him to the clinic to have it removed. I honestly believe she was highly gifted, but she lost that power after the rattlesnake incident.

I have also tried stargazing, but it scared me. I used to use the sun, instead of the stars, but did not realize how damaging it was to my eyes. This was a natural gift bestowed upon me and not something I had to learn or ask for. I used sun gazing for about ten years to detect what was killing a patient. I used it as a healing object for someone who had hope for life. It is totally impossible to look at the sun with your naked eyes, but I used to do it. I prayed and sang as I gazed at the sun, until it darkened my sight. Then from out of the darkness, a stream of white light bounced to the earth. The earth, in turn, changed its form to fit the shape of the sun. As I stared at the sun, it no longer shone brightly but became dark, as black as a piece of black cloth. When the white stream descended, it drew an image of the earth and all the things on it, just like a topographical map is made with rivers, hills, and mountains. It drew just a little section of it and magnified it

Men outside a shade house. John identified these men as (left to right) Leon Bradley, Gray Whiskers, and the Man Who Coughs. J.H.: "I have also tried stargazing, but it scared me. I used to use the sun, instead of the stars, but did not realize how damaging it was to my eyes." (Photo NAU.PH.413.142, Cline Library Special Collections and Archives, Northern Arizona University)

even more to show what the patient was suffering from. It showed what it was, but I still needed to guess.

Once I identified the ailment, the whole image disappeared. If I did not guess the answer, it started manipulating me for an answer, just as with hand trembling. Then I saw, as if on a screen, the problem or ailment of the sick patient. This is how I used to do it, until I started having sight problems and had to quit that business.

Others use stargazing. I have tried that, too. It has the same white stream of light that the sun sends forth, revealing the problem of the patient. I have used it many times. Another medicine man, Jack Gillis, used to be a true stargazer, and I have gone with him on many occasions. Some medicine men use stars as part of their ceremonial rituals. The Pleiades has a song that starts from the earth and goes up to the heavens and names all the stars. This song is used in the Blessingway and names the Dippers, Man with Spread Legs [Corvus and Orion], [body of Scorpius], First Slim One [Orion], and Awaits the Dawn [Milky Way].[4]

PEYOTE

Our people have become involved in a new religion called Peyote [Native American Church].⁵ It comes with many different rituals, like other religions. The medicine men ask for large fees when they practice. "Give me $500, then I will perform for you," they say. I do not know their purpose, but I was told to never ask for so much money; it was forbidden. The patient should decide the price to pay and what he can afford. I was taught these things and still practice them today. Some medicine men say, "Give me a cow with her calf, and I will take out the bundle of evil curse buried against you," or "If you pay me so much, I'll take out that piece of evil bone from your body so you can be healed."⁶

These teachings began just recently, and I personally do not believe in many of them because of my experiences. Several years ago, I became ill, tried a variety of rituals, but many did not work for me. Only a few were helpful. From what I know, the suction removal of foreign objects from the body worked only when the ailment pertained to the blood.⁷ The Paiutes, Utes, and some Navajo medicine men once practiced the true suction removal ritual. No one has really relearned that technique or uses it in a true way. At present, many claim to know it, but that, of course, is just like everything else.

Metal Teeth taught me that the Lifeway medicines were planted under the direction of the Medicine People. At the very end of the creation of many of the plants, another one came along. These medicines were like people and lived where they could survive, but this last medicine, Peyote, could not be with the rest of them. The environment around here was not suitable for it, so the Medicine People sent it south, where it was hot year round.⁸ As the Peyote People left, they said, "Someday in the future, when the People have gone astray, no longer respect their clans, have gone crazy on drugs, and everything is in chaos, we'll come back and save the People. We'll teach them to respect their clans again. When the People have forgotten the sacred songs and prayers, we'll be back to restore it all." This is what the Peyote People said as they journeyed south.

When we first heard that the Utes were using peyote, my grandfather said that it was probably the return of the Peyote Medicine People. He believed peyote would not harm you.

The Utes who lived in Allen Canyon west of Blanding used peyote. They would lie on their sides, beat a drum, and take peyote. It is said that long ago, a Ute man named Little Sioux (Naałání Yázhi), from Blue House [Towaoc], and Thin Yucca Fruit from Beclabito, east of Teec Nos Pos, went to work in Oklahoma, where they took peyote. Both men worked on the railroad among the Sioux. While they were there, the two of them attended the peyote meetings quite often, and soon they learned how to perform the ceremony.

Upon their return to the Navajo Reservation, they brought back peyote buttons and the songs, prayers, and medicine bundle. When they first arrived with these things, they took them directly to the top of White Ridge to the home of the late White Spot on His Back (Hane'łikizh), where his widow lived. It was from there that the peyote religion started, and not from the Utes.[9] The Utes used it, but without sacred rituals and a tepee. They just used it and beat the drum. The real peyote religion came from the Sioux Tribe and was brought back to the Navajo Reservation by these two men. The peyote religion then spread throughout Navajo land to Oljato and Monument Valley.

When the peyote religion first came to Monument Valley, I attended a meeting on the south side of Train Rock. Some of us were arrested by the police and taken to jail in Tuba City, Arizona, the next morning, because the Navajo Nation prohibited using peyote. The police said we were drunk on peyote, as if we had been drinking alcohol or getting high on drugs. They claimed it was not good for us and was hazardous to the public. This treatment was happening all over the reservation, with people being arrested and taken to jail.

Nobody was held in jail very long. There was no good reason for them to spend time in jail when they had not done any harm to anyone. The officials did not hold a real trial for us, since the judge only asked the police supervisor some questions about our arrest. Why had we been arrested? None of the people brought in were staggering or falling or acting strange. The supervisor said, "They were arrested because they had partaken of peyote," and that was his only reason. Then the judge asked, "How do you know? Have you taken some yourself? And did you get drunk on peyote or become 'crazy'? Is that why you prohibited the peyote ceremonies?" He answered, "No, I don't use it and never have." That was the end of that; he was cornered by those questions, which he could not answer. We were set free because there was really no reason for us to remain in jail or have a trial. Later I was again taken to jail for attending a peyote meeting but was let go with the same defense.

I am not educated and do not know how to read and write English, but I was asked to take on a project to study and legalize the peyote religion for American Indians. Many of our sacred prayer bundles have been taken away and lost. The Indian people and government wanted to retrieve these confiscated items, so they asked me to be on the committee. I told them that I was uneducated, not knowing how to read or write. "What good will I do to be on this type of project? It's no use. I don't understand what people talk about when things are discussed in English. I usually sit there puzzled and listen to the 'noise.' So how will I be of any use to you on this project?"

Their response was, "We need your wisdom, songs, prayers, and traditional beliefs in the Great One. It's all based on these very important assets to accomplish this project. That is why we need you to be a part of this committee and to help us. You have great knowledge in traditional beliefs, what the sacred prayer bundles contain, and what they represent. We need your help."

I tried to tell them to leave me off the committee, but they still put me on.[10] I was asked to talk about the history and beliefs of peyote and how it originated, going back to the beginning of Creation. I explained how the peyote plant came into being; why it was holy; how it grew into a plant through holy songs, prayers, and the blessings of many other plants, corn pollen, and rain water, which fostered growth on this earth. The researchers still put me on the committee, and I have served for several years now.

The research committee decided that some other Navajos and I should attend important meetings to settle this problem. We went to Washington, D.C., Denver, Phoenix, and the "state of the peyote" [Texas or Oklahoma], where we purchased peyote buttons. The government decided to study peyote and its ceremonies. The Native American Research Organization provided funds for this purpose. I do not remember the name of the grant that paid for the study, but once we requested the money and it was approved, Washington, D.C., provided the funds.

Identified by John as Herbert Cly. This photo was taken in 1938. J.H.: "Visitors came in pairs, and we had a couple of them attend a ceremony at Herbert Cly's house."

The research began with Public Health medical teams assigned to attend peyote ceremonies all over the reservation. These visitors came in pairs, and we had a couple of them attend a ceremony at Herbert Cly's house. During the first half of the night, they took notes on all that went on, and then decided to drink some peyote juice. Shortly after midnight, they quit taking notes, sat quietly, and observed until daybreak. When the ceremony ended, they made a statement: "This peyote is great. It really makes one think and talk about life and the good way of living. We don't see anything hazardous about using it. It is harmless to the human body and is good. The Peyote Ceremony comes with sacred songs and prayers that do not harm anyone. It is good."

The two medical researchers turned in their reports to Washington, D.C. After all the reports were in from across the reservation, the government "approved" the peyote religion and legalized it. Now we have the right to use the ceremonies based on the depth of study and research from this project. Once it was legalized, we were able to practice this religion, just as any other faith, to enrich our lives in holiness. That's how it happened.

I once got very, very sick with a bad cough, aching back, and inability to get out of bed. A man named Chee Yabney, from Teec Nos Pos, came to see me. He often attended peyote meetings around here and told me that he had gone to Texas, where it grew, and had picked a large burlap sack full of those buttons. He brought me some in a bag and said, "My son [he belonged to the same clan—Within-His-Cover People—as my father], you drink this and you will get better. You drink it in the morning, noon, evening, and at bedtime, and you will recover soon. Drink it until it is all gone." I drank it every day during most of the winter and into the spring; the sickness from uranium contamination came to the surface of my skin. It came out in sacs that had been formed around the sickness. When I went to the hospital, I was checked and told my lungs had been infected with sores but were now healing, and the coughing stopped.

Peyote is a real medicine that worked for me when I was sick, but it was not made to be abused. Because of my back problems that I have now, I want to try it again. Still, I dread it because it is very bitter. I do not know why, but when I used it before, I did not notice the taste that much. More recently, I have attempted to drink some but cannot stand the taste. I hear it is normal to go through this experience of not wanting it later. This has happened to many people like me who have used it.

I never became a peyote medicine man. I attended the meetings but did not partake and usually just slept. I have not been to a peyote meeting for five years now [in 1991]. When I was using it, however, I would go anywhere and everywhere just to attend.

Peyote is good because it helped restore our society. People around here were going crazy, acting badly, and had even forgotten their livestock, sacred songs, and prayers until peyote came among them. We were all drunk and alcoholics, living in turmoil. We had messed up our songs and prayers. Our young people no longer wanted to bother with the livestock or ride horses, had lost interest in material goods, and went in the wrong direction.

Peyote put them back on track and changed many lives.[11] Once again we had community activities, like field days and rodeos. Those involved in peyote drove nice vehicles and had high-paying jobs. They set liquor aside and changed for the better. I could tell the difference between those who drank and those who used peyote. The drunks had a bunch of old cars sitting around their homes like a car lot; those using peyote kept everything around their homes clean. It is a good thing that peyote came here when it did. If one were to have 100 percent faith in it, he or she would have a successful life.

UNCOVERING WITCHCRAFT

As a student learning to be a medicine man, you learn many things from your teacher. The instructor warns you against harmful rituals that may be encountered while practicing medicine. "Someday, you'll be chosen to do a prayer or sing to cure someone or ward off evil spells," the teacher would say. "You never say the accused person's name straight out, especially if you're not sure if he is practicing witchcraft. The patient might say so-and-so is doing witchcraft on me. Can you counteract the situation and reverse the spell?" The teacher told us, "Never name the accused person, unless you absolutely witnessed his actions and know he is at fault for your patient's sickness. This is crucial. You cannot guess or be suspicious about someone, then sing against him. That is wrong. Why should you do that to an innocent person?"

I was warned never to go in the direction of bewitching or cursing others. It is forbidden and deadly. "The sacred songs and prayers you have learned shall never be misused against any of your people," my grandfather told me. "Is there such a thing as skinwalkers?" "Yes." "Can someone bewitch or curse you?" "Yes." "Can someone bewitch you into deviant sexual destruction?"[12] "Yes. You are strictly forbidden to use your songs and prayers in these cases. If you do, you will kill someone. But you are limited to only four. If you destroy a fifth time, it will be you who will die. If you don't die, you'll likely end up paralyzed or a total beggar. 'While everyone else travels by horseback, your one-sided footprints will be seen along the roads,' is a saying that applies. Your tracks will be straight and barren, barefooted alongside the happy, wealthy, knowledgeable people who ride on their healthy horses. So never misuse what you've learned. Use it only to help and heal your people, or to ask for rain when there is drought in the land. These are more important and the good way. So leave all the evil doings alone!"

When a white man hates or is envious, he will shoot and kill the person. A Navajo, if he is a medicine man, has the ability to destroy life with his rituals and songs. Anyone is vulnerable to going in the wrong direction; even a medicine man can become his own worst enemy if he starts practicing evil. If you try it, you might be successful in destroying a life, then a second, and a third, but that could be the end, and you will lose all you have. All of your happiness, wealth, and sacred knowledge of prayers and songs will become as nothing, and you will be walking in an empty life, having lost your sacredness, your mind, your voice, and your body to evil. This is what happens to those who dwell on witchcraft and the like. This is what I was taught.

True medicine men do it the right way. They have prayers and songs that can lead to a suspect. It is like the police and FBI, who investigate incidents. They search for evidence of the person responsible for the sickness or problem. The search-and-locating prayers and songs are done for the client. Once it is known who is at fault, it will be apparent when the guilty one soon reveals himself. Even when the suspect becomes known, the medicine man should not directly accuse him, because the evildoer will naturally suffer from his own guilt and sometimes perish.[13]

Witchcraft is difficult to detect; it is hard to see such things that are unexplainable. If an evil person envies a beautiful person, he will bewitch him or her. It will make the beautiful person wild until he or she is ruined. There are many envious people who are obvious and can be picked out of a crowd. They are the poor straggly-looking ones who have nothing, no family (because they deserted them), and no livestock. They roam the road with packs on their backs, are jealous, and are the worst kind.

Changes in traditional medicinal practices have caused false accusations and the introduction of other rituals. Peyote branched off to sucking bewitched objects from the body. There are also crystal gazers and people who retrieve buried patient's belongings. These are all a part of what changed the real medicine into accusation-filled practices. People claim them to be true ceremonies when they are not. These newly created practices incriminate people, whether they are innocent or guilty. Someone will say, "That person is a witch; he is the one who put a spell on you, and that is why you are sick." Based on that assumption, the injured party prays and sings against the accused, putting evil on him without really knowing it is true. I am sure I have been accused of that too. These rumors can break up a circle of friends, family members, or a household.

If one person starts accusing another of witchcraft, relations are soon fragmented. Some children are told by their parents, "So-and-so's mother, father, grandfather, grandmother, uncle, is involved in witchcraft." The children believe this, and before too long, two groups of children will be arguing and fighting. This started happening not too long ago. Back when I was growing up, we did not hear of such incidents. It was not the thing to say or do.

Offenses happen fast and quietly, so quietly that one wonders why people are suddenly no longer talking or visiting each other. Rituals like sucking out evil, crystal gazing, and retrieving cursed bundles have caused broken homes and relationships.[14] The "medicine man" would say, "The man or lady over there buried your belongings in a grave. That is why you are sick. I can retrieve the cursed bundle for you, but you will need to pay me $1,000 and a brand new rifle as payment up front."

These new ceremonies came into existence not too long ago. They are new and have destroyed a lot of homes and torn apart communities, because of these witchcraft accusations. Even a husband's and wife's relationship is destroyed because one accused the other of witchcraft and was diagnosed by a so-called "medicine man." "You, my husband, your mother-in-law, and your brother and sister-in-law are all witching me."

Several years ago, this happened to me. My wife and her family were against me, and a "medicine man" wanted to retrieve the "cursed bundle." He said it was buried somewhere, and that it was going to kill me if not removed. I did not bother with it; I paid nothing and told them I was not interested. This is what destroys many close-knit families and friendships. It is awful, but that is how it happens all the time.

Sometimes one of these "medicine men" will say to a person, that he or she said a prayer or song the wrong way, but that he can correct it if paid. Many of them accuse each other, saying they made mistakes and therefore the patient is still sick. This overwhelms the patient. There is also too much said about skinwalkers. It is terrible, awful, and I do not like it.

When I attend big meetings with other medicine men, I speak out on such issues. I tell them outright how some of them are completely off course from the real medicine. There are usually many crystal gazers, retrievers, and suckers in these meetings, but I still speak my feelings and beliefs. "You have totally destroyed our people by your false practices," I say. "You have led them astray."

The younger generation of medicine men claim to have stronger and more effective rituals, whereas the older ones, like me, are not supposed to be as powerful because it is "old stuff." They also say the older men are liars. People start believing the young people are right and pay $700 or more for their help. This is all headed in a different direction.

All I have learned is how to pray and sing for protection against evil curses and rituals. I do such sings for victims who are dying from the effects of these curses. I was allowed this special gift, and I use it with great respect.

SKINWALKERS

I have also used my medicine practice to see if skinwalking was real.[15] The power said, "Yes." "What about witchcraft?" "Yes, it's true," was the reply. "What about the type of witchcraft where witches bury a person's belongings and talk one into the ground?" "That's true too." "What about where skinwalkers sprinkle a deadly potion on someone to make them sick or die?"[16] "That's true too."

My grandfather said to me, "You're not the kind of person who would deal in this type of witchery. It's never revealed to the loud ones, the one who is part of the crowd and laughs out and jokes around. For those who do such things, they tend to carry out their cursing rituals through other people. No, it's not for you. You're not cut out for it. It is for the quiet one, male or female, young or old, or loner; the one who doesn't mingle with the crowd. They are the ones who perform all the witchcraft, make deadly potions, and collect one's belongings to bury as waste," said Grandfather. "If I were to tell you anything about how it's done, you'd probably throw a coyote's skin on your back and claim to be a skinwalker.[17] But don't ever say you know how and take a skin. You're not that crazy. Don't be that stupid! I'm not going to enlighten you on such things. It's worthless, worthless! I know about it, but I don't work with it," he said to me. "And you will not work with it either. I am here to protect the people from harm. I'm here to heal the sick and those who have hope for life. That's what I am here for. That's what you'll be here for, too. So leave it alone; it's bad." I was told not to indulge, not to talk about such things, and just leave it alone or else I would never reach old age.

I was one of those people who did not believe in skinwalkers. I have herded sheep all by myself, ever since I was a small child, and never once had I seen a skinwalker. One spring, the goats wandered up on the side of a mesa among the big boulders. I searched for them, and when I found the lost goats, I saw a big dog walking among them. Its face was black and white, and it had a wide white ring around its neck. It kept its hind end away from me and backed off as if it were hiding its backside, then lay down behind the bushes and kept its distance. That was all I saw of this strange dog. I observed it, but I never saw it from behind, and it stayed when I herded the goats off the mesa.

About twenty years later, I heard a woman had died. Her relatives burned the ceremonial hogan she had died in, but next to it there was a summer shelter. As I took the sheep to water, I passed the hogan and there, in the middle of the shelter, sat the same dog that I had seen twenty years before. It was still hiding its backside. My donkey was scared of it, blowing and snorting through its nostrils. It had been a long time, but here it was again, just as I had seen it before. Yes, it was a skinwalker; they exist.

Another time, we were living in a male hogan and had a lot of sheep. We did not have a corral, so the sheep slept in the open. It was early spring and still cold. My sister said, "We get cold at night. What about you?" I went over and took a fresh sheepskin off a log, where it was hanging to dry. I put it on top of her and the children and returned to my own bedding of sheepskins on the other side of the hogan.

That night we were awakened by the continuous barking of the dogs. They sounded as if they were chasing something away from our camp, while others stayed close and kept barking. We again awoke, this time to the sound of footsteps. They were loud, like a horse walking, but had the pattern of a human's footfall. It was not a dog's tread, because dogs walk softly. The footsteps came closer and closer, then climbed onto the hogan. I prepared by grabbing a club and the fire poker; my shotgun lay too far away in the corner. The ceiling of the hogan was very low.

As the footsteps got higher and higher on the hogan, I prepared to whack him on the head when he appeared in the smoke hole. The sound came closer and closer; then I saw his head with a coyote's face. I must have died. I froze with club in hand and tried to yell but could not move or make a sound. I was horrified. The creature disappeared from sight and scrambled down the hogan, as sand and gravel fell on us. The debris made a loud noise as it plopped down on the fresh, hard sheepskin that I had given to my sister. Again, we heard the loud footsteps of the skinwalker as he hit the ground running. The dogs nearby, and those in the distance, kept barking and sounded like they were fighting with something.

The next day I looked for tracks. There had been two skinwalkers that came to our camp that night, leaving two sets of tracks coming and going. We had a dog that was very mean and fought with the skinwalkers. This dog died a little ways from home and had blood coming from its ears, mouth, and nose. The other sheepdogs came home and were not harmed. We looked around and saw bits of soft skin scattered on the earth. I followed one set of tracks that led to another set on top of the hill. It looked like one of the skinwalkers had sat and waited for the second one to arrive.

From there, the two went all the way to a deserted hogan, where someone had been buried, a custom practiced long ago. The two skinwalkers went inside, then left for another burial hogan. Their tracks went toward Gathering of Water and on to Kayenta. At one place, I

Male hogan and visitor. John said that on the other side of this rock, there is a cleft where people practicing witchcraft meet. J.H.: "The two [men] went all the way to a deserted hogan, where someone had been buried, a custom practiced long ago." (Photo 14499, used by permission, Utah State Historical Society, all rights reserved)

found two pieces of shoe leather that had been undone and must have been lost along the way. I do not know where they got it. Further on, I saw a long strip of assorted color cloth that looked as if it had come from a Navajo shirt. As I continued to search, I found a large ball of it sitting in the bushes. They must have left this, too. "This is ridiculous. What am I doing tracking these things out here," I told myself, then turned around and went home.

Not until I experienced and saw for myself did I believe in skinwalkers. They exist, and a person has to be tough and brave to face one. When you see one, you cannot move or scream or you will freeze up. That is how skinwalkers are.

Long ago I heard of sanctuaries where witchcraft was performed.[18] People used to say there was such a place on Navajo Mountain, another at Group Chased Up by the Mexican, also at White Streak of Cattail

Coming Out in Monument Valley. This was only hearsay, and I do not know if it was true. I have never personally seen one of these places.

Another site where witchcraft was performed was atop Table-Shaped Mesa, located below Many Farms, Arizona. It is said that a man once saw many tracks leading into the red sandstone of this mesa, so he decided to follow and investigate. On his way up, he met two normal-looking men descending. They suggested the three of them go back up the wash to see the "voodoo sanctuary."[19] The man noticed boulders neatly set a few feet apart in a row all the way up.

When they came close to the base of the mesa, he saw a cave where many horses were tied close to the entrance. Before going inside, the men told him, "As you enter, you will notice a pile of sacred mountain bundles sitting around, but there will be one shabby-looking one, which is the most important and oldest one of all. Grab it and run." The men made further plans for him. "Once you snatch the old sacred mountain bundle, run back down this same wash and hide from them at the farthest end. We will be right behind you."

The man entered and was startled to hear his own sacred hogan song. "Everyone, sing," the crowd was told. The man sat hiding behind the two men, and while everyone sang, they motioned to him and pointed to the old bundle. The rituals must have been going on for several days and nights, because some people fell asleep. He also noticed a couple, a man and woman, trying to dress in their coyote skins. Suddenly, everything stopped. For some reason, the singing was not working. The witches complained, "Something is wrong; maybe someone is looking at us, someone who does not belong here." They tried to find the problem but were too tired and fell asleep.

At that instant, the man grabbed the old bundle and ran as fast as he could. "Watch out, grab him!" everyone shouted, but it was too late. He ran down the wash with the two men right behind. They had changed into their coyote skins! The man reached a greasewood bush and scrambled inside. He heard many of the witches, now dressed in their coyote skins, looking for him. They searched his home but never found him. After the commotion quieted, the man left, bringing the old sacred mountain bundle back to his hogan.

People say that the leader of this group of witches had always lived in that cave. He was born there, married there, and ate there, too. The man found out later that this "master" had died of a heart attack the moment he stole the bundle. Many people were astonished at the brave man's act and named him Boy with the Witchcraft Bundle (Ashkii Anit'ịịhii). I only heard this story, but it is true. There are such things as skinwalkers and witchcraft sanctuaries where people make curses through witchcraft. That is how it is.

CEREMONIES

There was a time when there were many medicine men who knew the sacred ceremonies. Ceremonies are just like a man and his wife—one is male, the other female. These two are Holy Beings, although they are not human. When a ceremony is performed, we offer our prayers and songs to either the male or female god. Some of these rituals were part of the Holyway, which has several different ceremonies under the same category, such as Navajo Windway (Níłch'ijí), Male Mountain Topway (Dziłk'ijí Biką'jí), and Female Mountain Topway (Dziłk'ijí Ba'áádjí).[20] Those belonging in the Evilway categories include Big Starway, Red Antway (Wóláchíí'jí), and Enemy Monsterway (Yé'ii Hastiiník'eh). The Red Antway is used for people who have nightmares or are attacked by ghosts. It chases the evil away. The Enemy Monsterway protects against all illnesses, like flu and colds, and helps a person through old age.

All of these ceremonies had different prayers and songs, sacred stories, and medicinal plants that were kept a secret. Now they have all disappeared from our culture. These sacred prayer rituals involving herbal plants, rocks, and the mountains where offerings are made were kept so secret that when the elders died, they took this knowledge with them. Nobody cared to share their knowledge with the younger people, so it is mostly gone, with only a few medicine men still living to tell some, but not all, of these teachings.

To me, it is sad that it is like that, so I try to tell others what I know. Our elders kept it a secret, and nothing became of it, so there is nothing left. If we want this sacred knowledge and these ceremonies to remain, then we have to teach our children about them, so that the knowledge will remain alive. I believe that is how it should be done.

If people want to learn, then teach them the sacred ways of life. Medicine men who are stingy with their songs and knowledge are not right. I do not want this wisdom to cease, so I tell everyone when they ask me about different things. Some people do not agree or favor certain beliefs, but that will not keep me from doing what I think is best. I want to leave a legacy and the knowledge for my people. I want to be remembered even after a thousand years. Someone might dig up books with my name and stories in them, and the teachings will still be alive in another lifetime. Who knows what is in store for the future?

The sacred songs and ceremonies are all different. As we live on this earth, we might have strange dreams about death, someone killing us, falling off a cliff, or something harming our immediate family members. For this reason, we give offerings of sacred stones to Mother Earth, asking for safety and well-being. These bits of sacred stones consist of turquoise, mother-of-pearl, white shell, jet, coral, blue corn pollen, and other sacred pollens. All of these things are given to Mother Earth in prayer. Whatever evil my dream is telling me will be prevented from happening. We pray, "I bring you this gift in payment, so you will not let it come to pass."

Every one of the ceremonies, whether it is the Blessingway, Big Starway, or Lightningway, is within Mother Earth. We, therefore, pay tribute and give offerings to it to heal and protect us. We also say our prayers to the heavens, mountains, mesas, and trees. Trees that have been burned because of lightning are of the black clouds, so we give offerings to them. We also present our offerings to other clouds and rain, to greasewood brush, the young juniper tree, and different kinds of young pine trees.

Cornmeal is used at prayer time without a special sing. At dawn, one awakens to sprinkle white cornmeal during the prayer; at noon, corn pollen is used; and at sunset, yellow cornmeal. This is similar to how white men pray every day, except we use cornmeal and pollen. We do not see much of this type of prayer anymore, our people having practically done away with it. When one is in desperate need of something—a decent life, work, money, livestock, crops, or rain—that person should offer cornmeal and pollen at daily prayer times. That person will be blessed.

The use of cornmeal and pollen is similar to the white man's beliefs in the cross. To one point of the cross, we offer white cornmeal; to the other end, to the south, we put yellow cornmeal. At the other end, we make offerings to the heavens, then to the end that sits in the ground, we offer blue corn pollen. So the prayers are made in all four sacred directions.

Woman harvesting corn. J.H.: "Cornmeal is used at prayer time without a special sing. . . . The use of cornmeal and pollen is similar to the white man's beliefs in the cross." (Photo NO 5-29, Milton Snow Collection, Navajo Nation Museum)

I only perform the Blessingway, which covers many things. It is used for psychological healing, for renewing or strengthening the holy power in a person's prayers and songs, and for blessing a person's possessions and surroundings—home, corrals, cornfields, horses, sheep, goats, cattle, donkeys, mules, automobiles, and money. Sometimes, people will fail at everything, their luck will give out, and they will be without work and have nothing. A husband and wife might both work, but they will accomplish nothing. This is when they need a Blessingway sing to help them prosper again.

JOHN CURES ANGLOS

One day in the late afternoon, a white lady from Washington, D.C., brought her two daughters to my home. I guess another woman who had been here before told her about me. The lady with her two daughters had flown from D.C. to Cortez, Colorado, and rented a vehicle to get here. The mother explained that her oldest daughter had problems with nightmares, could not sleep at night, and had to be held down when she had these dreams. This was all too much for her. She also explained how they saw two figures walking around in the dark, but when they turned on the lights, the door opened, and they would disappear. This certainly called for the Evilway because it involved ghosts.

The lady who introduced them to me was from a group of health officials who had come to visit during the summer. When these health people came, they had a lot of questions about medicine men and health issues, so I showed them many of my things, except for the most sacred articles. Among those things they saw were the Charcoalway ceremonial items, which included the leather-covered rattle, charcoal, the bull roarer, and a few other objects. I demonstrated how I used them during a ceremony, and how they had the power to chase away evil when someone had problems with ghosts.

When this lady told the other woman, they decided to come see me because she was desperate to cure her daughter's problems. She offered me $1,000 for the ceremony. I started right away and did everything for them. I used all the required items and made the sacred herbal drink Lightning-Struck Rock Plant. They all drank and splashed it on themselves. Next came the application of grease, charcoal, red clay, and the attachment of the sacred stone; then feathering the air; and finally the end of the ceremony. The mother had undressed herself and applied all the grease and charcoal on her face that she could, so that only the whites of her eyes were visible. It looked funny. Her daughter, the primary patient, had to do the main ritual.

When they prepared to leave, they packed the remainder of the charcoal and herbs to take with them. I told them to sprinkle these things inside their house when they got home and to use the eagle feather to spread out the ashes. She said she had one at home, so they used it to complete their ceremonial equipment. They followed all of their instructions, and some time later, she called back to inform us they were healed, and there were no more ghosts. They were amazed at the effectiveness of the ceremony.

Long ago, a white man named Hungry Boy lived at Goulding's.[21] Because he was Harry Goulding's brother-in-law, Harry gave me $50 to perform a special song and prayer for him, because he was leaving for Germany to go to the war. Money was scarce then, so $50 was like $2000 now. I sang the special song for him, and he left, but later, when he returned after serving his time, he came back to tell me that he did not have any problems anywhere. During heavy artillery, men were killed or injured all around him, but he did not get hurt and came home safely. These songs and ceremonies are very sacred, and people can be strongly affected by them. They work for foreigners, white men, and even the Utes, Sioux, and Apaches. I have done ceremonies for all of them, and they treat the ritual as very holy, so it works for them.

HERBS AND SACRED SMOKE

Plants and herbs are gathered in a sacred way for religious purposes. This is very true of herbal smoke taken from the vegetation atop the black volcanic rock point on White Spruce Mountain.[22] My paternal grandfather used to get his mountain smoke from there, gathering the herbs, using offerings, songs, and prayers. The plants are still there. All of the herbal medicines that were used in earlier times still grow. Medicine men still gather the Lifeway medicinal herbs, and the general public can, too, if they know what to say to the plants. All that is required is sacred corn pollen and knowledge of what and how the herb is going to be used. First one prays to the plant, naming it once it is seen, but before picking it. It does not have any special names. A person just says how it will be used and who will use it. The plants can be gathered even by a person who does not know the ways of a medicine man by just identifying the healing process, the extent of its use, and who it is for. Then a simple prayer and sprinkling of corn pollen on the plant is all that is needed.

One ceremony I perform that uses these plants is called the Sacred Smoke. It is also referred to as People's Smokeway, Mountain Smoke, and Deer-Smoking Herbs. The ritual is named after the herb used in the smoke and may also be called the Deerway Ceremony. The prayers are called To-Talk-It-Back- [through prayer] to-Where-It-Came-From Ceremony (Łéyahdę́ę́'). The plants are collected from atop the Bears Ears or other mountains and are made into a special mixture. If a person makes a mistake while deer hunting or has a curse put on, he or she will be healed from this physical or mental harm. This protects one from all the evil things on earth.

The plants are picked by presenting corn pollen and sacred stones to deer-antler markings, because these animals belong to Talking God.[23] The special herb is then prepared through prayer to treat people who have become psychologically disoriented. In this prayer, Talking God is asked to restore the sick person's mental stability and activity. "The herbs I take from you will now heal this person when he or she smokes it. Heal him with your sacred songs and prayers, through your herbs, through your pipe, through your tobacco, cleanse and purify his body and mind of all impurities that make him sick."[24] The herb is then brought home, and the sick person drinks, bathes in, and smokes it, swallowing the smoke, which, in turn, induces vomiting of everything—liquids, solids, blood, and bile. Once that is over, a sacred prayer is performed for him, healing his body and mind.

There are two basic reasons for using the Sacred Mountain Smoke. One is for curing a person of deviant behavior and substance abuse. I have helped people with problems of drug and alcohol abuse, using the Sacred Smoke ritual and prayer to straighten out their lives. Many young boys and girls from Tuba City to Chinle, as well as from around here, come to see me for this treatment and healing.

The other reason is to bring about the four principles found in the Blessingway. First, it is used for receiving blessings, valuable things, and good luck. For instance, if a person were to enter his name in a drawing to win a car or horse trailer by paying two dollars, he would win. The smoke is done with a prayer for blessings and gifts in the Blessingway. The second category is protective smoke against evil. Sun Bearer gave this sacred smoke to his sons, Monster Slayer and Born for Water, when they went to visit him. The smoke was to help them kill all the feared ones below. It was for their protection and was unseen in the process of destroying the monsters. Navajos use it to protect against those who think or say evil things against them. The third is for protection against those who bewitch through their songs or prayers. The fourth category is to prevent sexual bewitchery through plants such as *Datura meteloides*. Plants like this are used in bewitchery [Frenzy Witchcraft], which causes a man or woman to crazily indulge in sexual practices. For this, the same sacred herb is smoked and bathed in for a cure. For some people, the sickness gets really bad, to the point where they will chew on themselves, pull on their body, and throw objects.

Once the ceremony is performed, the patient will resent participating in what he or she used to do—drinking, drugs, uncontrolled sex, running off to Squaw Dances, and the like. I have done this for many young people. One woman from Tuba City came to see me about her problem. She said she was out of control, running away from home at midnight and joining wild people at parties. I performed this sacred ritual with the assistance of my son, who usually helps in these sings. The young woman came back to tell me that she had been cured and no longer desired to attend dances or social activities. Instead, she does beadwork and has a small business selling her crafts. In fact, she became so isolated that she asked me to undo some of the things I did for her. "Grandfather, open up just a little bit of my activities again," she begged. I refused: "If I did, I'd be a liar on my part," I told her, "and you will be right back where you were before."

Herbal smoke can assist with other problems. For instance, difficulty can arise when a mother- and son-in-law see each other. This affliction goes back to the beginning of time. Many different things—such as the stars; people; ceremonies such as the Enemyway, Mountainway, and other nine-day ceremonies—started in a sacred and holy manner. These things were not to be done side by side or performed in sight of each other. Likewise, in-laws are not to see each other. The stars First Big One and Man with Legs Spread are not to see each other. For the same reason, one is forbidden to carry a live deer across the San Juan River. We are said to live within the female mountain, or female earth—a young girl. And on the other side of the river is the male earth. The male and female are forbidden to see each other. We were created accordingly, and this has always been the law. One of my clan mothers, Cheerful Woman (Asdzáán Baa Hózhóní), Lettie Atene, still observes this tradition and has never formally seen her son-in-law, LaMar Bedonie, although sometimes they sneak a peek.

If a woman and son-in-law want to see each other, they share a smoke of the sacred mountain herbs. These plants are rolled up in a corn leaf, which is lit and passed back and forth through a hole in a curtain of tanned deerskin. The mother- and son-in-law pass it to each other four times, then the deerskin is removed, and the two shake hands. If you are a medicine man, and your mother in-law becomes your patient, you sing on her and shake her hand. Doing these things will permit the in-laws to see each other forever.

In addition to the Sacred Smoke Ceremony, I also perform a prayer called Take It Away through Prayer. This is a protection prayer used to prevent harm from witchcraft, a curse, or a bad dream. I perform this only occasionally. The Kinaaldá is another ceremony I know because it ties in with the Blessingway. Women do their part by making the corn cake, while I do the singing and prayers. Few people, no matter what the race, can withstand the effects of being filthy rich. Most people go berserk! But if a person has a Blessingway performed, he or she will be better in handling wealth. People die from heart attacks or loss of sleep over money. These deaths are said to be from not having the Blessingway.

A former trader from Oljato, Big White Man, died in Kayenta when he opened a large box of money. It was too much for him. But if a person has the Blessingway, he will have a strong mind and body to withstand anything. That's why we give sacred offerings to the earth. The sacred prayers work in the same way. As long as you have the sacred songs and prayers performed, you will endure everything.

I have no knowledge in conducting the Enemyway, Mountainway, and nine-day ceremonies. I am only involved in the Blessingway, the Sacred Smoke, and protection prayers. My ability to perform these rituals has given me the opportunity to travel to many places as I treat those in need. Recently, due to health problems derived from working in the uranium mines, my travels and performances have been greatly reduced. If it had not been for that, I would still be strong and capable.

TRAINING FOR THE FUTURE

There is a lot of truth in what I have been taught, so I continue to teach my children the same thing. Most of them are adults now and work for a living. They have all gone to school; I never let them lie around the house. All that my father has taught me, I have taught them, such as caring for livestock, planting cornfields, hauling wood and water—it is all part of learning to make a decent living. I have raised all my children accordingly. I taught with love and kindness, but when needed, I used the whip. But as my father used to do, I followed it with explanation and more love.

It takes both parents to discipline and teach their children; neither person should take sides with the child or it spoils the teaching. "Discipline" is not "abuse." It is a way for people to better themselves. I am criticized by my older children because I am not as strict with the younger ones. They encourage me to use the whip more often, like I used to when they were small. I believe children today can relearn our traditional values only if the parental right to discipline is restored. This major shift would certainly change our younger generation for the better. It is impossible to continue on like this; it will destroy our youth and society.[25]

As you have probably noticed, we now have many housing areas on our reservation. Anybody could be tempted to move into one of these homes. If I were to do so, I would have to leave all that I have—my house, hogan, livestock, and livelihood—in exchange for convenience. This would be a place where I would do nothing but sleep and sit around and look out my window, and beeline for every activity that came my way. If the parents set this example, their children get into a habit of sleeping all day, and then go out for the nighttime parties and

Baxter Benally visiting with John. J.H.: "Remember that the root of our culture starts here [home], with sacred prayers and songs. Responsible parents do their part for children in many ways. Even a simple prayer, song, and sprinkling of pollen can be done for a child as he or she is leaving to catch the bus." (Photo by author)

activities. That is how most communities operate these days. It is not good, yet these ideas and planning originated from our officials in our government. Maybe, just maybe, a few will change for the better.

Remember that the root of our culture starts here [home], with sacred prayers and songs. Responsible parents do their part for children in many ways. Even a simple prayer, song, and sprinkling of pollen can be done for a child as he or she is leaving to catch the bus. This should be done whether the child will be gone for the day or a year, on or off the reservation. As a father, I have always done this for my children. If I fail to do it, eventually they will write and say, "Father, I am not doing so well, because I left without your sacred song and prayer," so then I follow through with it at home, and before too long, they are back to overcoming their hardships and challenges. This is true for everything we do in our daily lives. The answer lies within the songs, prayers, and corn pollen. We need to recognize and remember the important meaning behind these sacred rituals. It is the only way.

Some people are very appreciative when they hear these teachings, but others could not care less. Some of the most intelligent people, whether male or female, tend to overlook this knowledge and make unnecessary remarks about what you tell them. There are others who come right up to your face to observe and absorb everything you say. They are the interested ones. It is easy to distinguish one from the other.

Other Navajos say, "We have lost all aspects of our traditional religion. No one has gone back to 'relearn' the real beliefs, and no one is willing to learn the sacred songs and prayers that once protected our livelihood. We have lost our medicine men's true practices of faith, which gave us wealth in livestock and a decent life. This is why we want to join another religion that promises to give us back the valuable things that we have lost from our lives."

It is worrisome to think about the future of our people, because once the teachings are gone, that is it! This loss is happening now and will continue, which worries me. For this reason, we have been holding meetings in Window Rock for two years. We applied for a grant, which was approved, to help those interested in learning the medicine man way.

I was asked to be on this committee by the Navajo Nation and to bring back prayer bundles to the people. Many of us elders wrote the grant and sent it to Washington, D.C. The committee asked the government to give the Navajo Nation funds to establish scholarships for those interested in relearning traditional religion and medicine. The president passed it, and there was plenty of scholarship money to teach those interested in becoming a medicine man. The medicine man organization began recruiting students, offering approximately $300 per month per student to relearn the lost traditions.

Then word came that the funds were depleted or stolen, and arguments followed. Another organization formed and wanted to control the money. Several medicine men, including me, were asked to take their students to Window Rock. I had a few but did not bring them, because none of us was interested in going there. Now, the funds for students are on hold because the other organization wants to be in charge. I hope the grant does not expire.[26]

I have one young man, living west of Kayenta, who is from my father's clan, so I call him my dad. He is a great-great-grandson of Metal Teeth, my former teacher, who taught me everything about being a medicine man. The young man's grandmother knew I had learned from Metal Teeth, so she insisted he relearn his grandfather's sacred ceremonies and prayers. He came to me on New Year's Eve a year ago, has since learned a lot, and is on the verge of completing his lessons on some of the sacred ceremonies. This New Year's Eve [1999], we spent the night performing a Kinaaldá. He is an excellent student and asks a lot of questions. We also did a ceremony out on the plains near Rough Rock. He is about ready to go on his own.

This young man works for Peabody Coal Company and pays me well for his training. He wanted to learn the horse song and gave me a really nice two-year-old palomino stallion for the teachings. The horse is in my corral now. He also gave me a turquoise necklace, turquoise and silver watch bracelet, $200 in cash, and said he would pay me more once he begins singing on his own and has learned everything. He comes to see me all the time and spends nights here when we have lessons.

A student who is really serious about learning from a medicine man has to do several things. Some people will think this is gross, but the medicine man puts corn pollen on the tip of his tongue and the student has to kiss it four times. This sounds strange, but that is the required ritual. After kissing the tongue, the medicine man applies sacred corn pollen all over the student, who is then prepared to follow and do ceremonies everywhere. This ritual initiates the student and makes him or her holy to practice along with the teacher.

I have another student who lives past Gallup and has already performed three ceremonies by himself—one in Monument Valley, another near El Capitan, and one at Tsegi, west of Kayenta. This student gave me a bull, turquoise earrings, and cash. These two students are very good and have learned quite well. As for my own boys, they sing while doing sweat baths and are pretty good. One of them might get into learning these things seriously. None of my daughters has tried it, but they ask a lot of questions on how to deal with certain situations in daily living and raising children. They want to know what songs or prayers to use for different things, so I tell them and hope they are learning something.

My wife's little brother was also interested in songs. He started out well, learning the Blessingway, but then turned to peyote ceremonies.

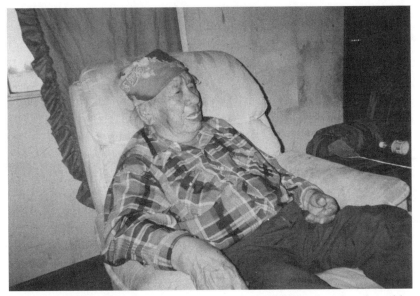

John Holiday in 1999. J.H.: "My voice, my stories, will be heard and read by people to the ends of the earth. Many of them will like this book and teach from it. That is what I want." (Photo by author)

Just when he reached his goal and started his wealthy practice, he began drinking alcohol, and that destroyed him. I do not know if he still practices; I have not heard. A person has to be able to handle his emotions and have a strong will to control success; if he cannot, he will destroy himself. This person had begun to establish a nice home with livestock that he received from his clients and was doing well, but it all was ruined. Money is something else. If one does not control it, it can make a person crazy. Even having a fifty-dollar bill in one's pocket can be disturbing. It is evil and bewitching to the mind and can mix it up, unless a person knows how to handle it.

There was a time when we totally outgrew everything; nobody cared to ride horses or own one. But today, we are gradually coming back to it. Occasionally, we see our young people riding their horses around. Some are participating more and more in the rodeos and livestock activities. Eventually, this will cause them to return to their traditional ways. I hope that they will. We have to be careful in accomplishing this goal.

As for me, I agreed to write this autobiography. I have told stories about myself and about what others have told me. I want to be remembered, too, like my grandfather before me. My voice, my stories, will be heard and read by people to the ends of this earth. Many of them will like this book and teach from it. That is what I want. I am looking ahead for many years to come, many generations to come. That is where my thoughts are, not just here to the ends of my eyelashes, but further, out there. I have told you a lot of myself and want to share this with those who want to know. That is it.

NOTES

PREFACE

1. Robert S. McPherson, *A History of San Juan County: In the Palm of Time* (Salt Lake City: Utah State Historical Society, 1995).

2. Robert S. McPherson, ed., *The Journey of Navajo Oshley: An Autobiography and Life History* (Logan: Utah State University Press, 2000); Charlotte J. Frisbie, *Tall Woman: The Life Story of Rose Mitchell, A Navajo Woman, c. 1874–1977* (Albuquerque: University of New Mexico Press, 2001).

3. See Walter Dyk, *Son of Old Man Hat: A Navajo Autobiography* (1938; repr., Lincoln: University of Nebraska Press, 1996); Walter Dyk and Ruth Dyk, *Left Handed: A Navajo Autobiography* (New York: Columbia University Press, 1980); and Walter Dyk, *A Navaho Autobiography* (New York: Viking Fund, 1947).

4. Charlotte J. Frisbie and David P. McAllester, *Navajo Blessingway Singer: The Autobiography of Frank J. Mitchell, 1881–1967* (Tucson: University of Arizona Press, 1978); Franc Johnson Newcomb, *Hosteen Klah: Navajo Medicine Man and Sand Painter* (Norman: University of Oklahoma Press, 1964).

5. Robert S. McPherson, *Sacred Land, Sacred View: Navajo Perceptions of the Four Corners Region* (Provo, Utah: Brigham Young University, 1992).

6. Keith H. Basso, *Wisdom Sits in Places: Landscape and Language Among the Western Apache* (Albuquerque: University of New Mexico Press, 1996).

INTRODUCTION

1. Leslie Marmon Silko, *Ceremony* (New York: Penguin Books, 1977): 2.

CHAPTER 1: DAWN

1. Clans are the glue of Navajo cultural and social fabric, which links individuals and families to others through biological and mythological relations.

Each person belonging to a clan traces ancestry back to the time of the myths and the origin of that clan. By belonging to both a mother's and father's clan, a person has an extensive web of relations on both sides of the family. Connections to these clans define certain relationships and responsibilities with extended family members as well as anyone else who belongs to the clans. An individual's mother's clan is predominant. One is said to be "born into" it, and "born for" the father's clan.

John's introduction of his identity begins with his clans. This definition is as much a spiritual declaration as a biological, historical, and mythological statement. Following proper Navajo etiquette, he establishes his roots for all to know. For anyone belonging to his clans, there may be social, religious, or economic responsibilities once this tie is established.

2. In a clarification interview, John told why he appears to be older on some official documents. "I was told that I was born one year [1919] after the influenza epidemic [1918], when many people perished from the illness. That was also during the time when men worked for one month for a sack of flour. [Later], my brother-in-law worked at Mexican Water, Arizona [for the Civilian Conservation Corps], and I had to take him some food. I rode my donkey over there after it was packed with meat. When they asked how old I was, my brother-in-law told them I was several years older than I actually was, because he wanted me to work as a water boy. With these additional years, I am eighty-nine years old today. We lied to the government, and I was hired. . . . I worked all summer through mid-winter, when the snow began to fall. Without the added years, I am probably eighty-three or thereabouts."

3. In 1961, when the Land Claims Commission interviewed Billy Holiday (Billy Holiday interview, July 21, 1961, Doris Duke Oral History Project #668, Special Collections, University of Utah, Salt Lake City, pp. 1–2), he said that he was a seventy-eight-year-old medicine man. Part of his testimony states: "I was born on Douglas Mesa. When I was young, my father had farms on both sides of the San Juan River and we lived on both sides at various times. We lived north of the San Juan at Bears Ears for a long time and we ran sheep and stock in the Bears Ears area for many years. I have been all over the Navajo Reservation . . . [and] learned this area by going with my father, who was a medicine man and was called to many places to perform ceremonies.

My mother's name is Warrior Woman Going By Something. She told me she was born at Dove Spring and the forked pole hogan is still there. I am not sure when she was born, but she told me that she did not go to Fort Sumner but stayed in the Oljato Creek area during that time. . . . My father went to Fort Sumner and returned to the Upper Chinle area when he returned."

4. Navajo family relations can be very complex. They fall into what anthropologists call the Iroquois classificatory system, defined as: "A system of kinship

terminology wherein one's father and father's brother are referred to by a single term, as are one's mother and mother's sister, but one's father's sister and one's mother's brother are given separate terms; parallel cousins are classified with brothers and sisters, while cross cousins are classified separately but not equated with relatives of some other generation." William A. Haviland, *Cultural Anthropology*, 8th ed. (New York: Harcourt Brace College Publishers, 1996): 292.

Woman Who Was Hit provides a good example of how descent can become even more complex. John explained how she received her name when she teasingly took her little grandson's hand and he hit her face. He then went on to say: "She had been married before and had daughters. In those days, it was normal for the man to marry his stepdaughter, which Aching Stomach did. My father came from this union, as did a sister, but she died. So my biological paternal grandmother had two children, a boy and a girl. Then Aching Stomach left his wife and married her younger sister and remained with her until they grew old. I do not know their English names, but my paternal grandmother's name was Woman Red Mustache (Asdzáán Dághaa' Łichíí'ii) because she married a man named Red Mustache (Dághaa' Łichíí'ii)."

5. John did not know her name. The genealogical information is somewhat confusing because of the marriage of different people who, through other marriages, were already conjugally related. For instance, a man may marry his wife's daughter from a previous marriage or her sister. Because of divorce and remarriage, there may be more than one mother and father, with their extended family, which further confuses a lineal tracing of descent. Also, the more generic English terms of aunts, uncles, cousins, and so forth lack the specificity of the Navajo language, which makes distinctions between the maternal and paternal side of a genealogical chart. Thus, John's relation to the foregoing people has been clarified to the best of his knowledge, but there are obviously some loose ends that need to be connected.

6. Táchii'niitó Nát'oh Dine'é actually refers to the Tobacco People (also Naat'ohnii Táchii'nii), a related subset of the Táchii'nii (Red-Running-into-the-Water People) Clan.

7. Navajo Oshley was a young man, probably in his twenties, when John was born. Oshley played an important part in John's youth, forming a close bond of friendship. According to John, Oshley probably got his name from a white man he worked with for a long time. "His name was I Want Sheep (Dibé Nisin), because he used to haul groceries around to trade for livestock. So the Navajos named him I Want Sheep. He and Oshley teased each other, Oshley calling him I Want Sheep, and the white man calling him One Who Sleeps a Lot (Ayóó Ałhooshii). The name 'Oshley' derived from Navajo, saying 'I sleep'—'osh leep'—a poor English pronunciation because of problems with teeth and misunderstanding. These two men named each other, but it came out funny."

See Robert S. McPherson, ed., *The Journey of Navajo Oshley: An Autobiography and Life History* (Logan: Utah State University Press, 2000).

8. "The One Who Goes Up and Down walked like he was riding a horse." J.H.

9. John is referring to the Navajo practice of sometimes marrying a mother and her daughter simultaneously. John's mother was the daughter and so his father, by marrying both, had married John's grandmother.

10. Again, John did not know her name, most likely because he used a kinship term to address her. He identified her only as "Billy Nash's wife." To non-Navajos this may seem strange, but some elders, during interviews, did not know the names of their wives because they always addressed them using a kinship term.

11. Changed Clothes Again is a shortened name more accurately glossed as Changed Uniform to Navajo Clothing, alluding to the fact that he served as a policeman in the Kayenta area. He belonged to the Red-Running-into-the-Water People. Billy Holiday interview, July 21, 1961, Doris Duke Oral History Project #668, Special Collections, University of Utah, Salt Lake City, p. 3.

John explained that the name Haawoohi came from a place called Red Rock Going Down in Mystery Valley, a side canyon in Monument Valley, where a water hole is located. At this spring, located beneath a rock ledge, there lived some birds ("a type that you usually hear in the forests on the mountains") that made the sound "haawoohi." One could hear the echo of the bird's call in that thicket around the water hole, which is how the site got its name. Since the man had a home in this area, he also was named after the bird's call. John's father, Billy, said of this individual: "Mystery Valley Man's clan was the Bitter Water People. He did not go to Fort Sumner, but stayed in the El Capitan area at that time. He was also an outstanding stockman. He died and is buried at El Capitan." Billy Holiday interview, July 21, 1961, Doris Duke Oral History Project #668, Special Collections, University of Utah, Salt Lake City, p. 3.

Billy Holiday said: "I knew Giving out Anger (Angry Man) whose clan was Red Running into the Water People. He was an outstanding trader and visited many parts of the reservation, especially the area around the San Juan River. He went north of the San Juan River to trade with the Utes and Paiutes who had moved in the area around the Bears Ears. He also went as far west as Kanab, Utah." Billy Holiday interview, July 21, 1961, Doris Duke Oral History Project #668, Special Collections, University of Utah, Salt Lake City, p. 2.

The One Who Did It was Giving Out Anger's son, belonged to the Reed People Clan (Lók'aa Dine'é), and is buried a few miles northwest of Kayenta. He received his name because of his involvement in the killing of two miners, Samuel Walcott and James McNally, on March 31, 1884, in the Navajo Mountain–Monument Valley region. The name One Who Did It implies the difficulty that Agent John H. Bowman had in bringing him to justice, a feat he never accomplished. For a full explanation of this event, see J. Lee Correll, "Navajo Frontiers in Utah and Troublous Times in Monument Valley," *Utah Historical Quarterly* 39, no. 2 (Spring 1971): 145–61.

12. The Navajo practice of having a winter camp that provided good range for the stock, shelter from the winds and snow, plentiful firewood, and ease of travel was coupled with the summer camp usually located at higher elevations, where water and grass were available. Seasonal migrations to these areas gave the range a rest and fostered the use of a variety of resources.

13. Apparently John is suggesting that the elderly couple would eventually die in the kiva, and then be taken out for burial.

14. "Metal Teeth received his name when he went to Gallup, New Mexico, and had some dental work—gold crowns—put on his teeth. He went to a place called Big Mexican for this work. Back then, hardly anyone had gold or metal dental work done, and his teeth were made of gold." J.H.

15. The mountain soil bundle contains material gathered from the four sacred mountains of Blanca Peak (Colorado), Mount Taylor (New Mexico), San Francisco Peaks (Arizona), and the La Plata Mountains (Colorado). The bundle holds protective powers and blesses the home in which it resides.

Charlotte J. Frisbie writes in *Navajo Medicine Bundles, or Jish: Acquisition, Transmission, and Disposition in the Past and Present* (Albuquerque: University of New Mexico Press, 1987), "Today the powers of First Man's corn bundle are symbolized in the mountain earth bundle which is an exclusive in Blessingway ceremonies. . . . This bundle represents Changing Woman's bundle which was brought to the Earth's surface by First Man and which was the source of all surface life. The mountain earth bundle contains earth collected from the four (or six) sacred mountains. Pollen is applied to the earth from each mountain and each is wrapped separately in unwounded buckskin and tied with buckskin thongs. A precious jewel is attached to each of the resulting pouches to indicate its directional association. Between these pouches are placed stick-like cylinders of mirage stone (aragonite), agate, and quartz. Stone figures of horses, game, and other things are also added. Then everything is covered with pollen and all of the individual pouches are wrapped in unwounded buckskin to form the bundle. . . . As [Sam] Gill (1981:64) says, 'The mountain earth bundle's structure represents in its jewels and soils, the substance from which life is given form, and in its stone cylinders the animating forces of life, long life and happiness. Its shape and design are that of a world created in beauty, and correspond with other manifestations of that shape in the ceremonial hogan and the surface of the earth itself'" (19–20).

16. Most of John's training is in the Blessingway ceremony (called Hózhǫ́ǫ́jí, but John's reference to Bijí is to the day on which the ceremony is held), which

actually comprises several ceremonies, as Leland C. Wyman, an anthropologist who specializes in Navajo ceremonial classification, describes: "The Blessing-way rites, of which there are some five kinds that differ only slightly from each other, are used for a multitude of reasons; in general they are not for curing but 'for good hope,' for good luck, to avert misfortune, to invoke positive blessings that man needs for a long and happy life and for the protection and increase of his possessions. Thus they are used to protect livestock, aid childbirth, bless a new hogan, consecrate ceremonial paraphernalia, install a tribal officer, protect a departing or returning soldier, strengthen a neophyte singer, and consecrate a marriage." Leland C. Wyman, "Navajo Ceremonial System," in *Handbook of North American Indians—Southwest*, vol. 10 (Washington, D.C.: Smithsonian Institution, 1983): 539–40.

17. Ntł'iz is a mixture of sacred white shell, turquoise, abalone, and jet that is used as an offering to the Holy Beings for assistance and protection. These materials correspond with the four sacred mountains, the cardinal directions, and extensive references in Navajo mythology and teaching. They are basic representations of a multiplicity of values.

18. "A game of stick dice is frequently played by Navajo women around a circle of forty stones. Three billets of wood are thrown upon a flat stone in the center of this circle, so that they will rebound from a suspended blanket and fall within the circle around which the gamblers are seated. Small twigs placed between the stones are used as counters and moved back and forth according to the fortunes of the game. The winning count is forty, the winner taking the stakes deposited under the stone in the center. The circle is divided into four groups of ten each with an opening left between, or at the cardinal points, and the scoring twigs are placed at the opening next to the player. The billets may be flattened on one side and rounded on the other, or slightly rounded on both sides, in which case they are colored with two and three black bands in water color to distinguish them. Accordingly, when all flat sides are turned up, the count is five points, while all round sides up scores ten counts. Similarly, all three bands up count ten, all two bands count five; one two band with two three band or vice versa, count three. Points are lost by dropping the sticks outside the stone circle. The game is not played after sunset and is a woman's game." Franciscan Fathers, *An Ethnologic Dictionary of the Navajo Language* (1910; repr., Saint Michaels, Ariz.: Saint Michaels Press, 1968): 481–82.

19. "Woman Who Became Fat Again was a Ute. When she was young, she almost died, but One Who Plucks His Whiskers (Dághaa' Yiits'ii'ii) performed a ceremony, and she recovered. When she regained her strength and weight, she received this name." J.H.

20. Little Boy and Slim Woman were John and Louisa Wade Wetherill, who had initially moved to the Oljato area in 1906, then changed the location of

their post in 1910 to Kayenta, Arizona, about twenty-five miles away. They not only were a successful trading couple, but also fostered the tourist trade to Rainbow Bridge, did some early mining in Monument Valley, and became respected spokespeople for the Navajo. See Frances Gillmor and Louisa Wade Wetherill, *Traders to the Navajo* (Albuquerque: University of New Mexico Press, 1934). Tall White Man was probably Clyde Colville.

21. The rule of mother-in-law avoidance was widespread among the Navajo at this time. The translation of the name for mother-in-law used by the son-in-law is One Whom I Do Not See. John later tells of a ceremony that is performed if the two relatives do have contact.

22. Rug and Old Coyote built a post approximately a mile northwest of the contemporary Oljato Trading Post (founded in 1921) and across the Oljato Wash. Thus, there were three posts in the Oljato area at different times. John later explained: "That is the stone house that Mrs. Sloan Haycock lived in. The water was brought down from up where the present trading post is located. The two men built a canal underground, down the wash, and then to this location. I was five years old when this happened. There was also a trading post [1906–1910] by the Oljato Reservoir, where the big old oak tree is. Those traders were Slim Woman [Louisa Wetherill] and John. After these traders moved away, the other trading post at Old Coyote started. The present trading post [in Oljato] was barely going too. [This post was started in 1921 by Joseph Heffernan, who kept it until 1936, when he sold it to another trader, named John Taylor.] There were first only tents at both places. The two men at Old Coyote used to hunt coyotes from there, and so that is how that place got its name. Rug was a trader who always asked the Navajo women if they had finished any more weaving, and so they gave him that name."

23. The Yé'ii Bicheii Ceremony, more properly referred to as the Night Chant, takes nine nights to perform and culminates with masked god impersonators who bless participants. This ceremony is performed in the winter and is used to cure rheumatism, head ailments, and general sickness.

24. "Woman Heat received her name from her grandchildren, when she asked them to build a summer shade because it was too hot [living in the hogan]. They teased her by giving her that name." J.H.

25. A log leaning against a door is a sign that no one is home.

26. John says of the Bears Ears, a prominent rock formation west of Blanding, "The bear is lying down. One of its ears is male; the other is female."

27. Hand trembling, a form of divination, determines the origin of an illness through supernatural communication with the spirits. Once the cause of the sickness is revealed, an appropriate cure can be determined.

28. Yellow Eye is most likely nightshade (*Solanum elaeagnifolium*). "Below elevations of about 6,500 feet, silverleaf nightshade grows on coarse and medium

soils along roadsides, trail sides, cultivated field margins, edges of washes, and rims of swales. [It] is used as a remedy for sore eyes, and when dried and pulverized, as a remedy for nose and throat trouble." Vernon O. Mayes and Barbara Bayless Lacy, *Nanise: A Navajo Herbal* (Tsaile, Ariz.: Navajo Community College Press, 1989): 70.

29. There are a number of different understandings among the Navajos concerning the cause of the influenza epidemic of 1918. They were aware of the use of poison gas in World War I and reached the logical conclusion that somehow the gas left the battlefield and came to the United States, where it infected the People. For a comparative study of the Navajo, Ute, Mormon, and non-Mormon response to this pandemic, see Robert S. McPherson, "The Influenza Epidemic of 1918: A Cultural Response," *Utah Historical Quarterly* 58, no. 2 (Spring 1990): 183–200.

30. Underground bread, actually translated as Round Thing (Dough) under the Ground, is made from a ground-corn and water batter that has burnt juniper leaves added as a type of baking powder. The loaf of dough is prepared, placed in a heated pit from which the live coals have been removed, covered, and baked. Once the loaf is cooked, the sand is brushed off, and the moist bread is eaten.

31. Achxǫǫh is jerky that has been pounded and fried, then used as trail rations. It can be made out of any kind of dried meat (sheep, deer, horse, donkey, beef, etc.). According to John, "They [Navajos] use it as an expression: 'Bring out your achxǫǫh [lunch].'"

32. Mexican Hat Rock is a well-known geographical landmark, deriving its name from a balanced rock that looks like a sombrero. The name Metal Pipe Going Across refers to a water system built in the early twentieth century to bring water to the homes in the community that were established during the oil boom. In 1910, a regional newspaper, *Grand Valley Times* (December 2), boasted among other things that the town had a "water system with eight hundred feet of pressure." This was achieved by having two tanks placed just below the rock, and then extending a pipe to the village, located at some distance—thus Metal Pipe Going Across. Names for the dominant hill, or syncline, located across the river from the rock are Mountain That Is Coiled, Navajo Blanket, and Swirling Mountain. This latter name is derived from the red, gray, and brown sands that make dramatic vertical patterns across the hill.

33. According to Richard F. Van Valkenburgh, Mountain Sheep's Testicles "refers to Upper Comb Wash Drainage and specifically to a rock formation in Arch Canyon which resembles sheep testicles. The area is broken red slickrock canyons immediately east of Bears Ears, Utah, and breaks out from the base of Elk Ridge escarpment." White Sheep interview, Doris Duke Oral History Project #687A, March 13, 1953, p. 2.

John has a different idea about the origin of this place name: "Navajos gathered sumac berries there in the canyon. People tell the story about some hunters who had killed a mountain sheep while others collected berries. One of the hunters decided to roast and eat the sheep's testicles, and so he put them in the coals to cook. They got very hot and exploded, giving the site its name."

Next to this rock formation is Sheep's Testicles Trail, also known as Posey's Trail, named after a Paiute who used this trail and was killed in 1923. In an unpublished field article on Sheep's Testicles Trail, Joe Merritt, a Navajo man involved in identifying Navajo archaeological sites, is quoted: "'We used the trail in 1917 while herding sheep here.'" The article continues, "According to [Merritt's] uncle, White Sheep of Dennehotso, the Navajos used this as a foot trail for a long time. It had been developed for horse travel long before Fort Sumner, with the Navajos making repairs and improvements as time and necessity allowed. It was a very dangerous trail and many horses fell and were killed on the west side of the ridge [Comb]. The Navajos used to camp near the spring at the foot of the trail in Comb Wash Canyon. From here a trail led down Comb Wash to Mexican Hat." "Sheep's Testicles Trail," Site N LSJ CC K, *Field Book 24*, p. 164, Navajo Land Claim File, unpublished document, Navajo Nation government, Window Rock, Arizona.

34. Annie Wauneka, born in 1910, was the daughter of Henry Chee Dodge, first tribal council chairman. In 1951, Annie began her lengthy tenure of service in the tribal council and became best known for a long crusade to bring Anglo-American health-care services to the Navajo people. Among her many accomplishments, she helped lower the infant mortality rate, introduced practices that curbed tuberculosis, provided a radio program with health practices broadcast in Navajo, and in 1963, received the Presidential Medal of Freedom Award, the highest honor given to civilians in peacetime. She died November 10, 1997. For a brief synopsis of her life, see Virginia Hoffman and Broderick H. Johnson, *Navajo Biographies*, vol. 2 (Rough Rock, Ariz.: School Board, 1978): 90–105; for a more detailed account, see Carolyn Niethammer, *I'll Go and Do More: Annie Dodge Wauneka, Navajo Leader and Activist* (Lincoln: University of Nebraska Press, 2001).

John's chastisement of her is associated with her work on behalf of schoolchildren. He blames her for removing some of the discipline that was so important in traditional Navajo culture. (See John's teaching about discipline and the whip for examples of what has been lost.) The chaos that seems to reign in today's schools, and the fact that punishment appears to be a thing of the past, can be traced back to Annie Wauneka's efforts to do away with corporal punishment and other methods associated with the boarding-school era.

35. Peeking Bobcat, also known as Wildcat Guts, received its name during the time of Creation. As the Holy Beings traveled about placing geographical

features on the land and naming them, they approached Bodaway Mesa. "It was said that Wildcat was getting tired. Then they came this way (east) and across into [the] Red Lake [Tonalea] area. At that time it was noticed that Wildcat was completely exhausted, that his feet were very worn, and that he had laid down. He only stuck up his head behind a ridge and said that he could go no farther. That is why the place where he laid down is known as [Peeking] Wildcat Peak." Karl W. Luckert, *Navajo Mountain and Rainbow Bridge Religion* (Flagstaff: Museum of Northern Arizona Press, 1977): 58.

CHAPTER 2: LIVING WITH GRANDMOTHER

1. Gary Witherspoon, "Language and Reality in Navajo World View," in *Handbook of North American Indians—Southwest,* vol. 10 (Washington, D.C.: Smithsonian Institution, 1983): 571.

2. The chronology in this part of John's life is rough. He believes he was about five or six years old when he started living with his grandmother, and that it was his idea to do so, even while his parents were still together. The shifting of children from the biological family to extended family members was a common practice. Grandmothers and grandfathers had experience and stable homes, and they needed the help that younger family members could provide. John expressed strong love and appreciation for Woman Who Owns the House, who with Metal Teeth, his paternal grandfather, had the greatest impact on his development.

3. San Juan [River], whose English name was Billy Water, was John's clan brother. He was born into the Many Goats Clan (maternal) and for the Folded Arms Clan (paternal). "He was a medicine man who performed many ceremonies and moved around quite a bit. He stayed in this area until his wife passed away; then he moved to Shiprock, New Mexico, where he remarried and lived until he died of old age. He got his name because he married a woman in Montezuma Creek and had two children. He left [ran away] from this family and returned home, so everyone called him San Juan River, identifying that he was from that place." J.H. For more about this man, see Robert S. McPherson, *The Journey of Navajo Oshley: An Autobiography and Life History* (Logan: Utah State University Press, 2000).

4. Little Mexican (Harry Nakai Yazzie) had a deformed leg that required a shoe with an elevated heel and, at least in his later life, the use of crutches. He lived his last years in the area south of Bluff, Utah.

5. This ceremony is held after a girl's first menses, around the age of twelve or thirteen. The four-day ceremony is part of the Blessingway. During this ritual, the girl assumes the attributes of Changing Woman, the most beneficent of Navajo deities. She shows that she is capable of nurturing life, helping others,

and taking on the tasks of motherhood. For a detailed explanation, see Charlotte J. Frisbie, *Kinaaldá: A Study of the Navaho Girl's Puberty Ceremony* (Middletown, Conn.: Wesleyan University Press, 1967).

6. War and warrior names such as this were often given to women. They were titles of power recognized by the Holy Beings during ceremonies and were considered sacred. Not all Navajos adhered to this or any other particular naming scheme. Names for everyday use were tied to kinship; they clearly identified a person based on to whom they were related.

7. "White Streak of Cattail Coming Out, or Meadow of White Cattails, is close to the VCA mine site. There was once a spot where there was a meadow of cattails, but it has since disappeared." J.H.

8. Exactly who these people were is unknown. The wagons and horses, the whole "Wild West" scene, is baffling, given the time frame of the mid-1920s. They were possibly a group of Mormons heading north from the colonies in Mexico or from settlements in Arizona.

9. The name Lived in the Same Place is a clan name given to a woman by the Holy Beings at the beginning of Creation. "She bore her children, and they became that clan. All different clan names were given to the people during this time, and they still exist to this day." J.H.

10. Assuming John is talking about these towns in the 1920s, his knowledge of them was limited. According to a local publication of the time, Monticello had a population of 1,400 people, three general merchandise stores, two restaurants, a barber shop, a printing plant, garages, and a flour mill. Blanding's population was 1,100, and the town boasted "good grade and high schools, water works, and electric lights, . . . stores, garage, flour mill and all other town facilities which may be needed by its inhabitants." *San Juan County, Utah* (Monticello, Utah: San Juan County, 1920): 18–20.

11. "Fremont Goosefoot or Fremont Pigweed seeds [are] black and small like mustard seeds and are used in much the same manner as corn. They are ground to make tortillas, bread, and almost everything for which corn is used. They were used long before flour came into use. Glucose is obtained by parching handfuls of seed meal." Francis H. Elmore, *Ethnobotany of the Navajo* 1, no. 7 (Albuquerque: University of New Mexico Bulletin, December 1943): 44.

12. Rabbit thorn, or boxthorn, is translated to mean "God food." "The fruits are eaten as they come off the bush, or they are boiled into a soup. They are picked in the summer and boiled to the right consistency and spread on the rocks to dry. When dry, they are stored until winter, then eaten dried or made into a soup. The flavor is rather flat. The fruit is also sacrificed to the gods." Ibid., 74.

13. "The western chokecherry is called by the Navajos 'coyote's corn.' When its blue berries ripen, the coyotes eat them. Medicine men take its pliable

branches and fashion a hoop (called 'round wood') for people to pass through during ceremonies." J.H.

14. "Folded Metal Belt, my maternal grandfather, was the oldest blood brother to One Who Plucks His Whiskers, and three sisters, Woman Who Owns the House, Streak Running Red Grass, and Mourning Dove, in that order of birth. Folded Metal Belt always used to wear a large, wide leather pouch belt that had spoons, knives, and a cup hanging from it. Inside the pouch were his miscellaneous food items—coffee, homemade creamer, flour, jerky, cornmeal, and so forth. At the top of the pouch and around the edges was leather fringe with rolled metal ornaments and bells on the tips. It made a loud noise when he moved around. He wore it when he traveled; otherwise, he hung it on the wall.

"When he gave me my name the Mean One I Fought For, he actually was speaking of himself. He fought the enemy when he was only fifteen years old. He carried two bags of arrows and could shoot an arrow while hanging from beneath his running horse. He rode all the way from Escalante, Utah, to Fort Sumner, New Mexico, to sneak in and visit the prisoners." J.H.

15. Big White Man was Arthur Spencer. John remembers this early post: "The Navajos were living around that area back then, in the red rocky hills west of Mexican Hat Rock. We used to live there, too. The store was small but nice. The people made an irrigation ditch all the way from the San Juan River by Hat Rock to the store, so that they could have a supply of water. He [Spencer] used to buy sheep and goats from the Navajos, so he kept his store well supplied with flour, potatoes, and other groceries. I only bought striped candy canes, since I was still a little boy. People bought things over the counter, while the trader stood behind it. The store seemed large and was built of rocks. There was also a guest hogan for the Navajo customers. The hogan was built halfway up with rocks, and the rest was made of logs, bark, and sand."

16. VCA is the local name given to the large uranium mine known as Monument II, which was run by the Vanadium Corporation of America (VCA) in the 1950s. The mine has since been closed and had toxic materials removed. It is located in Caine Valley, beyond the Navajo Tribal Park.

17. O. Hansen Bayles received the name of Four Fingers from the Navajos because of an accident he had while living in Parowan, Utah. According to family members, Hansen was very handy with a whip, which he often secured to his middle finger. One day, as he was popping the mice and rats that were fleeing sheaves of grain being fed into a threshing machine, the whip became entangled in the blades and drew Hansen's hand into the machinery. The first two joints of the finger were removed initially, and after a few days of suffering, Hansen's father removed the remaining stump with a chisel behind the woodshed. Eventually, the other fingers moved over to replace the missing appendage, and the hand became very strong. The Navajos, always observant, were duly impressed

and gave him the name. Finley Bayles, Four Fingers's grandson, telephone conversation with author, April 5, 1996.

18. This is a difficult name to translate into English. John explained it as follows: "This is a place where there is a flat cliff that has a trail that cannot be seen until you see a person moving on it. The name Seeing a Moving Speck [Person] on the Face of the Rocks describes what one views from a distance as someone descends the cliff."

19. The use of the term "Coyote" refers to the incorrigible trickster in the teaching tales that is always doing stupid, crazy things with disastrous effect. Coyote's experimentation with the forbidden serves as a model of what not to do, but here, John and the boys are acting just like him.

20. "Boasts about Himself received his name from being a sophisticated person who told stories in which he praised himself. Mister Horn probably got his name from his hair, which stood up like horns. When a person does not take care of himself, his hair becomes wild and sticks up. Towering House received his name from his clan." J.H.

21. On a number of occasions, John was asked to clarify what were the young male and young female of venereal disease. His descriptions were too vague to ensure accuracy.

22. The connection between venereal disease and deer hunting is not often discussed in the literature and is not entirely clear from what John has said. Certainly, sexuality and hunting are connected through various practices done before, during, and after hunting. One possible explanation is provided by Karl W. Luckert in *A Navajo Bringing-Home Ceremony: The Claus Chee Sonny Version of Deerway Ajiłee* (Flagstaff: Museum of Northern Arizona Press, 1978). At the time of creation, when Black God and Talking God released these animals for human use, there were the Deer People, guardian spirits, who traveled about visiting their animals' future haunts. These Holy Beings eventually returned to the sweat lodge, where Talking God introduced them to both medicinal and poisonous plants. Luckert then writes: "So the young man and young woman (young Deer people) became crazy, and they began living together with one another as crazy people. As brother and sister they began having sexual intercourse with one another. They became crazy because of the poisonous plants. . . . So it is up to Talking God and Black God to also cure again [through medicinal plants] the people who are affected by eating the meat of wild animals" (28). Thus, deer may represent the potential for sexual excess and misguided action and may help identify plants that cure.

John's mention that the diseases went to the north, and that meat must be prepared according to traditional teachings, refers to the fact that the San Juan River is the northern boundary of protection of Navajo land. To disregard the instructions of the Holy Beings, including the Deer People, by bringing the

meat back intact opens an individual to disease and other curses. John believes
this has been done by too many hunters, creating today's problems.

23. When John was asked to clarify this statement, his response drew upon
the Creation story and events in the worlds beneath this one. Although it raises
other questions, his answer gives a glimpse into the depth and kind of knowledge that medicine men have on such rarely discussed topics. He said: "There
were four levels of immersion before we came up to this earth. On the first
level [world], the Man [form of venereal disease] came about. In the next level,
the Woman; next the Young Male; and on the fourth level [world], the Young
Female. So now we have all four here on earth. Changing Woman [associated
with Mother Earth] came up through all four levels. Changing Woman was the
leader. The Navajos were told that if a woman ever became a leader within the
four sacred mountains [Navajo lands] again, we would be cursed with these illnesses. This is what appears to have happened when Annie Wauneka became a
tribal leader. We encountered cancer, high blood pressure, diabetes, and arthritis, all four illnesses that are upon us now. We let it happen."

John's comments about women in politics again hearkens back to the Creation story, the separation of the sexes, and the subsequent definition of gender
roles when men and women were reunited. Traditionally, government, as well as
hunting and war, have been the man's domain. Today, as roles become fractured
and reversed, imbalances and problems arise. I have been told of a meeting held
a number of years ago at the Oljato Chapter House, when a female tribal official
presented a plan to the participants and was doing quite well until one of the
elders stood up, challenged her right to present this information as a political
figure, and by doing so, closed down any further discussion. While this may be
an exception to the rule, it illustrates traditional views of gender role separation.

24. The term "homosexual" is used here without necessarily having a sexual
connotation. In Navajo culture, there were those who chose to assume the
duties of the opposite sex. The term "nádleeh," or "changed," is how they are
known. The change can be performed through a ceremony, after which a man
or woman can perform the chores of the opposite sex. There is no stigma
attached to such a person because these roles have been carefully delineated
since the beginning of time. Indeed, nádleeh hold a great deal of power, both
spiritual and economic, are believed to have good luck, and hold the keys to
wealth. Weaving, a woman's domain, and ceremonial knowledge, usually a
man's concern, can be combined, as it was for Hosteen Klah (Hastiin Tł'a),
about whom Franc Newcomb wrote. Their status is recognized and is not the
butt of humor. See W. W. Hill, "The Status of the Hermaphrodite and Transvestite
in Navaho Culture," *American Anthropologist* 37 (Summer 1935): 273-79.

25. "Rocky Ground Waterfall is located in the bed of Laguna Creek, the deep
wash that comes down from Kayenta. The trail went across Laguna Creek,

where the Extended Gray Hill meets Black Rock [a volcanic rock formation northwest of Baby Rocks]. The trail crosses above the wash, where the creek bed has an all-rock floor with a little waterfall. The name Rocky Ground Waterfall describes this area along the trail." J.H.

26. White Sheep was born into the Water's Edge People and for the Deer Spring People Clan. He was born in 1869 around Bluff, Utah, at White Rock Point, south of the San Juan River, and spent much of his life around Dennehotso. At the time of his interview, he was living in Kayenta, Arizona. White Sheep interview, Doris Duke Oral History Project #687B, January 6, 1961, p. 1.

27. "The water hole called Spring without a Penis received this name because it provided cold, clear drinking water that was so pure and good that it was just like eating castrated or purified calf meat." J.H.

28. "People used to tease one another a lot, just like I tease Mister McPherson. This man named Wow, That's Great always used to use that expression whenever he wanted to praise something. For instance, if he saw you saddling or roping a horse, he would say 'How great!' or 'Wow! That's great.' Even when he greeted people, he would use that expression but not say hello.

"There was another man named And Then (Áádóóyíni), because he used that expression at the beginning of every sentence. He would tell someone about a trip he had gone on with his wife and say, 'And then we left from home and slept at Mexican Water, and then we went on to Rock Point and slept there, and then we went to Chinle, and then to Gallup,' and so forth. That is why people called him And Then.

"Another man was named That Is the One (T'áábii). He also used this expression all of the time." J.H.

29. The ubiquitous use of corn pollen for religious observance is a part of everyday life. It is employed in daily prayers, ceremonies, and blessings, and as an offering to the Holy Beings. Even Coyote, the trickster, known for causing trouble and for antisocial behavior, understood its power and use.

30. This explanation came as a surprise, since warfare and killing are the traditional domain of men. John tells why this ceremony was necessary. "The Enemyway was held for Woman Who Owns the House and took place when I was very young. She had the ceremony performed on her because she killed some enemies long ago, and this was bothering her health.

"When she was just a young girl, before the Long Walk period, she was traveling with some relatives to Big Mexican, a trading post in Gallup, to sell wool. The people were encamped east of Ganado, Arizona, when five enemy held them at gunpoint. Grandmother happened to be out scouting, but when she returned, she saw what was taking place. With her bow and arrows, she sneaked up and shot them all—two Mexicans and three white men. They had been scouting on Navajo land. She became a warrior from that incident alone, but because of it, she became sick and had to have the Enemyway. Following the ceremony, she lived to an old age."

John further explained that the name Many Enemies has the feeling of a gathering, or army, of enemies. "This is the name given to the Plains Indians. They had more distinctive characteristics, especially their noses, which were larger and arched. But today, they have all changed and no longer have these characteristics, because they have intermarried with other races. These Plains Indians were our enemies at one time."

31. The Enemyway Ceremony was formerly used to protect warriors from enemy ghosts killed in battle. Today it is used as "a cure for sickness thought to be caused by ghosts of non-Navajos. It is classed with the other Ghostway (Evilway) . . . ceremonials" and may last either three or five nights. Leland C. Wyman, "Navajo Ceremonial System," in *Handbook of North American Indians—Southwest,* vol. 10 (Washington, D.C.: Smithsonian Institution, 1983): 541.

The ritual is based on a myth in which Monster Slayer, a slayer of evil, is cleansed from sickening influences after killing monsters inhabiting the earth. The ceremony is often called a Squaw Dance in English because of a social feature in the evenings at which a girl chooses her partner for a dance. Many Navajo people use the term "squaw" and are not offended by it.

32. The differences between a male and a female branch of a chant, in this case the Enemyway, are slight. Leland C. Wyman writes: "Navajos may differentiate chants according to the ritual governing them, male and female branches (a distinction probably depending on the sex of the protagonist of the myth and marked by comparatively slight differences in procedure), and a few other considerations, so that from forty to fifty names for song ceremonials are used by them." Ibid., 542.

When John was asked whether there is a difference between a male and a female ceremony, he replied: "Yes. Like everything else, all things come in pairs—male and female. We have two eyes. A female's left eye is the girl, and the right eye is the boy. A male's left eye is the boy, and his right eye is the girl. Then we have nostrils, a pair of holes. We have a pair of everything throughout our whole body. Plants come in pairs, male and female. The ceremonies and sings are also male and female. The Blessingway has a male and female ceremony.

"It was said that long ago there stood a female plant all alone. The Coyote came by and saw the single plant and said, 'You [unclear] did not plant the male plant by it.' Then he took out of his bag something and put it in the ground beside the female plant. 'There. This is the male seed, which will help it to reproduce itself,' he said and went on his way. From that time on, the plants have been reproducing themselves."

When asked if a female had to have a female sing and a man a male sing, John said, "No. They can have one or the other; it does not matter."

33. Kneel-down bread is made from a ground-corn and water batter that is poured into green corn husks, wrapped and tied, and then placed in a heated pit from which the live coals have been removed. The husks are then covered and allowed to bake. When removed from the pit, the husks are taken off and the bread eaten.

34. "Horse Jumping Up Steps received its name from the rocky step-like formations that a horse had to hop up as it ascended before reaching a smoother part of the trail." J.H.

35. Harry Goulding played a prominent role in the history of Monument Valley during John's lifetime. An excellent book about this trader and entrepreneur, who was heavily involved in the movie industry, encouraged the uranium industry, and fostered the development of tourism, is Samuel Moon, *Tall Sheep: Harry Goulding, Monument Valley Trader* (Norman: University of Oklahoma Press, 1992).

36. This is an often-told story by Navajo people about this young girl, Mike (a.k.a. Leone), being carried piggyback by her husband. According to Harry Goulding, he first saw Monument Valley in 1921, married Mike in 1923, and came to settle and trade there in 1925. Mike was born in 1905, making her twenty years old at the time John describes, hardly a youth. She died at the age of eighty-seven on November 26, 1992, at her home in Monument Valley.

Harry confirms John's mother's description of where they first lived, before moving to the present location of Goulding's Trading Post: "When Mike and I drove down to Monument Valley in the fall of 1925, there was a place where we could live on snow. Up near Mitchell Butte there's a wash that comes down, and there were a couple of trees growing; one is still there. There was a nice bend in there and a little shelter from the wind. We just camped under those trees close to that wash. We wintered on snow that first year, melted snow for water. . . .

"We just stayed there that winter. Then we prospected around a little bit, and there was a spring back up that canyon where the hospital is now, not in the main canyon, but right in against them cliffs there's a little canyon off to the left. There was a spring in there, but in the summer it'd dry out. I figured I could develop it and make enough water to take care of us, and even water our sheep, so we stayed over where we were until we got this spring developed to where we could get clean water. When we got done, we moved over there with our tent and store tent and all, and old Jose was with us and put his tent up. It was right down at the mouth of the canyon where the old corral is now." Ibid., 8.

37. Most likely, Mister Hungry's Son-in-Law refers to Cord C. Bowen, who moved to the Mexican Hat area in 1926 and built this post. He mentions living

near the suspension bridge but stated that his home was 200 feet from the river, on the hill. Bowen first came into San Juan County, Utah, in the early 1900s from Jewett, New Mexico, where he had helped his father run a trading post. His wife, Augusta Honaker Bowen, was the daughter of A. C. Honaker, who came into the Mexican Hat area during the gold and oil rushes at the turn of the century. If John is referring to Bowen, then Mister Hungry would be Honaker. See C. C. Bowen, *United States v. Utah* (1931), Colorado River Bed Case, Utah State Historical Society, Salt Lake City, Utah, 1190–91.

38. Big White Man, or Arthur Spencer, was operator of the Mexican Hat post since 1914. The store was built in 1911 by John H. Oliver, who leased it to Spencer. There are no remnants of it today, but it used to be located directly across from Mexican Hat Rock, next to where the paved road is now, and approximately two miles north of where Bowen's post was established. It appears that by 1926, Spencer and Oliver had abandoned this particular business.

Ugly Back of the Neck was probably John H. Oliver, owner of the post. Charles L. Bernheimer, a wealthy "explorer" of southeastern Utah from the East Coast, met Oliver on May 29, 1920. Bernheimer made the following journal entry, which describes both post and man: "J. H. Oliver, a Mormon and the first 'Wilson Democrat' I met on my travels, . . . cheerful, pleasing, if filthy personality. All he had was a one room wooden shack built from the lumber of deserted gambling dens that at one time existed there [Mexican Hat village] 20 years ago during an oil boom. The chairs were boards nailed together, so was his table and bed. Many hundreds of empty tin cans lay around, and as far as the eye could reach there was neither tree nor bush to break the monotony of this rusty tin can trading post. . . . A couple of cheap Navaho horses, a dozen head of cattle, and $1,500 worth of goods in his trading store seems all the income producing values he possesses; besides, he was lame." Cited in Doris Valle, *Looking Around the Hat: A History of Mexican Hat* (Mexican Hat, Utah: Self-published, 1986): 17.

39. John did not explain the connection between acting like a coyote and rain, but Navajo teachings are clear that Coyote, the trickster, had strong supernatural powers that he used in both a sacred and a profane way. One story, in particular, tells of how Coyote prayed, using his powers to flood the land, and with the subsequent water, to float and travel with ease. Coyote's qualities can thus represent the best and worst of human nature's use and abuse of power.

40. John says he knew that Woman Who Owns the House was dying because her skin peeled off easily. This is a sign to the Navajos that death will soon come to an old person.

CHAPTER 3: GRANDFATHER TEACHES THE WAY

1. To understand the chronological sequence, the reader needs to recognize the fluid social and economic situation that characterized Navajo visiting

practices. There was constant interaction among extended family members, as well as nonmembers, as people joined forces during different seasons of the year. Although John's statement seems to indicate that Metal Teeth now started to play an important role in his life, in reality, this paternal grandfather had been doing so during previous years. When speaking of the time that his grandmother assumed responsibility for his care, when he was five, John said: "It was also during this time that Metal Teeth used to come and live by us. He would come to live at either my father's or my grandmother's camp for a week or two, and then move on. I was small, but he would tell me stories and teach me a lot of things. I learned a lot of winter stories from him.

"He used to live around Lukachukai, where his wife was originally from. They would drive their wagon to [Monument Valley] to visit us, and sometimes they remained at my father's camp for several years at a time. I was about seven years old when Metal Teeth really started teaching me about Navajo medicine. I was very young, but I had already learned a lot while I was living with my aunt in Tuba City. The Hopi [priests] taught their traditional ceremonies in a very strict manner. I was disciplined to learn. The Hopi children are educated at a very young age, so I was very small when I began too."

2. Obviously, John is exaggerating, but as a medicine man, he is well traveled, and his services are sought by people near and far.

3. "Good-bye Cattails is located on Black Mesa at Where the Boat Sits. This place once had a spring in the canyon with a lot of large cattail plants around it. Suddenly these plants disappeared or died, so the people called it Good-bye Cattails." J.H.

4. There are four types of Navajo divination or diagnosing—listening, stargazing, crystal gazing, and hand trembling—all of which are related and serve similar functions. They are used to examine the unknown, find lost people or objects, identify a thief or witch, locate water or other desirable resources, prevent danger and evil, and, most frequently, determine the cause of an illness in order to remedy it.

5. That Which Is Taken from Underwater "refers to the small black particles or debris floating on top of the San Juan River. This is used in the rain ceremony. Many medicine men will ask for a share of this debris and use a small-sized strainer to have enough to go around." J.H.

6. Navajo elders often express the belief that water, livestock, riches, and so forth exist on the tips of the trees and other plants. This reference is comparable to the belief that "sheep are life" for those engaged in a livestock economy. Wealth, prestige, and power come from the herds, just as they come from money in white society. Water exists in the vegetation, waiting to be called forth through faith.

7. In Navajo thought, even when a tree is cut and becomes a log, the "growing end" should still be placed either down toward the ground, or, if building a

hogan and placing it horizontally, in a clockwise direction. John is referring to seeing this pattern reversed. For further explanation of this and other organizing principles in Navajo intellectual thought, see Maureen Trudelle Schwarz, *Molded in the Image of Changing Woman: Navajo Views on the Human Body and Personhood* (Tucson: University of Arizona Press, 1997).

8. These two youths not only represent but become the deity associated with two types of rain. Female rain is a soft, soaking, nurturing rain that nourishes plants and animals as it gently falls upon the land. Male rain is powerfully driven in torrential downpours that are much more violent and potentially destructive.

9. Sacred names are bestowed upon the young and serve as a spiritual identification that is used only in a ceremonial context. The name is an individual's sacred and secret identity recognized by the Holy Beings.

10. Lightning and lightning-struck objects hold powers from the Holy Beings. They can bring sickness and injury or healing when used in the hands of a medicine man who understands how to control the power. Knowledge is the key to safe use. Just as the Twins used lightning to rid the earth of monsters and evil, so, too, lightning can represent protection and healing as well as danger and death.

11. "One Who Gropes Around with His Hand had an encounter with a woman whom he accidentally scratched and so received this name." J.H.

The Nightway Ceremony is used to heal loss of hearing, eyesight, and other senses caused by misusing ceremonies, abusing paraphernalia associated with them, or improper dancing. This nine-night ceremony culminates in the famous Yé'ii Bicheii Dance, when ancestral Holy Beings come to bless the participants. For further information, see James Faris, *The Nightway* (Albuquerque: University of New Mexico Press, 1990).

12. "One of a Kind was one of Mister Endesh Chii's children. The son named One of a Kind had many brothers and sisters, but he said there was only one of him." J.H.

13. "The Little One Who Hears understood the English language and so was given that name." J.H.

14. A person does not wear wealth or waste things when in pursuit of game. The Holy Beings will see that he already has a lot of riches and so does not need help in obtaining the game. Metal Teeth is acting contrary to this notion.

15. John is talking about things that are in direct violation of traditional deer-hunting practices. To understand the philosophy behind the ritual practices, see W. W. Hill, *The Agricultural and Hunting Methods of the Navaho Indians* (New Haven, Conn.: Yale University Press, 1938); Karl W. Luckert, *The Navajo Hunter Tradition* (Tucson: University of Arizona Press, 1975); and Robert S. McPherson, "Navajo and Ute Deer Hunting: Consecration versus Desecration,"

in *Navajo Land, Navajo Culture: The Utah Experience in the Twentieth Century* (Norman: University of Oklahoma Press, 2001): 21–43.

16. Whenever one invites the Holy Beings to participate, there is always the possibility of making mistakes, offending, and suffering the consequences. The same is true in weaving. Some women say that they do not use the traditional prayers and songs, even though there is the chance of creating a far better rug by using them. The risk is too great.

CHAPTER 4: THE WORLD OF WORK

1. John is referring to an area of between 100 and 150 miles in circumference. The life of a Navajo sheepherder at the turn of the century was dependent on mobility and skill in finding resources for the sheep.

2. The Mokee Dugway (known locally as "Moki," but spelled "Mokee" on most maps) is approximately eight linear miles from Goosenecks of the San Juan State Park, located near Mexican Hat, Utah. The Dugway is a dirt road built in the 1950s for trucks loaded with uranium going to the mill in Mexican Hat.

3. John is apparently referring to Lee's Ranch, in the Valley of the Gods. He said he was eighteen years old at the time, which would make this around 1937. Buck and Clarence Lee (brothers) built the ranch around 1930, with the intent to graze cattle in the area. When that proved unprofitable, they promoted their establishment as a guest ranch until they left in 1940. Mountain Sheep thus may be one of the Lees. See Doris Valle, *Looking around the Hat: A History of Mexican Hat* (Mexican Hat, Utah: Self-published, 1986): 29–32.

4. "The name Tangle People comes from his clan of the same name that was formed at the time of Creation. His people were made from a combination of stones, all mingled together. There were the mirage stones, turquoise, white shell, black onyx, and abalone shells, mixed with the sand of the earth. This is where the clan's name comes from.

"The name Tall Red Under also comes from a clan. The Red House People were created first. One of their women had a daughter who ended up living alone and had one goat tied up at her home. A newly wed couple became her neighbor, and the bride became jealous of the single woman and told her husband, 'You go back to that woman's home, the one that has the goat.' This is where the Many Goats Clan started. The Many Goats woman had a daughter who had more in-laws. They moved to a place called Red Bluff. Those living at Red Bluff separated and lived by themselves. One of their girls was herding sheep and, while walking, fell into the mud. She must have sat in it, because her bottom got all red. That is where the Red Bottom Clan (Tł'ááshchí'í) began. This line of clans is all one; they were derived from the same source." J.H.

5. John Hunt and his boys were well known on the northern part of the reservation because of their involvement in the trading business. John Hunt had owned and operated stores in Teec Nos Pos, Mexican Water, Fruitland, Aneth, and Bluff, and Ray, his son, spent a lot of time in Mexican Hat. Ray's Navajo name, Swinging Arm, came from a withered and shortened left arm, the result of a childhood disease. Ray also worked as a trader in Oljato, Mexican Water, Gouldings, Chilchinbeto, and Gallup. See Ray, Grace, and Emery Hunt interviews, Southeastern Utah Project, Utah State Historical Society and California State University–Fullerton Oral History Program, a series of interviews between 1970 and 1987.

6. Probably Harold R. Butt, a stockman who lived in Blanding at this time.

7. "The man called Twenty-Five Cents received his name from the silver quarters sewed on his shirt and the pockets of his vest. People used to wear vests a lot back then." J.H.

8. A number of chants are part of the Holyway (Hodiyinjí) subgroup and may be used to cure the effects of lightning, such as Red Antway (Wóláchíí'jí), Shootingway (Na'at'oyee), and Windway (Nítch'ijí). "Each chant is concerned with particular factors that are thought to cause the disease or diseases for which it is believed to be an efficacious cure. In fact the ceremonial is directed toward appeasing or exorcizing such factors rather than toward treating the physical symptoms of the illness itself. There are a multitude of things with which improper contact is believed to cause sickness. . . . [by] natural phenomena [like] lightning (Thunder) and winds predominating." Leland C. Wyman, "Navajo Ceremonial System," in *Handbook of North American Indians—Southwest*, vol. 10 (Washington, D.C.: Smithsonian Institution, 1983): 543–44.

9. The humor in this is found in the Navajo practice of having a son-in-law in a family do a lot of the work, almost as a hired hand, or slave, to the family's wishes.

10. Father H. Baxter Liebler was an Episcopalian priest who came to southeastern Utah in 1943 and established the Saint Christopher Mission in Bluff and a number of satellite parishes, one of which is near Oljato. For more information about his work, see H. Baxter Liebler, *Boil My Heart for Me* (Salt Lake City: University of Utah Press, 1994), and Robert S. McPherson, "He Stood for Us Strongly: Father H. Baxter Liebler's Mission to the Navajo," *American Indian Culture and Research Journal* 23, no. 2 (August 1999): 109–26.

11. The livestock-reduction program, which took place when John Collier served as the commissioner of the Bureau of Indian Affairs, was one of the two most traumatic events in Navajo history. The other was the Navajo exile to Fort Sumner (1864–1868). Livestock was literally and philosophically life to the people. When the government decreed that large portions of the herds had to be destroyed to save the land from overgrazing and consequent erosion, resent-

ment and friction grew to new heights. Most of the reduction occurred during the 1930s, as the American economy languished in the Great Depression. By the time this program had run its course, in many instances, the herds had been cut by more than half, forcing the Navajos out of economic independence into an off-reservation wage economy and dependence on the government. Collier's name became synonymous with all the hate the program created. For a view of the program's impact on Navajos in southeastern Utah, see Robert S. McPherson, "Navajo Livestock Reduction in Southeastern Utah, 1933–1946: History Repeats Itself," in *Navajo Land, Navajo Culture: The Utah Experience in the Twentieth Century* (Norman: University of Oklahoma Press, 2001): 102–20.

12. Ibid. John is not just making an idle comparison. To many Navajos, livestock reduction was comparable to the Long Walk. Rounding up the livestock was similar to the gathering of the people in the 1860s—history repeating itself. It was another government attempt to destroy the Navajos and their way of life.

13. "Flips like a Rope received his name from his paternal grandfather, who had the same name and was very mean. He would flick his whip at anyone who gave him trouble. They also called him One Who Whips You, but shortened it to Flips like a Rope.

"Yellow Yucca Fruit's name goes back to the All Mixed (Stones) Clan. One of their women was at home with her granddaughter on a foggy day. The girl went outside and walked around the hogan, looking for her grandmother. Because she did this, she gave the name of Go around You (Hoonaadałí) to her clan. This same girl had a daughter and moved to a place where there were many yucca plants. Yucca bear banana-like fruit, and so the people coming from this daughter became known by this fruit's name.

"Crazy One received his name when the authorities sent him to the Tuba City Jail. He escaped on his horse, and although the police searched, they never captured him.

"One Who Does Not Fall was Crazy One's brother. When he wrestled with others for fun, no one could bring him down. They tried to throw him, but he stayed up." J.H.

14. John may not have been aware that a group of Navajos from Oljato apparently went to Washington. Mildred Heflin, who with her husband, Reuben, ran the Oljato Trading Post at that time, recalls the incident. "The Indians at Oljato got very upset about the Stock Reduction. They formed a delegation and sent them back to Washington to see Eleanor and President Roosevelt. Well, they did get to see Eleanor Roosevelt, but of course they didn't accomplish anything. They stayed back there about two weeks.

"I can't remember who all went along. John Fat and John Chief and his wife went. They had quite a few sheep. I don't remember all the other people who went. There were about five or six of them. Several people from the Kayenta area went along, too. They pawned their jewelry to the poor old traders (laughter). We could have gotten in very serious trouble over it, because here we were going against what the United States government was telling them to do. The Indian Agent was quite upset, of course. Fortunately, he blamed the missionary [Shine Smith who came to Oljato around 1937 and accompanied the delegation] more than he did us." Samuel Moon, *Tall Sheep: Harry Goulding, Monument Valley Trader* (Norman: University of Oklahoma Press, 1992): 97.

15. The law that John refers to are the rules of life established by the Holy Beings. There are laws established in the stars, in the teachings, and by the People that govern proper relations in all things.

16. John's reaction to the age of this girl is understandable. In traditional ways, a girl is not of marriageable age until after she has had a Kinaaldá following her first menses, usually around the age of twelve or thirteen. Ages fourteen to sixteen were considered preferable for marriage in the old days.

17. The politically preferred term for the conglomerate group of American Indians whom John calls Anasazi, who inhabited the Four Corners region from roughly 1000 B.C. (Basketmaker) to 1300 A.D. (Pueblo), is Ancestral Puebloans. However, because of the long-term use of the Navajo name Anasazi, glossed as Ancestral Enemies, and because this is the word that John used, I have decided to employ it in this book.

18. "What the Heck received his name from what he used to say all of the time—'My goodness, what the heck, just let it be that way.' His language became his name." J.H.

19. Traditional Navajo culture stresses modesty in dress. John's shock about this physical inspection is not surprising and was just one of his many new experiences in the white man's world.

20. Big White Man in this instance is not Arthur Spencer, from the Mexican Hat post of earlier years, but Reuben Heflin, who owned the post until 1944. The missionary is probably Shine Smith.

21. Wolves, by the early 1940s, had been mostly, if not entirely, eradicated. Whether this fear was real or imagined, John felt it necessary to be armed.

22. When a sheep is butchered, little is wasted. There are a number of different ways of using sheep intestines and other internal organs after they have been thoroughly cleaned. For instance, the small intestines can be wrapped around a length of fat and roasted on a grill. The intestines may also be cut into small pieces and fried or used as a long container in which water, meat, and fat are added, the ends tied, and the entire organ placed in the coals. Blood sausage is made by turning the washed stomach inside out and filling it with blue cornmeal, fat, bits of meat, some of the sheep's blood, and water, then tying both ends and boiling it. The liver may be thinly sliced and roasted with fat taken as a large sheet off the sheep's underside. And the sheep's skull is cooked in coals, removed from the fire, and cracked open for the brains.

CHAPTER 5: WORK IN THE LATER YEARS

1. The chronology in this section can again become confusing because of John's shifts in different types of employment. For instance, he was involved in herding, the movie industry, and vanadium and uranium mining off and on over a lengthy period. In order to avoid excessive jumping around, certain types of experiences have been consolidated. While John states that he was mining vanadium in 1938, most of his experience was during the post–World War II 1950s era, when the uranium business was booming. He was probably married in the mid-1940s, because he was single when he was at Belmont, working in the war industries, and so the reader should understand why certain elements in the chronology have been juggled.

2. John worked in the mines during two different stretches of time. This first one, as he said, was for three years. He was most likely mining vanadium in a mine called Utah One, on the eastern tip of Oljato Mesa. This was leased in 1944 from the Office of Indian Affairs in Window Rock by Wayne Carroll and Lee Shumway, who bid $505 on the forty-acre claim. The mine yielded fifty-two tons of vanadium the first year. William Chenoweth, "Early Uranium-Vanadium Mining in Monument Valley, San Juan County, Utah," *Survey Notes* 18, no. 2 (Summer 1984): 3, 19.

3. The Glen Canyon Dam was completed in 1963, with the subsequent creation of Lake Powell out of the dam's backed-up water. Paiute Farms, shared by Paiutes and Navajos at different times, was a favored agricultural spot. Tucked in the small valley bordering Nugget Creek, a tributary of the San Juan, Paiute Farms sat about a half mile from the river. It provided only a few hundred yards of planting space, with sufficient water to grow corn, pumpkins, and melons. White men passing through the area in 1894–1895 noted Navajo homes scattered among the stands of large cottonwoods. They also mentioned a conspicuous absence of willow. The flood of 1911 washed out these farms. James Aton and Robert S. McPherson, *River Flowing from the Sunrise: An Environmental History of the Lower San Juan* (Logan: Utah State University Press, 2000): 85.

John's discussion of Paiute Farms leads one to believe that his camp was in the area, but perhaps not exactly at, Paiute Farms. His proximity to the river and the size of the fields he planted suggest a larger bench nearby.

4. "Dan and I are both in-laws to Spring under the Cottonwood." John explained, "Relatives say a phrase when teasing or making an unkind comment to a brother-in-law." Next in this chapter, John explains the origin of this phrase.

5. Derivation of these Navajo names is as follows: "Yellow Water lived at a place on Black Mesa, Arizona, where there was yellow water. Short Hair received his name after he and some other men returned from prison in Salt Lake City for

stealing cattle from the Mormons. He had short hair at a time when everyone else wore the traditional hair bun. The One Who Hits was a sensitive, quick-to-anger person and fought with people who criticized him. Among the Greasewood's Son's father came from a place of that name, which is located near Tall Mountain, northeast of the Shonto Trading Post." J.H.

6. The Holy Beings established a Navajo tradition through the pattern of doing something—saying prayers, making a request, singing a song, and so forth—four times. If a person is asked four times, this last time, the request is granted. Coyote is using this practice to get what he wants.

7. Charlotte Frisbie, an expert in the use and care of medicine bundles, writes: "Jish [medicine bundles] must be assembled, in whole or in part, in a ceremonial context. They are usually blessed with corn pollen and other substances when used. . . . Jish, their associated ceremonials, and the people who conduct them occasionally need renewal. The most frequently held ceremony for jish is renewal through Blessingway . . . . The purpose of the renewal ceremony is to 'make you and your bundle strong,' 'to re-bless it and to increase its power,' 'to revitalize those things,' 'to make your knowledge fresh, strong, sharp,' 'to bring life back into those things.' . . . Many singers said that renewal must be done on a regular basis—such as after every four performances of each ceremonial or 'once every two years' or 'once every six months.' All said that renewal ceremonies could be held more often if any of their patients died or if they, their families, or their possessions (including their jish) suffered any misfortunes." Charlotte J. Frisbie, *Navajo Medicine Bundles, or Jish: Acquisition, Transmission, and Disposition in the Past and Present* (Albuquerque: University of New Mexico Press, 1987): 108–109.

8. "Tobacco Mountain is on the road as one drives to Cedar City and goes through Page, Arizona, over the old, old bridge. Wide Willow Prairie is north of Kanab, Utah. It is a place where the Utes used to live and has sand dunes and lots of trees." J.H.

9. In addition to being a terribly unpleasant task, this type of involvement with the dead is entirely against Navajo tradition. Navajos went to great lengths to avoid contact with the dead, especially those who died a violent death. Fear that the spirit of the deceased would come back was prevalent.

10. This machine is a total mystery. I have asked John to clarify what it was, and he has done the best he can, but what it actually was and how it worked really tell more about Navajo perception than about the machine. Mexicans, because of their mythological and historical interaction with the Navajos, have been classified as a powerful, but often untrustworthy, people. The explanation that this machine could actually differentiate between the two races hints of deep-rooted feelings about ethnicity.

11. Navajo avoidance of the dead is well known. Why John did not follow this teaching seems strange. Certainly there are examples in other Navajo auto-

biographies in which people have worked with corpses of the Anasazi or from other Indian tribes. John knew from his training as a medicine man and from the reaction of the older Navajos there that this work detail should be avoided. Enemyway or Evilway ceremonies are required to exorcise the spirits of the dead from the patient, which can be a lengthy and expensive process.

12. John later added an interesting interpretation concerning his sickness. He said: "We have different kinds of electric currents in our bodies. Illness caused by contact with Mexican flesh is much more difficult to detect than Anasazi illness. The sickness hides itself and cannot be detected by crystal gazing or hand trembling. What nearly killed me came from the Mexican. It turned my legs dark and was very, very painful."

13. The scalp, or hair, as well as a bone or some other part of an "enemy" is sung against, shot, and ritually destroyed, representing the destruction of the enemy (spirit) that is bothering the patient.

14. The tenacity of the Mexican's flesh can be attributed in part to the Navajo teachings about the Great Gambler, or One Who Wins You as a Prize. This story, set in Chaco Canyon, tells of an extraordinary Anasazi person who gambles and wins control over everyone and everything until he is finally defeated by an impoverished Navajo, with the aid of the Holy Beings. The Great Gambler is banished from Earth but promises to return one day as a Mexican. See Robert S. McPherson, *Sacred Land, Sacred View: Navajo Perceptions of the Four Corners Region* (Provo, Utah: Brigham Young University, 1992): 87–89; and Aileen O'Bryan, *Navaho Indian Myths* (New York: Dover Publications, 1993): 48–62.

15. Although there were others who filmed in Monument Valley prior to John Ford, he is the most prominent. His first film produced on location was in 1938, his last in 1964. For Navajo reaction to this era, see Robert S. McPherson, *Navajo Land, Navajo Culture: The Utah Experience in the Twentieth Century* (Norman: University of Oklahoma Press, 2001): 142–57.

16. "Man between the Rocks was my mother's husband. He used to work at Goulding's Trading Post, and so that is how he received his name. The location of the post is close to the opening between two big rocks, or mesas." J.H.

17. "Wooden Hat wore a stiff military-, police-type hat." J.H.

18. John is referring to the Navajo belief that if a person thinks or acts out a certain scenario, even if make-believe, it will come true. Other Navajos concur that because some of the people used in the movies were often involved in death scenes, they died young.

19. Peter McDonald served as chairman and president of the Navajo Nation from 1971 to 1982 and again from 1987 to 1988, until he was found guilty of corruption and placed in federal prison.

20. "Cottonwood Coming Up is a place between Dennehotso, Arizona, and the Mexican Water Trading Post. It received its name because cottonwoods grow along the canyon almost to its top." J.H.

21. Bit'ahnii Lók'aa Dine'é refers technically to the Reed People, a subset of the Bit'ahnii, or Folded Arms Clan (also known as Within-His-Cover Clan).

22. The San Juan River, the northern boundary of Navajo land, has a protective spirit that can help travelers once they leave the safe confines of the reservation. Beyond the river is the land of foreigners and enemies—Utes, white men, and other non-Navajos. By appealing to this spirit of the river through prayers and corn pollen, one can enjoy a safe journey and accomplishment of goals.

23. A brief overview of the miners' experiences in Monument Valley can be found in Robert S. McPherson, "Digging the Bones of Yee'iitsoh: Navajos in the Uranium Industry in Southeastern Utah," in *Navajo Land, Navajo Culture: The Utah Experience in the Twentieth Century* (Norman: University of Oklahoma Press, 2001): 158–78.

24. In an interview with Samuel Moon, Fred Yazzie confirms what John says. Speaking of the discovery of Monument II mine, Fred said: "Two Indians, I think it was Little John [Holiday], he's the one that saw the uranium, Little John and Luke Yazzie, two men. They showed him [Harry Goulding]."

According to Luke Yazzie, he was the one who showed the mine to Harry Goulding and later Denny Viles, field manager for VCA. Luke subsequently received little for his efforts. He thought he would become rich, but all he received was a job working in the mine he promoted.

As a sidelight, John was one of a number of miners who signed a letter to President Dwight D. Eisenhower in the summer of 1943, showing support for the war effort and the uranium industry in Monument Valley. Samuel Moon, *Tall Sheep: Harry Goulding, Monument Valley Trader* (Norman: University of Oklahoma Press, 1992): 175–85.

25. Removing an object shot into a person through witchcraft is not a ceremony typically performed by Navajo medicine men, and so John went to a Hopi practitioner. Behind this cure is the belief that an enemy can, through prayer and ritual, shoot a stone, bone, needle, and so forth into a person who has offended. The object is removed through the supernatural aid of a shaman.

26. Shooting an object into someone is a form of witchcraft performed through songs and prayers directed against an individual. To counter this, a shield of songs and prayers can be used to protect a person and can even redirect the evil back to the person who originated it. Some medicine men specialize in the protection against witchcraft.

27. The uranium-processing mill in Mexican Hat (actually Halchita–Red Land, approximately two miles away) opened in 1956 and closed in 1969.

28. Congress passed the Radiation Exposure Compensation Act of 1990, stipulating an award of up to $100,000 to deserving miners, widows, and children if the parents were deceased. President George Bush signed the law, and Congress eventually appropriated money for the compensation, but many miners complain

that there is too much red tape and that the pay is slow in coming and insufficient. John certainly agrees.

CHAPTER 6: TEACHINGS FROM THE FEARING TIME

1. "Woman Who Watches observed things—people, landscape, everything—when she traveled. Loud One talked a lot. Yellow Forehead probably had some blond hair on his forehead, and Ropey was named after the rope. Little Bitter Water received his name from his clan." J.H.

2. This is a surprisingly long distance from the main activity of most Navajo people south of the Four Corners region. Although southeastern Utah had small scattered bands living within its confines, the Henry Mountains and Richfield area are west and north and are in traditional Ute and Paiute country.

3. Part of the traditional wedding ceremony entails the couple feeding each other ground cornmeal mush, symbolizing their commitment and ability to care for each other.

4. Conflict between the U.S. government and the Navajos started shortly after the Treaty of Guadalupe Hidalgo in 1848, which ended the Mexican War. By the early 1860s, friction had increased to the point that the military, New Mexicans, and Indian auxiliaries began active field operations to round up the Navajos and incarcerate them at Fort Sumner, located on the Pecos River in eastern New Mexico. This period, known as the Fearing Time, and the subsequent Long Walk saw many Navajo groups decimated, impoverished, and in exile from their homelands. Those that did not go to Fort Sumner, also known as Bosque Redondo, fled to the hinterlands to escape military pressure. From 1864 to 1868, over 8,000 Navajos lived under the soldiers' watchful gaze until released to their newly established reservation on the boundary between New Mexico and Arizona. Books concerning this period include Lynn R. Bailey, *The Long Walk* (Los Angeles: Westernlore Press, 1964); Lawrence C. Kelly, *Navajo Roundup: Selected Correspondence of Kit Carson's Expedition Against the Navajo, 1863–1865* (Boulder, Colo.: Pruett, 1970); Frank McNitt, *Navajo Wars, Military Campaigns, Slave Raids and Reprisals* (Albuquerque: University of New Mexico Press, 1972); and Clifford E. Trafzer, *The Kit Carson Campaign* (Norman: University of Oklahoma Press, 1982).

5. John makes an interesting point. Today, much of the blame for the Navajo war, resulting in the incarceration at Fort Sumner, is placed on American military policy, misunderstanding, and betrayal. Although this is undoubtedly true, a number of Navajo elders have provided oral testimony saying that many of the problems were caused by the Navajos. For additional information supporting both views, see Broderick H. Johnson, ed., *Navajo Stories of the Long Walk Period* (Tsaile, Ariz.: Navajo Community College Press, 1973).

6. "Silversmith the Arrow Way received his name because he was injured by an Apache arrow." J.H.

7. "Yaahoo'a'í" means literally "to be raised with." John is saying that Woman with the Four Horns learned, as a young girl, a short, individualized sacred prayer of protection from her grandmother. As she was escaping, it protected her. This prayer, a very concrete reality, was answered through guidance of Woman with the Four Horns as she evaded her pursuers.

8. Many objects and animals have sacred names that are used only in ceremonies or on special spiritual occasions. These names were bestowed during the time of Creation and are used to call forth the sacredness of the object, so that its spiritual power will be made manifest. This is often done in mythic stories, where the hero or heroine is saved by this power.

9. "Peyote is a small, low-growing, hairy cactus whose flesh and roots are eaten by members of the [peyote] cult. The flesh looks like a small pincushion, and when dried, rather like an overcoat button. It grows in Texas and Mexico, in an area approximately bounded by Corpus Christi, Texas; Deming, New Mexico; Durango, Mexico; and Puebla, Mexico. It contains eight alkaloids, 'the most important of which is mescaline.'" David F. Aberle, *The Peyote Religion among the Navaho*, 2nd ed. (Norman: University of Oklahoma Press, 1982): 5.

10. "This mixture is created by first praying and giving sacred pollen to the vegetation, then gathering the tips of certain plants and flowers in the mountains or wherever the sacred plants grow. They are very tiny bits of these plants—some yellow, blue, green, or red—that are gathered. This collection of material is also called Living Plants with Tips of Beauty Mixture." J.H.

11. This part of Woman with the Four Horns's story employs a number of mythological motifs. Animals often assist heroes and heroines in their escape from evil or through trials. Gladys Reichard points out that "owls of one kind or another give information and ceremonial properties: One came to the hero of the Night Chant and told him the formula for incense which the gods fear. One covered Rainboy with his (skin as a) blanket; another on a different night, brought him a cottontail ready to eat, and covered him with his blanket." Gladys Reichard, *Navaho Religion: A Study of Symbolism* (Princeton, N.J.: Princeton University Press, 1963): 456.

12. "Wolf is a contrast to Coyote in that he is considered dependable. He is the leader of the hunting animals." Ibid., p. 501.

Karl Luckert writes: "All told, it appears that among the four-legged predators, Wolf has risen highest on the scale of divine mediatorship. Hunters identified with him in a song, albeit now disassociated from the Huntingway which is named after him; but he bestowed his mythical name on all human and animal hunters together; in addition, human hunters imitate his call. But since memorable times Wolf has remained fixed to his animal form. And this is the boundary which has severely limited his career as a divine mediator." Karl W. Luckert, *The Navajo Hunter Tradition* (Tucson: University of Arizona Press, 1975): 173.

13. For a history of some of the Navajos who did not go to Fort Sumner but remained behind in southeastern Utah, see Robert S. McPherson, *The Northern Navajo Frontier: Expansion Through Adversity* (Logan: Utah State University Press, 2001): 5–19.

14. "Bluebird Mountain is a name given by the Holy Beings at the time of Creation. There are many flocks of little bluebirds sent there by the Holy Beings." J.H.

15. Although John is very specific about who went to Washington, it is doubtful that some of those he mentions actually did. There is no doubt, however, that a contingent went before the signing of the treaty of 1868. Gerald Thompson, historian, writes: "Late in April of 1868, Manuelito, Barboncito, and several other Navajo headmen, accompanied by interpreter Jesus Arviso, were taken by Agent [Theodore H.] Dodd to Washington, D.C. They talked in person to President Andrew Johnson, but the Great Father refused to make any promises. The Navajos wanted to return to their ancestral lands, but the president explained to them that the Peace Commission would make that decision. Upon returning to New Mexico, the Navajos came to feel that if the commission did not give them justice (return them to their homelands), the entire tribe would bolt the reservation. Manuelito and Barboncito spoke in favor of fleeing, if the talks should fail." Gerald Thompson, *The Army and the Navajo: The Bosque Redondo Reservation Experiment 1863–1868* (Tucson: University of Arizona Press, 1982): 151.

16. Navajo Mountain, with Rainbow Bridge located at its northern end, is associated with protection as a refuge during troubled times. According to local beliefs, Navajo Mountain was the birthplace of Monster Slayer, who helped make the world safe for the Navajo people in mythological times. During the Fort Sumner period, many Navajos fled to this isolated region, believing the powers of the mountain and Monster Slayer served as a protective shield against the forays of the Utes, Hopis, and U.S. military. As John is pointing out, Navajos climbed the mountain and offered prayers to "talk back the people who were captured." Buck Navajo, interview by author, December 16, 1991, transcript in possession of author.

17. John is suggesting that through witchcraft and other evil means, this man was able to curse the Navajos into captivity. But just as words can create this situation, they can also correct the problem, once people realize the cause.

18. Dogs are said to have special powers to discern spiritual things connected to future events, people who practice witchcraft, and approaching danger. Here, the dog recognizes the fate of Mountain Boy, warning him of impending doom.

19. John later mentioned another reason for the incarceration of the Navajos at Fort Sumner, associated with the loss of a sacred bundle. He explained: "The Earth's Sacred Shake-offs, the Heavenly Sacred Shake-offs, and the Female Mountain Shake-offs were in a bundle made for the protection of the land we live on. The bundle defeated our enemies and prevented them from taking the land. But once the bundle was stolen, our people suffered the Long Walk. When it was gone, no one said the sacred songs and prayers, so the people were without the protection for the land or themselves. The Navajos suspected a couple of men—Little Bitter Water and Ropey—of taking it. From what I understand, the sacred bundle has been located. One of these days it will be brought back to this hogan, and there will be a renewal ceremony for it.

"The sacred bundle contains the shake-offs of the lightning, sunrays, rainbow, mirage, dawn, sunset, and sunshine. Other shake-offs were made from the Bear (performed near Circle of Black Rocks), Big Snake (associated with Navajo Blanket, east of Mexican Hat Rock), lightning (near Sitting Stars at a spot called Blue Sandstone), and the Holy Wind (taken near Tuba City at a place called Complex Land Formation—an intricate combination of land formations containing hills, washes, valleys, and rocks). A blue bird is the lightning, its color as dark as the moss in water. The Holy Wind is a pure, clear crystal that popped out of a hole in the earth when the medicine man prayed. The medicine men present spread a white cloth on the ground and did the shake-off of the crystal stone, which then went back into the hole with a 'toosh' sound. This was the Holy Wind escaping from that hole. There is another place where air escapes near Totem Pole Rock, on the way to Paiute Farms." J.H.

20. "This mountain has stones that are dark in color, and when cracked, they break off with square, sharp corners. The rock looks like marble, and so the mountain was named for it." J.H.

21. "The Navajos prayed through Holy Wind to the inner spirit of their white captors that they would feel mercy and sympathy for us, have remorse and cry, then set us free. Two days after they performed the ceremony, the People were freed." J.H.

22. In a clarification interview, John provided additional information and suggested that the shields, or ones like them, have since been discovered. As for the medicine bundle mentioned previously, he is not aware of its whereabouts. "The Navajos created a sacred earth bundle from a buffalo skin and its contents of sacred offerings. There is also one for the heavens. We cannot see their shields, but they each have one as their protector. The sky had the cattail shield, the mountains have their shield, both of which were given to the Navajos. So the Navajos made their own sacred bundle, protective shield, too. It was made in the likeness of the real one, belonging to the earth and sky. These shields were huge and had strings attached to them on the inside. The earth

shield had the mountains and vegetation depicted on it. The mountain shield had lightning, sunrays, and rainbows, while the sky shield had all the heavenly bodies and stars on it. These shields were big, and nothing could penetrate them—neither bullets and arrows, nor evil and witchcraft. They are shields against all things that can harm a person.

Many Goats with White Hair, eight generations ago, had the sacred bundle when it was created. It was made up in the mountains near Richfield, Utah, but when the Navajos were being taken to Fort Sumner, Ropey hid the bundle. When he went back to get it, he could not find it, so it was lost. The shields have now been found and are in a museum in Tucson, Arizona. All of these sacred shields protect the earth and sky every day, but we as humans cannot see them. They are holy and sacred." J.H.

In winter 2001, Professor Lawrence L. Loendorf, of New Mexico State University, contacted me concerning these shields because of my association with John. An excerpt of his e-mail follows: "I am particularly interested in the Pectol shields. My interest dates back several decades and includes my successful petition to Capitol Reef National Monument [Utah—approximately sixty miles straight-line distance from Richfield] to remove a sample of a strap for radiocarbon dating. According to the three separate (and overlapping) radiocarbon dates, the shields were made about the time horses were introduced to the Southwest. The size of the shields and the designs on them are consistent with this date. Sometime last year, in an effort to learn cultural affiliation of the shields, the Navajo claimed them. I do not have a clear story but apparently the shields were buried after a battle with the Spanish. . . .

"Recently John Holiday was taken to Tucson, where the shields are currently housed in the National Park Service archives, to view the shields. In inquiring about this visit, I was told that you have worked with Mr. Holiday."

The dates of these shields do not appear to coincide with John's account, and only one seems to have the pictorial elements he mentions. The three Ephraim P. Pectol shields were discovered in 1925, wrapped in cedar bark a foot and a half underground, in a rock shelter in the Capitol Reef National Monument. Early carbon dating placed construction of the buffalo-hide shields between 1650 and 1750; a more recent dating of three samples clusters around 1500; and Dr. Loendorf, in the latest study, has settled on the time frame of 1550–1650. Entrance of the horse mentioned by Loendorf would coincide more with the earliest carbon dates; however, the shields were large and designed for foot soldiers, not equestrian warfare. Still, the existence of such shields lends an interesting note to the story that John tells about those constructed during the Long Walk era. For further reading, see Lawrence L. Loendorf and Stewart Connor, "The Pectol Shields and the Shield-Bearing Warrior Rock Art Motif," *Journal of California and Great Basin Anthropology* 15 (Spring 1993): 216–24; and

Lawrence Loendorf, *The Pectol Shields: A Repatriation Study* (an unpublished interim report, 2001), in possession of Loendorf and McPherson.

23. Lines and circles are used in Navajo thought to either encircle and trap or keep out evil influences. The well-known practice of leaving an opening in a rug, basket design, enclosure, and so forth is the inverse of this practice, always allowing evil and thoughts an avenue of escape from something that is good. John is suggesting that the line drawn by these medicine men separated the Fort Sumner experience, with all of its horror, from the People as they departed, no longer to be influenced by it unless they willingly returned. Unfortunately, that is what has happened.

24. Not everyone agrees with what John says. In a public meeting in Blanding on January 26, 2001, a man named Ben Silversmith reacted to John's statement. He explained that he and other medicine men had held discussions about whether they should return to Fort Sumner. They agreed that they could, but it must not be under the same conditions, that is, as captives. Consequently, they did. He told of camping there and how, late at night, he heard many voices, some close by, others distant, but all were indistinct yet definitely Navajo. These were voices from the past.

He went on to say that the reason for the Fort Sumner experience is rooted in a Navajo word that means "none of your business." At the Creation of the earth, Mother Earth and Father Sky said to each other, when discussing what was going on in their respective spheres, "None of your business." This was not good. Later, during the separation of the sexes in the underworld, a similar thing happened between the men and the women. Before Fort Sumner, the old men were worried about what was taking place with the young men, who were raiding the white man and different Indian tribes. Again, the young men told their elders, "None of your business." The white man became angry, and the experience at Fort Sumner resulted. Now, a similar problem exists with young people telling the old people that what they are doing is "none of their business." That is why there are the problems that exist today.

25. Rather than a place to be shunned, Fort Sumner has become a shrine. Articles and editorial comments about Fort Sumner constantly appear in the *Navajo Times*. For instance, in a single issue on May 31, 2001, commemorating the signing [June 1] of the treaty of 1868, there were the following headlines: "A 'Baking Flat Plain': A First Visit to Bosque Redondo" [by a Navajo woman]; "Navajo Holocaust: Route of Long Walk Proposed for Designation as National Historic Trail"; "Grandmother's Advice: Rap Singer to Honor Ancestors." A caption on one of the pictures says, "The Navajo Traveler's Shrine at Fort Sumner State Monument, where stones from all parts of Dinetah were placed by Navajo Visitors." In the same article one learns that "thanks to a 1993 New Mexico Legislature resolution and a $2 million federal appropriation last year,

plans are in the works for a larger monument that will tell the story of the Long Walk and Bosque Redondo concentrating on the Navajo and Mescalero Apache viewpoints." Busloads of schoolchildren as well as tourists now frequent the site. When compared with what John has suggested, the opposing views are self-evident.

CHAPTER 7: JOHN TEACHES OF THE LAND

1. Additional information about many of the mountains, rock formations, plants, and animals discussed in this chapter can be found in books such as Robert S. McPherson, *Sacred Land, Sacred View: Navajo Perceptions of the Four Corners Region* (Provo, Utah: Brigham Young University, 1992); Laurance D. Linford, *Navajo Places: History, Legend, Landscape* (Salt Lake City: University of Utah Press, 2000); and Klara B. Kelley and Francis Harris, *Navajo Sacred Places* (Bloomington: Indiana University Press, 1994).

2. A frequent motif in Navajo mythology is the testing of the protagonist. When Monster Slayer and Born for Water started on their journey to meet their father, they were challenged by encounters with monsters and difficult situations along the way. Once they reached Sun Bearer, he too gave them a series of tests to prove that the Twins were who they said they were. The switching of the mountains was one of these.

3. During a clarification interview, I asked John to explain more about how the Twins are connected to tornadoes. His reply shows the power behind this type of knowledge: "I am only to tell what I've already told you. I cannot go into detail because of its sacredness and harm. When someone talks of this, it will happen. My wife does not like it when I talk about it, and my family members are afraid too. Every time I do, a tornado comes, so I cannot say anything. After the last interview when I spoke about them, we had one come through here. It broke our windows and tore out some of the trees." J.H.

4. The control of winds and other types of weather is a common practice among older medicine men. For other examples of this practice, see Robert S. McPherson, *Sacred Land, Sacred View: Navajo Perceptions of the Four Corners Region* (Provo, Utah: Brigham Young University, 1992): 41–47.

5. This story is repeated by many people—Navajo and Anglo alike—who worked in the film industry. Big Man became famous for his control of the weather and was said to be one of the highest paid Navajos on Ford's employment list. For further information, see Robert S. McPherson, *Navajo Land, Navajo Culture: The Utah Experience in the Twentieth Century* (Norman: University of Oklahoma Press, 2001): 151–53; and Samuel Moon, *Tall Sheep: Harry Goulding, Monument Valley Trader* (Norman: University of Oklahoma Press, 1992): 152–56.

6. One of the most complete and available references on star lore in Navajo culture is Trudy Griffin-Pierce, *Earth Is My Mother, Sky Is My Father: Space, Time, and Astronomy in Navajo Sandpainting* (Albuquerque: University of New Mexico Press, 1992).

7. Revolver here means that during seasonal changes, these two star patterns revolve around the North Star, which remains fixed.

8. To call someone a ghost is strong language, bordering on a curse, because of the association with the dead.

9. For further information on the connection of the Colorado and San Juan Rivers and Rainbow Bridge, see Karl W. Luckert, *Navajo Mountain and Rainbow Bridge Religion* (Flagstaff: Museum of Northern Arizona Press, 1977).

10. In a clarification interview, John explained further how this and other concepts discussed in this chapter work: "The Holy Man named Talking God owns all the wild animals—mountain sheep, antelope, buffalo, rabbits, prairie dogs, birds, and the yellow, blue, and black coyotes and wolves. These are all his animals, which he controls. That is why humans do not regulate their breeding seasons. People do not personally separate these animals, nor put them back together, because Talking God does that in his own spiritual, holy way. From the time that the animals have their young ones to the day they will breed again, the Holy One automatically regulates that by the monthly moon. Then all the other animals were given to the human race by the Holy [Changing] Woman. She gave us sheep, goats, cattle, horses, donkeys, and mules—all the domesticated animals. These animals are 'crazy' like us humans and just like the yellow-nosed billy goat who breeds in all seasons and puts forth his young into the freezing cold or hot weather.

"The hunt for the Holy One's animals should be done very carefully and with holiness. These are his animals, and we take them from him, because he herds and cares for them. He breeds them by the monthly moon. Each full moon has a name; we name them by the month in Navajo, too. The moon goes from a narrow shape called Sitting Thin or Skinny to the full moon named Full Round Setting. The Holy One will "close" the male animals from the females by the moon setting or month. He will not let the males go until a certain period, which is timed by the moon, which acts like a door or gate controlled by the Holy One.

"That is why the Navajos are very cautious in their hunting rituals. If we make mistakes and have no respect, it will affect our lives later; it may even kill a person. This is what Navajos should believe and practice. But the white people hunt their own way. Who knows—this could be the reason why so many of them die, without them realizing it.

"For Navajos, it is dangerous to hunt and butcher in 'our own way.' This can harm and blind us if we mistreat the eyes of the animal. If we do not remove the bladder correctly, it will affect our own bladder and organs. That is why Navajos are afraid to make any mistakes. We have to learn how to do it properly. It is a learning process, something passed down from our elders. The dissecting of the sacred animal parts is a different procedure from that of the sheep."

11. John is referring to the slaying of two police officers, Andy Begay and Roy Lee Stanley, on the evening of December 4, 1987. The two officers came upon an illegal beer party, were shot and killed, then were placed in their police van, which was ignited and sent over a cliff in Copper Canyon, near Lake Powell. Four Navajo men were indicted, with two convicted and sentenced to life imprisonment. Because of the close family ties of the policemen and the assailants from within the community, the incident had a large, unsettling impact.

12. The issue of hunting deer off the reservation is a long-standing problem, going back well over a century. For a historical perspective as well as a discussion of the cultural and environmental complexity involved in this dispute, see Robert S. McPherson, "Navajo and Ute Deer Hunting: Consecration versus Desecration," in *Navajo Land, Navajo Culture: The Utah Experience in the Twentieth Century* (Norman: University of Oklahoma Press, 2001): 21–43.

13. From the perspective of the Division of Wildlife Resources, the issue was evidence of the sex of the animal killed. Utah state law requires that, unless a special permit is acquired, only male deer with antlers be taken. Traditional Navajo practices require removing the head and sex organs and cutting the meat up in such a way that sex cannot be determined.

On October 27, 1990, Eddie Holiday was cited for failure to tag a mule deer. When this case went to court, on February 26, 1991, it became a test case to determine if traditional practices could be followed. The attorney general felt that the infraction had been minor, and so he dismissed the case without going to trial, and Eddie's rifle was returned. This particular issue continued to be deliberated for a number of years and entailed other concerns as well. Eventually, in 2001, an additional 275 permits could be purchased by American Indians who had not already obtained a permit for the hunt in the southeastern Utah region. This was in addition to the 11,500 resident and 1,500 nonresident permits already available. The only extension of hunting privileges for American Indians beyond normal hunting rights was a strip of land approximately fifteen miles wide west of Highway 191, extending to Lake Powell, in which these 275 permits could be used. Field officers of the Division of Wildlife Resources have also been instructed to work with Navajo hunters who have harvested and butchered deer in the traditional manner. However, if there is a clear indication that a doe has been killed, citations will be issued. Lieutenant Mike Milburn, law enforcement supervisor of the southeastern region of the Utah State Division of Wildlife Resources, telephone conversation with author, January 8, 2002.

14. Although the connection between rabbits and rain is not entirely clear, one suggested explanation links both rabbit and deer to moisture. Both animals are said to have the marks of rain—and in particular, lightning associated with rain—in their legs. This is what allows them to bound. Deer also have lightning marks on their antlers, where lightning strikes during a storm, which allows them to remain unharmed. Clouds and cloud cover are also associated with these animals, and that is why the Holy Beings direct that mating take place when clouds are present in the mountains during the fall and when storms are prevalent. The creation of human life is also supposed to take place at night, or in the dark, away from sunlight, otherwise an albino child will result. The reason for this is that the sun is said to be the eye of the Creator, who would be offended if he witnessed the sexual activity. Rabbit hunts take place during different seasons, but the spring hunt, after the corn has been planted, helps bring critical rains for crop growth.

15. "The Mud Dancers are holy men who participate in a ceremony for all of the people in attendance. Before going into the crowd at an Enemyway, these men have a ceremony performed on them. Then they run through the audience, and catch certain individuals, and throw them in a manmade mud puddle. Any person who gets thrown in has to help catch others and toss them in, too. The person who gets thrown in the mud puddle gets this special ceremony and is blessed by it. This strengthens a person's body and bones so that he or she will not break a bone or receive bodily injury if something happens, like being kicked or falling off a horse. This is a Lightningway type of ceremony and is also part of the Enemyway. If a person handles a dead body, he or she will not be affected. It also keeps witchcraft and evil things away." J.H.

16. Like deer, mountain sheep live in the mountains and are protected by lightning and thunder. Called Walk in Thunder, they are said to be immune to the effects of lightning, have strong supernatural powers, and create thunder when rams butt heads. Although the meat is not eaten, the hide is used to make medicine bags, which can protect a home from lightning. The skin between the horns on the forehead is massaged on aching muscles to relieve pain, and the fat is mixed with red and black pigments to drive evil away from a sick person. Jim Dandy, interview by author, December 4, 1989, transcript in possession of author.

17. John is referring to the last night of the nine-day Mountainway Ceremony, in which specially prepared participants perform the Fire Dance. The charred remains from the bark torches carried by the dancers are given to the spectators for use as medicine to heal mental and physical infirmities.

18. John is suggesting the possible effects of witchcraft used to curse this man's flocks and herds.

19. "Mixed waters is used for similar purposes as pollen. Originally these waters were gathered at Navaho Mountain, San Francisco Mountains, San Juan

Range, Pelado Peak, Mount Taylor, Taos, river forks in the south, and from waters in the west and north; from salt lakes below Zuni, or rather from the springs at the female and male mountains at the salt lakes. To this was added clay from the bottom of water, pollen, water pollen, and flag pollen." Franciscan Fathers, *An Ethnologic Dictionary of the Navajo Language* (1910; repr., Saint Michaels, Ariz.: Saint Michaels Press, 1968): 400.

20. In this and subsequent notes, unless otherwise indicated, additional information about the rock formations in and around Monument Valley is taken from ethnographic information collected by Stephen C. Jett, a noted scholar of Navajo geography. Stephen graciously provided this unpublished information based on interviews with local elders and a search of the literature.

Other names for Eagle Mesa include Wide Rock and Trees Hanging from Surrounding Belt because there used to be a lot of trees around the mesa. Standing beside the main mesa is a slender pinnacle that looks like an eagle, hence the name Eagle Mesa. Navajo names for this rock include Eagle along-side Mesa, Standing Slim Rock Alongside, and Big Finger Is Pointed.

21. "Owl Rock also known as Spindle (wool-twiner) and Slim Rock, according to Blessingway Singer Billy Yellow is a spindle left behind by the Holy Beings. The feature is a pinnacle of sandstone standing atop, and on the edge of, a mesa in the southern part of Monument Valley." Jett notes.

22. "El Capitan is an extraordinarily dramatic, pointed tuff-brecia volcanic neck rising from the floor of southern Monument Valley. [Robert W.] Young stated that it is the center of the world, and the pedestal for a Sky Supporter, who holds up the sky like an umbrella. However, according to Monument Valley Blessingway Singer Billy Yellow, this function actually belongs to Chaistla Butte, another neck not far to the south. El Capitan was formerly used to communicate with the Sun, First Woman, and White Shell/Changing Woman in her home in the ocean and possibly with other holy beings above.

"Paul Blatchford stated that an elderly singer had told him that El Capitan and Tuba Butte are the breasts of the great recumbent Female Mountain figure. Another statement is that it is female and paired with the male Shiprock.

"El Capitan has close associations with the Western Water Clans created by Changing Woman. Some of their number arrived at Oljato, via here, and settled there for a while. During their stay, they sometimes camped around the pinnacle for hunting purposes. Hides from the game secured were scraped on the rocks, and tanned then made into clothing by the women; the wind blew the hair all over the peak until it was almost covered, giving the landmark its name." Jett notes.

23. John's reference to having sheep in the area relates to the Navajo concept of keeping domestic livestock and wild animals separate. The two should not be mixed, even in the preparation of food. When sheep come in contact with deer hair, they become unruly and wild, requiring ceremonial cure.

24. Chaistla Butte is a black volcanic neck located a mile east of U.S. Highway 163 and five miles north of U.S. Highway 160 in the Little Capitan Valley, southeast of Monument Valley. "On one side of the rock is the form of a snake. According to Blessingway Singer Billy Yellow, should this butte fall, the world would end. The rock's name, To Support the Sky's Underside, implies that it is one of the Sky Supporters. I think there are five sky-supports, and the middle or central one stands on El Capitan." Jett notes.

There are many teachings about Shiprock, a dramatic 1800-foot-high volcanic neck in the corner of northwestern New Mexico. Among those cited by Jett are (1) the remains of a dark birdman who helped a Navajo fleeing from his Ute captors. "[The birdman's] sharp tail feathers became the two points of the pinnacle and his wings trail out on the ground, forming the lone, wall-like dikes extending southward and westward from the butte." (2) A family, fleeing from enemies, is offered a ride by a giant bird who promises to bring them to safety as long as the man does not look at his mother-in-law. He does, however, and the bird sets them down where Shiprock rests. (3) When the Navajos were at war and needed protection, "singers prayed and a piece of land rose with the Navajos, moved like a great wave to the eastward, and settled down to become Shiprock. The people lived on top, descending only to tend their fields and to obtain water. One day, lightning split off the trail and some old people and children were trapped on top and starved. Navajos today do not want anyone to climb the rock lest the ghosts be stirred up." (4) The best-known story is that Shiprock was the home of two human-eating birds that carried their prey to this location until Monster Slayer killed them. (This is the narrative of which John is speaking.) (5) "Shiprock is said by some to be one of the pinnacle arrows guarding the great Male Mountain figure [Chuska-Tunicha Range and Carrizo Mountains]. Shiprock and El Capitan are said to be paired, Shiprock being the male, El Capitan the female." Jett notes.

25. "Rain God and Thunderbird Mesas are the homes of thunderstorms and lightning, and have War God associations. People should not go on top of these mesas. Billy Yellow attributed the crash of a B52 bomber near there to the plane having flown too low over these mesas and their power having prevented it from ascending rapidly enough." Jett notes.

26. John is referring to the open area and rock formations to the southwest of Rain God Mesa, around what is referred to as the Hub.

27. John gave the following information as he stood at the southeast corner of Rain God Mesa, looking directly east at Totem Pole Rock. The rock formations he refers to start on his right and go to his front (Totem Pole Rock). As travelers then follow the road to Artist's Point, they will see an abandoned, weathered male hogan surrounded by a fence, to which John refers. Once at Artist's Point, one can see White-Tipped Mountain, a sandstone formation on the desert floor to the north.

28. Water Sprinkler is the clown at the Fire Dance. His actions are contrary to those of the other dancers, appearing to undo through opposition what the others are doing.

29. Paul Jones served as chairman of the Navajo Nation from 1955 to 1963. John is referring to the work he and other Navajos did during the land claims cases that were part of the Indian Claims Commission's hearings. The commission, founded on August 13, 1946, and closing on September 30, 1978, had the responsibility of listening to various claims by tribes across the United States. Many of these claims centered on ownership of Indian lands—disputes raised over both prehistoric and historic occupation and use. In the early 1960s, the Navajo Nation began a wide-sweeping effort to establish its ancestral boundaries. Archaeology, site surveys, oral and documentary history, as well as other proof, were submitted to federal courts for examination and approval in delineating the tribe's boundaries. John, as a knowledgeable medicine man and traveler through Navajo country, took part in this process.

30. Boundary growth on the northern part of the reservation led to two additions (in 1905 and again in 1933). Part of these new lands produced large amounts of oil that provided royalties to both the tribe and the local people in the Montezuma Creek–Aneth area. John is referring to the mistrust of local people for Window Rock, believing that the Utah Navajos do not receive full benefit. In 1971, the Utah state government formed the Utah Navajo Development Council (UNDC) to render a variety of services—health care, education, housing, livestock, and agricultural assistance—by using these funds. At its zenith (1976–1979), UNDC was an effective organization, but it has dwindled, though it is still in existence.

31. The 94,000-acre Monument Valley Navajo Tribal Park was dedicated in May 1960. Included in the initial cost of $275,000 was the construction of a visitors' center, campgrounds, and a network of roads that wind between and around some of the most heavily photographed monoliths and mesas in the world. In 1999 alone, 380,575 people visited the park, according to statistics on file in the Economic Development Office, Monticello, Utah.

CHAPTER 8: A CHANGING WORLD

1. Most likely, Navajos assigned these names to the car because of the "chi-chi-chi" sound of the engine. Some scholars suggest that another possible origin of the name could be the Navajo verb "nishjiid," which means "it sits or squats"; others believe the word comes from "dilchiid," which means "to point at something quickly." For more about Navajos' first reactions to the automobile and airplane, see Robert S. McPherson, "The Chidi and Flying Metal Come to the Navajos," in *Navajo Land, Navajo Culture: The Utah Experience in the Twentieth Century* (Norman: University of Oklahoma Press, 2001): 84–101.

2. Shake-offs are comprised of dust or light materials taken from an object and have the power and characteristics of the object because of the shake-off's close association with it. The anthropological term "synecdoche," meaning a part can represent the whole, is a basic principle expressed in various forms in Navajo culture and philosophy.

3. The Paiute people living in the area of Monument Valley, Douglas Mesa, and Allen Canyon for the most part belong to the San Juan Band. For an excellent study of these people and their history, see Pamela A. Bunte and Robert J. Franklin, *From the Sands to the Mountains: Change and Persistence in a Southern Paiute Community* (Lincoln: University of Nebraska Press, 1987).

4. Posey is a celebrated personage in southeastern Utah. He is most famous for his resistance to white encroachment on Ute and Paiute lands in the last quarter of the nineteenth and first quarter of the twentieth century. He was killed in 1923, during what has been termed the "last Indian war" in the United States, but this conflict has been badly overrated. One book, Albert R. Lyman's *The Outlaw of Navaho Mountain* (Salt Lake City: Publishers Press, 1986), is written about him, though it tends toward the dramatic and contains some inaccuracies.

5. John has confused his chronology concerning Ute-Paiute conflicts with neighboring Anglos. Posey did not kill a white man in Bluff but rather helped a Ute, who had killed a Mexican, escape from the law. This occurred in 1915. Eight years later, the Posey fight centered around Blanding (twenty-five miles north of Bluff). In the ensuing fracas, Posey received a gunshot wound and, a few weeks later, died.

6. John is referring to the influenza pandemic that occurred at the end of 1918 and 1919. The spread of this disease was rapid and highly destructive on the Navajo Reservation, though an exact death toll will never be known. The armistice ending World War I had just been signed (November 11, 1918), around the time this disease broke out. As mentioned in an earlier note (note 29, chapter 1), Navajos associate it with gas warfare used in this conflict.

7. "How Great, or My Goodness, used to say these words at the beginning of each sentence, so people began calling him that name. This phrase can be used as an expression of regret or praise, depending on the situation. People used to tease each other, just like I tease Mister McPherson. How Great would use this expression whenever he wanted to praise something. For instance, if he saw a person saddling or roping a horse, he would say it. Even when he greeted someone, he would not say, 'hello' but 'how great.'" J.H.

8. "There is a place north of Gallup, New Mexico, that Navajos call the Continuous Hills. A man from Dennehotso married a woman who lived there and had a son. The couple moved back to Dennehotso, and the people there named the boy Continuous Hills, because that is where he was born." J.H.

9. Towaoc has been the Ute Mountain Ute Reservation headquarters since 1914. The Navajo name Blue House was derived from the color of the agency's main building, and Towaoc, a Ute word, means Just Fine. See Virginia McConnell Simmons, *The Ute Indians of Utah, Colorado, and New Mexico* (Boulder: University of Colorado, 2000): 235–36.

10. The Utes and Paiutes in southeastern Utah received allotments and quasi-reservation status in Allen Canyon, located west of Blanding, in 1923. Visitation of Navajos with the Utes was a fairly common practice.

11. Many Navajos believe that contact with the Anasazi, or the dead in general, will sicken or kill the contaminated person. Ceremonial exorcism and cleansing is the antidote to prevent harm. The fact that his family members hunted for Anasazi artifacts illustrates that not all Navajos abided by these beliefs, and some were enticed into forsaking the practice for monetary motives. For other examples, see Robert S. McPherson, *Sacred Land, Sacred View: Navajo Perceptions of the Four Corners Region* (Provo, Utah: Brigham Young University, 1992): 113–17.

12. "One of the oldest traditional ceremonies belonging to Utes is the Bear Dance. . . . The Bear Dance involved the entire community. It celebrated the coming of spring with the bear coming out of hibernation; the awakening of spirits; winter returning to its home in the north; and the return of summer from the south, both summer and winter being guardians of the world." Forrest Cuch, ed., *A History of Utah's American Indians* (Salt Lake City: Utah Division of Indian Affairs, Utah State Historical Society, 2000): 219.

Today the Utes at White Mesa in southeastern Utah hold it in the fall to accommodate Ute ceremonies held elsewhere. John may be referring to this.

13. "Each needle is worth points, so when either of the opposing teams scores, the team counts and carries across the same amount of yucca stems. There are usually four shoes, 102 yucca stems, and a token. The two teams will take turns guessing which shoe contains the token. If they choose the wrong or empty shoe, they lose their points [yucca stems]. Depending on which shoe they choose, they can lose from four to ten points. The team whose turn it is to guess will say or bet four, six, or ten points on a particular shoe. Sometimes people will guess that the yucca ball is not in any shoe. If they are wrong, they will lose ten points. This betting or guessing is called 'to guess,' but the words are actually describing the cutting motion of an axe or hatchet. Another term used for the guessing is 'give me' so many points. The team that hands over all its yucca stems first, loses." J.H.

The yucca ball is the object hidden in the shoes. It is carved out of the tip of a yucca root.

14. "During the shoe game, the teams take turns hiding the token in different shoes, then the opposing side has to guess which shoe it is in. When the

opponents hit the wrong shoe, it costs them ten dollars. In gratitude for winning this money, a man on the winning team would grab the token from the shoe and sing a ceremonial song on someone who is sick on the opposing side. It could be a person with a headache or who is ill in some other way. The two teams do this to each other during the game, and that is what cured my sickness." J.H.

15. The following sections are filled with traditional Navajo values derived from life during the early livestock industry. If some of the teachings appear harsh, it is only because life can be that way. There are historical instances where Navajos actually starved to death because of circumstances out of their control. Preparation for the rigors of survival may seem excessive in today's plush society, but they were a necessity in times when there were no government programs and social nets to buffer against hardship. For an excellent summary of traditional values that parallel what John says, see Richard Hobson, *Navaho Acquisitive Values*, Peabody Archaeology Papers 42 (Cambridge, Mass.: Harvard University Press, 1953).

16. The fire poker is both a practical instrument used to stir the coals and bank a fire and a tool that holds many sacred teachings and powers. It is a protector of the home and has prayers associated with the hogan's well-being. To hit a person with it turns its sacred protective powers against the individual and the home.

17. Education reform of the militant boarding-school practices was a long time in coming. Although John blames Annie Wauneka for the shift away from harsher discipline, she was only one among many who worked for this change. Perhaps John's focus on Annie is because she was one of the first, and is definitely one of the best known, Navajo women in tribal politics—a practice that went against traditional beliefs outlined in the teaching stories. For a brief, accurate summary of changes in tribal education at this time, see Peter Iverson, *Diné: A History of the Navajos* (Albuquerque: University of New Mexico Press, 2002): 232–36.

CHAPTER 9: TEACHINGS OF LIFE

1. This well-known practice of telling certain things or holding ceremonies only at a specified time of the year is done to avoid offense to animals or Holy Beings. For example, Coyote (trickster) tales are told after there is frost on the ground and before the first lightning and thunder in the spring. This period is when creatures like spiders and hibernating animals are not around and so will not be offended.

2. Sometimes non-Navajos think of this transaction as purchasing information, but that really misses the point. Holy Beings are aware of how much

value is placed on sacred things. To provide a worthy amount for the transfer of knowledge is to recognize the value of what is being said.

3. Arrowheads serve as a protective device in ceremonies and medicine bundles, and as individual charms. "[An arrow point] may be secured to the forelock of the patient in the course of some ceremonies. By some they are worn even after the ceremony, when the charm is designated as a mark indicative of a holy rite." Franciscan Fathers, *An Ethnologic Dictionary of the Navajo Language* (1910; repr., Saint Michaels, Ariz.: Saint Michaels Press, 1968): 411. Navajo elders speak of these four arrowheads protecting Navajo lands against foreign invasion and evil.

4. "There are only vague descriptions of Begochídí [Bik'égochiidii]. He is not represented by any masked characters in the ceremonies, or by any picture in the dry-paintings. No description of his appearance has been recorded except that he looks like an old man. . . . Some say that Begochídí made all the animals whose creation is not otherwise accounted for in the myths. Others say that he and the Sun made the animals together. Others again limit his creation work to the larger game animals and the modern domestic animals. . . . Some say he is the same as the God of the Americans." Washington Matthews, *Navaho Legends* (1897; repr., Salt Lake City: University of Utah Press, 1994): 226.

5. The reed rattle "is a type of rattle and is called Tail Decorated with Feathers. It is used by a medicine man for ceremonies and is made out of a piece of cattail or reed, is decorated with feathers, and contains some peyote inside. There are usually two of these rattles—one decorated in turquoise, the other in white shell." J.H.

6. This is a confusing passage because it is incomplete and somewhat at variance with other published accounts. In similar versions of the Creation story, Locust emerges from the reed into this, the Fifth World, and encounters loons or ducks or grebes, who challenge him to a contest of passing arrows through the body. Locust successfully wins the contest and secures the right of the Navajos and associated Holy Beings and animals to reside in this world. For examples of this story, see Jerrold E. Levy, *In the Beginning: The Navajo Genesis* (Los Angeles: University of California Press, 1998): 62–64; Washington Matthews, *Navaho Legends* (1897; repr., Salt Lake City: University of Utah, 1994): 76–78; and Paul G. Zolbrod, *Diné Bahane': The Navajo Creation Story* (Albuquerque: University of New Mexico Press, 1984): 76–78.

7. Many versions of the Navajo Creation belief tell how everything was made spiritually before physically. Part of this process took place in the three or four worlds (depending on the version) beneath this world. Part of the process continued after the Emergence. The role of the Holy Wind, which exists by itself as well as in every living human, is central to spiritual expression. For additional information on this pervasive spirit, see James Kale McNeley, *Holy Wind in Navajo Philosophy* (Tucson: University of Arizona Press, 1982).

8. Male and female hogans are determined by shape, not function or who uses them. The conical male hogan, with an extended entryway, generally provides less space and is considered the older of the two forms. The female hogan, with its cribbed roof, is more spacious and more prevalent on the Navajo Reservation today. For a complete treatment of these structures, see Stephen C. Jett, *Navajo Architecture: Forms, History, Distribution* (Tucson: University of Arizona Press, 1981).

9. For an extensive treatment of the belief that every person's body is divided equally between male and female parts, see Maureen Trudelle Schwarz, *Molded in the Image of Changing Woman: Navajo Views on the Human Body and Personhood* (Tucson: University of Arizona Press, 1997).

10. "A mirage is when a person sees an object higher than it normally is or water on the road where there really is none. This is a Holy Being that exists in such areas of the mirage. We can only see the distortion. Females' bones are made from the holy mirage." J.H.

11. John clarified this thought by saying: "Only one strand was separated from the rest, and fourteen of the Holy Wind help us move around with bodily motion. It is the hair itself, on the scalp. These Holy Beings are standing on our hair. It comes out in the four sacred directions—the twirl [cowlick] on the crown of our head. Four come out, then four more, and four more—all together there are twelve of these Holy Beings."

12. This is the best-known story in Navajo mythology, encapsulating the birth of Changing Woman, the creation and rearing of the Twins, the visit to Sun Bearer, the receipt of weapons, and the killing of the monsters. A lot of Navajo ceremonial knowledge and philosophy spring from this story, which is told in much greater detail by other medicine men. Two easily accessible versions with variations are Aileen O'Bryan, *Navaho Indian Myths* (New York: Dover Publications, 1993); and Paul G. Zolbrod, *Diné Bahane': The Navajo Creation Story* (Albuquerque: University of New Mexico Press, 1984).

13. There are a series of stories about the Great Gambler, an Anasazi man who had significant supernatural powers but used them to enslave his own people as well as the Navajo. He is an example of a person who had the potential to be good but turned to a life of coercion, power, and corruption, ignoring even the wishes of the Holy Beings. Consequently, he lost his power and was banished from earth. Works cited in note six for this chapter have different versions of the Great Gambler story. See also Aileen O'Bryan, *Navaho Indian Myths* (New York: Dover Publications, 1993) for another concise explanation.

14. When asked to clarify this idea, John said: "The mountain [Sleeping Ute] is a man and a woman lying side by side. Long ago, legend says that this place involved something like gambling—just like the casino. [Today, the Ute Mountain Casino, on the Ute Mountain Ute Reservation, is located on the east

side of Sleeping Ute Mountain.] Many people were drawn to this place, and they all encountered some misfortune. It was like a trap. Because of this problem, a Holy Being [John referred to this person as "Someone"] was sent there. This Holy Being went to the place by standing atop a rainbow. The mountain, the place, did not see the Someone on the rainbow who came to him. It was a surprise attack. The Holy Being touched the ground as he stood on top of the rainbow and won the game. He won back all of the earth, mountains, and people. He beat the Great Gambler (One You Gather Everything For). They played like a person plays with cards, and the Holy Being won the game. He then put the loser [the Great Gambler] on the rainbow and shot him down into the depths of the earth. As he was descending, the people heard him speak in English, the white man's language. There were no white men then, but he spoke in English and said, 'I will come back. I will be back to beat you at the game. I will win back your language, your mind, your sacred songs, and prayers.' And that has happened. Today, the white men are here, and he [Gambler] has all that he said he would win back."

15. This is a common theme with elders. Loss of language equals loss of identity and the essence of being Navajo. As use of the Navajo language continues to decrease on the reservation, in spite of tribal and nontribal efforts to preserve it, the elders interpret this as a move toward the end of the world as it is now experienced. John describes later in this chapter what the final result will be.

16. John is mixing some of the teachings about the Anasazi with Mexicans who came later, but who are sometimes intellectually associated with the earlier Indian group. For an explanation of Navajo thought concerning the Anasazi, see Robert S. McPherson, *Sacred Land, Sacred View: Navajo Perceptions of the Four Corners Region* (Provo, Utah: Brigham Young University, 1992): 77–127.

17. "If, accordingly, in fancy one is pursued by foreigners such as Americans, Comanches, Utes, Pueblo, Cliffdwellers, or others, and is indisposed on this account, he calls upon the war singers to destroy these enemies. This accounts too, for the custom of coveting a tuft of hair, a piece of bone or clothing belonging to an Apache, Ute, or other foreigner, or purchasing them when seen at a curio shop. . . . At present the trophy is inserted with the bundle of weeds and on the final day of the ceremony [Enemyway], when the blackening of the patient has taken place, they are carried out some distance from the place of final gathering and deposited upon the ground by the singer. The throng surrounds the trophy at a respectful distance, while the singer takes a pinch of ashes and sprinkles the trophy with it, exhorting the visitors not to gaze upon it while this is being done. When the patient, too, has sprinkled ashes on it two of the visitors rush up and discharge their guns (formerly their arrows) upon the trophy. They then sing the praises of the patient in slaying or running the

enemy down." Franciscan Fathers, *An Ethnologic Dictionary of the Navajo Language* (1910; repr., Saint Michaels, Ariz.: Saint Michaels Press, 1968): 375.

18. When John was asked if a woman gave birth to her baby during either the full moon or skinny moon, he replied: "It can be either one. Women were made like that ever since the creation of mankind. The Holy One made women so that they would have their menstruation in monthly intervals in a cycle. Menstruation is called 'the Woman's Ruler.' A woman can get pregnant one day after she stops menstruating; then she will have her baby about the same moon in the full moon–skinny moon cycle."

19. The entire birthing process is filled with significance, explained in the teachings surrounding the role of Changing Woman, the exemplar for Navajo women. An excellent analysis of this symbolism is found in Maureen Trudelle Schwarz, *Molded in the Image of Changing Woman: Navajo Views on the Human Body and Personhood* (Tucson: University of Arizona Press, 1997): 61–112.

20. Herbert Redshaw served as a government farmer for the BIA in Aneth from 1914 to 1931. He was generally liked by the Navajos, who gave him the name His Own Devil (Abiich'įįdii)—an inexact translation—which is now the title of the Aneth Chapter. The name refers to how he walked, with a Frankenstein-like sway, but it was not considered a negative epithet. For more information about Redshaw, see Robert S. McPherson, "Government Farmers and the Navajos: The San Juan Experience, 1892–1933," in *Navajo Land, Navajo Culture: The Utah Experience in the Twentieth Century* (Norman: University of Oklahoma Press, 2001): 44–64.

21. For a detailed explanation of the symbolism of the Kinaaldá and the role of Changing Woman as the model for pubescent girls, see Maureen Trudelle Schwarz, *Molded in the Image of Changing Woman: Navajo Views on the Human Body and Personhood* (Tucson: University of Arizona Press, 1997); Charlotte J. Frisbie, *Kinaaldá: A Study of the Navaho Girl's Puberty Ceremony* (Middletown, Conn.: Wesleyan University Press, 1967); and Ruth Roessel, *Women in Navajo Society* (Rough Rock, Ariz.: Navajo Resource Center, Rough Rock Demonstration School, 1981).

22. Although John wishes to stress the propriety of past generations in "dating," there are certainly examples provided in other Navajo autobiographies to suggest there were those who did not practice the same strict moral rules. For examples, see Walter Dyk, *A Navaho Autobiography* (New York: Viking Fund, 1947); Walter Dyk, *Son of Old Man Hat* (1938; repr., Lincoln: University of Nebraska Press, 1996); and Walter Dyk and Ruth Dyk, *Left Handed: A Navajo Autobiography* (New York: Columbia University Press, 1980).

23. An associate of John's, Ervin Hanley, commented in a casual conversation that John is always the philosopher. Ervin heard him counsel a married couple, saying that the man should put "blue" (meaning turquoise) around a

woman's neck, and not around her eye (black and blue from abuse). This is the way couples should treat each other—with respect, gentleness, and love, not violence and hate.

24. As noted previously (note 23, chapter 2), nádleeh (literally, to revert or change back to a previous state) has a different connotation than "homosexual" does in the dominant culture. Additional information is found in W. W. Hill, "The Status of the Hermaphrodite and Transvestite in Navaho Culture," *American Anthropologist* 37 (Summer 1935): 273–79.

25. The Enemyway is used to dispel the ghosts or evil influences that can be bothering an individual. The origin of the ceremony goes back to the time of Monster Slayer and Born for Water, when they killed the monster Yé'ii Tso. They returned to Changing Woman and were recounting their deeds when they became faint and required a healing ceremony. The stick created for this ritual is a highly decorated object, with elements of a bow, various feathers, plant material, blacking from burnt weeds, deer hooves, sacred buckskin, yarn, and other cordage, which symbolize healing elements from the myth. The stick becomes a powerful force within the ceremony to ward off evil. See Franciscan Fathers, *An Ethnologic Dictionary of the Navajo Language* (1910; repr., Saint Michaels, Ariz.: Saint Michaels Press, 1968): 366–68.

26. Thought, prayer, and song cause physical things to happen. This theme is found throughout the Creation story, as the Holy Beings thought and planned before an object, ceremony, and so forth became a physical reality. John is saying that because of these songs, Navajo society changed for the worse.

27. "When it rains in the surrounding mountains, there are many small streams coming down to form one river. These are all from the surrounding sacred mountains. All of these rivulets join in the San Juan and Colorado Rivers; then these two rivers meet. This is where the name comes from. It is like someone taking a variety of canned foods and mixing them with a blender." J.H.

28. "Son of Coyote Pass People received his name from his father's clan." J.H.

29. "Muddy received his name from his clan, the Mud People, and I'm Worried About always ended his sentences with these words." J.H.

30. For a more detailed explanation of the Holy Wind, see James Kale McNeley, *Holy Wind in Navajo Philosophy* (Tucson: University of Arizona Press, 1982).

31. When asked to clarify this life-and-death process in greater detail, John replied: "When a baby is born, he is given a Holy Wind from the Holy One. When it enters the baby's body, the child makes its first cry. The male Holy Wind fills the left lung, then the female Holy Wind fills the right lung. This pair of Holy Winds gives life to humans, lasting into old age. When the day comes that a person dies, these Holy Winds will return to where they came from in the beginning of that person's life. The Holy Wind goes back to a beautiful place

down below the earth somewhere, and when another baby is born, a pair of Holy Winds will go there again. It could be the same pair or another. That is what I was told by the elders. It is almost like the Christian belief. There is much to say about the teachings of life and death, but it is very sacred, and it is not allowed for conversation. I can tell only the general things."

32. Additional information about life after death is found in Berard Haile, *Soul Concepts of the Navaho*, Reprint ed. (Saint Michaels, Ariz.: Saint Michaels Press, 1975).

33. "It has been 1,000 years since that happened, and now we are in a different era. Nowadays you can see pottery shards all over the world, everywhere. The end came suddenly, like lightning, and turned the earth once. This happened all too fast, and the Anasazi vanished. Legend says the same will happen again once we outgrow our Navajo language, traditions, sacred songs, and prayers. It nearly happened two or three years ago, when the earth almost collided with [Halley's comet?]. But the two objects missed each other, and we were spared. We were probably saved because we had a strong culture. If we had collided, there would not be anything on this earth now." J.H.

34. John is referring to when the Twins visited their father, Sun Bearer, and received the weapons necessary to kill the monsters on earth. After this was done, the weapons were placed in the ground so that they could not be used to hurt the People. The white man, however, gained access to them, and now they are available in our world.

CHAPTER 10: THE MAKING OF A MEDICINE MAN

1. For another explanation of how hand trembling works, from a practitioner's perspective, see Robert S. McPherson, *The Journey of Navajo Oshley: An Autobiography and Life History* (Logan: Utah State University Press, 2000). Oshley confirms many of the things John mentions, and discusses the effects of age and other circumstances on the medicine person.

2. A person who has the gift of hand trembling is believed to have been selected by the spirit, or power, of the Gila Monster deity. The hand trembler determines the patient's illness as the practitioner's right hand passes over and above the patient's body and reads the signals. The mythology surrounding hand trembling is "short and poorly integrated into the larger corpus of Navajo myth. It features a supernatural Gila Monster, who figures prominently in only one other ceremony, Flintway." Jerrold E. Levy, Raymond Neutra, and Dennis Parker, *Hand Trembling, Frenzy Witchcraft, and Moth Madness: A Study of Navajo Seizure Disorders* (Tucson: University of Arizona Press, 1987): 41, 46.

3. The Seventh Day Adventist Hospital opened its doors in 1950, dating this incident to around that time.

4. For a complete study on star lore, see Trudy Griffin-Pierce, *Earth Is my Mother, Sky Is my Father: Space, Time, and Astronomy in Navajo Sandpainting* (Albuquerque: University of New Mexico Press, 1992).

5. For a full treatment of the growth of the Native American Church, see David F. Aberle, *The Peyote Religion among the Navaho*, 2nd ed. (Norman: University of Oklahoma Press, 1982); and Omer C. Stewart, *Peyote Religion: A History* (Norman: University of Oklahoma Press, 1987).

6. John is referring to practices attributed to witchcraft, where materials are prayed and "worked" against an individual and buried near his or her dwelling as part of a curse. The second evil is where an object is projected, through song and prayer, into a person and is removed by sucking it out.

7. "Sucking Way is the cure for Wizardry. The sucker normally cuts the place which hurts and sucks out some foreign object. It is usually mentioned that blood was sucked out a number of times before the object was obtained. The sucker sang and usually applied some sort of medicine to the wound.... All informants agreed that there had been a great efflorescence of sucking in the period between roughly 1870 and 1910. A very large number of informants volunteered skepticism about suckers. Suckers were generally held to be wizards themselves or in league with wizards. They were held to be charlatans in that they had prepared in their mouths the objects which they were going to 'suck out.'" Clyde Kluckhohn, *Navaho Witchcraft* (1944; repr., Boston: Beacon Press, 1970): 51–52.

8. "[Peyote] grows in Texas and Mexico, in an area approximately bounded by Corpus Christi, Texas, Deming, New Mexico, Durango, Mexico, and Puebla, Mexico." David F. Aberle, *The Peyote Religion among the Navaho* (Norman: University of Oklahoma Press, 1982): 5.

9. Aberle and Stewart take a different approach, saying that the Utes in Towaoc were the prime movers in bringing the Native American Church to the Navajo living in the northern part of the reservation. The earliest introduction of the religion in Utah was around 1915, and by the 1930s, it had become fully developed.

10. Exactly which committee this was is difficult to determine. From the 1950s to present, there have been numerous investigations involving Navajos and participant testimony. Omer C. Stewart, in *Peyote Religion: A History* (Norman: University of Oklahoma Press, 1987): 293–317, identifies many of these different groups.

11. The Native American Church has no specific dogma but incorporates many important teachings from general American Indian culture, specific Navajo principles, as well as Christian teachings. Among those teachings are beliefs in strong families, sharing, inner peace, brotherhood and sisterhood, environmental stewardship, abstinence from alcohol, and respect.

12. "Frenzy witchcraft is primarily the Navaho 'love magic.' This and the use of a group of plants, of which Datura is the most prominent, are its most distinguishing features. . . . The basic technique is that of administering the plant through food, in a cigarette, by kissing, or simply by contact on the person or with objects. . . . Frenzy witchcraft is a malevolent activity directed especially against the rich; the killing of a sibling is the price of initiation; there is the tie-up with incest, especially with the sister; there is collusion with singers and diagnosticians." Clyde Kluckhohn, *Navaho Witchcraft* (1944; repr., Boston: Beacon Press, 1970): 40–41.

13. For a graphic example of this, see Robert S. McPherson, *The Journey of Navajo Oshley: An Autobiography and Life History* (Logan: Utah State University Press, 2000): 60–61. In this incident, a person practicing witchcraft against Oshley was exposed, although not physically present, through a ceremony and died when a medicine man turned the evil power against him.

14. One means of witching a person is sorcery, defined here by Clyde Kluckhohn: "Sorcery is essentially an enchantment by spell. The Sorcerer does not need to encounter his victim personally at all. He must merely obtain a bit of the victim's clothing or, better, personal offal (hair, nails, feces, urine, body dirt). This will be buried with flesh or other material from a grave or buried in a grave or under a lightning-struck tree. The Sorcerer will then recite a spell, often setting the number of days after which the victim is to die. The incantation may be recited as a prayer in a chant or may be a song or both songs and spoken formulas may be employed." *Navaho Witchcraft* (1944; repr., Boston: Beacon Press, 1970): 31.

15. Another form of witchcraft practitioners are called skinwalkers or were-animals. Good information on this topic can be found in Clyde Kluckhohn's *Navaho Witchcraft* (1944; repr., Boston: Beacon Press, 1970); Margaret K. Brady, *Some Kind of Power: Navajo Children's Skinwalker Narratives* (Salt Lake City: University of Utah Press, 1984); and William Morgan, *Human Wolves among the Navaho* Yale University Publications in Anthropology 11 (New Haven, Conn.: Yale University Press, 1936).

16. John is referring to corpse poison. Kluckhohn describes it as follows: "A preparation is made of the flesh of corpses. The flesh of children and especially twin children is preferred, and the bones at the back of the head and skin whorls are the prized ingredients. When this corpse poison is ground into powder it 'looks like pollen.' It may be dropped into a hogan from the smoke hole, placed in the nose or mouth of a sleeping victim, or blown from furrowed sticks into the face of someone in a large crowd. 'Corpse poison' is occasionally stated to have been administered in a cigarette. Fainting, lockjaw, a tongue black and swollen, immediate unconsciousness or some similar dramatic symptom is usually said to result promptly. Sometimes, however, the effects are less obvious.

The victim gradually wastes away, and the usual ceremonial treatments are unavailing." Clyde Kluckhohn, *Navaho Witchcraft* (1944; repr., Boston: Beacon Press, 1970): 25.

17. The term "skinwalker" is derived from the belief that the witch practitioner actually puts on the skin of a wolf, coyote, or some other such animal, and by doing so, assumes supernatural qualities used against an individual. Through evil prayer, ritual, and knowledge, the skinwalker performs antisocial acts shunned by a "normal" person.

18. Although witchcraft can be practiced anyplace, Navajos will often identify local spots where witches are said to gather. Here they work their powers against victims before going out at night to perform their evil.

19. These sanctuaries, translated into English as "home of witchcraft medicine," are hidden sites that may take special powers to enter. For instance, an entryway may be a very thin crack that no humans could fit through unless they had witchcraft powers. Then they can easily enter. The crevice then opens into a large chamber where the witches congregate.

20. For the full range of Navajo ceremonial classification, see Leland C. Wyman and Clyde Kluckhohn, "Navaho Classification of Their Song Ceremonials," *Memoirs of the American Anthropological Association* 50 (1938; repr., Millwood, New York: Kraus Reprint Company, 1976).

21. Hungry Boy was Maurice Knee, who tells how he got his name: "My Navajo name is The Hungry One. If I had a store full of Indians, and they were standing around visiting and not trading, just buying candy and pop, pretty soon upstairs Mike would hit on the floor. 'Dinner's ready, come and get it!'

I'd say, 'Hey, I'm going to go eat now, I'm hungry. Go outside.'

Well, that's when they all wanted to trade. At two o'clock I'd finally get up to eat. So at ten o'clock in the morning, I started saying, 'Well boys, I'm awful hungry, you're going to have to go,' and then I got out by noon.

Three o'clock in the afternoon I'd say, 'Whew, I'm awful hungry, you're going to have to go now,' and then they'd trade and I'd get out by six, six-thirty.

'That white man sure eats a lot,' they'd say. 'He eats all the time! He's Hungry One.'" Samuel Moon, *Tall Sheep: Harry Goulding, Monument Valley Trader* (Norman: University of Oklahoma Press, 1992): 62.

22. "White Spruce Mountain—Chuska Peak in the Chuska Mountains—has a lot of these trees growing on it. This is where people gather materials for the sacred smoke." J.H.

23. Claus Chee Sonny, a practitioner of the Navajo Bringing-Home Ceremony, provides the mythological explanation for the Mountain Smoke Ceremony and its connection to deer: "When the Deer People were cured [following a ceremony] they left the hogan, asking, 'How do we go?' 'Where do we go?' 'Where can we be?' And Wind spoke to them. He put down mountain tobacco. From the plains

he took and laid down Cloud Tobacco. These are the two which were laid down. They were given to counteract the two great killer plants which drive people crazy–Blue Locoweed and *Datura meteloides,* the latter being the most dangerous.

[Next follows an explanation about medicinal plants; how the mountains were not sure where they should be located; and how animals, trees, rocks, and so forth were also unsure of their role. Talking God, by using mountain smoke, settled the situation.] Upon receiving their information, the deer went to where the mountains were placed. To the south, to another mountain, went the elk, to the plains (in the west) went the antelope. To the north, to another mountain which was there because of a smoke ring, went the different cats—such as Lynx and Mountain Lion—and Coyote. . . . [Next follows a song.] This is the song that was used to place first the mountains and then to place things which are on them. Then, in time, food and water were brought to the hogan. [Luckert's note: "'In time, food and water were brought to the hogan' means that people began to dwell in houses. This craziness is identified with being 'out there' in the wild. With songs and prayers the patients are brought back home, which means that they are healed."] But all those who have gone crazy are out there. (With this ceremony) they are brought back this way (toward the hogan). . . . So, tobacco was used to lay down all the things on earth, as well as to prepare a way for people for their walk through life. Each person, each plant, each game animal, as well as the tobacco was put there for them. That is how it is." Karl W. Luckert, *A Navajo Bringing-Home Ceremony: The Claus Chee Sonny Version of Deerway Ajiłee* (Flagstaff: Museum of Northern Arizona Press, 1978): 43–51.

24. "A pipe is filled with this mixture [mountain tobacco] and lighted with punk made of corncob pith. The pipe is stemless, conical in shape, and provided with a hole in the bottom to draw the smoke. When necessary they are made of clay mixed with crushed broken pottery, though frequently pipes found in old [Anasazi] ruins are made to answer. The singer smokes this pipe facing east, and blows the smoke first downward to the earth; then to the sky, in front of himself, to his right, rear, and left side, and finally from above downward. This is repeated in turn by the patient and all present." Franciscan Fathers, *An Ethnologic Dictionary of the Navajo Language* (1910; repr., Saint Michaels, Ariz.: Saint Michaels Press, 1968): 395.

25. Even a casual reading of the newspapers confirms John's fears, as articles appear weekly delineating the problems. The headline of a recent article in the *Indian Trader* (May 2001, p. 5) tells the story "No Longer Interested in Making Pottery or Doing Crafts, a Lot of Navajo Youth Struggle with Violence" with the subtitle, "As violence across the country dips to record lows, youth on Navajoland are coping with a reservation that has become decidedly more threatening." The author, Pauline Arrillaga, writes: "With jobs scarce on reservations, poverty and unemployment levels are the highest in the nation. Alcoholism is

an epidemic, and domestic violence is soaring. 'Add cultural confusion to the mix, and you've got a generation of 'stuck-between-two-worlds,' says Tom Goodluck, a counselor at the Four Corners Regional Adolescent Treatment Center in Shiprock, New Mexico. . . . The center treats about 80 Indian teenagers annually for chemical dependency and mental health problems. 'Most of the patients don't speak Navajo and know little about their culture,' Goodluck says. 'I see a lot of people come in with no spirituality, no belief in a creator,' he says. 'They don't even know how to pray. These children are hungry for something.'"

26. In the December 2000 issue of *American Indian Report* (24–25), Daniel Kraker wrote an article entitled "Running out of Medicine: Navajo Nation Recruits Traditional Healers." In it he states: "Twenty years ago, there were 2,000 medicine men (and women) practicing on the Navajo reservation in the arid Four Corners area of the Southwest. By 1995, the next time a survey was conducted, the number had dwindled to 300, many of whom were in their sixties or older. . . . Of the more than 300 ceremonies used to treat a variety of ailments, only 34 remain—and at least six of these are near extinction. . . .

"The Navajo Traditional Apprenticeship Program, now almost two years old, provides $350 to medicine men who agree to provide up to 24 hours of training a month, and $300 a month to apprentices who study under them. . . .

"[Eddie Tso, who directs the program,] has thus far enrolled between 50 and 75 apprentices in his program—mostly people in their thirties—but he knows the number must increase. 'We're losing them quickly,' he acknowledges. 'If we don't do anything about it, and we look back in 20 years, there won't be any ceremonies left.'"

INDEX